NEW DIRECTIONS IN SCANDINAVIAN STUDIES

TERJE LEIREN AND CHRISTINE INGEBRITSEN,
SERIES EDITORS

NEW DIRECTIONS IN SCANDINAVIAN STUDIES

This series offers interdisciplinary approaches to the study of the Nordic region of Scandinavia and the Baltic States and their cultural connections in North America. By redefining the boundaries of Scandinavian studies to include the Baltic States and Scandinavian America, the series presents books that focus on the study of the culture, history, literature, and politics of the North.

Small States in International Relations edited by
Christine Ingebritsen, Iver B. Neumann, Sieglinde Gstohl, and Jessica Beyer

Danish Cookbooks: Domesticity and National Identity, 1616–1901
Carol Gold

Crime and Fantasy in Scandinavia: Fiction, Film, and Social Change
Andrew Nestingen

Selected Plays of Marcus Thrane translated and introduced by
Terje I. Leiren

Munch's Ibsen: A Painter's Visions of a Playwright
Joan Templeton

Knut Hamsun: The Dark Side of Literary Brilliance
Monika Žagar

*Nordic Exposures: Scandinavian Identities
in Classical Hollywood Cinema*
Arne Lunde

Icons of Danish Modernity: Georg Brandes and Asta Nielsen
Julie K. Allen

Danish Folktales, Legends, and Other Stories
Timothy R. Tangherlini

Icons of Danish Modernity

GEORG BRANDES AND ASTA NIELSEN

Julie K. Allen

UNIVERSITY OF WASHINGTON PRESS   *Seattle and London*

MUSEUM TUSCULANUM PRESS   *Copenhagen*

THIS BOOK IS MADE POSSIBLE BY A COLLABORATIVE GRANT
FROM THE ANDREW W. MELLON FOUNDATION.

This publication is supported by a grant from the
Scandinavian Studies Publication Fund.

© 2012 by the University of Washington Press
First paperback edition 2015
19 18 17 16 15   5 4 3 2 1

All rights reserved. No part of this publication
may be reproduced or transmitted in any form or
by any means, electronic or mechanical, including
photocopy, recording, or any information storage or
retrieval system, without permission in writing from
the publisher.

University of Washington Press
www.washington.edu/uwpress

Library of Congress Cataloging-in-Publication Data
Allen, Julie K.
Icons of Danish modernity : Georg Brandes and Asta
Nielsen / Julie K. Allen.
  p. cm. — (New directions in Scandinavian studies)
ISBN 978-0-295-99483-3 (paperback)
1. Brandes, Georg, 1842–1927—Criticism and
interpretation. 2. Brandes, Georg, 1842–1927—
Friends and associates. 3. Nielsen, Asta, 1881–1972—
Friends and associates. 4. Denmark—Civilization—
20th century. 5. Denmark—Intellectual life—20th
century. 6. National characteristics, Scandinavia.
I. Title.
PT8125.B8Z6125 2012
306.09489—dc23   2012018870

The paper used in this publication is acid-free and
meets the minimum requirements of American
National Standard for Information Sciences—
Permanence of Paper for Printed Library Materials,
ANSI Z39.48 1984.∞

To Brent, who may not have realized what an odyssey he was signing up for but has been an incomparable traveling companion all the same.

CONTENTS

Preface ... ix
Acknowledgments ... xi

Introduction ... 3
1. The Critic and the Actress: Crafting Art and National Identity ... 16

PART ONE
Georg Brandes

2. The Literary Revolutionary: Marketing Danish Modernity in Imperial Germany ... 47
3. The Outspoken Radical: Political Journalism and Provocative Pacifism ... 87

PART TWO
Asta Nielsen

4. The Danish Diva: Identity Games in Prewar Silent Cinema ... 127
5. The New Woman: Enacting Scandinavian Modernity on Screen ... 178

Conclusion ... 227

Notes ... 233
Bibliography ... 261
Index ... 279

PREFACE

Whenever I mention this project to Danes, the most common initial response I get is the surprised query, "Georg Brandes and Asta Nielsen together?" The eminent scholar Jørgen Knudsen, who has written more about Brandes than anyone in the world, exclaimed, "Well, that's going to be a very short book!" As these comments suggest, my decision to pair the cantankerous literary and social critic Brandes with the glamorous silent film diva Nielsen may not, at first glance, seem intuitive or substantial enough to justify an entire book on the subject. I am convinced, however, that the parallels between Brandes's and Nielsen's lives and works emerge quite clearly upon closer investigation, particularly when viewed through the theoretical lenses of celebrity power and metacultural influence. It is common knowledge that Brandes and Nielsen were pioneers in their respective professional fields, but very few people, especially in the English-speaking world, are aware either that their personal lives were intertwined or that their celebrity personas are closely connected to contemporary and ongoing discourses of Danish national identity construction and social liberalization.

My own path to this realization was fairly circuitous, starting in German literature and ending in Danish film. I first began researching Brandes's role in the marketing of Scandinavian literature in Germany in connection with my doctoral dissertation, which dealt with depictions of Denmark in German and Austrian literature of the late nineteenth and early twentieth centuries. I had not intended to write an entire chapter about Brandes, but his larger-than-life stature among the German-speaking authors of the time gave me little choice. His name cropped up everywhere, in widely disparate contexts, and nearly everyone I read about had a strong opinion about him. Regardless of whether they loved him or hated him, everyone who was anyone in northern European intellectual life at the end of the nineteenth century knew Brandes. When I began studying Nielsen several years later, I encountered the same phenomenon. She was ever-present in early German cinema, her name uttered with reverence by critics from Willy Haas to Siegfried Kracauer. The more I learned about these two brilliant, controversial individuals, the more I came to regard them as a team, working for a common cause, despite the differences between them. The sheer scale of Brandes's and Nielsen's international celebrity placed them in a category of their own among Danes of the time and demonstrated conclusively their representative function for their country and their culture in the world. Yet at the same time, the fact that their countrymen had such a hard time accepting them made it clear that their iconic status was contested at home, posing an irresistible riddle. This book is an attempt to solve that riddle by considering the similarities in the modernist orientation of their works, their fame abroad and conflicted reception at home, and, finally, their significance within the context of some of the larger social trends and issues that were at work in late-nineteenth and early twentieth-century European and American society.

ACKNOWLEDGMENTS

This book has been a long time in the making and I have received a tremendous amount of assistance and encouragement along the way. There are not worlds enough or time to thank everyone who deserves my thanks, so I ask forgiveness in advance for any omissions. When I started researching Georg Brandes while a graduate student in the department of Germanic Languages and Literatures at Harvard University, I benefited from the constructive criticisms of many distinguished scholars, including my doctoral advisors Maria Tatar, Judith Ryan, and Stephen Mitchell. I am deeply indebted to Per Dahl at Aarhus University, Denmark, for inviting me to spend 2002–2003 working in the Brandes Archive and for the many years of mentoring and hospitality that his initial invitation led to, as well as to his colleagues in the Institut for Litteraturhistorie at Aarhus University and to Olav Harsløf at Roskilde University, Denmark, for their excellent advice and insights into Danish culture, literature, and politics. Among my many helpful colleagues at the University of Wisconsin—Madison, I must particularly thank Susan Brantly, Tanya Thresher, Tom DuBois, Scott Mellor, Kirsten Wolf, Nete Schmidt, Peggy Hager, Jim Leary, and especially Judy Anderson for boundless professional and personal support. I would also like to thank Marc Silberman, Jørgen Knudsen, Colin Cameron, Jennifer Black, Jillana Peterson, and Claire Thomson for their very helpful feedback on various drafts of this book, as well as the editors and anonymous reviewers at the University of Washington Press and the Modern Language Initiative who have so ably shepherded my manuscript all the way to publication.

    I was able to conduct the extensive archival research necessary for this project thanks to generous financial support from Harvard University, the Fulbright Program, the American Scandinavian Foundation, and the University of Wisconsin Graduate School, College of Letters and Science, Center for European Studies, and International Studies. While any errors are my own, the accuracy of this project is due in no small measure to the unstinting assistance of the archivists and librarians at the Brandes Archive in Aarhus, the Danish Film Institute and Danish Royal Library in Copenhagen, the Deutsches Institut für Filmkunde and Kinothek Asta Nielsen in Frankfurt, and the Deutsche Kinemathek and Bundesfilmarchiv in Berlin. This book has also been significantly improved by the opportunities I have had to present bits and pieces of my research to very knowledgeable and helpful audiences at various conferences, among others the First and Second International Georg Brandes Conferences, the Importing Asta Nielsen Conference organized by Martin Loiperdinger, and meetings of the Nordic Society for Comparative Literature (NorLit), the Midwest Modern Language Association, and the Society for the Advancement of Scandinavian Studies. Preliminary versions of some of the material in the book have appeared in the proceedings of both international Brandes conferences and NorLit 2007, as well as in the journals *The Bridge*, *Scandinavian Studies*, and *The Journal of Scandinavian Cinema*.

I can't possibly enumerate the many friends in Denmark, Germany, and throughout the world who have sustained me during many research and conference trips with meals, hospitality, and stimulating conversations, but I am thankful for all of them. Most of all, however, I am grateful to my family for supporting and putting up with me through this whole process: my husband Brent Allen; my parents Phillip and Ruth Ann Smith; my in-laws David and Susan Allen; my sisters Nicole Soh, Erika Garnica, Jennifer Black, Liesl Buskirk, Kim Smith, Bethany Curd and brother Bryant Smith; and my four amazing children Clark, Emily, Soren, and Alice Allen, who have never known a time when I wasn't working on this book in some form or another but have not allowed me to lose sight of what really matters.

Icons of Danish Modernity

Introduction

As a small, peaceful country perched on the northern edge of continental Europe, Denmark tends to take up very little space in the imagination of the American public. Perhaps because of the alliteration between the terms Danish and Dutch or the prevalence of windmills in both countries, Americans often confuse Denmark with the Netherlands. When former Danish prime minister Anders Fogh Rasmussen came to Washington, DC, in May 2004 to receive president George W. Bush's thanks for Denmark's staunch support of the American invasion of Iraq, the Danish television journalists who accompanied him were hard-pressed to find anyone on the streets of the US capital who was aware that Denmark had aligned itself with the United States in the war, let alone that the Danes had committed both ground troops and naval forces to the endeavor. Even undergraduate European history majors at American universities are, as a rule, amazed to learn of Denmark's prominent role in European politics and economics over the past thousand years, as demonstrated by Denmark's dominance in the Baltic Sea region during the late Middle Ages, King Christian IV of Denmark's leadership of the Protestant armies in Germany (to defeat, it must be confessed) during the Thirty Years' War, and the fact that the ever-popular LEGO toys were invented in Denmark.

Yet despite a general ignorance of specific details of Danish politics, history, and geography, Americans do tend to have a mental image of Denmark as being quintessentially "modern," in the sense that Denmark is reputed to be in the vanguard of such "liberal" social, economic, and political movements as gay marriage, sustainable energy, and universal health care. While this perception of Denmark owes a great deal to the country's leading role in the creation of the type of social democratic welfare state that has come to be known as the Nordic model,[1] it is also a result of the international reception of Danish cultural products, ranging from architecture and design to literature and film, as inherently innovative and trendsetting. Alongside such world-famous luminaries as author Hans Christian (H. C.) Andersen (1805–1875), whose charming but complex fairy tales have lent themselves to a variety of Hollywood film adaptations, and philosopher Søren Kierkegaard (1813–1855), whose challenging theological and literary masterpieces continue to intrigue scholars across disciplines around the world, a sample list of some of the most internationally famous Danes of the past two centuries whose works have been heralded as "modern," despite the significant chronological and aesthetic differences between them, might include composer Carl Nielsen (1865–1931), painter Peder Severin (P. S.) Krøyer (1851–1909), novelist Karen Blixen (1885–1962), film director Carl Theodor Dreyer (1889–1968), designer and architect Arne Jacobsen (1902–1971), and poet-mathematician Piet Hein (1905–1996). Such a list could go on and on, but these few examples should serve to illustrate the prominent role of individual Danes in shaping global perceptions of Danish culture as cutting edge. Although very few, if any, of the writers and artists named above would have considered themselves Danish nationalists or regarded their work as nationalistic, their public image and their works have nevertheless played a central role in the development of popular conceptions, however vague or inadequate, of Danish national identity, both within and beyond Denmark's borders.

Although artistic and literary works are often perceived as being unrelated to national politics, the cultural dimensions of national identity give such works an inherently political dimension, precisely because they help individuals to conceptualize the world they inhabit. Danish historian Søren Mørch explains that the function of culture "is to produce meaning, order, and coherence in human existence. This cannot be done completely individually, independent of others, because the phenomenon itself can only be understood . . . in relation to others' [view of] meaning, order, and coherence."[2] The emergence of social groups based upon particular shared cultural attributes, from language to religion to foodways, underlies the modern conception of the nation. Anthony D. Smith argues for the inextricability of culture from national identity, explaining that "national identity comprises both a cultural and political identity and is located in a political community as well as a cultural one," such that "any attempt to forge a national identity is also a political action with political consequences."[3]

The political and cultural work of forging of a national identity necessarily takes place in the public sphere, a space that Jürgen Habermas has defined as a social imaginary derived from the circulation and discussion of novels, newspapers, journals, and magazines.[4] Similarly, Benedict Anderson asserts that such "national print media" as novels and newspapers provide the "technical means for 're-presenting' the *kind* of imagined community that is the nation."[5] Although neither Habermas nor Anderson explicitly addresses film, cinema functions in a very similar, perhaps even more immediate, way because of its emphasis on visuality. Greg Urban builds on Anderson and Habermas with the argument that the mass subjectivity of a national people is formed by the "performative ideology of reading that is at the heart of the public sphere and modern citizen-state. . . . Nationalism is thus a particular example of the semiotic constitution of community, a social imaginary created out of the semiotic mediation of circulation."[6] The influential role of culture in imagining national communities, on which all of these theorists agree, means that each stage in the production, dissemination, and reception of a cultural text has the potential of contributing to the emergence of particular national and cultural identity constructions.

Although no such thing as an a priori or unified Danish national identity exists, Danish society has long operated on the assumption that certain values, beliefs, and practices are intrinsic to membership in the imagined community of the Danish nation. It is difficult to pinpoint exactly when this notion of a Danish national community first emerged—Ole Feldbæk argues for its manifestation in certain elite circles as far back as the 1740s[7]—but it is closely associated with the "modern era." It is equally challenging to determine what values and characteristics such a conception of Danish national identity presupposes, since one of the hallmarks of modern Danish life is the almost infinite array of choices in shaping one's individual identity.[8] It is clear that Danes nevertheless subscribe to the idea that a distinct Danish national identity defines them as a nation. Since the 1970s, the nature and status of Danishness (*danskhed*) has been a topic of frequent discussion and debate in Denmark, a phenomenon that anthropologist Steven Sampson attributes today in part to the popular perception of Danish identity as being threatened by Denmark's integration into the European Union and its increasingly multiethnic population.[9] Throughout the centuries, the perceived threats to Danish society have taken many forms, but public discussions, Sampson explains, tend to focus less on the particular content of Danishness than on the concept of Danishness "as an object in itself."[10] He explains,

> Danskhed seems to have several characteristics, being both a category, a "tilstand" [condition], and a "størrelse" [extent]. Danskhed is something one "has." If we are not careful, danskhed can be "lost." Danskhed is valuable and fragile. It must be "protected." . . . But danskhed is also a quantity. There can be more of it or less of it. It can be "weakened," and it must be "preserved." Like a glass full of water we can measure it.[11]

The discourse that Sampson describes of Danishness as a tangible, quantifiable element testifies to a pervasive belief in a distinct, recognizable Danish national identity that continues to serve as a unifying force in Danish society today, even as its nature has shifted radically over time.

Yet, as demonstrated by the escalation of Denmark's preoccupation with its national identity in recent decades in response to a perceived threat, imagined national communities do not exist in a vacuum. On the contrary, the existence and specificity of a particular imagined national community are predicated upon comparison, by both insiders and outsiders, with other imagined communities and their perceived characteristics.[12] For example, while Danes of one era imagine their national community in particular ways, neighboring Germans in the same period may regard it completely differently. The creation of competing models and interpretations that this situation entails results in a range of (possibly conflicting) constructions of a given national identity by various groups. The difficulty of imagining any entire national community is often resolved by the common, though not always entirely conscious, practice of defining national groups by the celebrities who represent them in the public sphere. The iconic quality of such famous individuals allows them to channel beliefs, observations, and stereotypes about the cultures that produced them.

Using the reception of two prominent Danish celebrity icons as a focusing principle, this book explores the tension between collective conceptions of Danish national identity in the late nineteenth and early twentieth centuries that fall into three categories: first, views held by Danes about their own culture, which I refer to as "endo-stereotypes"; second, judgments about Danish identity made by non-Danes, or "exo-stereotypes"; and third, beliefs among Danes about how their culture is viewed by outsiders, or "meta-stereotypes." In the following discussion of the transformations of Danish society and culture around the turn of the twentieth century, I analyze the existence and power of such descriptive and prescriptive conceptions of Danish national identity, both singly and in interaction with each other, while acknowledging that these constructions are necessarily artificial and inherently unreliable, particularly because of their tendency toward slippage over time. Each generational cohort of Danes reaches its own, often conflicting, conclusions about what traits and traditions do and do not constitute the view of Danishness it espouses, which means that the same qualities or ideas might be embraced by one group of Danes as the incarnation of Danish national identity, only to be rejected by another group as antithetical to Danishness.

While the creation of endo- and exo-stereotypes, both deliberate and inadvertent, local and global, is not a process exclusive to a particular era or place, the spread of popular conceptions of national identity has been closely linked to the rise of the nation-state, although theorists of nationalism disagree about the extent to which the nation is a distinctively modern phenomenon. Ernest Gellner articulates the modernist position with the argument that the nation is a sociological structure made possible by the conditions, practices, and institutions of modernity,[13] while John Hutchinson defends the primordialist stance that insists on the inherent possibility of nationhood outside the context of modernity, based on a premodern common ethnic heritage.[14] Regardless of whether some sense of a Danish national identity existed among Danes before the emergence of a self-conscious Danish nation, however, it is incontrovertible that the defining features of Danish society and culture in the twenty-first century, in particular the currently prevailing endo- and exo-stereotypes of Danishness, were profoundly shaped by the events, individuals, and trends associated with Denmark's gradual political, social, and cultural modernization over the course of the preceding two centuries.

Benedict Anderson's work reconciles the primordialist and modernist positions to a certain degree by demonstrating how the mechanisms of modernity rework preexisting collective identities. He emphasizes that imagined national communities do not simply replace the religious communities and dynastic realms that provided the parameters of collective identity in earlier ages. He notes that the concomitant decline of such communities and the rise of nationalism reflect instead "a fundamental change . . . in modes of apprehending the world, which, more than anything else, made it possible to 'think' the nation."[15] A primary factor in the transformation of nineteenth- and early twentieth-century Denmark was the emergence of a variety of mass media, particularly newspapers and film, which dramatically increased the speed and geographical breadth of the dissemination of endo-, exo-, and meta-stereotypes about the modernity of Danish culture.

Given that "modernity" is a highly contested term with a vast possible range of culturally and historically specific connotations, it is necessary to define how it functions in this book. On a broad historical level, I use it to refer to the profound disruption and reinscription of the collective status quo that took place in Denmark between the late eighteenth and late twentieth centuries. A series of social, political, economic, and cultural shifts during this period brought about Denmark's gradual transformation from a highly agrarian, socially stratified, almost feudal state under the rule of an absolute monarch, with a mandatory Evangelical-Lutheran religious orientation, into the secular, egalitarian, social democratically oriented constitutional monarchy that Denmark is today. "Modernity" thus denotes a process of systemic upheaval that continues into the present day, destabilizing received truths and revolutionizing living conditions.

On a thematic level, however, I use the term "modernity" as the designation for the overarching orientation of the new sense of collective national identity that was gradually interiorized by Danes over the course of the late nineteenth and early twentieth century. This identity was derived from the processes of liberalization, decentralization of authority, and individual empowerment that belong to modernity, but it also incorporates nostalgia for the idealized, irretrievable past. The specific character of "modernity" in Danish society at any given time is of course contingent upon and specific to that particular time, giving rise to conflicting interpretations of modernity that will be treated in more detail as they become relevant to the narrative, but one common element is the initial, often negative, reaction to and yet ultimate acceptance of change and the ever-increasing multiplicity of individual choices. Although "modernity" in this context denotes primarily the shaping of social mores and cultural orientation, it also encompasses the effects of such political, economic, and infrastructural developments as the establishment of universal suffrage and democratic governmental processes, the constitutional guarantee of such civil rights as freedom of the press and freedom of religion, the twin trends of industrialization and urbanization, the (partial) replacement of class and gender hierarchies with universal education and meritocratic institutions, and the spread of systems of rapid, relatively inexpensive transportation and communication.

Although modernity thus defined spans several hundred years of Danish history, this book focuses on the final decades of the nineteenth century and initial decades of the twentieth, a period when domestic and international conceptions of Danish national identity were particularly fluid as a result of recent foreign political events and their repercussions in Danish cultural politics. From the vantage point of the present, with our ability to craft a master historical narrative post hoc, it becomes apparent that the national losses that Denmark endured in the early and mid-nineteenth century, including its navy (seized by the British in 1807), control of Norway (granted as the spoils of war to Sweden in 1814), and the fertile, densely populated duchies of Schleswig and Holstein (captured by Prussia in 1864), were not just a series of unfortunate events that cost the Danes blood and money. Instead, these events proved to be significant stations along the path of Denmark's displacement from its erstwhile position of regional military and economic power, which accordingly destabilized its relationship with its neighbors, first and foremost the German-speaking states to the south. Denmark's final defeat by Prussia in particular deflated the nationalistic euphoria that had emboldened Danish foreign policy in the mid-nineteenth century and prompted a chastened revision of Denmark's self-image. During the final decades of the century, Danish society turned dramatically inward, making a virtue of national self-sufficiency and a low international political profile.[16] The widespread perception among Danes in this era that Danishness faced an existential threat from German aggression aggravated the effects of modernity and ensured that the preservation of an authentic, neoromantic Danish national identity became a national preoccupation.

Denmark's intermittent progress toward social and cultural modernity in the decades surrounding the year 1900 was thus profoundly affected by its precarious geopolitical position in the shadow of the recently united and rapidly militarizing Germany, the dangers of which were illustrated by the Prussian military's decisive role in the two wars it fought with Denmark in the mid-nineteenth century. After the economically and psychologically devastating loss of Schleswig-Holstein in 1864, Danish politicians gauged every foreign policy decision by the reaction it was likely to provoke in Berlin. At the same time, Denmark's cultural intelligentsia found itself torn between the desire to differentiate its artistic and literary products from German norms and the concomitant realization that success in Germany was the gateway to international recognition and financial success. Centuries of cultural influence from Germany could not be undone, but the fear of being swallowed up politically by Germany provided powerful motivation for Danes to develop their own brand of modern literature and art. The increasingly prominent role of social democracy in Danish politics after 1900 heightened the perception of nearly unbridgeable ideological differences between Denmark and a Germany dominated first by authoritarian imperialism and then by National Socialistic fascism. Denmark's political weakness ensured that the country could not take any drastic steps to distance itself from Germany, as evidenced by Danish neutrality during World War I and the (ultimately futile) German-Danish nonaggression pact of May 1939 on the eve of World War II, but it did not preclude tumultuous artistic, literary, and public debates over how to maintain Denmark's cultural distinctiveness and national character.

Disagreement among Danes over which direction Danish culture should follow grew so intense that not one but two periods in the late nineteenth and early twentieth centuries are characterized in Danish intellectual history as "culture wars" (*kulturkampe*). Ironically, the term itself is derived from German chancellor Otto von Bismarck's struggle to dominate the Catholic Church in Germany in the 1870s. In the Danish context, however, it applies to the turbulent cultural discourse surrounding two decisive political transformations. The first is the conflict between National Liberalism and Brandesianism in the 1880s and 1890s that accompanied Denmark's shift to a true parliamentary democracy. The second is the leftist "cultural radicalism" (*kulturradikalisme*) movement that emerged in tandem with the rise of the Danish welfare state in the 1920s and 1930s and became an outspoken opponent of the fascist ideology emanating from Germany.[17] A central common feature of both culture wars was tension between tradition and change, specifically with regard to the effects of modernity on Danish national identity. Although these culture

Introduction

wars were primarily of interest to Danes themselves, who championed competing endo-stereotypes of Danishness, they were also influential in shaping exo-stereotypes of Denmark, particularly in Germany, which was simultaneously Denmark's nearest neighbor, one of its most important trading partners, and its greatest foreign political threat.

Despite the historical importance of the sweeping geopolitical and ideological narratives I have just outlined, the story of how Danish culture came to be *perceived* as modern is ultimately less concerned with facts than with the way Denmark was regarded in the public sphere, which was determined to a large extent by iconic Danish celebrities of the time. The democratization of European society over the course of the nineteenth century facilitated the rise of a culture of celebrity that challenged traditional hierarchies of social power by elevating ordinary individuals to public prominence on the basis of merit and popularity rather than birth or wealth. In *Celebrity and Power,* P. David Marshall identifies the nineteenth-century origins of the contemporary usage of the term "celebrity" to denote public individuals whose status is attainable, at least in theory, by the masses.[18] Although celebrities generally have little actual political power, they possess enormous emblematic importance as representations of both the masses themselves and the potential of capitalism to destabilize social hierarchies; in short, "the celebrity embodies the empowerment of the people to shape the public sphere symbolically."[19] In this way, modern celebrities become signs that represent something other than themselves; in the age of democratization and social upheaval, they can function as both a product of the dominant culture and a vehicle for the aspirations of subordinate cultural groups. The career of the writer Hans Christian Andersen provides a compelling example of this phenomenon. Born into decidedly lower-class circumstances, Andersen became one of the greatest Danish celebrities of the nineteenth century, especially outside Denmark, but his lifelong struggle for acceptance in class-conscious Danish society remained a central theme in many of his fairy tales and autobiographical works. His fame and the upward social mobility it facilitated represented both a validation of his literary gifts and a challenge to the preeminence of the Danish bourgeoisie.

Since Andersen's death in 1875, very few Danes have attained a comparable degree of international celebrity, with two exceptions: literary critic Georg Brandes (1842–1927) and silent film actress Asta Nielsen (1881–1972). Like Andersen, neither Brandes, a middle-class Jew, nor Nielsen, a working-class woman, belonged by birth to the Danish educated elite, and their rise to prominence presented an implicit challenge to the Danish social power structure. As celebrities, artists, and media personalities, Brandes and Nielsen were intimately involved with the production of both exo- and endo-stereotypes about Danish modernity. During the period 1870 to 1930, which encompasses the most productive years of both Brandes's and Nielsen's respective careers, most of the leading Danish artists and intellectuals, such as journalist Henrik Cavling (1858–1933) and author Hans Kirk (1898–1962), were household names in Denmark but little-known beyond its borders. By contrast, Brandes and Nielsen were prominent enough in other countries, particularly Germany, to function as de facto ambassadors of Danish culture to Europe and the rest of the world. As global celebrities, they had access to a wider scope of activity and agency on the world stage than their countrymen whose fame did not transcend Denmark's borders, and their representation of Danish culture carried significant weight with international audiences. Marshall notes, "Within society, the celebrity is a voice above others, a voice that is channeled into the media systems as being legitimately significant."[20] Given the discursive power imparted by their celebrity status, examining Brandes's and Nielsen's professional activity and reception abroad can illuminate not only their individual careers but also, to a certain extent, the nature of the image of Danish national identity they mediated to the rest of the world and the ways in which that image was incorporated into both exo- and meta-stereotypes of Danishness.

Yet while both Brandes and Nielsen were undeniably talented individuals who achieved phenomenal professional success and renown, they were quite distinctly products of their respective times. Their accomplishments and failures reflect not only their own abilities and limitations but also those of the sociopolitical environments in which they lived and worked. The history of their reception at home in Denmark, in particular, sheds light on their involvement in resolving Denmark's conflicted relationship to modernity and the gradual emergence of new endo-stereotypes of Danishness that incorporated elements of social and cultural modernity. The highly public nature and wide distribution of their work in the mass media makes them particularly valuable for this study as imagining subjects, the nature of whose relationship to Denmark and its cultural climate was potentially influential for the millions of people who read or viewed their works, and whose views are readily accessible through their archived professional works and personal documents.

Brandes and Nielsen were close friends for nearly two decades, but their names have rarely been linked together, due to the fact that they were born a generation apart and worked in disparate professional fields. However, compelling similarities in the ideological and geographical trajectories of their lives and careers elide those apparent gaps and suggest a shared involvement in crafting both internal and external perceptions of Danish national and cultural identity. As outsiders in Danish society, Brandes and Nielsen had to struggle to earn their countrymen's acceptance, which was predicated upon the shifting sociopolitical context of the time. Brandes was embraced by the workers' movements in the 1870s as a social reformer who challenged the hegemony of the Danish elites, but rejected by them two decades later as a bourgeois individualist.[21] While Danish film was in its heyday in the 1910s, Nielsen was celebrated at home as a Danish movie star who had conquered the German market, but her continued success in Germany in the 1920s, after Danish film had lost its privileged standing there, earned her the disdain of her countrymen.

Both Brandes and Nielsen faced professional obstacles in Denmark that prompted them to work in Germany for significant periods of time, although they did not sever the emotional ties that bound them to their homeland. As literal and metaphorical border-crossers (*Grenzgänger*), their experience of living in a foreign environment forced them to take a conscious position with regard to their national and cultural identity as Danes, which gave them the requisite emotional distance to regard their native culture objectively and constructively. They each achieved a remarkable degree of professional success and international celebrity, yet encountered hostility from many of their countrymen for their performative embodiment of controversial aspects of modernity, which thereby became associated with Danishness Their individual stories raise common issues of nationality, national character, and national belonging, with a paradoxical twist: Brandes and Nielsen were forced into positions as outsiders *inside* Danish culture and society at the same time as they served as celebrity representatives and advocates *outside* Denmark for the very culture that rejected them. The ongoing story of their reception in Denmark has nearly as much to do with Danish society's perception of itself as with its estimation of Brandes's or Nielsen's work.

This book, drawing as it does on discourses of celebrity, modernity, national identity, history, literature, and film, is neither a traditional biography of Brandes or Nielsen nor solely an investigation of either their relationship or their works. Instead, their respective, distinctive life stories and artistic oeuvres serve as cultural-historical case studies of the development of Danish cultural modernity in an era when Denmark was struggling to determine both its place in the new global political order and its attitude toward the sweeping social and aesthetic changes that followed in the wake of its political and economic modernization. It is, of course, important to remember at this juncture that the way in which modernity was understood in Brandes's time is not the same as it was by Nielsen's generation nor as it is today. Through his literary-critical work, Brandes was instrumental in transforming the meaning of the term "modern" in Germany from a primarily chronological designation into an ideological position in opposition to the status quo. However, as Malcolm Bradbury and James McFarlane point out in their guide to European modernism, the idea of "the modern" changed radically between the 1880s and 1890s, losing its "confident faith in social advance" and acquiring overtones of nihilism and irrationality, so that by the early twentieth century, "modern" had "become the sign of all that was old-fashioned and bourgeois, a term the connotations of which suggested nothing so much as exhaustion and decay."[22] Yet by the time "modern" fell out of favor with the European intelligentsia, it had become ubiquitous among the general public, especially women, many of whom were eager to be "modern" and have "modern" lives. Through her films, Nielsen served as a model for her fans of what a "modern" woman and a "modern" life looked like. Despite the semantic differences between the meaning of "modern" in their respective historical contexts, Brandes's and Nielsen's stories share enough ideological common ground to allow us to trace the trajectory of their contributions to the evolution of Danish, German, and European discourses of modernity over the span of more than a century.

Although Brandes and Nielsen are treated relatively autonomously in most of the book, Brandes in part 1 and Nielsen in part 2, chapter 1 provides brief biographical sketches of both protagonists and an overview of their friendship, examined within the framework of their mutual project of crafting and disseminating an image of Danish cultural modernity to the world, primarily via mass media in Germany. In part 1, chapter 2 documents Brandes's efforts in the final decades of the nineteenth century to foster the development of a realistic literary aesthetic in Denmark and to promote Scandinavian literature in Germany and Austria as quintessentially modern. Chapter 3 focuses on the later decades of Brandes's life, when he became an impassioned advocate for the rights of oppressed minority peoples across Europe and an outspoken opponent of the imperialism that led to the outbreak of World War I. In part 2, chapter 4 deals with the unexpected beginning and rapid development of Nielsen's multifaceted early film career and international stardom, while chapter 5 explores the ways in which Nielsen's later career was characterized by the redefinition of her relationship to both Germany and Denmark, in particular the restructuring of the German film industry after World War I, Nielsen's declining popularity in Denmark concurrent with the decreasing influence of the Danish film industry abroad, and the rise of National Socialism in Germany.

While Danish and German scholars have taken a renewed interest in both Brandes and Nielsen in recent years, there has been very little written about them, individually or together, in English. This book begins to remedy that deficiency, not just by documenting their lives and professional accomplishments but also by demonstrating the significance and continuing relevance of their contributions to European culture and national identity constructions, particularly with respect to the way their celebrity functioned as a tool for presenting an image of Denmark that fuses a portrayed modernity and a portrayed nationalism. Although they did live colorful, often scandalous lives that make entertaining reading, Brandes and Nielsen were more than the early twentieth-century equivalent of reality television stars—they were gifted artists and skilled communicators, whose work and mass media presence reflected not only their personal abilities and ambition but also their investment in the sociocultural development and modernization of their homeland and the world.

CHAPTER ONE

The Critic and the Actress

Crafting Art and National Identity

When the Hamburg-America Line launched its newest and largest-ever passenger ship, the *Vaterland* (Fatherland), in May 1914, the company faced the daunting public relations task of helping potential passengers overcome fears stemming from the disastrous sinking of the *Titanic* two years earlier. To boost customer confidence, officials invited celebrities from across Europe to come along on the transatlantic maiden voyage of the *Vaterland* and gave leading European and American newspapers generous access to these celebrities to ensure that this message would reach the masses. Among the luminaries chosen for this task were two of the most famous Danes of the era, the literary critic Georg Brandes and the silent film actress Asta Nielsen. The elderly but consummately elegant Brandes was the fashionable Miss Nielsen's table companion on board. Press photographs show Nielsen and Brandes promenading on deck, accompanied by Nielsen's first husband, director Peter Urban Gad, and the journalist Josef Melnik. Although Nielsen disembarked when the ship docked at Southampton due to the constraints of her filming schedule, Brandes continued on to New York for a lecture tour across the United States.

The maiden voyage of the *Vaterland* was notable both for its successful marketing tactics (which were, however, soon undermined by the outbreak of World War I[1]) and as an end point of Europe's belle époque, during which period Brandes's and Nielsen's respective international reputations were at their height. Their inclusion on the celebrity guest list of the *Vaterland* transmitted a public relations message independent of the Hamburg-America Line's agenda about the safety

Figure 1.1. As celebrity guests on the maiden voyage of the transatlantic ocean liner the *Vaterland,* Asta Nielsen and Georg Brandes helped to reassure would-be passengers about the safety of ship travel in the wake of the *Titanic* disaster. This image shows the journalist Josef Melnik, Nielsen, Brandes, and Nielsen's husband and director, Peter Urban Gad, on board ship. Credit: The Royal Library, Copenhagen, Department of Maps, Prints, and Photographs

of sea travel; it confirmed the view of newspaper readers across the globe that these two individuals were the preeminent representatives of Danish culture abroad. As German journalist Friedrich Sieburg noted in an article in *Die Weltbühne* in March 1925, "There are many people outside of Europe who know little more about Denmark than that not only Asta Nielsen but also Georg Brandes was born there."[2] Brandes's and Nielsen's high profile in the mass media, shaped by both their own professional contributions and their coverage as celebrities by the press, positioned them as influential representatives of Denmark and Danish culture to the world, even when the image of Denmark associated with them diverged significantly from Danish society's self-image.

Nielsen's and Brandes's effect on exo-stereotypes of Danish national identity can best be understood as a metacultural phenomenon. "Metaculture" refers to the way in which individual cultural objects function as emblems of broader cultural trends and characteristics, a process that is closely linked to the mass reproduction and wide distribution of cultural objects associated with modernity. Greg Urban argues that one of the central ways in which culture becomes shared, both within nations and across borders, is through "[extraction] from cultural objects involved in mass dissemination, where the dissemination is relatively uncoupled from replication."[3] The images of a particular culture that are extracted from mass-produced cultural artifacts are laden with value assessments that give rise to metacultural discourse. In his foreword to Urban's book, Benjamin Lee defines metaculture as "judgments people make about similarities and differences, [when] they judge token instances of cultural production to be manifestations of the same cultural element."[4] In essence, the part stands in for the whole: audiences extract meaning about national identity from the particular instances they encounter of a nation's cultural production. The more ubiquitous the products, the more effect they have on endo- and exo-stereotypes of cultural identity.

Although not necessarily the most popular cultural productions in Denmark itself, Brandes's and Nielsen's works were so successful and widely distributed internationally as to render them the best-known token instances of Danish cultural production, from which European, particularly German, audiences derived a conception, however artificial, of the essential nature of Danish culture and national identity in this period. Although the artistic merit of Brandes's texts and Nielsen's films has been well-established in literary history and film scholarship, the significant metacultural implications of their works have received little scholarly attention, particularly in English. The perceived modernity of their works among international audiences contributed to the development of a generalized exo-stereotype of Danish cultural modernity, while the far more ambivalent reception of their works in Denmark reflects both resistance among Danes at the time to the implicit meta-stereotype of Denmark as an exemplar of modernity and the prevalence of a rival endo-stereotype of Danish society as self-consciously conservative.

The significance of Brandes's and Nielsen's involvement in the creation and popularization of an image, however contested, of Denmark as culturally innovative and socially liberal has a great deal to do with timing. Their careers coincided with an era of tremendous political and social upheaval in Denmark, which involved both an inward-oriented contraction of Denmark's political agenda and an outward-oriented expansion of the distribution of Danish cultural products. These competing tendencies set the stage for the implicit debates over the nature of Danish national identity in which Brandes and Nielsen participated on a metacultural level. During the three-quarters of a century preceding Brandes's public debut as a literary critic in 1871, Denmark had suffered a precipitous decline in status and influence as its position in European politics became increasingly peripheral. With the acquisition of Norway, Iceland, Greenland, and the Faroe Islands in the late fourteenth century, Denmark had been one of the first European colonial powers, but the loss of Norway to Sweden in 1814 and Schleswig-Holstein to Prussia in 1864, as well as the sale of a string of small colonies in India and West Africa to Britain in 1850, marked the decline of its colonial ambitions, although not the end of the Danish empire, which persists today in the form of the limited political union of Denmark, Greenland,[5] and the Faroe Islands.

Paradoxically, however, Danish cultural production flourished during the same period as its foreign political influence dwindled, illustrating the principle that became Denmark's unofficial motto: "That which is lost outwardly must be gained inwardly" (*Hvad udad tabes skal indad vindes*).[6] During the first part of the century, this flowering of Danish culture, which has been somewhat grandiosely christened Denmark's Golden Age (*Guldalderen*), remained primarily confined to Copenhagen. By contrast, the results of Denmark's naturalistic literary renaissance during the latter half of the century, a movement known as the Modern Breakthrough, enjoyed unprecedented popularity abroad, particularly in Germany, and compensated to some degree for Denmark's political weakness. This shift in Denmark's national preoccupation, from the pursuit of imperial greatness to cultural rejuvenation, had a tremendous effect on domestic conceptions of Danish identity.

Yet Denmark's centrality to the international success of the Modern Breakthrough in Scandinavian literature, which took continental Europe by storm during the late nineteenth century, was by no means self-evident. The most prominent figures in this literary movement, a judgment reflected at least in part by the enduring heft of their reputations, were, in fact, the Norwegian Henrik Ibsen and the Swede August Strindberg, who came to represent a much larger and widely disparate grouping of Scandinavian artists and authors, including the Danes Jens Peter (J. P.) Jacobsen and Herman Bang. Nevertheless, as I demonstrate in chapter 2, Brandes's pioneering role in introducing the writers of the Modern Breakthrough to continental readers had the effect of irrevocably linking his name and nationality to the movement's agenda. The fact that Brandes came to embody Denmark's cultural and artistic modernity in the European public sphere, although his own literary-critical works are not generally representative of modernist aesthetics, serves to further underscore the gap between reality and perception that is so central to the formation of exo-stereotypes. By endorsing and promoting the literature of the Modern Breakthrough, Brandes contributed to shaping popular German views of Denmark as a progressive, artistically vibrant culture, which in turn created a market for Danish cultural productions, notably literature and film, that conformed to this image.

Historical perspective is critical for interpreting the reception of texts, as initial judgments about them by contemporaries are often quite different from the way they subsequently come to be perceived. The most significant literary and artistic works in any given national canon are frequently revolutionary, advancing stylistic and ideological changes that threaten to disrupt the status quo, rather than representing an established cultural tradition. Although often celebrated as national masterpieces by later generations for their enduring aesthetic or social significance, forward-thinking works are often initially out of step with the views of the mainstream public they purport to represent. As assessments of these works shifts over time, so too do their metacultural associations.

A striking example of this process of shifting reception is the scandal caused by Ibsen's acclaimed drama *Ghosts* (*Gjengangere*) when it was first published in Copenhagen in 1881. The director of the Nya Teatern in Stockholm, Ludwig Josephson, condemned the play as "one of the filthiest things ever written in Scandinavia,"[7] while a reviewer in London's *Daily Telegraph* denounced it, in 1891, as "an open drain; a loathsome sore unbandaged, a dirty act done publicly. . . . Ibsen's melancholy and malodorous world . . . [is] absolutely loathsome and fetid."[8] Yet a few contemporary critics recognized the drama's inherent quality. In the London *Star,* Arthur Bingham (A. B.) Walkley exhorted,

> Do these people really find nothing in *Ghosts* but a mere hospital ward play? Is it really for them nothing but a painful study of disease? Have they no eyes for what stares them in the face: the plain, simple fact that *Ghosts* is a great spiritual drama? Like nearly all the other great masterpieces of the stage, it is a drama of revolt—the revolt of the "joy of life" against the gloom of hidebound, conventional morality, the revolt of the natural man against the law-made, law-bound puppet, the revolt of the individual against the oppression of social prejudice.[9]

In the 130 years since its publication, *Ghosts* has earned its place as one of Norway's greatest dramas, while Ibsen himself, who lived in self-imposed exile from his homeland for more than thirty years, has become one of the most distinguished representatives of Norwegian literature. This chronological disparity in the reception of revolutionary texts demonstrates the difficulty of judging the value of contemporary cultural artifacts as representative of the national cultures of their creators.

As was the case with Ibsen and Norway, the tensions inherent in the task of constructing an image of Denmark's national identity that was attractive to the larger world but still an accurate reflection of prevailing endo-stereotypes of Danishness has frequently led to conflict between Danish society and the standard-bearers of Danish culture beyond Denmark's borders. At issue is most often the question of authority to define Danishness. During his lifetime, Hans Christian Andersen, who has since become Denmark's most favored son, was far more renowned and admired in Germany and Britain than in Denmark, in part because of the working-class background that rendered his works unpalatable to many of the Copenhagen bourgeois elite. Similarly, neither Nielsen nor Brandes enjoyed the same degree of popularity at home in Denmark as they did abroad. Much like the ugly duckling in Andersen's fairy tale, an analogy that several contemporary critics applied to Nielsen, Brandes and Nielsen found the Danish duckyard both unappreciative and limiting, a situation that forced them to go out into the wider world to achieve recognition.

However, even after the rest of the world had recognized them as swans, many Danes still regarded Brandes and Nielsen as ungainly misfits undeserving of recognition or respect and unqualified to represent their home country. The most significant of the many reasons for this was that the exo-stereotype of Danish modernity evoked throughout Europe by the metacultural associations of Nielsen's and Brandes's work did not yet correspond to the self-perception of mainstream Danish society, which was still caught in the throes of its prolonged transition from a provincial, conservative culture into the liberal, modern country Denmark has since become. Although much of the criticism Brandes and Nielsen faced in Denmark took the form of very personal attacks or professional disapproval, their divisive reception functioned to a significant degree as a manifestation of ongoing struggles over competing narratives of Danish cultural identity, between top-down pedagogical models supported by the educated bourgeoisie and performative avant-garde challenges to them. Examining the disjunction between European and Danish perceptions of Brandes and Nielsen in this period, as well as the way in which the controversiality of the image of Denmark that they mediated is gradually eroded, offers valuable insights into the competing exo- and endo-stereotypes of Danish national identity in late nineteenth- and early twentieth-century sociopolitical discourse. Both Brandes and Nielsen were closely associated with Scandinavian modernity, the former for his impassioned advocacy of a socially engaged modern literature, the latter for her compelling cinematic depictions of strong-willed, sexually emancipated women.

Brandes and Nielsen contributed to the emergence of an exo-stereotype of Danish cultural and national identity as freethinking and permissive at a time when social and cultural conditions in Denmark did not yet embody these qualities. Their transmission of a culturally modern and socially progressive image of Denmark in Germany during this period of Danish political diminution affected European views of Denmark and Scandinavia as well as Denmark's self-image around the turn of the century, projecting an image of de facto Danish modernity, although Danes were still deeply divided over the question of modernization. Although many Danes at the time rejected the liberal causes that Nielsen and Brandes represented, the fact that Danish society today so closely resembles the image of Denmark popularized by Brandes and Nielsen suggests that their efforts to influence the cultural geography of Denmark were neither futile nor misguided, despite the opposition they encountered at home. In this way, although one cannot assert that they were directly responsible for the actual establishment of political and social modernity in Denmark, their performative enactment of this modernity before it became widely accepted positioned Brandes and Nielsen as representative icons of Danish cultural modernity as seen from abroad.

By its nature, culture is both a reflection of the past and a product of the present. The term "national culture" can designate many things, including a given country's predominant beliefs, habits, preferences, and values, as well as the relationship between the various political, economic, and intellectual realms within a given society. It has, however, no ontological reality or temporal permanence on its own; it exists only in the minds and practices of its bearers. Urban explains that "culture is necessarily characterized by its 'onceness.' It has been. But culture is also on its way somewhere—whether or not it gets there—and hence, it is also characterized by its futurity."[10] The dynamic nature of culture means that it encompasses both traditional and progressive elements, despite the protests of the adherents of one mindset or the other. Thus, at the same time as public figures affect external perceptions of their national cultures, they are also engaged in shaping the internal development of those same cultures, as evidenced by the gradual disappearance of the discrepancy between the conservative social climate of early twentieth-century Denmark and the controversial modernity of the image of Denmark associated with Brandes and Nielsen. Opponents perceived their progressive views and unconventional lifestyles as threatening to the familiar, traditional Christian morals of nineteenth-century Danish society, while their supporters celebrated the liberation of Danish society from outmoded, restrictive social mores. Over time, as Danish culture gradually embraced modern views in such areas as secularization, democracy, civil rights, and sexuality, disapproval of Brandes and Nielsen gave way to approbation for their pioneering efforts in imagining and performing modern Danish identity.

One reason why Brandes and Nielsen were able to mediate and disseminate ideas about Danish national identity so effectively was their use of mass media. It is a common complaint in today's society that the purveyors of mass media shape public opinion in support of particular agendas, but this is by no means a new phenomenon, as the targeted advertising of the *Vaterland*'s voyage in 1914 illustrates. The mass media are both a byproduct and agent of modernity, in the sense that their very existence presupposes the rise of the masses as consumers of information and culture, while their function is to disseminate seemingly endless streams of information to ever-larger groups at ever-increasing speeds.[11] The scope and complexity of modern life make it impossible for individuals to form firsthand opinions about every issue, with the result that people have little choice but to base their opinions of much of the world around them on the information they receive through the media: newspapers, magazines, television, film, and the Internet. It is inherent in the nature of mass media to transmit not only information but also value judgments about that information that shape its interpretation and perceived significance. In the 1940s, Frankfurt School philosophers Theodor Adorno and Max Horkheimer coined the term "the culture industry"[12] to describe the influence of mass media on the public's cultural norms and political views. Although mass media are frequently subject to government censorship—whether in Denmark in 1799 or Syria in 2012—for their role in circulating revolutionary ideas, Adorno and Horkheimer warn that mass media foster homogeneity and standardization by making culture complicit with capitalism in order to "sell" very specific identity constructions to their audiences. By controlling the origination, popularization, and interpretation of the ideas, objects, practices, and values that define specific national cultures, mass media are instrumental in establishing the very cultural and social norms that they often appear to challenge.

Brandes's and Nielsen's use of mass media to publicize their preferred model of Danish cultural identity was therefore integral to the perceived modernity of that identity construction. Danish film historian Mette Hjort identifies two possible foci for the study of culture: the content of cultural productions, on the premise that transmission of culture is a form of duplication that leaves the content unchanged, and the processes of transmission themselves, predicated on the belief that such processes "reflect the particularities of cultural forms."[13] Her analysis complements and completes media theorist Marshall McLuhan's slogan "the medium is the message," which encapsulates his assertion that "the real import of media technology is not their apparent content ... but rather their material presence, as discrete technologies, and more importantly, the reticulated networks of production and consumption they create."[14] McLuhan's ideas, in turn, are prefigured in Walter Benjamin's seminal 1936 essay "The Work of Art in the Age of Its Technological Reproducibility" (*Das Kunstwerk im Zeitalter seiner technischen Reproduzierbarkeit*). Benjamin argues that the mechanical reproduction of art dislocates it from space and time, making it instantly and infinitely accessible wherever a reproduction is found.[15] In the case of Nielsen and Brandes, both content and form are important: the mechanically reproducible nature of their articles, books, and films enabled them to reach a widely dispersed audience, who formed opinions both about the subject matter being treated and, particularly as a result of the illusion of intimacy fostered by the apparent immediacy of film, about the creators of the works themselves.

Despite the many differences between the newspaper and film genres in which Brandes and Nielsen were active, they are both highly influential forms of mass media that have had a profound effect on the way culture is transmitted and its influence on how modern societies perceive the world around them. In much the same way that Benedict Anderson identifies the newspaper as a quintessentially modern genre that has played a pivotal role in changing the way its readers conceive of time and their relationship to the societies in which they live,[16] film scholars such as Mary Ann Doane and Philip Rosen argue that the cinema creates modernity by renegotiating collective perceptions of time, space, history, and identity.[17] Both of these media facilitate the metacultural process that Urban describes as "[etching] an image of [cultural] objects ... onto the diaphanous membrane of intelligible understanding."[18] While the images generated by newspapers in the period under consideration were primarily mental, aside from occasional woodcuts, lithographs, and later photographs, the cinema, then as now, showcases prefabricated images of reality that essentially dictate their own reception and interpretation. Urban explains how this process of cultural transmission functions: "One sees a film, and one is able to pull culture out of it—to recite or employ lines from it, to model one's behavior or clothing or hair styles on characters in it, to script one's interaction with others according to the plot that organizes it."[19] This process is a highly individual one, albeit replicated simultaneously thousands of times in theaters across the globe at any given moment.

On the level of collective cultural identity formation, newspapers and film share many of the formal attributes that Anderson ascribes to the newspaper as a facilitator for the emergence of imagined communities. Anderson describes the newspaper as a "one-day best-seller," "a book sold on a colossal scale, but of ephemeral popularity," that is consumed almost simultaneously by thousands of individuals, each of whom "is well aware that the ceremony he performs is being replicated simultaneously by thousands (or millions) of others of whose existence he is confident, yet of whose identity he has not the slightest notion."[20] The cinema also facilitates simultaneous, communal consumption, both in actual movie theaters in a particular city or country, where viewers immerse themselves in a specific imagined community cheek by jowl with dozens of strangers, as well as in the global circulation of films during specific, limited time periods. In certain respects, early silent films transcended the ability of newspapers to convey information, for they were capable of the kind of photographic realism that newspapers in the early twentieth century were not and enjoyed a wider circulation than newspapers that were generally restricted to a single city or region.[21] Robert C. Allen goes so far as to describe very early silent film, as far back as 1898, as a "visual newspaper,"[22] a judgment that derives in part from a statement by Harry Marvin, the first president of Biograph, that "the public demanded of us the prompt and reliable service of the daily newspaper.... The public has expected us to gather the news in a pictorial way and disseminate it at once."[23] Reading the same newspapers and seeing the same films can contribute to group coherence by preferentially popularizing certain values and ideas. Yet since neither the newspaper nor the film industry is ideologically unified, the nature of the values and ideas being conveyed to audiences relies to a large extent on the choice of media outlets, which, in turn, is closely linked to the individuals associated with particular media vehicles.

Due to the rapidity and vast geographical extent of the circulation of modern mass media, the high public profile of media personalities, whether entertainers, journalists, or reality television stars, generates a self-reinforcing global cult of celebrity that endows its members with disproportionate influence over public opinion. Marshall notes that "the celebrity is, in fact, by definition a fundamentally intertextual sign," configured by the interplay between the achievements upon which their fame is based and the circulation of information about them as individuals in the public domain.[24] Celebrities receive media attention simply because they are already well-known, thereby becoming more famous and therefore more valuable for conveying connotative meaning, as illustrated by Brandes's and Nielsen's invitation to participate in the maiden voyage of the *Vaterland*. Famous individuals are not only frequently endowed with an air of authority, deserved or not, as a result of their position in the public eye, but are also often associated with particular behaviors, values, ideologies, and cultural traditions. Such associations are not entirely arbitrary but are derived from the cultural products with which the celebrities are affiliated. Marshall explains that "celebrities function in consumer culture as a connecting fiber between the materiality of production and culturally contextualized meaning of consumption and its relation to collective identity."[25] In light of Urban's discussion of metaculture, one could argue that celebrities embody particular models of cultural identity that are performatively constructed through their participation in mass media but often uncritically emulated by their fans.

Fame is, of course, an age-old phenomenon, but modern celebrity distinguishes itself from earlier periods not only by the sheer amount of personal information about famous individuals that is made public but particularly by its integral role in the commodification of culture. With its calculated, market-driven creation of movie stars, the film industry played a central role in the industrialization of the cult of celebrity in the 1910s and 1920s. The resulting mass production of iconic celebrities thus had little to do with an individual's contributions to politics, science, or industry, as had been the case in former times. Instead, as Paul Taylor and Jan Harris explain, with reference to sociologist Leo Lowenthal's study of the American film industry between 1901 and 1941, "Consumption became the overarching frame of reference for understanding public figures. The idols of consumption Lowenthal described represented an early example of the much more sophisticated role played by today's celebrities as embodiments of commodity values."[26] The corresponding cultural shift from dispassionate awareness of agents of social production to emotionally charged admiration for agents of social and individual consumption allows celebrities to be manipulated by the culture industry for commercial purposes, a process that relies on the viewer's desire to identify in some tangible way with the object of admiration.

The cult of celebrity creates an illusory sense of intimacy between creators and consumers of culture that can distort audience members' perception of the reality of their relationship with a particular celebrity. For example, although Brandes maintained a prolific correspondence with dozens of individuals he knew personally, it was through his newspaper articles that his views reached and influenced millions of strangers, some of whom came to adore him and others to loathe him. Likewise, both Nielsen's films and the newspaper coverage of her personal and professional life contributed to giving audiences across the globe a sense of closeness to her, which occasionally manifested itself in bizarre ways. One anecdote that Nielsen was fond of retelling took place in 1913, when a man in a small town in Spain attended a showing of one of her films each night for a full week; on the last night, he pulled out a revolver and shot her image on the screen.[27] She learned about the incident from the newspapers and published a statement in the newspaper to assure her fans that she "didn't feel the least bit shot."[28] This encounter demonstrates the difficulty faced by early fans at deciphering the ontological status of the celebrities they knew only from the screen. Both the shooting itself and the resulting, implied concern among Nielsen's fans for her well-being that prompted her public response testify to the deeply personal connection consumers felt (and still feel) toward celebrities.

The story of Brandes and Nielsen, both as celebrities and as close personal friends, illuminates the way in which metacultural coverage of Denmark in the international media contributed to the development of both exo- and endo-stereotypes of Danish national identity. As Marshall notes, "The power of the celebrity . . . is to represent the active construction of identity in the social world, . . . to embody or help embody 'collective configurations' of the social world."[29] Therefore, the key to understanding Brandes's and Nielsen's contributions to perceptions of Danishness lies in the way in which the works they produced shaped such identity constructions, individual and collective, within the social worlds they both inhabited and represented. In the years between the invasions of Denmark in 1864 and 1940, two conflicting images of Scandinavia competed for the imagination of German media audiences. One was a romanticized view of simple, hardy descendants of Vikings living among rugged, alpine Nordic landscapes, an image popularized by newspaper and film coverage of Kaiser Wilhelm II's annual pilgrimages to the Norwegian fjords and reinforced by the graceful but often grim fairy tales of Hans Christian Andersen. The other approach transformed admiration for the gritty realism and progressive social agendas of such authors as Ibsen and

Strindberg into a conviction of Scandinavia's intrinsic cultural modernity. Both Brandes and Nielsen promoted the latter view, which, by the mid-twentieth century, ultimately emerged as the dominant image of Scandinavian culture, both in rejection of the tainted Aryan racial narrative promoted by the Nazis in the 1930s and '40s and as a reflection of the widespread political and socioeconomic changes in postwar Scandinavian societies and governments that positioned them as champions of individual liberties, social welfare, and humanitarian causes.

Brandes's and Nielsen's respective careers fall into two parts, each phase demarcated by both a particular historical period and a distinctive orientation of his or her work. In Brandes's case, the first phase extends from his controversial debut as a literary critic in Copenhagen in 1871 until the mid-1890s, while the second phase encompasses his literary and sociopolitical work from the turn of the century up to his death in 1927. Nielsen's early career spanned the years 1910 to 1919, from the introduction of the feature-length film through the end of World War I; her later film career took place primarily from 1919 to 1937, from the beginning of the Weimar Republic through the onset of the Third Reich, although Nielsen continued to work in a variety of public media, including newspapers, literature, and documentary film after her return to Denmark in 1937, where she lived until her death in 1972. Despite the wide disparity in their ages, the friendship between Brandes and Nielsen, which began near the beginning of Nielsen's career and toward the end of Brandes's, lasted for nearly two decades and offers an intimate view of the burden of personal success and patriotic sentiment that these two famous Danes shared.

Georg Brandes was a highly visible figure throughout Europe long before Asta Nielsen's birth, in particular after he attracted both acclaim and notoriety in 1871 for his famous condemnation of Danish literature as stagnant, uninspired, and forty years behind the rest of Europe in his highly influential literary survey "Main Currents in Nineteenth-Century Literature" (*Hovedstrømninger i det 19de Aarhundredes Litteratur*). Born in 1842 and raised in a middle-class, assimilated Jewish home in Copenhagen, Brandes completed a brilliant university career, making a name for himself in Denmark as a gifted literary and social critic. His lecture series, which introduced French literary naturalism to central and northern Europe under the banner of literary and cultural modernization, established Brandes as an authority on modern literature and quickly earned him a following

Figure 1.2. In contrast to his expectations of becoming a professor of aesthetics at the University of Copenhagen, Brandes's provocative lectures on modern European literature propelled him to the forefront of a literary and social revolution in Denmark that came to be known as the "Modern Breakthrough." Painted by Harold Slott-Møller, 1889. Credit: The Royal Library, Copenhagen, Department of Maps, Prints, and Photographs

of idealistic students and feminists. Brandes built his career on the interpretation of literature and commentary on social and political issues, but, over the course of the early 1870s, the combination of his radical program of literary modernization, his controversial views on social issues, and his scandalous private life proved too much for many of his bourgeois Danish peers.

While his realistic literary aesthetics resonated with many young Danish authors, Brandes's condemnation of religion and his outspoken advocacy for women's rights and civil marriage, in conjunction with his many extramarital affairs, earned him a reputation as a cosmopolitan liberal. This made him a persona non grata among the educated elite (*dannelsesborgerskab*) in Copenhagen, many of whom cited his Jewish heritage as evidence of his un-Danishness. This ideological and personal opposition manifested itself in the mid-1870s in economic ways, primarily through the denial of a coveted professorship at the University of Copenhagen and Brandes's exclusion from Copenhagen newspapers. Unable to make a living in Denmark as a result of the hostility of the Danish bourgeoisie, Brandes moved to Berlin in 1877, where he built an international reputation as a literary critic and promoter of the realistic literary style associated with the Scandinavian Modern Breakthrough, as realized in the works of Ibsen and Jacobsen, among others.[30]

As a Dane, and thus a bystander in the nationalistic cultural politics of the great powers, Brandes was in a peculiarly advantageous position to introduce Nordic interpretations of French literary modernism into German intellectual circles, which had been isolated from French cultural developments by the political and military hostility between the two countries in the 1860s. He built his reputation by means of literary-critical articles in widely circulated German cultural newspapers; lecture tours; monographs about Scandinavian, French, and Russian modernist writers; and a personal relationship with many of Germany and Austria's leading writers and thinkers. Although deeply involved in German cultural discourse, Brandes remained acutely aware of sociopolitical developments in Denmark, reflecting his personal investment in the liberalization of Danish society. He returned to Denmark in 1882, after a group of forty-eight anonymous private donors committed to providing him with financial support, at a level equal to a professorial salary, for a period of ten years. Brandes continued to visit Germany at least once a year, however, and more than seventy volumes of his works emerged from German presses between 1883 and 1900. Over the next several decades, Brandes's European fame continued to grow, especially after he became known as the man who "discovered" Nietzsche by offering the first public analysis of the German philosopher's work through a series of five lectures in 1888 that were published a year later under the title *Aristocratic Radicalism* (*Aristokratisk Radikalisme*).

By the end of the nineteenth century, when Denmark had begun to achieve a degree of social and political modernization in terms of the rise of democratic institutions and civil rights, Brandes turned his attention abroad once more, becoming known for his public activism on behalf of oppressed minorities in Europe, ranging from the culturally oppressed Danes in Schleswig to the violently persecuted Armenians in Turkey. Although Denmark was itself still a colonial power in Greenland, Iceland, the Faroe Islands, and the West Indies, albeit no longer in India and Africa by 1850, Brandes positioned himself as an outspoken opponent of European colonialism, imperialism, and nationalism. He sacrificed much of his European prestige and some close friendships with, among others, French prime minister Georges Clemenceau, by speaking out against World War I and refusing to choose sides, but he regained a position of influence in the interwar period, when he wrote prolifically for Danish, European, and American newspapers about world politics. By the time he died in 1927, a few weeks past his eighty-fifth birthday, Brandes was one of the most famous Danes of his time and a pillar of the European cultural establishment.

Brandes's legacy as a literary scholar and humanitarian activist turned out to be far from undisputed, however, both abroad and at home. The backlash against his refusal to take the side of France during World War I barred him from inclusion in French literary histories, while his chastisement of the Poles he had championed against Russia for their persecution of Jews during World War I placed him on the Polish intelligentsia's blacklist. The anti-Semitic policies of Nazi Germany in the years immediately following his death ensured that his substantial contributions to German cultural life were either erased or suppressed. In Denmark, meanwhile, the long-standing rivalry between Brandes's supporters and opponents became increasingly irrelevant in the social and political upheaval of the 1930s and 1940s. Yet the old pro- and contra-Brandes camps emerged once more after the war; when Danish author and literary historian Elias Bredsdorff (1912–2002) defended his doctoral dissertation about Brandes and Henrik Pontoppidan in 1964, one of the criticisms raised, by professor Paul Krüger, was that Brandes was not Danish enough.[31]

Asta Nielsen's path to fame was more precipitous than Brandes's, but no less challenging. Born into an impoverished blue-collar family in Copenhagen in 1881, Nielsen seemed an unlikely prospect for international stardom. Her mother hoped she would become a shop clerk, but instead her husky alto voice earned her a spot as a charity pupil at the Danish Royal Theater at age twelve. In 1901, at age twenty, Nielsen gave birth to a child out of wedlock, a daughter she named Jesta. She never named the father, but, according to her biographer, Poul Malmkjær, the most likely candidate was her acting instructor, the much older (and married) Peter Jernsdorff.[32] When she finished her training, Nielsen had trouble finding work in Copenhagen theaters, so, from 1905 to 1907, she toured Scandinavia with a group of young actors, earning the admiration of Norwegian playwright Thomas Krag and Danish author Herman Bang, but no theater contract.

Despite her talent as an actress, Nielsen was marginalized in the Danish theater world by her dark hair and dark eyes, which did not conform to the prevailing audience preference for the stereotypically Nordic ideal of blond, blue-eyed beauty. Fellow actor and lifelong friend Olaf Fønss described her as "a gypsy—a daughter of the South with wildness flashing from her curly, shining black hair and with the suppleness of a beast of prey in her slender body."[33] In his opinion, Nielsen's exotic appearance, combined with her strong personality, prevented her from achieving professional success in Copenhagen; he noted that "no one was as dramatically individualistic as Asta Nielsen—so dramatically that it was almost a handicap for her; for, as a result of her foreign-looking appearance and her bold manner, she stood out so distinctly from the other small Danish ducklings in the duckyard that she had trouble finding a place for herself."[34] In her later career, Nielsen exploited this perception of exoticism to enhance her mystique and never contradicted claims such as Robert Neiiendam's speculation that "gypsy blood" accounted for Nielsen's "exotic-erotic glamour."[35]

Nielsen attracted international attention with the spectacular box-office success of her first film, *The Abyss / Afgrunden* (Urban Gad, 1910), which led to contracts with several German film companies and a dazzling career in the German film industry over the next two decades. As a trailblazer in the field of realistic cinema acting and the beneficiary of the monopoly film distribution system's need for iconic "stars," Nielsen became one of the leading actresses in the German film industry before World War I, headlining an annual film series and earning an astronomical salary. Since its emergence as a popular and profitable cultural medium at the end of the nineteenth century, cinema has functioned as a vehicle for both entertainment and

Figure 1.3. Asta Nielsen's successful debut film put her in an ideal position to be launched as one of the world's first global movie stars, promoted worldwide by the German film industry's publicity machine. Reproduction of a postcard by Becker & Maass, Berlin. Credit: The Royal Library, Copenhagen, Department of Maps, Prints, and Photographs

education, offering viewers a glimpse of alternate realities and suggestions for how to shape their own lives. Nielsen's films are particularly noteworthy for her performative enactment of distinctly modern constructions of gender and shifting national identities. The war interrupted her career, but also enshrined her reputation as an international star, with her picture decorating trenches on both sides of the conflict. Although the conditions of filmmaking in Germany changed radically in the Weimar Republic, Nielsen succeeded in rebuilding her career in the early 1920s. Although she struggled to find acceptable roles during the late 1920s, she remained a high-profile star until her retirement from the cinema in 1932, by which time she had made nearly seventy films. During the late 1920s and 1930s, however, rising Swedish stars such as Greta Garbo, Zarah Leander, and Kristina Söderbaum took Nielsen's place as iconic cinema representatives of Scandinavian sensuality and modernity in Germany. Nielsen returned to Denmark in 1937, where she lived in quiet obscurity, punctuated by occasional flurries of media attention, until her death in 1972. She published a two-volume memoir, *The Silent Muse (Den tiende Muse)*, in 1945–46, as well as several short stories, but she received little recognition from the Danish film community until a few years before her death, when she directed a documentary about herself that premiered at the 1968 Berlinale.

Despite her undeniable significance to silent cinema, Nielsen's position in Danish national cinema history is still disputed, a paradox that offers insight into the role of national cinema in processes of Danish national identity construction in the early twentieth century, in particular the effect of politics of positionality on Nielsen's classification as a Danish film star. Danish film companies were leaders in early silent European cinema, far out of proportion to the size of Denmark's population and economy, but Danish film was eclipsed by the German and American film industries after World War I. The reception of Nielsen's German-made films in Denmark tracks this rise and fall: her pre–World War I films were heavily marketed and widely distributed in Denmark, but her films from the 1920s were rarely even screened in her homeland. Once Danish film lost its influential position in the European market and became a "minor cinema," Danish cultural critics and audiences were less tolerant of a Danish actress who had chosen to throw in her lot with the competition. Mette Hjort explains that "the term *minor* points . . . to the existence of regimes of cultural power and to the need for strategic resourcefulness on the part of those who are unfavorably situated within the cultural landscape in question, be it a national context or a more properly global one."[36] When Denmark's peripheral status in world politics in the 1920s eviscerated its ability to safeguard the export market of one of its most successful industries against the strong-arm tactics of the German government, Danish film producers and audiences turned inward, producing films primarily for domestic consumption and discounting the accomplishments of expatriate Danes such as Nielsen. Rather than her Danish nationality, the fact that Nielsen made the majority of her films in Germany became the decisive factor in determining her contributions to Danish national cinema.

The friendship between Brandes and Nielsen, which predated their voyage on the *Vaterland* by several years, rested on a foundation of professional respect and personal compatibility. Nielsen's spectacularly successful film debut had not only catapulted her into prominence but also led to her marriage to her talented director, Urban Gad. Gad was the son of Rear Admiral Urban and Mrs. Emma Gad, who were prominent figures in Copenhagen society, not least because of Emma's career as a successful playwright, journalist, and author of several books on domestic etiquette. Their home in Dronningens Tværgade 40 was a well-known salon for Danish literati, where Brandes was a frequent guest, alongside Gustav Wied, Sophus and Karin Michaëlis, and Henri Nathansen, among others.[37] Brandes met Nielsen at one such gathering in 1912 and found himself charmed by her wit and beauty. For her part, Nielsen recalled, "At that time I had just eagerly devoured most of his works and was delighted to learn later that he appreciated me."[38]

In subsequent years, they saw each other frequently in Berlin and Copenhagen, enjoying a light-hearted friendship strengthened by a similar sense of humor, as the following anecdote illustrates. On her mother-in-law's instructions, Nielsen made a point of serving Brandes an array of olives whenever he came to lunch. In 1916 she even smuggled a large jar of Spanish olives back through war-torn Europe to Copenhagen for him after a visit to Granada. In her memoirs, Nielsen describes the moment when she triumphantly presented the jar to Brandes:

> He looked at the jar with disgust, turned it a few times in his thin fingers, and asked, "Why in the world have you brought me these things?" "Because I know they are your favorite food." "I hate olives," he almost snarled. "Once, to be polite to the hostess, I

praised her olives, and since then these disgusting things have plagued me whenever I am seated at a table. I don't want to own them, take them back, just the sight of them makes me ill."[39]

Nielsen recalled the many times she had served him olives, which he had politely eaten, but realized, "At his own table, he wanted to be left alone."[40] This potentially awkward moment became an inside joke and a bond between them, a reminder that although they were both bound to try to obey social conventions, they each knew the other would understand and forgive any transgressions of polite society's rules.

Their preserved correspondence is not extensive, but it is heartfelt, showing the mutual respect, affection, and growing intimacy between them. The address "Dear Madam" of Brandes's early letters gives way to "Dear Asta Nielsen" and finally "Dearest Asta." In a letter from December 23, 1916, in which he belatedly and somewhat abashedly thanks Nielsen for the jar of olives, Brandes laments, "I am ashamed that I have never done anything at all for you, although I have always admired you."[41] In a letter dated December 24, 1919, written in response to receiving Nielsen's annual Christmas picture postcard of herself, he confessed,

> If only I were also lovely, Asta, I would also have a stack of pictures of myself lying around and could just take one and write "Merry Christmas" on it and show you thereby that I was thinking of you. But I am anything but young and lovely and guard myself well against giving pictures away and cannot express my warm feelings with such brevity. Dear Asta, dear Wingårdh, my heart belongs to you and there are, unfortunately, only very few people I care about, on the threshold to 1920.[42]

Brandes's relationship with Nielsen was clearly a source of comfort and happiness for him in the final decades of his life. In fact, his often flirtatious letters even suggest a touch of infatuation, which is not hard to understand, given Nielsen's beauty and vivacity. Although he was not generally a fan of the cinema, Brandes attended the Copenhagen premiere of Nielsen's controversial film version of *Hamlet* in 1921 to show his support for her. Nielsen's account of their relationship in her memoirs is equally affectionate, suggesting that Brandes's legendary charm was still as potent as ever, despite his advanced years. German film critic Willy Haas recalls Nielsen's description of Brandes as "my fatherly friend," and documents the emotional indebtedness expressed in her assertion that "everything that I have and that one can receive from another person, I have received from him."[43]

During the heady "Goulash Age" in Copenhagen during the first few years of World War I, a period of prosperity brought on by the astronomical profits of Danish merchants supplying foodstuffs—including canned goulash—to troops on both sides of the conflict, Nielsen would often invite groups of friends to her apartment on Vestergade, of which Brandes was the "luminous center."[44] Nielsen's descriptions of Brandes's behavior at her gatherings depict him as an elegant but energetic guest. Just as on board the *Vaterland*, he was very punctual. In her memoirs, Nielsen recalls, "Exactly three minutes after the appointed time, G. B. stood in my living room as the first guest, with the precision that is often characteristic of great men. Having little fondness for solitude, when he wasn't working, he was always in the mood for a cheerful little get-together."[45] She disputes the widespread charge that Brandes always sought to monopolize the conversation at parties and to gather all the guests around himself in an attentive circle, and poses the question whether anyone exists who did not enjoy "the magic of his speech, the life and spirit he radiated, and the charm with which he could accompany his own not always friendly comments."[46] She also praises his toasts for their wit and artistry, which enchanted his friends and enemies alike.

Brandes was likewise generous in his praise of Nielsen's accomplishments. At a party in Nielsen's honor in January 1918, Brandes made a speech, full of references to inside jokes between them, including her habit of avoiding him at parties, the ill-fated jar of olives, and a flirtatious conversation they had on board the *Vaterland*. He also articulated what has become one of the most often-quoted descriptions of Nielsen:

> Everyone is familiar with Asta's beauty. She is a full-blooded rose, a moor-rose. Everyone knows her expressive eyes, the versatility of her talent, the popularity she enjoys, her international reputation. If I rode on the wings of dawn to the outermost ocean, I would find Asta's name there as well.[47]

Brandes's praise of Nielsen is genuine but not fawning, capturing both his own admiration for her and the mark she had made on the world. In 1920, on the occasion of her divorce from Urban Gad and remarriage to the Swedish shipbuilder Freddy Wingårdh, he offered public recognition of her unique position in Danish culture, explaining,

"Many years ago in Paris, I read a sign projecting from a house, where fencing instruction was offered: There is *one* God, *one* sun, and *one* Lucioni, Fencing Master in the 1st Z. Regiment. Thus there stands written in flaming letters in the air over this bitter, ill-tempered city: There is *one* Asta."[48] Despite his masterful use of hyperbole in praise of Nielsen, however, Brandes disliked being made a fuss over. On the occasion of his own seventy-seventh birthday, at a party hosted for him by Gertrud and Otto Rung, Nielsen was given the task of crowning Brandes with a laurel wreath; when she tried to place it on his head, he tore it off and muttered, "What should I do with such finery?"[49] Nielsen noted dryly, "That is also far more characteristic of G. B's reaction to homage."[50]

After the war, their friendship continued until Brandes's death. Nielsen returned to Berlin to work and rebuild her fortune, while Brandes resumed the international traveling he enjoyed so much, often in the company of his secretary, Gertrud Rung, revisiting Italy, Greece, and, frequently, Germany. Nielsen spent many sociable evenings in Brandes's Berlin apartment, at one of which she met the Russian émigré Grigori Chmara, with whom she lived in a common-law marriage in Berlin for most of the 1920s and 1930s and who costarred with her in many of her films from this period. The end of an era was approaching, however, both in terms of Brandes's increasing frailty and a shift in Nielsen's professional orientation from cinema back to stage acting. Fittingly, Nielsen's last silent film, *The Dangerous Age / Das gefährliche Alter,* an adaptation of Danish writer Karin Michaëlis's controversial novel from 1910, appeared in theaters in 1927, the same year that Brandes died.

Although both Brandes and Nielsen are celebrated in Denmark today for their contributions to Denmark's cultural legacy and international renown, their reception in Denmark during their lifetimes was much more problematic. Each had ardent supporters and fans in Denmark, but, for the most part, their Danish contemporaries, particularly in the news media, regarded them skeptically, treating them either with distant politeness or outright contempt. Despite his high standing among the cultural and literary elite of Europe, Brandes never gained full acceptance in the social circles of the Copenhagen upper bourgeoisie. Throughout his life, he remained a polarizing figure who inspired the devotion of a few and the loathing of many. Nielsen did not inspire the same virulent hatred as Brandes, but she encountered a remarkable amount of disdain in her homeland. Although other factors certainly contributed, ranging from personal or professional jealousy to nationalistic antagonism toward Germany and all persons associated with it, Danish society's reluctance to accept both Brandes and Nielsen reveals certain similarities that suggest that the primary cause of this disconnect is, in fact, metacultural, originating in deep-seated tensions within Danish society over the ideal character of Danish national identity and anxiety over the way in which Brandes's and Nielsen's work shaped international perceptions of Danishness.

By 1871, when Brandes's career began in earnest, Denmark had become a small, homogeneous nation with a penchant for self-analysis. The disastrous foreign policy failures Denmark experienced in the early and mid-nineteenth century had led to "a constant diminution of territory and converging development of concentration on Danishness that met no or only small barriers of an ethnic and geographic kind."[51] Such national introspection, combined with a strong propensity toward socially conservative ideals, made Danes acutely sensitive to the way in which prominent individuals, such as Brandes and Nielsen, represented their homeland. Well before he made his fortune in Germany, Brandes's advocacy of liberal social reforms branded him the enemy of traditional Danish bourgeois morality, the embodiment of modernity's threat to traditional values, respect, morals, Christianity, and patriotism. His defense of such causes as women's emancipation, civil marriage, and atheism were interpreted as representative of a dangerous socialist movement that would corrupt Danish society with radical foreign ideas, including new sciences, social organizational forms, and a secular way of life. Similarly, Nielsen's eroticized film personas seemed to glorify the alluring dangers of immorality. In 1912 a major Danish newspaper argued that Nielsen was the "primary representative of the dangerous direction of 'sensual films,'" describing her as the "priestess of sensuality and a master in her field."[52]

In order to justify Denmark's rejection of its own most famous artists, the Danish press made a point of denying Brandes and Nielsen any claim to Danishness, on the basis of a perceived inherent foreignness about them. Leading nationalist newspapers such as *Fædrelandet* and *Dagbladet* denounced Brandes's international orientation as anti-Danish, arguing that his cosmopolitanism and Jewish heritage were fundamentally alien to the Danish national character. For her part, Nielsen's dark hair and eyes bore little resemblance to the stereotypical blond-haired, blue-eyed ideal of Nordic beauty, prompting many critics and biographers to insist that she must have more exotic ethnic origins, which could account for her blatant sensuality on screen.[53]

Further proof of Brandes's and Nielsen's lack of legitimacy as examples of Danish national identity seemed to come from their voluntary and prolonged association with Germany. Danish historian Claus Bjørn asserts that "throughout the last century, much of what the Danes have understood as characteristically Danish features can be understood as the opposite to the equivalent German traits. Danishness, as it were, had to be contrary to Germany and everything represented by Germany."[54] Nielsen and Brandes were by no means the only Danes to seek their fortune abroad, merely the latest in a long tradition of successful border-crossing Danes stretching back at least as far as Hans Christian Andersen and Søren Kierkegaard, but historical coincidence and their own success worked against them. When Brandes moved to Germany in 1877, the scars from the war of 1864 were still fresh, such that Brandes seemed to be going over to the enemy. Similarly, Nielsen chose to return to Germany after World War I, when nationalistic sentiment in Denmark was running high once more. Not only had Germany provided her with professional opportunities that Denmark did not and could not, she seemed to favor German culture over Danish, a preference that would later give rise to accusations, which Nielsen adamantly refuted, of being a Nazi sympathizer.

Behind these metacultural debates about Denmark's status vis-à-vis Germany, however, lies an even more basic question about the nature of Danish culture and society. Many of Nielsen's and Brandes's supporters felt that Denmark's unwillingness to admire their successes reflected a fundamental provinciality and small-mindedness inherent to Danes, that it was resentment of anyone else's success, of the violation of the unwritten Jantelov dictate "You must not believe that you are somebody" (*Du skal ikke tro, du er noget*),[55] that prevented recognition by their homeland. Acknowledging that Nielsen's Danish contemporaries treated her pettily, Malmkjær argues that

> [Danes] should have been proud of her, proud that the world had seen her eyes, that she made film acting art, that she showed that Denmark still had more to offer than a Heath Society and a Co-op movement. For she *was* Danish, and she remained Danish with a Danish passport and insurance, a taste for sausages, and eternal discontent with the weather.[56]

Nielsen's and Brandes's metacultural role in crafting international perceptions of Denmark may have disgruntled many Danes of the time who felt that they represented an excessively liberal or even immoral incarnation of Danish national identity, but their highly visible, if controversial, contributions to such discourses undoubtedly secured Denmark a position on the international stage far more prominent than the country's weakened political status warranted.

The groundbreaking professional success and international cultural prominence of individuals such as Nielsen and Brandes enabled Denmark to compensate for its peripheral geographic position and political weakness, at a time when the threat of complete domination by Germany was ever present. At the inauguration of the Herstedvester shortwave radio station in 1934, King Christian X thanked "[Our] countrymen in other countries . . . for preserving your love for the old country, the Danish flag, and the Danish language. Thank you for representing Denmark, Danish culture, and Danish throughout the world in a lovely and worthy manner. By your faithfulness, you have made Denmark greater."[57] In stark contrast to the fatalistic mood that pervaded Danish society in the aftermath of the German invasion in 1864, even the German occupation of Denmark from April 1940 to May 1945 could not destabilize the proud sense of Danish national identity that modern Danish literature and film had helped to shape. Denmark emerged from the war with a firm determination to create an equal-opportunity, socially responsible national community, which bore a striking resemblance to the image of Denmark presciently popularized by Brandes and Nielsen in the decades before the war.

Nearly a century after Brandes and Nielsen promenaded along the decks of the *Vaterland,* they are no longer the most famous Danes in Europe, but they have finally earned the respect of their own fatherland. In recent decades, Brandes and Nielsen have at last been claimed as part of Denmark's cultural inheritance. During the late 1950s and 1960s, the Danish press became increasingly sympathetic to Brandes's and Nielsen's plight, bemoaning the scandalous neglect to which they, particularly Nielsen, had been subjected. An upswing in popular-culture interest soon followed: in 1966, the highly respected director Theodor Christensen drafted a screenplay for a film based on Brandes's life, complete with a list of reasons justifying Brandes's relevance to the present day, but died before completing the project. In 1968 the young director Henrik Stangerup made a short film about Nielsen's life, which she at first collaborated on, then took over and remade to her own satisfaction. A veritable Brandes renaissance among Danish academics began in the late 1970s and continues through the present day, resulting in the publication of several volumes of conference proceedings, correspondence, anthologies, and biographies, most notably Jørgen Knudsen's comprehensive eight-volume biography, which appeared in installments between 1985 and 2004 and then as a condensed, single-volume edition in 2008. Nielsen has also received much more scholarly attention since her death. Film historian Marguerite Engberg has written several short biographical pieces about Nielsen, including a short book in 1966,[58] but it was not until 2000 that the first complete Danish biography of Nielsen appeared, written by Poul Malmkjær and titled *Asta: The Person, the Myth, and the Film Star* (*Asta: Mennesket, myten og filmstjernen*). In light of the renewed interest in Nielsen's life and work in Denmark over the past decade, Stephan Michael Schroeder suggests that the hegemonic influence of discourses of nationality on Nielsen's reception in Denmark has finally been broken,[59] but it may be more correct to say that Nielsen's self-affirmed identity as a modern, socially liberated Dane has finally been acknowledged by her countrymen as a distinguishing characteristic of her work, regardless of where her films were made. It took Denmark nearly half a century to recognize what Nielsen and Brandes may have felt all along—that no matter how far from home they traveled, how controversial their work appeared, or how famous they became, they could never divorce themselves from their national and cultural identities as Danes, and that their professional successes could enhance their homeland's prestige.

The progressive, free-thinking image of Danish national identity that Georg Brandes and Asta Nielsen transmitted to the world through their lives and works may not have reflected the conservative bourgeois society that dominated Danish culture in the late nineteenth and early twentieth century, but it resonates with Danes today, who have grown up in precisely such a secular, sexually liberated environment. While Brandes and Nielsen did not create this new society, their influential role in envisioning Danish cultural modernity is evident in the vitality and innovative character of modern Danish cultural productions, as well as their global marketability, from the insightful, thought-provoking films of Susanne Bier to the magical realism of Peter Høeg's novels to the lively reggae fusion music of Natasja Saad. As the international crisis that erupted in 2006 over the publication of cartoons depicting the Muslim prophet Mohammed in the Danish newspaper *Jyllands-Posten* reveals, Danish national identity is still a work in progress, subject to debates and disagreements over its actual and ideal nature, and the mass media continue to play a central role in mediating competing constructions of Danishness both within Denmark and throughout the world. It is, therefore, helpful to take a new look at these two talented individuals who played such central roles in enabling Danish culture and society to reach its present state, and to trace the trajectory of their lives and careers to see what we can learn from their examples.

PART ONE
Georg Brandes

CHAPTER TWO

The Literary Revolutionary

*Marketing Danish Modernity
in Imperial Germany*

The Danish literary critic Georg Brandes, who is widely credited with being the driving force behind the Scandinavian literary renaissance known as the Modern Breakthrough, was a provocative, paradoxical figure. In the first phase of his career, spanning roughly 1871 to 1891, Brandes established himself throughout Europe, despite fierce Danish opposition, as a leading arbiter of both Scandinavian and European modern literature, advocating a realist literary aesthetic and a correspondingly progressive social agenda. While his own professional success and financial security were always paramount, his engagement on behalf of Danish literature and culture was nevertheless a highly effective tool for rehabilitating Denmark's reputation in Continental Europe after a period of political decline. Brandes's life and views encompassed stark contrasts and contradictions with regard to social class, religion, national identity, personal beliefs, and political activity. He promoted women's rights but had a reputation as a callous philanderer. He advocated for the rights of the underclass and oppressed minorities, but admired "great men" such as Nietzsche and Bismarck. He came across as supremely confident, but was plagued by self-doubt in the privacy of his own mind. He was skeptical of all religion, including his own Jewishness, but was fascinated by religious thinkers ranging from Søren Kierkegaard to Jesus. He resented Germany's interference in Danish affairs and disdained its militaristic character, but moved to Berlin to advance his own career. He was a Dane who was most famous outside of

Denmark. He was regarded as unpatriotic by his countrymen, but he used his influence to the benefit of his country.

These incongruities are fundamental to assessing Brandes's effectiveness as the mediator of a modern Danish identity to continental Europe, for it is in the tensions between these contradictory facts and opinions about Brandes that the nature of his involvement in national identity construction is to be found. His name is rarely associated with Danish nationalism, except as a negative example, and he was often accused of being fundamentally un-Danish; yet analysis of his efforts on behalf of the modernization of Danish intellectual culture and the promotion of Danish culture abroad reveals that Brandes was in fact one of the most influential cultural nationalists in modern Danish history and that he played a central role in shaping exo-stereotypes of Danish national identity, particularly in Germany, in the late nineteenth century.

When Brandes was born in Copenhagen in 1842, his homeland was on the verge of a massive social and political paradigm shift. Denmark's military, economic, and territorial losses, a consequence of being on the losing side of the Napoleonic Wars in the first decades of the century, stimulated a cultural renaissance that came to be known as the Danish Golden Age. With the majority of the Danish bourgeoisie's intellectual energy being directed into cultural production rather than political activity, Danish culture reached unprecedented heights, fostering such literary luminaries as Johan Ludvig Heiberg, Adam Oehlenschläger, Hans Christian Andersen, and Søren Kierkegaard. Romanticism and nationalism flourished symbiotically throughout the first half of the nineteenth century, culminating in the rise of the National Liberal party that spearheaded the prodemocracy movement in the 1840s and oversaw Denmark's transition from an absolute to a constitutional monarchy in 1848. Despite the decisive role of Britain and France in bringing about the end of the first Schleswig war in 1852 and restoring the status quo ante bellum, the National Liberals claimed victory over the restive German-speaking minority in Schleswig-Holstein and its Prussian allies, cementing the link between nationalism and liberalism in mid-nineteenth-century Danish politics and setting the stage for the second Schleswig war in 1864.

The National Liberals' attempt to incorporate the duchy of Schleswig into the kingdom of Denmark by means of the 1863 November constitution violated the terms of the London Protocol and led to Denmark's second major foreign policy disaster of the nineteenth century. Coming to the defense of the German speakers in Schleswig and Holstein, Prussia and Austria invaded Denmark in December 1863 and decisively defeated the Danish army. With German troops occupying much of the Jutland peninsula, Denmark was forced to cede the provinces of Schleswig, Holstein, and Lauenburg to the German Confederation, losing 20 percent of its population, nearly 40 percent of its territory, and causing many Danes to fear that Denmark would soon cease to exist as an independent state.

The Danish political landscape post-1864 was strikingly different from the confident National Liberal alliance with romantic nationalism that precipitated the disaster. Denmark's politically humbling transformation from a multinational empire to a (nearly) ethnically homogenous nation-state exposed its vulnerability vis-à-vis Germany. Anger over Prussia's victory and subsequent annexation of Schleswig-Holstein with its significant Danish minority, paired with the fear of being subsumed politically and culturally into the rapidly expanding German Empire, whipped anti-German attitudes and Danish nationalism to extremes. During parliamentary discussions of the peace treaty in late 1864, politician Alfred Hage warned that not only was Denmark's political independence endangered, its national identity was as well; he prophesied that Denmark would slowly be "consumed by Germanness, by a Germanness that is unfortunately already far too widespread in all of Denmark, a Germanness that weakens us and steals our marrow and bone, and which is the cause of the whole terrible condition in which we find ourselves."[1] Although the combination of Germany's proximity, military might, and sheer size, especially after German unification in 1871, forced Denmark to follow Germany's lead in foreign affairs, Danes increasingly distanced themselves culturally from Germany in order to protect their political autonomy and concentrated on developing a more recognizably Danish cultural tradition.

Growing to adulthood in this environment, which paired rapidly fossilizing Danish Golden Age culture with desperate spasms of Danish nationalistic fervor, Brandes developed a strong sense of the flaws and shortcomings of his native culture at an early age. After completing his university studies in Copenhagen, he embarked on the traditional European Grand Tour, spending most of the late 1860s in Paris and London. Upon his return to Denmark in 1870, he began to position himself as an outspoken but influential literary and cultural critic. He began by publishing his doctoral dissertation,

Contemporary French Aesthetics (*Den franske Æsthetik i vore Dage*), which analyzed the contributions of Hippolyte Taine and Charles Augustin Sainte-Beuve to the development of realist literature and literary criticism. Shortly thereafter, he published a Danish translation of John Stuart Mill's *The Subjection of Women* (1869), in support of his own defense of women's emancipation and civil marriage. In the fall of 1871, he launched a polemical lecture series at the University of Copenhagen, which he later published as *Main Currents in Nineteenth-Century Literature* (*Hovedstrømninger i det 19de Aarhundredes Litteratur*). In *Main Currents,* Brandes outlines the stages of revolution and reaction that characterized the development of continental European literature in the late eighteenth and nineteenth centuries. Using the empirical method of historical positivism he had learned from Taine and Sainte-Beuve in Paris, Brandes contextualizes individual literary works in terms of their relationship to prevailing social and aesthetic norms, while continually drawing connections to the state of contemporary European politics and culture. He demonstrates how, against this backdrop, Danish culture, literature, and society appeared hopelessly backward and provincial, and calls for a literary revolution to revitalize Danish literature and society. The popularity and radicality of Brandes's views brought him to the attention of Denmark's educated bourgeoisie in a dramatic way and set the tone for the rest of his provocative and highly controversial professional life.

The literary reformers in Denmark that rallied to Brandes's standard dubbed their movement the "Modern Breakthrough." Among Brandesians, "modern" did not simply denote a recent or contemporary origin but rather an ideological position in opposition to the status quo. Thus the moniker "Modern Breakthrough" refers to the movement's focus on the rejuvenation and reorientation of Scandinavian literature and art in the late nineteenth century, conveying a sense of triumph at the rejection of romanticism and Biedermeier aesthetics in favor of direct engagement with social problems. This paradigm of literary modernity eventually encompassed the related movements of realism and naturalism and has become closely associated with the democratization and liberalization of Danish society and politics at the end of the nineteenth century. Brandes was by no means the sole architect of Denmark's literary renaissance, but he was a highly visible advocate of the necessity for Denmark's cultural renewal, both in Copenhagen and abroad.

Recognizing the significance of Brandes's role in this highly dynamic process requires us to first understand the nature of the relationship between Denmark and Germany in the period preceding 1864. The sheer scope and complexity of Germany and Denmark's social, political, and economic interactions over the centuries defy any facile description of their relationship, although the shift from a civic to a linguistic-ethnic conception of Danish nationalism in the late eighteenth and nineteenth centuries prompted a revisionist view of Danish history designed to prove that Germany has always been Denmark's most dangerous enemy.[2] Although the latter view ignores both Denmark's power struggles with Sweden and the many positive aspects of Denmark's interactions with German territories over the centuries, it is true that one of the defining characteristics of Danish-German relations between the mid-sixteenth and mid-nineteenth centuries was the cultural dominance of the German-speaking regions, far out of proportion to their relatively weak political power.

The longstanding imbalance in favor of German culture in Denmark makes it clear that traditionally benign assessments, such as Danish historian Vibeke Winge's references to a "German-Danish symbiosis," despite her own admission that "German literature dominated . . . the print market and German drama the theater,"[3] are inadequate to fully characterize the relationship between Danish and German culture in this period. Although such judgments may accurately reflect the perception of Danes at the time of a harmonious coexistence with German culture, they obscure the seminal and often obstructive influence that the wholesale importation of German culture over such a prolonged period of time had on Danish artistic production. In fact, although Denmark never came under overt German political control during this period, its predicament bears many of the earmarks of cultural imperialism identified by Edward Said in *Culture and Imperialism,* a study of the cultural dimensions of imperialism, in particular the imperialist nation's "power to narrate, or to block other narratives from forming and emerging" in the dominated area.[4]

Despite the obvious differences between Denmark's situation and that of a colonized country, most notably its political independence and its own continuing colonial pursuits, Denmark's cultural dependency on Germany resulted in an unequal relationship similar in this particular aspect to that of a colonized territory to its colonizer, which inhibited Danish writers from creating their own national narratives.

The lack of a formal political strategy or apparatus behind the dissemination and elevation of German culture in Denmark complicates the attribution of responsibility for the purported cultural colonization of Denmark, but the inhibiting effect on Danish cultural production is nonetheless apparent. For more than three centuries, European cultural trends reached Denmark primarily via Germany, with German functioning as the common cultural medium, while Danish literature defined itself in reference to German literature, like a satellite orbiting Germany's cultural sun, and adopted either German authors and German works or German literary ideals and movements. In addition to the aristocracy-sponsored influx of German writers and artists into Copenhagen society, the many Danish intellectuals educated at German universities acted as a conduit for introducing and establishing German aesthetic and philosophic trends in Denmark. Both the preeminence accorded German literature in Denmark and the need to compete in the German marketplace prompted Danish writers to model their work on German examples, which hindered the development of an independent Danish national literature.

Even when Denmark's imperial empire was at its peak, encompassing Norway, Iceland, Greenland, the Faroe Islands, Schleswig, Holstein, and colonies in the West Indies, Africa, and Trankebar, domestic Danish high culture was so heavily influenced by German customs, ideas, and cultural imports that Denmark itself appeared to many observers to be merely an extension of Germany. Uffe Østergård notes that eighteenth-century Denmark was "a fully equal member of the German-speaking cultural region of northern and central Europe."[5] Since Germany did not yet exist as a unified political entity, Germanness was primarily a matter of a perceived linguistic, cultural, and literary community. This inherent ambiguity allowed Johann Gottfried Herder to refer offhandedly to Copenhagen as "the Danish end of Germany" in his travel journal in 1769.[6] Similarly, the report of the Dutch traveler Johann Meerman in 1797 that "Denmark seemed to me in nearly all respects to be a continuation of Germany"[7] testifies to Denmark's prolonged cultural subsumption by Germany. All of these reports expose the tacit cultural hierarchy that existed in Europe at the time. While Denmark's colonies looked to Copenhagen for cultural guidance, Denmark itself followed Germany's lead.

With a disproportionately wealthy and well-educated German-speaking minority in Copenhagen actively fostering Danish cultural dependency on Germany, Denmark thus found itself in the historically unusual position of being an imperialist power under foreign cultural domination, but this was not perceived as threatening until the advent of ethnic nationalism in the late eighteenth century. Denmark's close cultural ties to Germany developed initially because of economic opportunities and dynastic alliances. Denmark's strategic position between the North Sea and the Baltic Sea had attracted German tradesmen since the days of the medieval Hanseatic League, while Germany's technical prowess created demand for German craftsmen in Denmark. After the Reformation, the considerable German contingent at the Danish court, a consequence of frequent marriages between Protestant Danish kings and German noblewomen, lent German enhanced status as the language of the cultural elite while Latin gradually lost its privileged status as the language of culture and power. The efforts of both the upper-class German-speaking population of Schleswig-Holstein and much of the Danish nobility to promote the spread of German culture in Denmark, by sending their sons to German universities and patronizing German artists, writers, and musicians, enabled German to become the primary language of such prominent cultural institutions as the military, the bureaucracy, the university, and the theater.

German influence on Danish politics and art climaxed in the second half of the eighteenth century, when King Frederik V placed German-speaking politicians such as Andreas Peter (A. P.) Bernstorff, Ernst Schimmelmann, and brothers Johan Ludvig (J. L.) and Christian Ditlev Frederik (C. D. F.) Reventlow in charge of the government. The king also sponsored the so-called German Circle, a group of influential German writers under his protection, including Johann Elias Schlegel and Friedrich Klopstock, who set the tone in literary circles. Danish writers who sought entrance to this elite group did so by way of the literary salons hosted by such Dano-German noblewomen as Charlotte Schimmelmann, Friederike Brun, and Sophie Reventlow, who regarded themselves as an extension of the Weimar salon centered on Goethe.[8] This cultural orientation on German norms was both an outgrowth of the perceived superiority of German high culture among educated Danes and a strategic course adopted by Danish writers, such as Jens Baggesen, who was equally fluent in Danish, French, and German and thus able to reach a much greater literary and theatrical public than little Denmark itself could provide.

Well into the nineteenth century, Danish authors remained highly dependent on the example and opinion of their southern neighbors for literary inspiration, as the enthusiastic adoption of German romanticism in Denmark demonstrates. The few Danish writers able to compete with German literary imports for prestige and commercial success, notably Ludvig Holberg, Adam Oehlenschläger, and Jens Baggesen, were strongly influenced by the German language and German intellectual developments. For example, Holberg's comedies often use German themes and German wordplay to achieve their comic effect; Oehlenschläger's famous poem "The Golden Horns" (*Guldhornene*) was the direct result of his introduction to Herder's philosophy by Henrik Steffens; and Baggesen wrote many of his works in German. In many cases, success in Germany was a prerequisite for recognition in Denmark, to such an extent that even the domestic renown of Hans Christian Andersen was predicated on his breakthrough in Germany.

Popular demands for Denmark's emancipation from Germany's cultural influence grew slowly during the eighteenth and nineteenth centuries, in tandem with a developing sense of Danish nationalism and, eventually, the emergence of a unified German nation-state. Since Denmark's loss of political power closely paralleled Germany's rise, the dominant position of German culture in Denmark gradually aroused fears that German cultural imperialism would lead to German military encroachment on Danish territory. With the benefit of postcolonial hindsight, Said warns that "culture is in advance of politics, military history, or economic process."[9] Danes at the time were not oblivious to either the interconnectedness of cultural and political imperialism nor the political danger that German cultural dominance entailed; the nationalistic overtones of Denmark's struggle to free itself from Germany's cultural control underscore contemporary Danish perceptions of Germany's cultural presence as threatening, particularly as a prelude to political intrusion.

The emergence of a conscious anti-German attitude in Denmark in the early 1770s accompanied a power struggle between the Danish bourgeoisie and the pro-German aristocracy that erupted when Johann Friedrich Struensee, the German doctor to the schizophrenic King Christian VII, seized power in 1770. Countless German-speaking bureaucrats had served Danish kings over the preceding centuries without arousing public disapproval, but Struensee's misadventures coincided with the shift from a civic conception of nationalism in Denmark to an ethnic one, making his linguistic identity as a German-speaker instantly suspect. Despite the enlightened reforms that he implemented, including freedom of the press, Struensee's nationalist opponents vilified him for his contempt of the Danish language and culture and made him a symbol for the dangers of German cultural imperialism. After his removal, the passage of the Citizenship Law in 1776 attempted to calm fears of a repeat German infiltration of the Danish court by barring anyone born outside the Danish kingdom from holding public office. When Crown Prince Frederik (later King Frederik VI) took control of the government in a 1784 coup masterminded by C. D. F. Reventlow and reinstated his aristocratic German-speaking protégés Bernstorff, Schimmelmann, and Reventlow himself, the controversy did not entirely subside. The prince's advisors were popular for their liberal views but despised for their Germanness. Subsequent efforts to replace German with Danish in public institutions underscored the increasing importance of language as a symbol for Danish national identity.

This paradigm shift had far-reaching consequences for the development of Danish literature as well. In March 1789 a year-long newspaper debate, known as "the German feud" (*Tyskerfejden*), erupted over a German-language production of Jens Baggesen's opera "Holger the Dane" (*Holger Danske*). Due to the central role of linguistic nationalism in the outcome of this cultural conflict, Østergård identifies the German feud as the "beginning of the process of differentiation and selection that one can call 'the invention of Danish national literature.'"[10] Despite its focus on the legendary Danish hero, Danish nationalists objected to the fact that Baggesen frequented German salons and was sponsored by both Count Schimmelmann and Prince Frederik's German brother-in-law, Frederik Christian of Augustenborg. In response to the anti-German tone of the reviews, Schimmelmann published an anonymous defense of Baggesen and his opera—in German—accusing the pro-Danish group of cultural mediocrity. Peter Andreas (P. A.) Heiberg, who would be exiled to France a few years later for disrespect to the king, published a parody titled "Holger the German" (*Holger Tydske*), as well as several articles demanding that all Germans in Denmark become demonstrably Danish in language, culture, and lifestyle, which exposed Danish frustration at being treated as culturally inferior.

The two mid-nineteenth-century Dano-German wars over the provinces of Schleswig and Holstein, in 1848–51 and 1864, erupted out of this tense situation. Nationalistic movements in Schleswig-Holstein in the late 1840s polarized political positions on both sides of the issue. Danish efforts to annex Schleswig, with its large Danish-speaking population, clashed with rising German nationalism in Holstein, which had joined the German Confederation in 1815. Wary of an expansionist Prussia when war broke out the first time in 1848, Britain, France, and Russia intervened to prevent a Danish defeat, but the terms of the 1852 London Protocol stipulated a restoration of the status quo ante bellum with no further attempts by Denmark to annex Schleswig. When Denmark's 1863 November constitution violated that provision, the second outbreak of war was inevitable. Germany's superiority in numbers and weaponry ensured a resounding victory, with momentous results for Denmark's economy, international political standing, and self-perception.

Viewed through this historical prism, Brandes's efforts at literary modernization in Denmark and the international marketing of Danish literature take on particular significance as steps in the process of asserting Denmark's cultural independence from Germany as well as compensating for Denmark's diminished political status. Having shifted his own academic focus from German to French criticism in the mid-1860s, Brandes strove to consummate Denmark's liberation from Germany's cultural domination by stimulating the development of a modern Danish national literature in the realistic, socially critical tradition of French and English naturalism.

Once the literary revolution of the Modern Breakthrough had caught hold in Denmark, Brandes set about reversing the long-established south–north current of cultural influence by marketing this new realistic Danish literature in Germany in order to both assert Denmark's cultural merit and compensate for Denmark's reduced political prestige. His strategy of seeking to validate Denmark's national identity by promoting its cultural products in the international arena conflicted with the prevailing standpoint in Copenhagen that the best way to preserve Danishness from German interference was isolation and self-sufficiency. Yet although his detractors labeled him antinational and excessively cosmopolitan, it is precisely Brandes's vigorous international engagement on behalf of Danish literature between 1870 and 1900 that confirms his instrumental role in the construction of a new Danish national identity—particularly vis-à-vis Germany—after 1864. Rather than cultivating Danish literature simply for domestic consumption, Brandes used it as a tool for rebuilding Denmark's self-image and international reputation by promoting Danish literature abroad as equal to the national literatures of the great European powers. Despite the opposition it provoked at home and its necessarily limited success abroad, Brandes's effort to establish Denmark's position as a culturally important and independent force in European intellectual life contributed significantly to an improved Danish national self-perception and a lessening of tensions between Germany and Denmark in the early twentieth century.

Comparing Brandes's encouragement and international promotion of an independent Danish national literature with the pattern Said maps out in *Culture and Imperialism* for the emergence of postimperial cultures reveals the geopolitical implications of Brandes's literary project. Said argues that subjugated societies cannot throw off the yoke of imperialism without men and women (such as Brandes) who are willing to stand up to the dominant powers and assert their national worth:

> These changes cannot occur without the willingness of men and women to resist the pressures of colonial rule, to take up arms, to project ideas of liberation, and to imagine (as Benedict Anderson has it) a new national community, to take the final plunge. Nor can they occur ... unless the rebellious "natives" impress upon the metropolitan culture the independence and integrity of their own culture, free from colonial encroachment.[11]

Since the late eighteenth century, Danish intellectuals had actively resisted the pressures of Germany's cultural imperialism and projected ideas of liberation from Germany's influence, but nationalistic sentiments first gained widespread currency among the common people in connection with the two Schleswig wars.

Despite having provoked the Prussian invasion of Schleswig-Holstein in 1864 by attempting to annex Schleswig in defiance of the London Protocol of 1852, Danes came to regard the war as a matter of defending themselves and their culture against Germany's oppressive influence. Although it was Denmark's military defeat and the ensuing threat of political obliteration that confirmed its will to resist German cultural imperialism, in contrast to many postcolonial scenarios in which armed liberation precedes cultural emancipation,

Denmark's situation largely conforms to Said's postimperial paradigm. Subsequent to Denmark's period of primary resistance, of "literally fighting against outside intrusion,"[12] Brandes played the part of the "rebellious native" engaged in secondary or ideological resistance, aimed at rebuilding and revitalizing the formerly subjugated national community. From this perspective, his struggle to construct a Danish national identity on the basis of an internationally acclaimed national literature appears simultaneously as an attempt to impress upon both Germany and Denmark the independence and integrity of Danish culture.

In attempting to help his countrymen envision a unique, postimperial Danish literary identity, Brandes expanded on the efforts of bourgeois intellectuals who had fought for Danish independence in the realm of popular culture, in particular the theater and literary newspapers, over the preceding 150 years. Already in the 1730s and 1740s, young Copenhagen intellectuals led by Ludvig Holberg had begun to criticize the prominence of foreigners in Danish cultural institutions, in particular the disproportionate influence of German speakers in the upper echelons of society. With pronouncements such as "German is a poison for the country—all of our woes are German"[13] in his 1772 play *Harlequin Patriot*, Danish poet Johannes Ewald gave voice to growing popular antipathy toward German involvement in Danish affairs, although he personally admired the German poet Friedrich Klopstock. Much like Hage's later depiction of Germanness as a deadly cancer, Ewald's metaphor suggests that German culture, like a lethal poison, posed a serious threat to Denmark's political existence, all the more so because of its invisibility and insidiousness.

Nineteenth-century Denmark owed much of its faith in the existence and importance of a uniquely Danish culture to the poet, educator, and theologian Nikolaj Frederik Severin (N. F. S.) Grundtvig, who took up the cause of Danish cultural nationalism in the early nineteenth century. In his compilations of Nordic mythology and folklore, Grundtvig glorified Denmark's heroic past in Herderian style and advocated intellectual independence from Germany by the cultivation of Danish folk culture and closer ties to other Scandinavian countries. Grundtvig's particular brand of nationalism was not political but cultural. Best known for his creation of the folk high school, he decried the use of Latin in schools in favor of the Danish "Mother Tongue," but he was equally opposed to the predominance of German culture in Denmark. In 1816 he founded the journal

Danne-Virke, named after the medieval embankment that protected Denmark's southern boundary, and marketed it as "a border embankment against German culture."[14] His 1832 collation and analysis of Nordic mythology contributed to a resuscitation of interest in Viking-Age Dano-Norwegian literature, and although much of his work was later appropriated by German scholars in the service of Teutonic glorification, its initial purpose was to assert the antiquity and quality of Nordic artistry and culture. Grundtvig was also a powerful advocate of a pan-Scandinavian union to offset Germany's growing power, an idea that appealed to many Nordic writers and intellectuals, including Henrik Ibsen. The dream of pan-Scandinavianism foundered, however, when no other Nordic countries came to Denmark's aid during the war against Prussia in 1864, a disillusionment that prompted Ibsen to exile himself from Norway for nearly three decades.

Entering the arena of Danish national identity construction shortly before Grundtvig's death in 1872, but with first-hand experience of Denmark's humiliation in 1864, Brandes's modus operandi differed from Grundtvig's, but his goal of reclaiming Danish culture from German control in order to strengthen an independent Danish national identity was the same. In Danish cultural history, Brandes is commonly regarded as Grundtvig's antithesis, a view that is exemplified by the manifesto "Grundtvig or Brandes?" (*Grundtvig eller Brandes?*), published in 1904 by a disaffected Brandesian, which frames the differences between the two men as a choice between populism and radicalism.[15]

Despite their ideological differences, particularly with regard to religion, the historical record confirms that Brandes was one of Grundtvig's most effective successors in the struggle to achieve Denmark's cultural emancipation and advancement. While Brandes shared Grundtvig's conviction that dependence on German culture had crippled Danish literature, he did not believe that rejecting it out of hand would solve the problem. Instead, Brandes aimed at fundamentally transforming the relationship between the two countries and their national literatures from one of imbalanced dependency to one of equitable exchange. Although Said does not explicitly address situations where cultural imperialism is not accompanied by political control, his contention that for a postimperial society "to achieve recognition is to rechart and then occupy the place in imperial cultural forms reserved for subordination"[16] illuminates the fundamental issues at stake in Brandes's self-conscious exertions to redefine Denmark's relationship to Germany and to itself. Since it was no longer necessary after 1864 to convince the Danish people of Germany's threat to their cultural autonomy, Brandes was able to take the next steps in the process of achieving postimperial equality with Germany, namely helping to promote an endo-stereotype of an aesthetically innovative Danish national identity and to achieve international recognition for Denmark's modern cultural output.

From this perspective, Brandes's promotion of Danish culture abroad can be seen as a means of compensating for Denmark's reduced geopolitical clout. Leopold Magon asserted in 1926 that Brandes's greatest contribution to Danish literary culture lay in his efforts "to enlarge the externally diminished Denmark by enlisting it in the cultural community of the 'most advanced' peoples of Europe."[17] The turn toward naturalist aesthetics and the critical treatment of social problems in Scandinavian literature was radical in itself, but it was Brandes's strategic marketing of this emerging literary modernism throughout Europe, particularly in Germany and Austria, as a "Nordic" phenomenon that contributed to the popularization of an image of Denmark as artistically and socially progressive in the public consciousness of continental Europe.

Although Brandes is remembered in Germany and Austria today primarily as the man who introduced the works of Henrik Ibsen[18] and Friedrich Nietzsche to German readers, his ambitions went beyond the achievement of personal prestige or financial gain to symbolic nation building on Denmark's behalf. The efficacy of his attempts to convey a view of Denmark as culturally and socially innovative to German-speaking Europe can be verified by the testimony of such writers as Stefan Zweig, who credited the Scandinavian literature introduced by Brandes with conveying "a powerful wind-gust of freer, more spiritual air"[19] into the German literary community. It is precisely the discrepancy between Zweig's opinion, which corresponds to the progressive image of Danish culture that Brandes tried to disseminate in Germany, and the actual highly orthodox character of the Danish political and literary landscape in the final decades of the nineteenth century, reveals the true nature of Brandes's efforts to influence Danish national identity. The image of an innovative, free-thinking, modern Danish state and literature that Brandes mediated to the world via Germany had little in common with the repressively conservative atmosphere in Copenhagen in 1870. In order to achieve Danish cultural parity with Europe's foremost nations despite such hindrances, Brandes disseminated the image of an imaginary

Denmark, characterized by the liberal values of realistic Brandesian literature, in hopes of it turning one day into reality.

By the time he presented the first of his groundbreaking lectures on "Main Currents in Nineteenth-century Literature" in 1871, Brandes had already begun to emerge as a highly controversial figure in Copenhagen society. His condemnation of Kierkegaardian Christianity, and his outspoken advocacy for women's rights, sexual freedom, and civil marriage, not to mention his affairs with married women, earned him a reputation as a cosmopolitan liberal. In conjunction with his Jewish heritage, this label was enough to make him a persona non grata in certain circles of the educated Copenhagen bourgeoisie (*dannelsesborgerskab*). Despite, or perhaps because of this reputation, his realistic literary aesthetics resonated profoundly with the emerging generation of young Copenhagen intellectuals, such as Holger Drachmann, J.P. Jacobsen, and Herman Bang, many of whom would later be regarded as pioneers in the Modern Breakthrough.

Drawing on the positivistic literary history approach pioneered by Taine, Brandes equated national identity with national literature, defined as "the complete history of a people's . . . opinions and feelings."[20] In what eventually grew to encompass six volumes, Brandes outlined the causes and effects of the major literary movements in France, England, and Germany from the French Revolution through the revolutions of 1848 in terms of each national literature's relationship to the Enlightenment ideals of unfettered scientific research and humanistic poetics. In particular, he praised the revolutionary quality of the works of authors who defended the causes of freedom and progress, such as Lord Byron's and Ludwig Feuerbach's challenges to religion, Ivan Turgenev's social critiques, and George Sand's challenging of gender roles.[21] Although the work is decidedly international in scope, the implicit references to Brandes's Danish context were unmistakable for Danish readers. Brandes biographer Jørgen Knudsen explains that the "basic pattern is, in fact, the Hegelian trinity of optimistic progress: from liberating revolution via (religious) reaction to new freedom and development—just with the polemical point, that Denmark has become stuck in the reaction, but from this day on, literature shall once more deal with reality instead of our dreams."[22]

Brandes's fundamental premise for literary modernity was the requirement that literature must be socially engaged in order to be meaningful: "The failure of a literature to debate problems is the same

Figure 2.1. Even as a young man, Brandes tended to inspire either fervent devotion or passionate enmity, with tumultuous consequences for his personal and professional life. He married the wife of his German translator, conducted numerous extramarital affairs, and was blamed for driving at least one woman to suicide. He was unofficially blacklisted by most Danish newspapers for several years because of his provocative critiques of Danish society. Photograph by H. Riise, 1889. Credit: The Royal Library, Copenhagen, Department of Maps, Prints, and Photographs

as losing all meaning."[23] Underscoring the political consequences of meaningless literature for the country that produces it, namely the loss of the ability to bring about development and progress, Brandes laid out a revolutionary course for Danish literature, toward a socially critical, realistic literature in the style of such French naturalist writers as Émile Zola. He foresaw a dire fate for Denmark of political, social, and even economic irrelevance if the moribund state of Danish literature was not remedied, prophesying that "the nation that produces it . . . will not be the kind of nation that controls development and progress, any more than the mosquito that believed it drove the wagon because it occasionally gave the four horses pulling it an insignificant bite."[24]

Brandes characterizes literary movements as essentially political events, a position that he made explicit in the foreword to the second German edition of *Main Currents*, where he states that "the orientation of the work is political, not literary."[25] This stance refers implicitly to the nationalistic character of his intention of using modern Danish literature to construct a modern Danish national identity, independent of German cultural influence. Since Denmark could not compete with Germany militarily, Brandes suggests, it would have to prove its worth on a cultural battleground. Although he stopped short of overt anti-German rhetoric, his call for the development of a new Danish national literature, independent of and in competition with German literature, capitalized on the political breach between Denmark and Germany by appealing to popular anti-German sentiment as justification for the necessity of literary modernization. His decision to conclude his survey in 1848, when "liberal ideas triumph even in Germany,"[26] was calculated to remind his Danish audience of Germany's continued supremacy in cultural as well as military matters and to provoke a competitive reaction. By way of contrast, he condemns the state of affairs in Denmark, where "the poetic production is as good as at a complete standstill . . . and the intellectual deafness has, like the deafness of a mute, produced muteness."[27] By promoting an independent, innovative Danish literature, Brandes aimed to help Denmark find its voice in dialogue with the great powers of Europe.

Although Brandes's agenda appears distinctly national today, particularly in light of its correspondence to Said's postimperial paradigm, and although it ultimately did gain some currency among liberal Danish politicians, the opposition Brandes encountered among his countrymen has long obscured his involvement in the construction of a modern Danish national identity. Danish politics in the 1870s were dominated by a conservative alliance between the powerful aristocratic landowners and the educated bourgeoisie, although fledgling leftist and social democratic movements began to arise in the 1870s. While travelling on the Continent, Brandes had moved politically to the left, "toward a European consciousness, while the Danish citizenry had moved at the same time to the right, toward national self-sufficiency, on heightened watch for all threats, known as well as unknown, ripe for an attack of 'moral panic.'"[28] Brandes's desire to export Danish literature conflicted with the leftists' insistence on Denmark making itself as unobtrusive as possible, as leading politician Viggo Hørup cautioned, "so that we are not in the way where someone might happen to step on us by mistake."[29] At the same time, the largely working-class social democrats were hesitant to claim Brandes because of his privileged academic background. Moreover, his self-identification as a "free thinker" put the conservative bourgeoisie on guard against potentially subversive ideas in his arguments and allowed them to dismiss his views as "mere agitation."[30]

Brandes's defense of such controversial causes as women's emancipation, civil marriage, and atheism were interpreted as representative of a dangerous socialist movement that would corrupt Danish society with radical foreign ideas, including new sciences, social organizational forms, and a secular way of life. By challenging the values and achievements of the powerful conservative bourgeoisie, Brandes antagonized the powerful National Liberals, who retaliated by denying his authority to interpret Danish society, culture, and character, often on the basis of his Jewish heritage. Prior to *Main Currents*, Brandes's Jewishness had not been a factor in his professional or personal life, but, as his notoriety as a critic and his following among Danes grew, his critics denounced him as "Jewish, *udansk* [un-Danish], foreign, European, Asiatic, oriental or—perhaps worst of all—French,"[31] charges that would recur with varying degrees of hostility throughout the rest of his life.

The result of Brandes's alienation from the Copenhagen bourgeoisie was his increasing exclusion from Danish intellectual life. One of the most personally painful evidences of this was his failure to be appointed to the professorship in aesthetics vacated by Carsten Hauch at the University of Copenhagen to which Brandes had seemed the heir apparent. By the mid-1870s, Brandes had been blacklisted by all of the major Danish newspapers and seemed to have no professional future in Denmark. Therefore, instead of comfortably ensconcing himself in an ivory tower at the University of Copenhagen as he had planned and hoped, he decided to seek his fortunes in Germany and found himself, at the age of thirty-five, starting over in a new city, country, and language.

The international dimension of Brandes's campaign to emancipate Denmark from German cultural control, which corresponds to what Said describes as the struggle to "impress upon the metropolitan [German] culture the independence and integrity of [Denmark's] own culture, free from colonial encroachment,"[32] was in many ways an even more precarious and delicate task than taking on the Danish establishment had been, since it required careful handling of two distinct audiences with very different expectations. On one hand, Brandes's international orientation was intrinsically suspect in the eyes of his Danish detractors, who were therefore predisposed to disapprove of his work in Germany. On the other, his position as a Dane, and thus a member of the perceived culturally inferior group, put him at a disadvantage in attempting to establish his credibility on the German literary market. The political tensions between Denmark and Germany, in particular the ongoing problems in Schleswig-Holstein, complicated all cross-cultural endeavors by fostering Danish resentment toward Germany while heightening patriotism among Germans, who regarded the territories as a rightful part of the German Empire. As a result, Brandes's efforts to promote Danish literature in Germany were frequently misconstrued by the Danish press, while German critics, despite their enthusiasm for his mediation of Scandinavian literature, generally failed to acknowledge the postimperial dimension of Brandes's work with regard to Danish-German relations.

One of the reasons that Brandes's legacy has been disputed in Denmark for more than a century is the fact that his move to Berlin was viewed by his countrymen through the lens of residual Danish antagonism toward Germany in the aftermath of the Second Schleswig War. Brandes was therefore regarded as a cultural traitor by his Danish critics, who took Nietzsche's admiring description of Brandes as "a good European" as proof of his dangerous cosmopolitanism. Although Berlin was the fastest growing metropolis in Europe with the greatest likelihood of welcoming Scandinavian literary exports, from a Danish perspective it was also the enemy's stronghold. The continued pervasiveness of anti-German sentiment in Denmark ensured that Brandes's decision to try his luck in Germany would be seen as a defection to the enemy, further alienating the Danish establishment. His critics interpreted his increasing involvement in German literary affairs over the course of the 1870s as a lack of sympathy with Danish grievances against Germany. His situation resembled the predicament Norwegian author Bjørnstjerne Bjørnson faced in 1872 when his suggestion of striving for spiritual and cultural rapprochement with Germany earned him the bitter charge that he had thereby chosen to "set his heel beside Bismarck's and stomp in time with him on Denmark's heart."[33]

Brandes could certainly understand his countrymen's feelings, since he himself had regarded the new German Empire with hostility and suspicion until a few years previously. In his autobiography, he reflects on his disgust for Germany in the early 1870s, recalling that "for me, the new empire represented the fortress of European reactionary ideas. The newly erected imperial throne was for me a well-crafted ancient seat from history's attic, freshly painted with noble blood."[34] By the late 1870s, however, his frequent visits to Berlin had mitigated his dislike of Germany, and his increasingly untenable position in Copenhagen required him to take drastic measures to ensure both his personal and Denmark's cultural survival. Always a pragmatist, Brandes set national grievances aside and concentrated on achieving his own career advancement in the place where it was most likely to succeed. The hope that, by so doing, he could also help to offset Denmark's centuries-long cultural domination and more recent military humiliation by Germany with a correspondingly significant triumph for Danish literature in Germany offered an additional incentive.

Yet when Brandes published an account of his years in Berlin in Danish in 1885, he did not condemn Germany for its nationalistic excesses, nor distance himself from it, despite the inevitable charges of cosmopolitanism that would follow. Instead he reprised the role he had played in Berlin, but in reverse, positioning himself, based on his credentials as "an adopted child of the city," as a mediator of German "spirit and nature" to Danes.[35] He admits to his readers that he had never expected to live in Germany, that he had not initially been drawn to Germany or Prussia. However, he explains, this attitude was altered by the calamitous consequences of Denmark's ignorance of Germany in 1864, which inspired in him the desire to understand Germany better in order to deal with it more effectively:

> When events of the era showed me with sudden clarity that we in Denmark had been living in thick and portentous ignorance of the nature of our large neighboring kingdom, and when the development of its political and military might, with which it astonished Europe, awoke my interest, there arose in me an urge to complete my knowledge of Romance cultures with a more substantial impression of Germanic life.... We Danes have, in the last half-century, as a rule only known Germany from its least sympathetic side, the one it has turned against us politically. Like many others, I see it as a necessity today to understand our most powerful neighboring state from the inside, from the center. In every case, there is a direct path away from monodimensionality and prejudice, forces that might seem to increase patriotism, but which most certainly do harm to the fatherland.[36]

As a Dane working in Germany, Brandes was able to promote his native culture and affirm its vitality; as an "adopted German" writing in Denmark, Brandes endorses the pragmatic approach of trying to understand one's enemy in order to avoid future defeats.

This strategy is revealing, for it confirms the preeminence in Brandes's mind of the cause for which he struggled, that of facilitating cross-cultural understanding and tolerance through cultural exchange, both for the sake of the human community at large as well as that of the individual observer. Like his countryman Søren Kierkegaard, Brandes endorsed an agenda of passionate inwardness and action in an age when empty rhetoric and lavish blame-laying served only to sap vitality from Danish society and culture.

Brandes's professional survival was his first priority, but his interest in self-preservation did not negate his potential for patriotism. As Knudsen points out, the demand that a leading personality fight only for causes in which he has no vested interests is unrealistic and counterproductive: "The *only* great battle for a cause that has a chance of success is one that draws at least some of its power from utterly personal ambition, and the only *small* battle for an individual that has the potential for more than a minor victory is one that is ennobled and justified by a greater, selfless cause."[37] In Brandes's case, the small battle for professional survival was ennobled by his determination to rebuild his country's literary reputation, which in turn was facilitated by Brandes's own ambition, despite the failure of his critics to recognize this causal relationship. Sven Møller Kristensen asserts, "Without the political fire, one cannot understand the connection between his life and philosophy, and without that perspective, one cannot explain why he continually aroused opposition and anger."[38]

In 1877 Brandes had many influential connections across Europe and harbored high hopes of being able to secure a professorship at one of the leading universities in Germany or Austria. In the meantime, however, in a move that enhanced his own career and reputation as well as that of his homeland, Brandes settled in Berlin and attempted to become a German journalist, capitalizing on the rising power of the mass media in Germany in order to both influence the development of a modernist German literary culture and help shape popular perceptions of Scandinavia as progressive and modern. Brandes became a regular contributor to various literary newspapers, including Julius Rodenberg's *Deutsche Rundschau*, which had pioneered the genre of the popular literary review, appealed to an educated middle-class audience, and positioned itself as an authority on cultural matters ranging from art to literature to academia. While his own success was certainly Brandes's primary concern, the fact that his triumphs would also serve as a means of compensating for the political diminishment of Denmark during the nineteenth century lent them added significance and provided powerful motivation for Brandes to achieve success.

Although no evidence suggests that Brandes had a systematic plan for promoting Scandinavian literature in Germany, he was still phenomenally successful, due to a combination of literary acumen, good timing, and a certain degree of liberality with the truth. Brandes attained a position of influence in German literary circles in the final decades of the nineteenth century such as few non-Germans have ever achieved. Tremendously popular in Germany, *Main Currents*, which Thomas Mann praised as "the Bible of young, intellectual Europe,"[39] inspired an entire generation of German and Austrian writers, as testimonials from authors as ideologically dissimilar as Gerhart Hauptmann, Friedrich Nietzsche, and Hugo von Hofmannsthal confirm, and brought Brandes into contact with many prominent German writers, many of whom found his confirmation of their own sense of being part of a historic ideological upheaval intoxicating.

By using this clout to promote Dano-Norwegian writers and works that he felt would strengthen Denmark's cultural position in Germany and to endorse particular German-speaking writers, Brandes was instrumental in guiding German literature in modernistic aesthetic and socially critical directions as well as raising the profile of Scandinavian literature abroad. Klaus Bohnen points out that German naturalism would have developed very differently without Brandes's mediation of the works of, among others, Ibsen, Taine, Zola, and Tolstoy to Germany, to say nothing of the decisive influence Brandes had on German literary history by introducing Viennese writers to J. P. Jacobsen's work and Nietzsche to Kierkegaard's.[40] Bernhard Glienke confirms Brandes's seminal effect on both the literary market in Wilhelminian Germany and the international prestige of Scandinavian literature, affirming that "the Wilhelminian Empire and the Brandesian literary movements were not just founded at the same time; they were connected from the beginning. . . . . The cultural signs of the times in the Bismarck era were, from its beginning, more or less dominantly, also Scandinavian signs. In this way, the Modern Breakthrough, by which the Scandinavian literatures attained world-class status, was also able to attain international legitimacy."[41] More than simply reflecting his intellectual acuity, however, Brandes's achievements owe a great deal to being in the right place at the right time to make his opinions heard. Germany's lack of a naturalist tradition of its own created a cultural gap that Brandes was ideally situated to fill. Both the conservative political situation in Germany and the entrenched authority of established literary traditions had inhibited the reception of French naturalist ideas, which allowed Brandes to associate the innovative ideas he advocated with the Scandinavian literary works he publicized.

Brandes had tested the waters of German literary criticism a few years prior to his move to Berlin, albeit indirectly. He had collaborated with Adolf Strodtmann, the German translator of *Main Currents*, on a survey of contemporary Danish culture, which appeared in Berlin in 1873 under the title *Intellectual life in Denmark (Das geistige Leben in Dänemark)*. Well-received in Germany, Strodtmann's book establishes Denmark's relevance to Europe on the basis of its artistic accomplishments, arguing that "a nation that produces within one generation painters like Carl Bloch, poets like Paludan-Müller and Henrik Ibsen, aestheticians like Kierkegaard and G. Brandes . . . occupies too important a position in the cultural life of the present for the rest of the world to ignore the tremendous creations of its artists and writers."[42] In addition to praising Denmark's artistic and literary prowess, however, Strodtmann also explicitly associates cultural production and political vitality. He declares himself appalled that even "the spokesmen of public opinion [in Denmark] have recently begun to accustom themselves to the idea that

Denmark's political existence could be over"[43] and challenges Danish artists to compensate for Denmark's political weakness, asserting that "they also fulfill a patriotic duty when they exert themselves to make the rest of the world familiar with the representations of beauty that they have created and thereby increase the fame and intellectual esteem of their fatherland abroad."[44] The similarity between Strodtmann's views and Brandes's is unmistakable, though Brandes's involvement is never openly acknowledged.

Brandes is not named as coauthor of the book, but Strodtmann functioned as a sort of ghostwriter for Brandes, echoing Brandes's judgments of Danish culture and literature. This state of affairs is confirmed by Brandes's letters home during an extended stay at Strodtmann's home in Steglitz, in southwestern Berlin, in the autumn of 1872. On October 3, 1872, Brandes asked his brother Edvard to send Strodtmann copies of three articles on Danish art written by Holger Drachmann, as well as a copy of Julius Lange's history of Danish art, because Strodtmann "needs these for what he is writing about Denmark, with which I must help him, if it is not to be terribly wrong."[45] On October 13, he reminded his parents not to mention to anyone that he was staying with Strodtmann, "for I have written out five to six pages of notes for his descriptions of Denmark and I want no one to say that they are from me."[46]

Brandes was justifiably wary of publicly acknowledging his involvement with the book, since Strodtmann's vehement defense of the German seizure of Schleswig-Holstein ensured the book's utter failure in Denmark, despite the otherwise positive view of Danish culture that it conveys. In private, however, Brandes defended his decision to assist Strodtman, explaining that "the amusing part is that it is my accomplishment alone that the book has turned out as positive about Denmark as it has. Everything that is written correctly about our art and our literature is my contribution."[47] Knudsen agrees that Strodtmann's book would undoubtedly have been worse without Brandes's help, but deems Brandes's involvement a grave and irresponsible miscalculation, judging that "if it was his intent to emulate H. C. Andersen or Ibsen and win a reputation abroad in order to use it to turn public opinion to his advantage at home, then he took the first step here as clumsily and unfortunately as possible."[48] However, this view of Brandes's collaboration with Strodtmann, while recognizing its harmful consequences for Brandes's personal situation in Denmark, fails to take into account the book's effectiveness at enhancing Denmark's international reputation by affirming Denmark's extraordinary intellectual and artistic vigor, a phenomenon that Strodtmann praises as "a flourishing overabundance of intellectual power and an independent sense of freedom . . . that has become truly rare in modern literature."[49]

When Brandes moved to Berlin, he enjoyed several advantages in his quest to establish himself as an authority on modern literature in general and Nordic literature in particular. He was already fairly well-known as a literary modernist, due to Strodtmann's popular translations of *Main Currents*, as well as the articles he had already written for the *Deutsche Rundschau* before leaving Denmark. Once established in Berlin, Brandes was finally able to arrange for the publication of German translations of many of his Danish works. Strodtmann's translations of volumes four and five of *Main Currents* appeared in German in 1876 and 1883, and volumes one through five were published in a second edition already in 1886. His Kierkegaard study appeared in Danish in 1877 and in German in 1879, his groundbreaking Ibsen essay in the November 1883 issue of *Nord und Süd*, and his biography of Ludvig Holberg in 1885. He worked frenetically on new books at the same time, producing a study of Esias Tegnér in early 1878 and his very popular biography of Benjamin Disraeli in just over two months in late 1878. He revised and expanded the Disraeli book for a German edition in mid-1879, which became the basis for an English translation a short time later. A German edition of *Creative Spirits of the Nineteenth Century (Modern Geister)*, his character sketches of leading nineteenth-century Scandinavian writers, such as Hans Christian Andersen, Tegnér, Frederik Paludan-Müller, and Bjørnstjerne Bjørnson, was published in Frankfurt in 1882. In addition, Brandes published dozens of articles in German-language newspapers about both French and Dano-Norwegian naturalists, from Zola to Ibsen, which established his authority on literary modernism so firmly that emerging German naturalist writers regarded Scandinavia as the cradle of naturalistic aesthetics.

One important key to the rapid growth of Brandes's reputation as a respected literary critic in German-speaking Europe is the remorseless pace of Brandes's output. In addition to writing for the *Deutsche Rundschau*, Brandes was also a frequent contributor to other German newspapers and literary journals, including *Die Tribüne, Nord und Süd, Das Magazin für die Literatur des In- und Auslandes*, and the *Frankfurter Zeitung*, as well as the Austrian papers *Wiener*

Abendpost, Wiener Allgemeine Zeitung, Wiener Montags Revue, and *Neue Freie Presse.* The ubiquity of his byline in the German literary press enhanced his own name recognition and the German public's awareness of modern Scandinavian literature, as well as boosting sales of books by Nordic authors. German authors Arno Holz and Johannes Schlaf's decision to make their naturalist debut under the ostensibly Norwegian pseudonym Bjarne P. Holmsen illustrates the extent of Brandes's success.

As an eloquent mediator of cutting-edge naturalism to Germany, Brandes helped to direct the literary culture of the newly united German Empire into modernist paths by promoting Scandinavian literary figures, such as Ibsen, Bjørnson, and Jacobsen, as representative of naturalist aesthetics. At the same time, due to both the nature of the authors he profiled and his own well-publicized transgressions of conventional opinions and morals, he also contributed to a popular European perception of Scandinavian culture as highly progressive. He used the mass media to transmit not only literary ideals but also specific metacultural conceptions about the national and cultural identities of Germany's Nordic neighbors.

As they had in Denmark, the liberal political ideas underlying Brandes's radical view of modern literature attracted elements of the bourgeoisie that were dissatisfied with the increasingly reactionary atmosphere in Germany and eager to use literature to challenge this state of affairs. In the *Frankfurter Zeitung* on March 13, 1884, Otto Brahm described modern Scandinavian literature as "a movement aimed at liberating spirits from deep darkness that makes its way with a lively boldness that shrinks before nothing."[50] He gave Brandes credit for this invigorating intellectual development, declaring that "only since Georg Brandes, about fifteen years ago, dared to tell his countrymen about the 'Main Currents' of modern literature, has a new epoch begun."[51] Not only liberal intellectuals appreciated Brandes, however. German publishing houses also welcomed his efforts to popularize Scandinavian literature, since the Scandinavian countries' failure to join the Bern Convention on copyright law until the turn of the century enabled publishing houses to print translations of Scandinavian texts cheaply. This had disadvantages for Brandes as an author, because he had to produce simultaneous Danish and German editions of the later volumes of *Main Currents* in order to make a profit, but it facilitated the marketing of other authors' works. With the support of both the cultural elite and the commercial sector, Brandes was well-positioned to market the modernity of Scandinavian literature and culture. What is striking, however, is the vehicle he chose to accomplish this task.

Brandes's close involvement with the *Deutsche Rundschau*, the leading German national liberal literary newspaper in the Wilhelminian Era and a major force in German national-identity development, provides a particularly revealing demonstration of his ability to use politically improbable means to achieve his nationalistic ends. Brandes's relationship to the National Liberals in Denmark had been markedly antagonistic, but when Julius Rodenberg invited him, already in 1874, to contribute to his newly established newspaper, Brandes eagerly accepted, putting political scruples aside in favor of his aesthetic and professional goals. The partnership proved mutually advantageous from the outset: Rodenberg, eager to compete with such cosmopolitan publications as *Revue des deux Mondes*, could boast of having the rising star of European literary criticism and the acknowledged expert on modern Scandinavian literature on staff, while Brandes gained direct access to the German public through one of the most widely read newspapers in the country, which enabled him to boost both his own and his country's reputation in Europe.

The *Deutsche Rundschau* proved invaluable to Brandes in making his name known among the educated German middle class and giving him a broad popular platform for promoting his literary agenda. Over the fifteen years of his collaboration on the *Deutsche Rundschau*, Brandes published essays on historical and literary figures as diverse as Ferdinand Lassalle (1875), Paul Heyse (1876), Esaias Tegnér (1878), Émile Zola (1888), Benjamin Disraeli (1879), Friedrich Nietzsche (1890), Ludvig Holberg (1887), Adam Oehlenschläger (1886), and J. P. Jacobsen (1883). The success of these articles gave Brandes's opinion on both literary and cultural-political matters such weight that Paul Heyse asserted, in a letter to Brandes from June 20, 1883, that "a recommendation from you is regarded as a trump card."[52] Deferring to the *Deutsche Rundschau*'s conservative moral position, however, Brandes generally downplayed his more liberal social views in his articles while emphasizing the literary modernity of each author, demonstrating once again the underlying pragmatism in his approach to his German audience.

Brandes's involvement with the *Deutsche Rundschau* was, however, ultimately unsustainable over the long term, given their very different approaches to the question of nationalism. Particularly in the early years of their collaboration, both Brandes and Rodenberg strove to make Brandes's literary ideas attractive to the educated German bourgeoisie by placing them in context of Germany's own cultural and political advancement, but theirs was a marriage of convenience, not conviction. By way of introducing Brandes to the journal's largely middle-class audience, the first number of the *Deutsche Rundschau* contained an enthusiastic review of Strodtmann's German translation of the first three volumes of *Main Currents,* which Friedrich Kreyssig praises as "the Dane's accomplishment."[53] Underscoring the Scandinavian character of Brandes's ideas and his courage in defying Danish prejudices against Germany, Kreyssig lauds both Brandes's ability to rise above Danish "national sensitivities" about Germany in his quest to abolish "rotten prejudices and spirit-killing habits" and his attempt to bring Denmark into the fold of the "great peoples of culture," alongside Germany.[54] Already prior to Brandes's return to Copenhagen, however, his own and the *Deutsche Rundschau*'s increasing emphasis on their respective conceptions of German and Danish national identity, in particular concerning the imperial destiny of the German people, brought about their gradual estrangement.

While Brandes had capitalized on the *Deutsche Rundschau*'s prestige and wide circulation to awaken interest in Scandinavian literature as the manifestation of a unique Scandinavian cultural identity, the *Deutsche Rundschau* had framed Brandes's contributions and the works he promoted as representative of a shared Germanic cultural heritage (*Kulturgut*). Founded just three years after German unification in 1871, the *Deutsche Rundschau,* which styled itself the first representative national German journal, vigorously promoted a common German national identity and later became a persuasive proponent of German colonial expansion as the logical and necessary outcome of the establishment of the German Empire. In its mission statement, the *Deutsche Rundschau* promised to occupy itself with "the scientific questions, the political, literary and artistic events" of the time, but, above all, "to be *German.*"[55] This conception of a united German national identity relied to a certain extent on a romantic concept of pan-Germanism, and by engaging Brandes for the *Deutsche Rundschau*, Rodenberg hoped to reinvigorate "the intellectual connections to the German peoples to whom we are genetically related" by offering insight into "the literatures of the Scandinavian North and the Netherlands which are so pleasing to us."[56]

Ultimately, however, it was not the *Deutsche Rundschau*'s rhetorical support for Germanic racial unity that brought Brandes's association with it to an end, but rather its increasingly reactionary political stance in conjunction with a fundamental revision of the understanding of modernity in German intellectual circles. When Otto Brahm left the *Deutsche Rundschau* to start the naturalist journal *Freie Bühne* in 1889, he courted Brandes assiduously but unsuccessfully. Brandes was hesitant about affiliating himself too closely with naturalism, but his primary reason for refusing Brahm's offer was the fact that one of his disaffected disciples, the Swede Ola Hansson,[57] was already closely affiliated with the *Freie Bühne*. Hansson, who openly contested Brandes's position as the unofficial ambassador of Scandinavian literature in Germany, represented both a new generation of Scandinavian writers and a new orientation within modern literature. The frenzied popularity of the "modern" in Germany had increased throughout the 1880s, a phenomenon symbolized by Eugen Wolff's invention of the term "die Moderne" in 1886, but concomitant semantic slippage in the definition of "modern" in Germany reached a turning point around 1890; in place of the positivist ideals of social progress and liberation that Brandes had championed in the 1870s and 1880s, "modern" became associated with nihilistic despair, irrationality, and ontological uncertainty. This paradigm shift is apparent within the Modern Breakthrough itself, as writers such as Strindberg, Hamsun, and Hansson surpassed Ibsen and Bjørnson in popularity. Although Brandes was closely associated with the earlier generation of Modern Breakthrough writers, particularly Ibsen, his central role in introducing Strindberg and Nietzsche to German audiences enabled him to retain his authoritative position as arbiter of modern literary trends even after the transition.

The competition between the Dane Brandes and the Swede Hansson also points to another decisive but rarely considered aspect of Brandes's mediation of Scandinavian literature in Germany, namely his deliberately undifferentiated presentation of the different Scandinavian national literatures. When Brandes turned his attention to conquering the German literary market for Denmark in the early 1870s, few Danish authors had produced any significant works of realistic literature. By contrast, an older generation of writers in Norway had already begun to cultivate the new literary ground Brandes had broken. Norway's early artistic avant-gardism was due in part to the fact that Norway's struggle to define an independent national cultural identity had begun half a century earlier than Denmark's, in the wake of its political liberation from Denmark in 1814. Yet despite his determination to assert Denmark's cultural autonomy, Brandes ignored similar attempts by Norwegian authors and subsumed modern Norwegian literature, which was still heavily reliant on a Danish-language model, into the Danish tradition he was striving to develop. The development of modern Swedish literature lagged somewhat behind the Danish curve, so even though Brandes did not need to co-opt Swedish authors in the same fashion, the perceived cohesiveness of the "Scandinavian Modern" movement ensured that their works would be viewed as part of the same category.

Since Bjørnson's and Ibsen's socially realistic dramas of the late 1870s exemplified his own literary principles, Brandes promoted Dano-Norwegian literature as a single cultural phenomenon. In his review of Bjørnson's dramas *Bankrupt* (*En Fallit*) and *The Editor* (*Redaktøren*) in the journal *Det nittende Aarhundrede* on June 2, 1875, Brandes heralded the beginning of a realistic literary tradition in Scandinavia, proclaiming, "Finally it seems as if we here in the North are also in the process of receiving a series of dramas in which the two great powers—the present and reality—are respected and given their due. Finally this most fertile of all fields has begun to be cultivated among us."[58] Brahm's comparison in 1884 of the fragmented literary scene in Germany to the apparently "unified literary movement [among the Danes and Norwegians], which aims at particular goals, and for which both great and humble, marching in lockstep, faithfully do their duty,"[59] confirms the efficacy of Brandes's tactic of marketing Dano-Norwegian literature as identical in purpose and style.

Bjørnson's and Ibsen's popularity in German theaters was decisive in advancing both German fascination with Scandinavia and Brandes's own reputation as a literary critic, but once Danish naturalism had come into its own, Brandes began to differentiate more sharply between individual national literary traditions and to emphasize the specifically Danish focus of his nation-building efforts. By the late 1880s Brandes regarded the Norwegians as Denmark's most serious rival for literary prominence in Europe. Concerned that Danish writers were being eclipsed in Germany by Norwegians, he warned his audience of Danish students in 1894 that "Ibsen's name has broken through [in Germany] and has carried numerous other Norwegian names with it,"⁶⁰ a feat which no Danish writer had yet been able to bring about.

However, Brandes's remarkable engagement on behalf of the Danish poet J.P. Jacobsen was intended to remedy that situation. In a letter to Theodor Wolff on January 22, 1889, Brandes frames Wolff's efforts to publish a German edition of Jacobsen's novel *Niels Lyhne* specifically in terms of the competition between Danes and Norwegian writers for German attention. Although he himself had contributed to the breakthrough of the Norwegian novelist Alexander Kielland in Germany, Brandes informs Wolff,

> It would please me, if you could succeed in awakening German minds to the strength and delicacy of Jacobsen's work. It is altogether ridiculous, that Kielland, who is so monodimensional, is known everywhere, is famous, while the much greater Jacobsen, with whom Kielland has never compared himself, remains unknown and misunderstood. In general, it is disheartening for us Danes to see how the Norwegians, for whom we ourselves laboriously prepared the way abroad, are now preferred to us everywhere.⁶¹

The nationalistic distinction Brandes makes between Jacobsen and Kielland in particular, and Danes and Norwegians in general, was absent from his early efforts to market Scandinavian literature in Germany, but it plays an unmistakable role in Brandes's promotion of Jacobsen, whom he selected as the likeliest candidate to establish Denmark's cultural standing in Germany once and for all.⁶²

Questions of inter-Scandinavian rivalry aside, Brandes's energetic sponsorship of Jacobsen also foregrounds his willingness to subordinate aesthetic concerns to his nationalistic cultural-political agenda, a strategy characteristic of his endorsement of Scandinavian literature in Germany. Brandes's recommendation of literary works was frequently determined more by a work's sociopolitical message than by its form or style,⁶³ as illustrated by his enthusiasm for Heyse's novel *Children of the World* (*Kinder der Welt*), "not so much because of its artistic prowess or literary qualities, but rather because he found in this book an 'urge for freedom' and a 'welcome independence from articles of faith and conventions,' in short, 'free thinking.'"⁶⁴ In Jacobsen's case, Brandes attempted to appeal to German modernists by emphasizing the originality of Jacobsen's use of language and scientific attention to detail, while downplaying Jacobsen's impressionistic aesthetics, which he personally disliked.

Although Jacobsen belonged to Brandes's clique in Copenhagen both by conviction and by virtue of his background in the natural sciences, atheism, and Darwinism, his elegant, melancholy narrative style has very little in common with the utilitarian realism Brandes demanded, a fact of which both Jacobsen and Brandes were aware. In a letter to Brandes's brother Edvard on March 30, 1880, Jacobsen admitted his unwillingness to conform to Brandes's demands for the explicit discussion of social problems, concluding, "I am too aesthetic in a good and bad sense to be able to join in such direct procurator-speech-type of works, in which problems are supposedly debated but actually are just postulated as solved."[65] For his part, Brandes described Jacobsen's novel *Niels Lyhne* in a postcard to Sophus Schandorph in 1881 as "a purely subjective, highly mannerist book."[66] Brandes's dismissal of the hero and the story itself as "depressing, not even really interesting" in his review of *Niels Lyhne* in *Morgenbladet* on February 9, 1881,[67] caused Jacobsen to complain to Edvard on February 22 that Brandes "personally does not like it or attribute it further value and essentially is disappointed by it."[68] Despite the discrepancy in their styles, however, Brandes invested himself wholeheartedly in bringing about Jacobsen's breakthrough in Germany, because of his conviction that the originality and sophistication of Jacobsen's work could enhance Denmark's image for cultural modernity abroad.

Brandes's confidence in Jacobsen's ability to establish Denmark's cultural modernity proved to be justified, but his very success in popularizing Jacobsen marked the end of Brandes's active promotion of modern Scandinavian literature in Germany. The incompatibility of Jacobsen's impressionistic style with prevailing naturalist tendencies in Germany in the early 1880s frustrated Brandes's initial efforts to introduce Jacobsen, which ranged from praising *Niels Lyhne* to Heyse in 1881 as the work of Denmark's "greatest artist and simultaneously greatest mannerist"[69] to arranging for the publication of two of Jacobsen's novellas in the *Deutsche Rundschau* in 1883: *Mrs. Fønss* (*Fru Fønss*) appeared in the April issue and *The Plague in Bergamo* (*Pesten i Bergamo*) in May, the latter accompanied by an afterword in which Brandes emphasizes Jacobsen's scientific credentials as a botanist and student of Darwin. Yet although Brandes praises Jacobsen as "the most outstanding prose writer" among the younger generation of Dano-Norwegian writers,[70] the sensitive simplicity of his prose initially awakened little popular response in German audiences accustomed to grittier fare.

Despite this initial disappointment, Brandes continued to insist on the radicality of Jacobsen's style. In his 1883 essay on Jacobsen, which appeared in the collection *The Men of the Modern Breakthrough* (*Det Moderne Gjennembruds Mænd*) alongside biographical sketches of Bjørnson and Ibsen, Brandes described Jacobsen's inventive use of language as a revolutionary act of literary modernism, "for just as no new generation can be satisfied with thinking the thoughts of a previous generation, so too can no new group of literary men use the language written by their predecessors."[71] This strategy finally paid off in 1888, when Brandes persuaded Theodor Wolff of Jacobsen's modernistic qualities and engaged him to take charge of publicizing *Niels Lyhne* in Germany, a task Wolff enthusiastically fulfilled with an admiring article about the novel in the *Berliner Tageblatt* on December 4, 1888, and a Reclam edition of *Niels Lyhne* in 1889. Brandes's reputation was crucial to *Niels Lyhne*'s initial reception, particularly since Wolff underscored the connection between Brandes and Jacobsen in his introduction to the Reclam edition and equated both with Denmark's recent literary prowess, claiming that "just as Denmark has produced, in Georg Brandes, the most sensitive critic, so too has J. P. Jacobsen developed there as the most sensitive poet."[72]

By handing the marketing of Jacobsen over to Wolff, however, Brandes also surrendered his authority over the way in which Jacobsen's work would be interpreted with regard to Danish national identity. Despite both Brandes's and Wolff's attempts to market Jacobsen as a naturalist, his work was almost immediately co-opted by symbolist and Jugendstil movements. The image of Denmark as radically progressive that Brandes had tried so hard to disseminate quickly gave way to a more diffuse, stylized perception of Denmark in keeping with Jacobsen's prose. Although Wolff, in his preface to a second, far more elaborate edition of *Niels Lyhne* in 1895, contested the symbolists' claim to Jacobsen, he had himself laid the groundwork for such an interpretation in his original introduction to the Reclam edition. Highlighting the national qualities of Jacobsen's work, in which, he claimed, "Danishness finds its pure expression," Wolff offered readers a generalized comparison of Danish and Norwegian literary styles, asserting that "everything Danish is round and soft and misty, while everything Norwegian is square and sharp and definite."[73] In contrast to Brandes's earlier attempts to introduce Jacobsen in Germany, Wolff's sponsorship of Jacobsen coincided advantageously with a shifting aesthetic mood in Germany. In

1889, with naturalism already past the peak of its popularity, Jacobsen's lyrical poeticism appealed to German readers because of its contrast to what Wolff condemns as the "dull reporter style" of naturalist texts.[74] Precisely because *Niels Lyhne* was an instant success, however, selling more than 10,000 copies in five years, the image of Denmark associated with Jacobsen in Germany and Austria took on a life of its own over which Brandes no longer had any control. The image of Danish culture being disseminated in Germany remained a modern one, but a different style of modernity than Brandes himself endorsed.

Nevertheless, the scale of Brandes's success in promoting modern Scandinavian literature in Germany is especially remarkable considering the language issues involved. Although fluent in German, Brandes did not write in German with the same ease and mastery as he did in Danish. Moreover, as a Dane, Brandes belonged to a group long perceived to be culturally subordinate to Germany, which put him at a disadvantage in attempting to establish his reputation as an authority on the German literary market. Brandes faced the dilemma—as many postcolonial writers have since then—of whether to write in his native language with its limited currency, the restrictive effect of which he complained about frequently in his correspondence, or in the language which had been the medium of Denmark's cultural oppression but which would also provide him with access to the minds whose opinion of Denmark he hoped to influence.

When he moved to Berlin, Brandes initially decided, as a matter of expedience and in the spirit of settling there permanently, to adopt the "imperial" language and establish himself as a German writer, because of both the time lag involved in translation and his bleak professional prospects in Copenhagen. Since his Danish works, with the exception of *Main Currents,* had not yet been translated into German, he was forced to attempt the task of reestablishing his authority as a literary critic in a new language, which he found very frustrating. In a letter to Heyse on May 29, 1878, he complained about the handicap he experienced as a result of entering the German literary market so late, of being "a worker of the final hour. The thought often irritates me that if I had written as many books and such of the same importance for the development of the country in German as I have in Danish, I would be, unlike now, a welcome beginner here."[75]

Ultimately, however, the challenge of attaining the same level of sophistication in German that he was accustomed to in Danish led Brandes to conclude that his attempts to internalize German were doomed to failure, that he would never feel at home in the German language. On February 29, 1879, he complained to Heyse that "I lose all linguistic refinement in German."[76] More than simply despair over semantics, however, Brandes's reaffirmation of Danish reflected his growing sense of being in exile from Denmark and his ongoing engagement with the development of Danish national identity. The experiment of trying to become a German writer taught Brandes that his professional and nationalistic projects could not be separated. Throughout his years in Berlin, Brandes had continued to contribute to Danish newspapers, including a series of articles describing conditions in the new German capital that were compiled in the book *Berlin as the German Capital* (*Berlin som tysk Rigshovedstad*) in 1885. Admitting to Heyse that his heart was still in Denmark, Brandes declared, "I want to gradually educate a new public in Norway and Denmark. The young generation in Germany is foreign to me."[77] Consistent with this desire to participate actively in national-identity construction in Denmark, Brandes resettled in Copenhagen in 1883. Even though he continued to contribute to the *Deutsche Rundschau* until 1890, he composed all of his subsequent critical works in Danish.

Long after his return to Copenhagen, Brandes continued to insist on the necessity of both liberalizing Danish society and promoting Danish culture abroad over the following decades. In a speech to the radical Student Society (*Studentersamfund*) in Copenhagen on February 1, 1894, which was subsequently published under the title "Concerning National Sentiment" (*Om Nationalfølelse*),[78] he defended his conviction that Denmark's political and cultural salvation lay in an enhanced Danish presence on the European cultural scene. Speaking precisely thirty years after Prussia's conquest of Schleswig-Holstein, Brandes deplored Denmark's loss of self-confidence after the political disappointments of 1864 and documented its negative effect on Denmark's reputation in Europe. Claiming a monopoly on patriotism, the National Liberals had undermined Denmark's ability to regain its self-respect by requiring that patriotic Danes ignore the rest of Europe, with the result that Europe lost interest in Denmark. Brandes reported that the only mention of Denmark in a review of the World Exposition in Paris in 1878 was the comment, following a lengthy description of the Swedish and Norwegian contributions, that "le Danemark s'efface." He interpreted the phrase as signifying Denmark's self-inflicted loss of stature, explaining that "Denmark is being erased, disappearing, leaving the story. Denmark remains in the wings, no longer appears on stage, or stumbles over its feet when coming and going."[79] By reminding his audience of the real possibility of Denmark's disappearance, both from European consciousness and the map, after 1864, Brandes underscored the harmful effect of Denmark's self-imposed cultural isolation from the rest of Europe, including Germany, and effectively legitimized his own efforts to rescue both Denmark's national identity and its very existence by promoting Danish culture internationally.

Having been attacked by the Danish press for a lack of patriotism whenever he published anything abroad, Brandes now turned the tables and accused his critics of being the primary obstacle to improving Denmark's international reputation. He gave his remarks an explicitly nationalistic context by comparing Denmark's situation with that of its former subject territory, Norway, which had achieved tremendous artistic renown in Germany, in particular because of Ibsen and Bjørnson. Brandes deplored the fact that while the Norwegians, who "understand completely the art of making foreigners aware of their significant talents, and their less significant ones as well,"[80] stood behind Ibsen, Kielland, and Jonas Lie and rejoiced in their international success, the Danish press was primarily concerned with criticizing the few Danish works that managed to find an audience abroad, greeting the courageous writers of the Modern Breakthrough, such as Jacobsen, Drachmann, and Schandorph, with contempt instead of praise.

Explaining that literary success abroad required domestic support, Brandes accused his detractors of the same antinationalism with which they so often tried to burden him, concluding,

> The Danes have complicated the sale of their literature at home, and done all that they could to make its success abroad impossible. In particular those who claim to represent national sentiment have demonstrated a lack of patriotism and waged a war against those spirits who have dared to defy convention, which has had a stultifying effect at home, while delaying and restricting recognition and authority abroad. No Danish name arrived abroad with unanimous Danish support, it came blackened and spotted and dulled. No Danish talent was carried by the estimation and overestimation at home that is often the first step to European fame.[81]

Laying the blame for the failure of Danish literature to achieve greater success in Europe squarely at the feet of conservative politicians, who had succeeded in their attempt "to spiritually ravage this country and lay it waste,"[82] Brandes reminded his youthful audience that, at the lowest point of Denmark's self-image in the 1870s, new literary efforts, such as Jacobsen's novel *Niels Lyhne*, had kept a belief in Denmark's vitality and potential alive.

Reprising his own argument from 1871, Brandes reasserted the role of national literature as the primary guardian of national identity, but also emphasized the crucial necessity of marketing it to the world, a position he had only implied in *Main Currents*. He warned that despite the emergence of a realistic Danish literary tradition, the war for Danish cultural independence was far from won, since, even given the European interest in Scandinavian literature at the time, Denmark's failure to lend its wholehearted support to its own national literature had prevented a specifically Danish breakthrough in Europe. In Brandes's view, Denmark's only hope of regaining a positive national identity lay in changing the country's attitude toward its own writers and recognizing the contributions of literature to national self-respect.

Brandes challenged his audience to fight for the twin causes of political freedom at home and literary recognition abroad in the service of their country, pleading, "Let us, with the desire and will to assert Denmark's name in foreign harbors once again, do what we can to develop daring and personal initiative among us as well.... For the present, we must do what we can to spread knowledge in Europe of what we already have, work to promote our own."[83] This charge in many ways summarizes Brandes's own efforts to market Danish literature and culture abroad while striving to liberalize Danish society. Although Brandes's opponents were particularly critical of his orientation toward Europe and dismissed it as unpatriotic Jewishness, the highly successful cosmopolitan aspect of his promotion of Danish literature sets his efforts apart from those of other Danish cultural nationalists.

While no individual can single-handedly determine a nation's perception of itself or its international reputation, the history of European national-identity construction over the past two and a half centuries should acknowledge not only the power of the collective imagining of national communities but also the influential contributions by individuals, whether statesmen, artists, or philosophers, to the way in which particular national groups imagine themselves and their neighbors. In the wake of the French Revolution and in tandem with the rise of the modern nation-state in the nineteenth century, Europeans were forced to abandon obsolete concepts of political legitimacy based on divine right or dynastic continuity and search for new foundations for their political identity. Intellectuals and politicians who took up the quest to craft new conceptions of national identity to buttress nationalistic movements turned to the realm of culture to find support for their new claims to national legitimacy in history, literature, art, mythology, and language.

Although scholars and critics have long ignored or misunderstood Brandes's nationalist agenda, his attempts to shape Denmark's self-image, both in terms of achieving literary modernization in Denmark and marketing Danish culture abroad, bear witness to his seminal participation in the development of a new Danish national identity in the tumultuous decades after 1864, when Denmark's very political existence hung in the balance. Particularly in terms of asserting Danish cultural independence from Germany's long-standing dominance, Brandes's literary and political agitation in and on behalf of Denmark should be understood as partaking in the process of imagining and establishing national communities that preoccupied Europe at the time. His endeavors were by no means conducted in a vacuum, but rather in implicit, if not overt dialogue with both Danish and German nationalists.

In trying to bring about Denmark's domestic liberalization and demonstrate its importance and independence in Europe on the basis of cultural rather than political vitality, Brandes was forced to contend against competing images of Denmark at home and abroad. Whereas many of Brandes's countrymen clung to an image of Denmark as a secure haven of bourgeois Christian values, many Germans viewed it as part of an idealized heroic pan-Germanic homeland and the cradle of Aryan civilization, a romantic fantasy that Richard Wagner's operas and Kaiser Wilhelm II's annual pilgrimages to the Norwegian fjords reinvigorated toward the end of the nineteenth century and the National Socialists later adopted and distorted. Brandes's carefully stage-managed depiction of Denmark as a progressive defender of free-thinking liberalism appealed to young Danish and German intellectuals and enjoyed a brief prominence near the end of the nineteenth century. Although this view ultimately failed to establish itself as the prevailing assessment of Denmark in Germany after the turn of the century, it continues to resonate with aspects of Denmark's self-image today.

Since Brandes was just one player among many in the complex game of national-identity construction and projection, it is impossible to isolate the specific effect of his nation-building efforts on Danish society or on Danish-German relations. The difficulty of documenting influence, however, should not be permitted to obscure the nature of his contributions to both the prominent position of Scandinavian art and literature in German-speaking Europe in the decades before and after 1900 or the lessening of tensions between Germany and Denmark after the formation of a liberal government in Denmark in 1901.[84] That same year, Brandes pronounced his dual strategy of achieving both Denmark's artistic liberalization and enhanced international prestige a success, concluding in an article titled "Danish Literature after 1870" (*Den danske Litteratur efter 1870*) that the Modern Breakthrough had succeeded in its attempt "to bring Denmark artistically forward to a level equal to the rest of Europe and now and then in certain aspects slightly ahead of certain larger countries."[85] Not only had Danish literature been thoroughly invigorated, as Brandes documents in the article, but Danish culture had accomplished the daunting but psychologically critical feat of having surpassed its larger, more powerful neighbors, particularly Germany. This augmented international stature made it possible for Denmark to relinquish some of its hostility and fear toward Germany.

Although Brandes's central role in achieving the breakthrough of Scandinavian literature in Germany has been well documented, little attention has been paid to how this transformation of Danish-German literary relations affected conceptions of Danish national identity. His efforts illustrate Said's theory that a culturally subordinate nation, in order to reinscribe its relationship to the dominant power, must "rechart and then occupy the place in imperial cultural forms reserved for subordination, to occupy it self-consciously, fighting for it on the very same territory once ruled by a consciousness that assumed the subordination of a designated inferior Other."[86] Brandes fought for Danish cultural equality quite literally on German territory, attempting to raise Danish literature to a position of influence equivalent to the one German culture once occupied in Denmark in order to counter perceptions of Danish cultural inferiority and irrelevance both inside and outside Denmark.

Assisted by his literary acuity, deft manipulation of reality, and fortuitous circumstances, Brandes assisted Scandinavian literature to unprecedented prominence and prestige in Germany, but such a position was impossible to maintain, given the disparity in size and power between the German Empire and Denmark. Nevertheless, Denmark's moment in the European spotlight, albeit as part of a perceived Scandinavian whole, had a decisive influence on the restoration of Danish national self-confidence and international esteem in the late nineteenth century. Furthermore, Brandes's cultural campaign can be seen as preliminary to the renewal of Danish demands for the return of Danish North Schleswig, a cause for which Brandes became an ardent spokesman, demonstrating his understanding of the fact that, as Said asserts, "the slow and often bitterly disputed recovery of geographical territory which is at the heart of decolonization is preceded—as empire had been—by the charting of cultural territory."[87] In response to Germany's aggressive attempts to forcibly eradicate Danish in Schleswig-Holstein, Danes invested the preservation of Danish culture in North Schleswig with immense symbolic and strategic importance, defining solidarity with their colonized countrymen as a matter of defending the language and history underpinning their common Danish national identity. Brandes's quest to motivate and advertise Denmark's cultural self-sufficiency helped pave the way for the eventual restoration of Denmark's territorial integrity, because in order for Denmark to be able to demand territorial concessions from Germany when the time came, it had to be able to demonstrate its national and cultural autonomy.

CHAPTER THREE

The Outspoken Radical

*Political Journalism
and Provocative Pacifism*

Nationalism, in its various guises, replaced literary modernism as the primary issue about which Georg Brandes spoke out most passionately in the early twentieth century; he was particularly critical of the symbiotic relationship between nationalism, imperialism, and ethnic oppression. After nearly a century of sporadic eruptions, nationalism had definitively emerged as one of the dominant ideological paradigms in European politics by the end of the nineteenth century. Despite a false start during the revolutions of 1848, proponents of a monocultural national ideal brought about the consolidation of a unified Italian state in 1861/1870 and a German one in 1871. Meanwhile, nationalist fervor sparked popular movements and uprisings in support of self-determination among ethnic minorities across Europe, which were, however, violently suppressed by centralized governments of multiethnic states such as Austria-Hungary and the Ottoman Empire.

Competition between the great powers for colonies, both as sources of raw materials for import and as markets for exporting finished goods, led to an arms race between Germany and Britain and played a role in triggering armed conflicts between colonizers and colonized peoples, including the Greco-Turkish War of 1897, the Spanish-American War of 1898, and the Anglo-Boer Wars of 1880–81 and 1899–1902, as well as the Boxer Rebellion in China in 1900. Although economic concerns played a central role in these conflicts, they were also physical enactments of psychological battles over the cultural hegemony upon which imperialism and colonialism implicitly rely for legitimacy. The self-legitimizing nature of nationalism required that colonial experiments validate the superiority of the colonizing power's culture, not simply its greater military might. It was in this minefield of cultural politics that Brandes emerged as an articulate defender of human rights.

Brandes's commentary on Kaiser Wilhelm II's "Hun Speech" is an excellent example of such activism. When 130,000 German volunteers embarked for China on July 27, 1900, to defend Germany's wounded honor against the Chinese rebels, the German leader's send-off speech employed precisely the kind of extreme nationalist rhetoric that Brandes abhorred, motivating him to write a scathing denouncement of the speech. Attributing Germany's accomplishments to the Christian foundation of its culture, the Kaiser charged the troops with the task of making the superiority of both Christianity and the name of Germany known in China by emulating Attila the Hun's merciless brutality and utterly destroying their opponents. In an attempt to counter such arguments with reason, Brandes points out that Chinese culture could hardly build upon a much younger religion and questions the unlikely affiliation of Attila the Hun with the cause of Christianity, since "it has not previously been thought that a culture based on Christianity must necessarily completely eradicate its enemies, whom an apparently outdated doctrine instructs them to love."[1] Brandes goes on to condemn the militarization of the German people in the service of nationalism and to warn that a nation that values inflammatory rhetoric and well-tailored uniforms above reason will come to grief.[2]

In Brandes's opinion, the perversion of nationalism in the manner demonstrated so starkly by Kaiser Wilhelm II on this occasion posed a major threat to the continued advancement of modern European culture. In his commentary on the "Hun Speech," Brandes notes sardonically, "The new century, which holds such promise, will apparently show that the old methods used by rulers twelve hundred to one thousand years ago to bring about the honor of God and the happiness of mankind are still in full force."[3] This assessment reveals Brandes's fear that nationalist excesses would arrest or even reverse the modernization of European culture to which he had dedicated his life and cause great human suffering as well. He was particularly concerned about the narrowing of cultural horizons brought about by national self-glorification and the destructive consequences of inflammatory, racialized nationalist rhetoric about the supremacy of one nation above others. Decades before the beginning of World War I, he predicted that the continued cultivation of nationalistic pipe dreams would lead to both a prolonged, devastating cultural crisis and an equally drawn-out, destructive physical war.

Although representative of a peripheral European country and writing in a minor language, Brandes was a ubiquitous participant in European cultural and sociopolitical discourse throughout the late nineteenth and early twentieth centuries. He is generally remembered in Europe today primarily as a literary critic and intellectual historian, but, like other prominent literary Europeans such as his close friend Anatole France, Brandes's radical views of literature accompanied ardent political opinions as well. He viewed culture and politics as inseparably connected, describing it as an author's "thankless task to prepare the way for politics by shaping and educating public opinion."[4] He believed that when a country's political discourse becomes poisoned with self-deception, bigotry, and oppression, its culture becomes equally corrupted. In order to prevent the destruction of both the modern Danish and European cultures he had worked so hard to foster, Brandes devoted himself to educating public opinion throughout Europe about the dangers of nationalism and its negative effect on the development of national identity and culture.

Brandes was critical of the mass media for pandering to nationalist agendas, but he nevertheless spent much of his adult life working as a political journalist and public speaker, debating international sociopolitical issues in addition to the literary-aesthetic matters on which he had initially established himself as an expert. He was particularly critical of imperialism, not only because of its exploitative economic foundations, but even more so due to the oppressive sociopolitical conditions that so often resulted from implementation of an imperialistic system. Although aware that an independent press did not yet exist in Europe, Brandes needed the global mass media to convey his words to a broad European and American audience, since he could have little effect on world events writing in Danish for Danes alone. His international stature ensured that many of his writings were translated into major world languages and picked up by publishers and newspapers across the globe, lending his opinions an influence disproportionate to his country's economic or military might.

Although his views were not lacking in internal contradictions or self-interest, Brandes worked to shape not just how the world viewed Denmark, but, more fundamentally, to redefine national sentiment as the representation of a country's values rather than the thoughtless espousal of nationalist propaganda.

Denmark had become intimately familiar with the dangers of nationalism during the Schleswig-Holstein wars in the mid-nineteenth century, which had had the immediate consequence of exposing Denmark's political impotence on the European stage and the longer-term outcome of subjecting tens of thousands of ethnic Danes in Schleswig to aggressive Germanization policies. During the two Schleswig wars, excessive nationalist zeal in Denmark had made the Danes far more eager to fight than their military capacity could justify, as their subsequent humiliating defeats by Prussia and Austria confirmed. However, those painful memories did not deter the Danish intellectual elite at the close of the century from continuing to embrace the ideals of nationalism and equating patriotism with unquestioning support for the Danish government and its policies. Brandes's unwillingness to endorse such blind nationalism, in conjunction with his penchant for continually challenging the Danish status quo, was one of the reasons many of his homegrown detractors labeled him "un-Danish." This implacable opposition to Brandes as an individual, rather than to his positions on specific issues, suggests that his critics' conception of Danish national identity, in contrast to his own, rested primarily on conformity to the prevailing conservative, Christian ideals of Danish society, which the king and Parliament felt duty-bound to preserve, rather than on a clear conception of what values an ideal modern Denmark should embody.

Brandes's energetic political activism, both in Denmark and abroad, from the 1890s through the 1920s, confirms that his disdain for unbridled nationalism did not signal a lack of loyalty to his homeland, nor preclude his vigorous involvement in the development of Danish national identity, a topic about which Brandes wrote many times. Steeped in the romantic nationalism of the nineteenth century, Brandes regarded culture as the basis for a nation's identity, but not a justification for delusions of superiority. His view of culture was fundamentally and irrevocably political, encompassing not only the artifacts of artistic and literary production but also social mores, gender relations, working conditions, and worldview. Brandes demonstrated this position by advocating causes and opinions that he believed would benefit his homeland, both in terms of its social awareness and its international image, even when his efforts alienated his erstwhile friends and supporters. In his opinion, the modern Danish culture that he had tried to foster at home and popularize in Europe went beyond a mere literary aesthetic to encompass the moral and ethical character of the Danish people, which is reflected in its cultural production. More specifically, Brandes believed that having the courage to protest injustice, even at great personal cost, was just as central to a grounded, enlightened Danish national identity as the development of the innovative literary culture to which his name had become so inextricably linked.

The simplistic equivalence of nationalist ideology and conservative politics that had dominated Copenhagen in the 1870s was weakened during the so-called provisional period (*provisorietid*) between 1885 and 1894, when Danish prime minister J. B. S. Estrup (1825–1913) repeatedly failed to get Parliament's support for his budget bill and passed it as a provisional law instead, thereby governing without the consent of Parliament. This unconstitutional state of affairs, along with other repressive measures restricting freedom of the press and the right to bear arms, led to increasing tensions between the entrenched conservative Right party (*Højre*) and the emerging liberal Left party (*Venstre*), led by Christen Berg and Viggo Hørup. This opposition culminated in the 1901 system change (*systemskifte*), after which the prime minister was no longer selected by the king but rather by the party with a majority in the lower house of Parliament (*Folketinget*), which resulted in the first *Venstre*-led government.

Although the two main parties differed considerably in their views of foreign policy—*Højre* supported the construction of defensive earthworks outside of Copenhagen, while *Venstre* advocated complete disarmament—both parties agreed on the necessity of keeping a low national profile in order to avoid attracting the attention of their powerful neighbors. Not surprisingly, this self-effacing approach to Danish foreign policy did not suit Brandes, whose idealism was unwavering, his style of self-expression confrontational, and, as his biographer Jørgen Knudsen puts it, whose ambition for his country was equal to his ambition for himself.[5]

As the Dane around the turn of the century with arguably the highest international profile, Brandes was recognized worldwide as a respected symbol of Danish culture, a role that he took seriously. He lived in Denmark permanently after 1883, but he toured Europe each year for months at a time, in part to visit his numerous illustrious acquaintances, such as French prime minister Georges Clemenceau, and in part to escape the petty scandals that continually plagued him in Denmark. While staying in Paris in June 1902, he estimated proudly, "I have been invited out for lunch and dinner every day for about eighty days, so I have met several thousand people, among whom . . . I have gotten to know a few dozen or so quite well. Of foreigners, I encountered mostly Armenians, Rumanians, and Englishmen."[6] He lectured on a wide range of subjects across the Continent; in 1912 he spoke in no fewer than forty-two European cities.[7] In addition, he corresponded with intellectuals and writers in Germany, Poland, Austria, France, and England, while publishing articles and books prolifically, often simultaneously in several languages. Danish political historian Uffe Østergård asserts that Brandes's "books and thousands of short and long articles in all of the dominant—and several of the minor—European languages gave him a political influence that has never been surpassed."[8] Brandes became so well-known that aspiring writers from half a dozen countries deluged him with manuscripts, while German, English, and American tourists in Copenhagen believed, as Brandes remarked in a letter to Asta Nielsen in October 1920, that "I belong to the sights of Copenhagen as much as the Round Tower."[9] His recommendation was sufficient to secure a publisher for an aspiring author, while his censure sent foreign governments scrambling for political cover.

As a result of his intellectual credentials, extensive media access, and celebrity status, Brandes's pronouncements on subjects as diverse as women's rights, drama, democracy, and philosophy were viewed by many non-Danes as authoritative articulations of Danish viewpoints, even when his positions aroused passionate opposition in Denmark, as they often did. The discrepancies between his views of Danish culture as he felt it should be and his countrymen's view of themselves are central to Brandes's project of shaping both the character of Danish society and international perceptions of Danish national identity in the early decades of the twentieth century. Brandes did not fit the mold of the ideal Danish nationalist, and the ongoing debates about him in Danish scholarship today rest in part on the still-disputed question of Brandes's patriotism, particularly the extent to which his political views accurately reflected Danish identity.

His opinions were often more extreme than those of the Danish intellectual elite, who frequently condemned his position on various issues. Brandes's many speeches and articles on nationalism reveal that he regarded himself as a patriot but not a nationalist, a defender of Danish culture and identity against small-minded idiots who failed to grasp the larger issues at stake in seemingly petty debates over behavioral norms. However, as the industrialization and liberalization of

Figure 3.1. The endless criticism and hostility to which he found himself subjected in Denmark took an emotional toll on Brandes, but did not dissuade him from continuing his prolific publications, extensive personal correspondence, or annual lecture tours. Photograph by Strelitsky. Credit: The Royal Library, Copenhagen, Department of Maps, Prints, and Photographs

Danish society accelerated after the turn of the century and recognition of Brandes's international fame began to permeate Danish society, the gap between Brandes's positions and those of his Danish critics narrowed. When the tide of European public opinion began to turn against Brandes in the mid-1910s as a result of his uncompromising opposition to World War I, he enjoyed more widespread, albeit far from universal, approval in Denmark.

Brandes even had the chance to appear on film, at around the same time as Asta Nielsen was launching her film career, though with less commercial success. Together with Danish Prime Minister Carl Theodor Zahle, engineer Valdemar Poulsen, and painter Kristian Zahrtmann, Brandes was selected as one of the handful of prominent people about whom the newspaper *Politiken* made a series of short documentary films in 1912–13 for the specific purpose of creating a national film archive. The brief clip shows a roomful of eager students at Copenhagen University, to whom Brandes delivers a short but highly animated lecture. The choice to depict Brandes in a university lecture hall confirms that his countrymen had not forgotten his contributions to Danish academics and literary history. Yet it was not until decades after his death, in the 1960s and 1970s, that the value of Brandes's contributions to the modernization of Danish society and culture became more generally accepted.

Although Brandes's literary criticism had long contained a distinctly political component, the latter half of his career involves a fundamental reorientation from what Danish cultural historian Olav Harsløf describes as "cultural-political criticism (ideology criticism) to political-journalistic criticism (social criticism)."[10] While he had always been concerned with how Danes viewed the world, he now became increasingly active in promoting particular political responses to social conditions and crises. The political radicalization of Brandes's orientation and production took place gradually over the course of several decades, but it characterizes a distinct second phase of Brandes's representation of Denmark abroad, as well as in his reception in Denmark. During this period, his tireless defense of minority rights and humanitarianism contributed to the evolution of international and domestic perceptions of his homeland as a prudent, peace-loving state, at a time when Danish public opinion was beginning to embrace the same ideals, leading to a sort of truce, if not true reconciliation, between Brandes and mainstream Danish society.

Many scholars have interpreted the shift in Brandes's focus during this period as confined to the literary sphere, involving a turn from critiquing individual literary texts to writing biographies of prominent historical figures. While it is true that Brandes produced a large number of biographies during this period, his literary endeavors took on a much more pronounced political tone than previously, and he devoted increasing amounts of time and energy to political journalism. While Brandes's most significant published monographs after the turn of the century consist of monographs of "great men," including Nietzsche (1889), Shakespeare (1897), Goethe (1915), Voltaire (1916), Napoleon (1917), Julius Caesar (1918), and Michelangelo (1921), the unifying theme in these texts is Brandes's admiration of his subjects' radical individualism and his conviction that all decisive change is accomplished by individuals rather than broad social movements. Illustrating his own belief, Brandes produced a prodigious quantity of political journalism designed to shape public discourse of social issues, not only for Danish and Norwegian newspapers but for French, German, British, and American newspapers as well. In addition, on his annual lecture tours through western, central, and eastern Europe, he did not spare his audiences the discomfort of his disapproval of repressive social conditions in each country, although Russian censorship of his speeches was particularly severe. His outspoken views on subjects as fraught and timely as the dangers of nationalism, the spread of anti-Semitism, the economic imperatives of imperialism, and, most famously, opposition to World War I earned him both global acclaim and transnational censure, by turns.

By the end of his life, Brandes had outlived most of his original supporters and critics, becoming a legend in his own time, to be evoked alternately to inspire or to terrorize. Nearly every opinion he voiced and endorsement he made carried metacultural import for Danish national identity, contributing to the way the world viewed Denmark and the way the Danes regarded themselves, if only in opposition to Brandes's views. Henning Fenger assesses the ways in which Brandes's views resonated with the Danish public, both positively and negatively:

> By the time he died, he was an institution, known, admired, rejected and worshipped in Denmark, famous, respected, feared and honored throughout the entire Western world. [He was] our only international name as a critic, prose author, and political writer. Thus his death in 1927 aroused violent reactions. The evil ones laughed and the

good ones cried, or the other way around, depending on whether the bereaved were conservatives or radicals.[11]

Fenger's description of Brandes as an institution is appropriate, for his name has become synonymous with the ideas he espoused and promoted. Yet Brandes's efforts to bring about both the modernization of Danish society and the spread of international perceptions of Denmark as a progressive, modern state were also deeply personal endeavors, occupying his thoughts and emotions throughout his long, tumultuous life and shaping his conflicted relationship to his homeland.

When Brandes returned to Copenhagen in 1883 after his five-year exile in Berlin, he resumed lecturing at the university and writing literary critiques, but he also became engaged in social debates and political activism in opposition to the right-wing National Liberal government of Prime Minister Estrup. Brandes's skillful and targeted use of mass media in the service of these aims accounts to a large degree for both his popularity among like-minded thinkers, particularly upper-class women and idealistic students, and his vilification by less sympathetic critics, such as Harald Nielsen, Johannes Jørgensen, and Vilhelm Andersen.

Although he was invariably associated with the *Venstre* party because of his defense of free thinking, Brandes never belonged to a political party or held political office, nor did he endorse a particular political platform beyond expressing support for such radical individual ideas as the establishment of a Danish republic and the complete separation of church and state.[12] Instead, Brandes seems to have acted out of the conviction that cultural liberalism was fundamental to the development of genuine political and economic freedoms. Consistently acting on this belief often placed him in uncomfortable situations that exposed his private life to public scrutiny, perhaps most notably in the "morality feud" (*sædelighedsfejden*) over gender roles and sexual mores that polarized Danish society between 1884 and 1887, in which Brandes defended the sexual liberation of women and the redefinition of marriage.

Brandes's political views were anchored in the bourgeois liberalism that motivated the European revolutions of 1848, an ideology pervaded by suspicion of democracy and socialism but committed to the empowerment of the common man by means of expanded personal freedoms and economic opportunities. By involving himself in domestic Danish political debates, Brandes hoped to motivate Danes to return to the liberal ideas of the 1849 constitution. Although the eventual victory of the liberal parties in Denmark testifies to the success of these ideas, he himself remained a controversial and polarizing figure, not just because of his Jewish heritage, serial adultery, and antireligious views, but also because of his contempt for people who disagreed with him. Knudsen notes that Brandes's opponents "regarded him as the ungodly and rootless Jew, the unprincipled seducer, the tyrannical destroyer, the unscrupulous plagiarist, while he despised them as slanderous, lying, money-worshipping idiots who had sold out."[13] He aroused so much public opposition in Denmark in the final decades of the nineteenth century that the Danish Parliament voted twice to refuse him the state pension to which his highly acclaimed works would seem to have entitled him. It was not until the "system change" that brought the *Venstre* party into power in 1901 that he was finally awarded the professorship at the University of Copenhagen that he had so long coveted.

In the political arena just as much as the literary realm, Brandes vigorously utilized print media to influence both national politics and the development of Danish national identity. The traumatic experience of being blacklisted by the Danish press in the mid-1870s had exposed how completely dependent Brandes was on being able to write for newspapers, both in terms of his financial stability and as a vehicle for disseminating his views of the world. Throughout his time in Berlin, he had worked on reestablishing his connections to Danish newspapers, with his brother Edvard's help, in part by writing articles analyzing the social and political conditions in the newly united Germany. Brandes used these articles to express his misgivings about German conservatism, militarism, and nationalism.

Still, once back in Copenhagen, there was no Danish newspaper on which Brandes could rely to consistently circulate and defend his radical views until, on October 1, 1884, his brother Edvard cofounded with Viggo Hørup the opposition newspaper *Politiken,* which rapidly established itself as the dominant forum for liberal political discussions in Danish society. Like other Danish newspapers of the era, *Politiken* was unapologetically polemical, but also very popular and influential. From an initial circulation of 5,000 in 1885, it grew to 23,000 by 1899 and 70,000 by 1915, not including newsstand sales (often to individuals who didn't want to have their names associated with the paper by officially subscribing).[14] Brandes's relationship with the newspaper soured somewhat after the turn of the century, both because of the paradigm shift that took place when *Venstre* came to power in 1901, which made

Politiken effectively the official governmental organ rather than the voice of the opposition, and the extensive changes that Henrik Cavling introduced when he became editor in 1905, which included removing cultural matters from the front page and deliberately representing a broad range of viewpoints. Nevertheless, Brandes continued to make frequent contributions to *Politiken* until his death, and to write for a range of other Danish newspapers as well, including *Tilskueren*, *Det nye Aarhundrede*, and even occasionally *Social-Demokraten*, despite his ideological reservations about the latter.

As a regular and prominent contributor to *Politiken* for more than forty years, Brandes used the newspaper as a vehicle for promoting his views on both social and political issues. Although he maintained a pretense of independence from the paper by never accepting a paid staff position and occasionally taking a hiatus from contributing, he was a constant presence, generally on the front page, with not only literary critiques and sketches but also travelogues, obituaries of leading authors, editorials, and polemical pieces about the provisional government and the morality feud, as well as a regular front-page Monday column from 1901 on. During the 1887 elections, for example, Brandes published twenty-one polemical articles in *Politiken* in support of the liberal cause. Although *Højre*'s resounding electoral victory dashed Brandes's hopes for an imminent shift in Denmark's political climate, many of the changes he advocated did ultimately come about in the early twentieth century, due in large part to the strategic compromises reached between Denmark's political parties in the 1890s that prepared the way for the 1901 system change. Internal divisions within *Venstre* led to the formation of the Radical Left (*Radikale Venstre*) party in 1905, in which Brandes's brother Edvard was a prominent member, and when the *Radikale Venstre* formed a government in 1909, several of Brandes's followers occupied leading positions, suggesting the long-awaited victory of Brandesianism.

Although Brandes both enjoyed unprecedented financial security and suffered from increasingly poor health by the turn of the century, his passion for inciting social change only increased in intensity. He viewed the nascent political changes in Denmark as long-awaited legitimization of his own views, the beginning of a new era in Danish society, but not an end in themselves. In a speech given in the town of Sorø in June 1902, Brandes exulted, "When the people stepped over the threshold of the new century, they became master in their own house for the first time."[15] At the same time many of his articles from 1901 and 1902 are highly critical of *Venstre*, in order to preemptively combat the complacency to which *Venstre*'s politicians might be tempted to succumb. Within a few years, however, with *Venstre* firmly entrenched in power, Brandes no longer found domestic politics to be challenging enough to engage his considerable analytical faculties.

After the turn of the century, Brandes began devoting much of his time and writings to analyzing the underlying causes of European social unrest and agitating for their correction. Specifically, according to Harsløf, he concentrated on analyzing "the components of this reactionary unity: racism, militarism, nationalism—and its origin: imperialism."[16] He identified concrete examples of this reactionary sociopolitical climate in the plight of oppressed minorities across Europe, ranging from the persecuted Armenians in Turkey to the Irish to Poles under Russian rule. Although these problems seemed to have little relevance to Denmark, with the exception of the forced Germanization of the Danes in Schleswig, Brandes regarded the ideological dangers of nationalism and imperialism as applicable to humankind as a whole, not just the countries currently perpetrating harm against minority groups. His brand of cosmopolitan nationalism privileged a conception of the nation as a civic union in which the rights of heterogeneous ethnic groups must be protected by the state to which they belong, regardless of that state's dominant linguistic and ethnic identity. Brandes demonstrated remarkable prescience in predicting the inevitability of international armed conflict as a result of unbridled ethnic nationalism and imperialistic excesses, a war that, when it came, did not leave Denmark unscathed, despite its official declaration of neutrality.

In addition to newspapers, another public venue where Brandes found tailor-made opportunities to disseminate his views to a diverse and generally sympathetic audience was the progressive-minded Student Society (*Studentersamfund*) at the University of Copenhagen, which he had helped establish in 1881 as an alternative to the conservative Student Union (*Studenterforening*). The *Studentersamfund*, which most of the future leading *Venstre* politicians frequented during their student days, reciprocated by providing Brandes with a consistently welcoming forum for articulating his views. As a result, Brandes made many of his most explicit pronouncements about nationalism and politics in this venue, giving at least one major speech annually and often participating in open discussions after other lectures. After the system change, the *Studentersamfund* dwindled, deprived of the rationale for its existence, until being dissolved during World War I, but it had been instrumental in educating several generations of Brandesians.

Though he was reviled throughout his life by his countrymen for his international orientation, Brandes's geopolitical concerns were linked to his preoccupation with the character of Danish national identity. Despite his critics' denial of his ability to understand the Danish mentality, Brandes felt intense loyalty to his homeland and his mother tongue, as reflected by his assertion in a letter to Henri Nathansen that "The Danish language is, in fact, my fatherland."[17] When *Venstre* divided into two camps known as "Danes" and "Europeans," respectively, in 1898, Brandes rejected this division and, in a speech to the *Studentersamfund,* described his sense of self as being constituted by a series of concentric, not mutually exclusive, identities: that of a private individual, a Dane, a Scandinavian, a European, and a citizen of the world. He admonished his audience to embrace this multiplicity rather than fearing it, explaining, "The fact that we are Danish does not exclude us from being Europeans. As is well known, Denmark is part of Europe. But neither does the fact that we are Europeans exclude us from being Danes. We don't speak European—there is no such language. We speak Danish and feel Danish."[18] Without resorting to nationalistic rhetoric, Brandes affirms here both his deeply rooted sense of belonging to Denmark and the importance of Denmark's engagement with the world.

Brandes was particularly concerned with reclaiming the idea of nationalism from the interpretative control of the conservative political establishment. In the pamphlet "Concerning National Sentiment" (*Om Nationalfølelse*), which began as a speech to the *Studentersamfund* in 1894, Brandes tries to liberate patriotism from the narrowly militaristic category to which it had been assigned by Denmark's conservative National Liberal intellectuals and politicians. Brandes argues that Denmark's liberals had abandoned their ideals out of fear of losing power, but, by so doing, had contributed to Denmark's sociopolitical stagnation and nationalistic blindness. In his view, nationalism was the inverse of patriotism, manifested as "a nation's aggressive assertiveness at the expense of other peoples and races."[19] It was against this destructive form of nationalism that Brandes became a crusader, driven by the hope that Denmark could be in the vanguard of sociopolitical reform and humanitarianism by embodying liberal ideals to the world. Thomas Nordby explains, "For Brandes, national sentiment implied a more comprehensive national loyalty, not least with regard to the tradition of liberal rights and freedoms that had, among other things, been concretized in the June Constitution [of 1849]."[20] In response to critics who disparaged his loyalty to his homeland, Brandes insisted that his life and works demonstrated his patriotism in this broader sense.

In a speech given in 1904 on the island of Møn, Brandes explicitly linked the personal and national dimensions of identity, articulating the connection he saw between his activism and his love of his homeland. He challenged his Danish listeners to live up to his expectations by demonstrating a global consciousness:

> All people feel great enthusiasm for their fatherland. . . . It is also a natural form of patriotism to praise a country's people, laud its accomplishments, and glorify its past. Yet this is not the highest form of patriotism. . . . It is . . . more important to develop a sense of freedom and justice among the people, not just for its own use. . . . Thus it was my ideal it should be known that, despite the small size of our country, men lived here who felt sympathy with all wronged individuals or oppressed peoples across the world and who lifted their voices, spoke on their behalf. . . . All Poles and Finns, Ruthenians, Georgians, Armenians should know that freedom and justice lived in Denmark. . . . This is modern patriotism.[21]

In his own interpretation, Brandes's insistence on the value of each individual human life, his support for every oppressed minority in its struggle for human rights, was a deeply patriotic act that reflected his Danish identity and values. In contrast to the desire for cultural hegemony demonstrated by the great powers, Denmark should distinguish itself by acknowledging and defending marginalized peoples. Knudsen points out the intrinsic link between Brandes's well-known advocacy of free thinking and his less-discussed support for the freedom of self-determination, noting that, for Brandes, "it was not enough to work for the freedom of the spirit; what mattered was working for the liberation of the nations' individualities."[22] In Brandes's view, freedom requires action, not merely philosophical discussion and the espousal of abstract ideals.

Yet in an era of national unification, expansive nationalist political agendas, and intense pressure to conform to an increasingly rigid national ideal, Brandes's task surely seemed impossible. Not only was he speaking as the representative of a politically insignificant nation, but he often found himself in the position of undermining his own hard-won popularity, particularly in Germany, by discussing unpleasant truths. However, although he recognized his own and his country's relative powerlessness in a global context, Brandes seemed to relish the challenge posed by occupying such a disadvantageous position. Brandes's personality and biography are riddled with paradoxes, not least of which is his combination of hard-bitten realism and incorrigible idealism, as well as his passionate engagement on behalf of specific national groups while shunning the self-aggrandizing tendencies of nationalism.

Well aware of the powerful economic and ideological forces used to justify the oppressive treatment of minority peoples across Europe, Brandes nevertheless made it a priority to denounce such treatment as often and as publicly as possible, regardless of the acceptability of his views to those in power. He was not a proponent of armed insurrection, but he did support minority groups that challenged the cultural hegemony of the groups dominating them, affirming their fundamental right to cultivate and maintain their own culture. He was highly sensitive to the dangers implicit in the ideologies of racial constructs and hierarchies that emerged as a result of heightened nationalism, particularly because of resurgence of anti-Semitism that targeted him personally. On occasion, Brandes found himself on the side of the oppressor, for example in the case of Iceland's desire to gain independence from Denmark, which Brandes denounced as a further diminution of Denmark's international prestige. However, Brandes's own fallibility aside, the aim of his provocative proclamations remained constant: to combat "the hatred of truth," which, he warned, often masquerades as "politeness, consideration, tact, piety, patriotism, and sparing other people's beliefs."[23]

As the turn of the century marked both the global saturation point of European colonialism and the increasing probability of an eventual global conflict over limited resources and markets, there was no end of work to be done, both for Brandes himself and for the countrymen he hoped to motivate. In a speech titled "Thoughts at the Turn of the Century" (*Tanker ved Aarhundredeskiftet*), given to the *Studentersamfund* in 1899, Brandes warned,

> The great powers are dividing the globe among themselves. They strive to do this as peacefully as possible, to the extent that they would like to avoid a world war. Yet they do it very ruthlessly all the

same, because they sacrifice for the sake of their economic advantage not only those unhappy peoples whom they subjugate with fire and the sword and all such horrors, but also all of the smaller peoples round about who are swallowed up for the sake of national unity or used as objects of barter or handed over to brutalization so that peace can be preserved. Thus, with the consent of Christian Europe, the Sultan had 300,000 Armenians murdered. We have seen Poland sacrificed and forgotten, have now also experienced Finland's demise, and observed the spread of political coarseness in southern Jutland.[24]

Brandes recognized that many of the atrocities being committed in the name of nationalism actually served to further the economic aims of the more powerful country or ethnic group. Implicit in Brandes's catalogue of injustices is the possibility that Denmark too could easily face a similar fate, swallowed up and subjugated by a powerful neighboring state. More importantly, however, he charged that by ignoring such atrocities, Danes made themselves complicit in them. Throughout his political writings, he reminds his readers repeatedly that political expediency, not morality, determines the actions governments undertake, but individuals have no such justification for tolerating or perpetrating injustice.

Defending the cause of oppressed minority groups was not an arbitrary decision on Brandes's part but was rooted in his pride in his own culture and his awareness of its precarious position in Europe. Having experienced Denmark's defeat and the German occupation of Jutland after the Second Schleswig War as a young man, Brandes was familiar with both the resulting decline in Denmark's national prestige and the growing tensions between German and Danish speakers in the former Danish provinces. As the German government's treatment of the Danes in Schleswig became increasingly oppressive, Brandes became a partisan for the Danes' right to retain their ancestral language and culture. He did not hesitate to champion their cause, even in the German capital itself. At a farewell gathering of one hundred prominent writers, politicians, artists, and nobility in his honor at Hotel Kaiserhof in Berlin on February 1, 1883, Brandes used the occasion to protest the conscription of Danish citizens into the German army, which had had the effect of forcing young Danish men to flee their farms:

> My heart cringes in my chest, when I think, that even now, as I voluntarily leave Germany, hundreds of Danish citizens like me, the sons of North Schleswig peasants, who believed that they had a right to

live on the land where they were born, must leave the country against their will and without fanfare. I don't dare speak to the legal question, but Germany seems to me to be strong enough to be able to demonstrate magnanimity.[25]

This initial sentimental appeal to a German sense of fairness had little purpose beyond its confrontational shock value, but Brandes's next salvo on behalf of his countrymen, the polemical article "Danishness in Southern Jutland" (*Das Dänentum in Südjütland*), published in Maximilian Harden's journal *Die Zukunft* in 1899,[26] was a much more forceful exposé of Germany's brutal repression of Danish language and culture in Schleswig. Brandes's outspoken advocacy for the Danes in Schleswig irritated many Germans, particularly German nationalists who had long disapproved of his liberal modernist agenda, but it also boosted his credentials in Denmark as "a good Danish man,"[27] lending him much-needed credence and public goodwill.

The ambiguous legal status of the Danes in Schleswig was one of the unanticipated outcomes of the 1864 war. Article XIX of the 1864 Treaty of Vienna had granted inhabitants of the duchies six years to opt for Danish nationality and transfer themselves, their families, and their personal property to Denmark, while keeping their landed property in the duchies. Furthermore, the article stipulated that "the rights of citizenship, not only in the Kingdom of Denmark but also in the Duchies, are preserved for all individuals who hold them at the time of the exchanges of ratifications of the present Treaty."[28] After Prussian and Austrian disagreements over the administration of the duchies resulted in the 1866 Prusso-Austrian War, Schleswig was ceded by Austria to Prussia on condition, stipulated in Article V of the Peace of Prague, that the populations of northern Schleswig be granted the right to a plebiscite regarding remaining under Prussian rule or returning to the Danish kingdom. Approximately one-third of the population of Schleswig, some 50,000 Danes, returned to Denmark to await the plebiscite.

However, jealous of its territorial gains, the new government of united Germany never granted the promised opportunity for self-determination and, in fact, formally renounced this clause in the 1871 Treaty of Versailles subsequent to Germany's victory in the Franco-Prussian War. When those Danish speakers who had initially left Schleswig accepted this disappointment and returned home, they found themselves in legal limbo, having lost their Danish citizenship by giving up their domicile in Denmark but excluded from German citizenship for having failed to apply within the stipulated six-year time frame. Having no guaranteed civil rights, the stateless Danes in Schleswig were subjected to particularly harsh treatment, including arbitrary home searches, arrest, and expulsion. Cultural nationalism complicated the political situation, however, as the Danes in Schleswig tried to maintain their language and cultural traditions in the face of an increasingly strict German governmental policy of mandatory assimilation, particularly with regard to the use of Danish in schools and churches. When Ernst Matthias (E. M.) von Köller became the prefect of Schleswig-Holstein in 1897, inaugurating what became known as the "Köller period," the official attacks on Danish culture, including the banning of all Danish songs, the use of the colors of the Danish flag, Danish-language literary lectures and theatrical performances, and so on, escalated into what Brandes described as "a war of extermination."[29]

In the essay "Danishness in Southern Jutland," Brandes bases his defense of the Schleswig Danes' rights on the uniqueness and vitality of their Danish culture. Recognizing the irrational partisanship inspired by nationalist fervor, he admits how little a single individual can accomplish against a nation, noting that "where nationalism is involved, people are deaf to anyone who pleads the cause of an oppressed neighboring people."[30] Nevertheless, he expresses his hope of reaching at least those enlightened Germans who are not blinded by nationalism. Beginning with a brief sketch of Denmark's historical bonds to Schleswig, he argues that the province, unlike the contested Franco-German region of Alsace, is completely Danish, "by history and tradition, as well as by the inclination of the heart."[31] Despite Denmark's diminutive size in terms of territory and population, he argues, the Danish language is a cultural language (*Kultursprache*) that gives voice to a distinct Danish culture. He acknowledges the debts that Danish literature, theology, and philosophy owe to Germany, but insists that Denmark has contributed equally to the enrichment of German culture, through such authors and artists as Ludvig Holberg, Søren Kierkegaard, Bertel Thorvaldsen, and Hans Christian Andersen. He highlights the respective strengths of the German and Danish cultures but rejects the notion that Danish culture is a satellite of German, warning against the tendency to focus exclusively on the "incontestable, but yet quite distant kinship" between Germans and Danes and ignoring the deep differences that divide them.[32]

To a certain extent, Brandes's ardent defense of Danish culture seems to place him in the National Liberals' camp, reinforcing his unintentional but undeniable kinship to Grundtvig, as discussed in the previous chapter, but his arguments do not posit the superiority of Danish culture, merely its uniqueness. In order to demarcate the intrinsic differences between Germany and Denmark that render Danish culture both admirable and unassimilable, Brandes praises the preeminence of Danish dairy and agricultural practices, the broad accessibility of higher education to peasants through Grundtvigian folk high schools, and the charitable public services rendered by Danish university students through organizations such as the *Studentersamfund*. He cites the 80,000 subscribers to the popular science journal *Frem* as proof of the widespread hunger for knowledge among the Danish people, and, echoing his own promotion of modern Danish literature in Germany in the 1870s and 1880s, reminds his readers of the innovative qualities of recent Dano-Norwegian literature, particularly the works of J. P. Jacobsen, and art, such as the luminous landscapes produced by P. S. Krøyer and the painters of the Skagen school in the 1880s and 1890s.

Yet Brandes, always a savvy marketer, is careful not to provoke his German readers too severely, even when asserting Denmark's cultural independence. He asks them to admit that "it was the literature of the North that set German spirits in motion and thereby left its traces on a wide range of German texts, while, on the other hand, the influence of German literature on Nordic was minimal, or, more accurately, nonexistent."[33] He calls into question the ethical and moral legitimacy of attempting to exterminate such a culture just because people who feel a sense of belonging to it, through their heritage and language, prefer it to German: "Indeed, they do not disdain German culture and do not reject it, but Danish culture simply speaks to their instincts."[34] He denies the propaganda that attributes to the Danes hostile attitudes toward Germany, noting that the Danes in Schleswig have never demonstrated the slightest disobedience or desire to rebel against German rule, only to preserve their cultural inheritance.

At the same time, Brandes does not mince words in his description of the cautious attitude of the inhabitants of Schleswig and, in solidarity, Danes in general, toward Germans. He expresses amazement that the German authorities in Schleswig, who harass and oppress their Danish subjects, are surprised that those same subjects do not love and admire Germany. Similarly, in response to complaints that German tourists are not universally beloved in Denmark, he protests that Germans are treated with kindness and fairness, but marvels at those who believe that Germany's violent conquest of two-fifths of Danish territory, annihilation of Denmark's international political standing, forcible separation of families on both sides of the new border, and sadistically creative persecution of the entrapped Danes in Schleswig should have entitled them to affection and respect in Denmark. Nonetheless, he asserts that the efforts of enlightened Danes had done much to improve public opinion of Germany in the decades since 1864, only to have their efforts sabotaged by the mistreatment of Danes in Schleswig.

The point of Brandes's essay is neither to salve nor wound the feelings of his German readers but to incite them to take control of the development of their own political culture and demand a change in governmental policy. To this end, Brandes, in the conclusion of the essay, drives home the metaphorical knife into the heart of German nationalistic pride. He points out that the Danes, having acquiesced in their inevitable military-political defeat, cannot possibly be expected to surrender a thousand years of linguistic and cultural identity on command, and that German efforts to force such a surrender expose Germany's fears about its own identity, despite the might of its "armored fist."[35] The frantic violence of Germany's oppressive measures suggests that Germany does not truly believe that the attractive force of "German power, German wealth, German military fame, German science and art and the fifty-million-strong German population" can outmatch the influence of "the powerless miniature state that bears the name of Denmark."[36] Rather than enticing and rewarding Schleswig Danes for accepting German culture, which would have led to the gradual abandonment of their Danish loyalties, the German authorities' decision to punish and persecute them for remaining loyal to Danish culture had the effect of strengthening the Danes' resistance and exposing Germany's deep-seated insecurities.

Brandes closes with the argument that, at its core, the situation of the Danes in Schleswig is not fundamentally about German or Danish culture or politics but the essential human desire for self-determination. The force that lends the Schleswig Danes the courage to resist German oppression is the desire to think for themselves, to assert their equality with all other peoples. This universal human desire is what Brandes believes is worth fighting for, regardless of the venerable history and linguistic uniqueness of a particular culture like that of the Danes. In consequence, Brandes's engagement on behalf of oppressed minorities was not limited to assisting other Danes but stemmed from his sense of self as a European and an ethical individual, which obligated him to help whomever stood in need, even when he did not believe that his efforts could make a difference.

Brandes's sustained engagement on behalf of the Danes in Schleswig established his credentials as a spokesman for persecuted minority groups, many of which sought his endorsement in order to draw attention to their plight. He was inundated with requests for aid, both financial and psychological, from every side. After his article on Danes in Schleswig was translated and republished in French, English, Czech, Polish, and Russian, impassioned pleas for help filled his mailbox, resulting in more than thirty articles between 1898 and 1909.[37] In selecting which causes to defend, Brandes was motivated not by pity for the victims of the miserable situations he read about but by admiration for a particular group's determination to fight for their rights, without becoming too aggressive. Østergård notes, "In his later years, [Brandes] constituted by himself a virtual European public, which many groups and individuals competed to attract."[38] Brandes was aware of how little influence he had as a private individual; he once explained his refusal to collaborate with a major foreign political organization with the comment, "In order to impact world events and make an impression on those in power, one must be situated differently than a private individual without power in a small land without influence."[39] Nevertheless, when speaking as the conscience of Europe, Brandes was able to shape public opinion in multiple countries, urging his readers and listeners to prevail upon their governments to intervene in the various situations of oppression that he so vividly described. Even when confronting the most powerful governments in the world, Brandes challenged their cultural hegemony and spoke out defiantly in support of ethnic groups whose causes he believed to be just.

Brandes demonstrated this strategy with his early advocacy for the cultural autonomy of Poles under Russian occupation. As a young man he had taken a sympathetic view of the Polish resistance fighters being provisioned in Copenhagen in 1863,[40] a sympathy that deepened into empathy during Denmark's occupation by German forces in 1864. Extended visits to Poland in 1885 and 1886 provided him with firsthand experience of the intellectual revolution taking place among the upper classes, which he documented in his 1888 travelogue *Impressions of Poland* (*Indtryk fra Polen*), the opening sentence of which declares, "This book deals with a people's struggle to preserve its nationality after its unity as a state has been forcibly dissolved."[41] Brandes knew that although culture may not be able to prevent military conquest, it is a powerful force for resisting foreign domination.

Brandes was one of the first prominent European intellectuals to argue the Poles' cause and was rewarded for his efforts with effusive gratitude. For his part, Brandes admired the Polish people's passionate struggle for freedom and self-determination, exclaiming in an article in *Tilskueren* in 1885, "What is it to love Poland other than to love freedom, to have deep sympathy with misfortune, and to admire courage and belligerent enthusiasm!"[42] In taking the part of the Poles, Brandes was challenging the might of "the Russian system, the heavy, mechanistic-seeming Russian system of force, the mechanism of clearing out and exterminating."[43] Although he pitied the Poles for the sterility and poverty of their public lives, his motivation for championing their cause was his belief that Poland's fate would be representative of the fate of justice and self-determination across Europe. However, concern for the possible repercussions of his defense of Polish revolutionaries, either in the form of the harassment of his Polish sources or denial of future travel permits to Poland, prompted him to delay the publication of *Impressions of Poland* in any major European language for a decade, until 1898, when it appeared in German and Polish, then in English in 1903.[44]

It is sadly ironic that Brandes later forfeited the positive opinion of his Polish friends and admirers by demonstrating the same courageous outspokenness that had won him their favor in the first place. When vicious anti-Jewish pogroms broke out in Poland in 1914, Brandes condemned both the mobs for their brutality against the Jews and the Polish intellectuals who not only failed to speak out against the pogroms, unlike such Russian authors as Maxim Gorki, but even emerged as leaders of the riots. In Brandes's eyes, this failure of Polish intellectuals to recognize and oppose the "medieval prejudices" underlying the pogroms demonstrated the weakness of Polish culture and its subordination to Russia.[45] Brandes's erstwhile Polish friends and admirers never forgave him this insult and suppressed all mention of his contributions, both to Polish literature and to the cause of Polish independence.

Brandes also antagonized his many supporters in Germany, not only by espousing the cause of the Danes in Schleswig but also by his condemnation of Germany's enabling role in the genocide being perpetrated against Armenians in Turkey. He lectured and published extensively about their situation between 1900 and 1919. He publicly rebuked Germany for the legitimacy that its friendly relations with Turkey lent to sultan Abdul Hamid, whom British Prime Minister William Gladstone had called "the great murderer."[46] He gave his most memorable speech on the subject in 1903, when he was invited by a group of Armenian students in Berlin to speak at the philharmonic. Several hundred prominent Berliners gathered to be painfully enlightened by Brandes's graphic depictions of the rape, torture, mutilation, and murder of hundreds of thousands of Armenians by Turks and Kurds. After several heart-wrenching depictions of such horrors, Brandes made the parenthetical notation in the published version of the speech that "many women cry; others stand up; more than a few leave the hall."[47] Brandes then exploits the sensitivity of his female listeners to make his point. He explains that "Armenians have had to suffer a hundredfold what Berlin ladies could not bear to hear about."[48] Acknowledging his own inability to change German foreign policy toward Turkey, Brandes instead appeals to his listeners to plead the Armenians' case to their own governments, to accept the responsibility of wearing the blood-soaked mantle of the Armenian victims as a reminder to demand "security and freedom for the survivors of the ancient, honorable Armenian people."[49]

Once again, Brandes does not invoke sympathy as the sole or even the primary reason for coming to the aid of the Armenians, but rather culture, both admiration for the cultural wealth created by Armenians over the past four thousand years and fear of the destructive effect of tacit complicity on European culture. He proclaims gravely, "Since Europe has not prevented the horrors being committed in Armenia and now in Macedonia as well, we cannot possibly claim that our time has any ethical advantage over the darkest eras of history."[50] He provides multiple examples of the high level of Armenian culture, from the Armenians' mastery of multiple languages to their oft-demonstrated ability to withstand conquest and integrate the culture of their conquerors into their own. He describes the Armenian people as the most European of all Eastern peoples and cites the central roles Armenians played in the Parthian, Byzantine, and Ottoman Empires, particularly in the areas of government, business, architecture, poetry, religion, and literature. Brandes's primary source of information about the atrocities being inflicted on the Armenians was the writer Avetis Nazarbék, whom he met in London in 1895 and who was murdered in 1903 for his relentless denouncements of the Armenian genocide. Nazarbék had published several histories of the Armenian people, which shaped Brandes's knowledge of Armenian culture and upon which he drew heavily in preparing his arguments.

Although Brandes was best known in continental Europe, he did enjoy a modest degree of influence and prestige in the English-speaking world as well. In the *American Review of Reviews* in January 1911, he was singled out as "the most valuable natural asset of his country" and "the most eminent living Scandinavian."[51] His monograph on Shakespeare had earned him credibility and admiration in Britain, while the large population of emigrant Danes in America ensured him a reading public there as well. Brandes visited Britain on a few occasions, but never established the kind of close personal or professional ties he had in France or Germany.

Brandes had an ambiguous relationship with America, which he regarded as a fundamentally Puritan society with little concern for individual freedoms. In particular, Brandes was disappointed by the American interpretation of freedom as "freedom to earn money without society's interference, not a freedom that promotes intellectual independence."[52] In a letter to Rasmus B. Anderson, professor of Scandinavian studies at the University of Wisconsin, in response to an invitation to lecture there in 1881, Brandes expressed his reservations about how American audiences would react to his style of lecturing, explaining, "I would fit damned poorly in a country where what matters is craftiness, working for one's own advantage, taking a businesslike view of things. I am afraid that I would be tricked wherever I went."[53] As a result, although some of his books were available in English translation early on, Brandes contributed very little to English-language newspapers until the last decade of his life, and visited the United States only once, just before the outbreak of World War I.

When Brandes finally visited the United States, in continuation of his celebrity turn with Asta Nielsen on the maiden voyage of the Hamburg-America passenger liner *Vaterland* in May 1914, his presence represented a boost for the Scandinavian camp in the American culture wars of the time, which often pitted immigrants against native-born Americans. Brandes was eagerly welcomed by Danish Americans as an icon of the high culture of their Danish homeland and its international prestige, a situation that illustrates his dual cultural and metacultural significance. Announcing Brandes's upcoming visit in the Omaha-based Danish American newspaper *Den danske Pionier*, editor Sophus Neble asserted, "When the Danish-Americans receive Georg Brandes as their guest, they will celebrate him in his dual capacity: as the countryman who has meant more for Denmark's development than any other in recent memory, and as the great international name which resounds across the entire civilized world."[54]

His visit was thus a momentous and historic event for the Danish American community. C. H. W. Hasselriis of the Danish-American

Association of Chicago, which sponsored and organized Brandes's lecture tour, telegraphed an announcement of the upcoming event to *Politiken* on May 8, 1914: "The announcement that Georg Brandes is going to pay a short visit to North America and come to Chicago has awakened lively interest among all Danes. It is a given that Brandes's appearance here will be the greatest event in the history of Danish-American organizations."[55]

The acclaim Brandes enjoyed also transcended the linguistic and cultural boundaries between the various American ethnic communities, reflecting the view that the honor of his accomplishments belonged not only to Denmark but also to the rest of Scandinavia, Germany, and Europe as a whole. According to an article in *Politiken* on May 23, a German American newspaper in New York, the *New York Staatszeitung*, had published a long article about Brandes and welcomed him to the United States on behalf of all German Americans.[56] Similarly, *Berlingske Tidende* reported on May 27 that "all newspapers have bid him welcome in front-page articles in English, German, French, Hebrew, and Polish. The *Tribune* calls him a Prince of Literature, the most notable living critic, while the *Herald* praises him as the first among Scandinavian writers."[57] During his visit, Brandes delivered his lectures alternately in English, Danish, and German, reflecting these multinational affiliations.

The timing of Brandes's visit was also significant, for it coincided with the high point of the numeric strength and cultural vitality of the northern European immigrant communities in America. The outbreak of World War I in August 1914 and the subsequent introduction of culturally repressive nativist legislation and restrictive immigration quotas led to a dramatic decline in immigration from Scandinavia over the course of the 1920s. H. Arnold Barton's assessment of the state of the Swedish American community in this period applies equally well to Danish Americans, if not more so, given the more widely dispersed settlement patterns among Danish immigrants to America:

> In 1917 Swedish America still represented natural, inherent ethnicity, based primarily upon the living experiences, customs, values, and language of Swedish-born immigrants, constantly reinforced by fresh blood from the homeland. By 1930 the Swedish-born were significantly fewer, older, and generally more assimilated into the American mainstream."[58]

The Danish American communities that Brandes toured in 1914 were flourishing, but by the time he died in 1927, Danish American identity was being inexorably transformed from a natural extension of Danish culture to "a matter of personal sentiment, family tradition, and vague nostalgia, no longer strictly tied to ancestral customs or language."[59] In this context, Brandes's visit to America can be regarded as heralding both the climax of the age of Danish American culture as an extension of the homeland and the dawn of a new age of Danish American identity on its own merits, as attested by the emergence in the 1930s of such notable Danish American authors as Sophus Keith Winther and Enok Mortensen.

Brandes's long-awaited visit was a major event: newspapers throughout the United States and Denmark reported on his every activity, invitations to more than 150 banquets poured in, and thousands of disappointed fans had to be turned away from his lectures. A few of the tributes to Brandes included a torchlight parade in Brandes's honor organized by Danes in Chicago and a gala hosted by the Academy of Arts and Sciences in Boston. In New York City, eight thousand schoolgirls performed Danish folk dances for Brandes in Central Park on June 8, 1914.[60] In an interview with the Danish American newspaper *Nordlyset,* Brandes complained about being hounded by reporters wherever he went in America, but thanked Danish Americans for their hospitality, noting, "I have never received a reception anywhere comparable to that which I have received from America's Danes."[61] In light of the fact that relatively few of his books and even fewer of his articles had been translated into English, the conclusion is inescapable that it was primarily Brandes's symbolic stature as a great Danish intellectual, whose fame reflected well on both his Americanized countrymen and their homeland, that merited such ardent outpourings.

An article in the Chicago-based Danish American newspaper *Revyen* articulates precisely this expedient view of Brandes's visit: "This is an opportunity that Danish Americans have awaited for many years. May it be fully utilized, now that our genial countryman's world fame is greater than ever and sheds glory over the Danish nation."[62] At a banquet in New York City, Echard V. Eskesen, president of the Danish American Society in the eastern US, described Brandes's visit as being "like a brilliant comet that only rarely appears in the heavens and then disappears." He continued,

> We have longed for years to see you over here, to speak to you about ourselves, our hopes and aspirations in this great new society. You were the inspiration and torchbearer of our youth and we have brought the thoughts and ideas that you once awakened in us with us over here and sought to transplant them in American soil. And we are vain enough to

believe that it was in part for our sake that you came and therefore we
thank you with all of our heart. We Danes who live over here are just
a small fraction of the entire American people, but we have no fear of
being swallowed up or destroyed in this large population, for we derive
strength from the rich culture we bring with us from our motherland,
a great fund of ideas and spiritual values—and it is our task to draw
from this well over here, to strive with all might to remain ourselves, so
that Nordic art and spirit can permeate the new society being erected
here. . . . May you, dear Doctor, live and work for the benefit of the
fatherland and for all people for many more years and may your flame
continually light the way for us, so that it melts the frost of the cold
nights in our hearts. Many have sung your praises and our voice is
so small and can only repeat what others have said. But we over here
can say one thing with authority and that is that you have taught us,
despite all of the foreignness around us, to love Denmark first of all
and be proud of its men and its banner-carriers.[63]

The effusiveness of Eskesen's remarks is characteristic of the speeches given at each banquet in Brandes's honor. In Chicago, Carl Antonsen strove to outdo Eskesen, claiming that "there is nowhere you have been that Danes of all camps and social classes have praised you in more sincere admiration and love and gratitude for what you have accomplished than here in Chicago."[64]

Yet many of those present knew little of Brandes's work; instead, they revered him for the prestige he brought his native land and, by extension, to all Danes throughout the world. A rare exception is Kate Parsons of the *New York Times*, who, in her full-page article on Brandes on May 31, 1914, credits him with being "the savior of [Denmark's] literary life."[65] By contrast, Antonsen made no mention of Brandes's works, but merely exulted, "Georg Brandes belongs to the entire world, but we Danes are still proud of the fact that you are *Danish!*"[66] Similarly, in his remarks, Hasselriis expressed the Danish-American Association's "pride that you are a Dane, and our gratitude for the glory you reflect on our mother country by virtue of your universal and eternal fame."[67] Despite his notorious irritability and individuality, Brandes seemed to accept, even welcome, this symbolic position, but not for himself alone. In his reply to a group of Danish choirs that serenaded him in Chicago, Brandes described the task of promoting Danish culture as a collective task:

Here, where we stand in the middle of the great ocean of humanity,
you have caused Danish songs to resound across the sea as a sign that
Denmark will never perish. You have sent back your thoughts to the

fatherland in the east, which neither you nor I can make larger, but together we have spread its renown, made it greater."[68]

At the same time, he also acknowledged his own particularly prominent role in this process, explaining somewhat whimsically, to great applause, that "over my cradle, invisible beings sang: Whenever your name is mentioned in foreign lands, Denmark's name will spring to people's lips everywhere. The prophecy has come true and thus it has been for forty-four years. The name of Denmark will come to sound over my grave as over my cradle."[69] In both the eyes of his Danish American audience and in his own estimation, Brandes's fame as an individual was secondary to his fame as a representative of Denmark.

Yet for all of the celebrations, speeches, and ceremonies, Brandes's visit to America did not have the lasting effect on Danish American cultural life that its organizers had hoped. One reason for this might be that the generation gap between Brandes and his audience ensured that his words, which had such a revolutionary effect in Copenhagen nearly a half century earlier, would make no lasting impression on his American listeners. As several of the banquet speakers noted, they had grown up with Brandesianism and the Modern Breakthrough as respected ideals to emulate, not the radical departures from convention they had once been. Moreover, Poul Houe argues that "behind all of his modernist rhetoric, Brandes was deeply anchored in the enlightened Romantic and Naturalistic culture of the old world."[70] Some of the press coverage of Brandes's visit in 1914 highlighted his famous temper, his impatience with mediocrity, and his skepticism of democracy, all of which served to isolate him from the Danish Americans clamoring for his approval. The outbreak of World War I less than two months after Brandes's departure dealt a more decisive blow to Danish American culture, particularly because of the dramatic increase in pressure on Danish Americans and other European immigrants to assimilate more completely into American culture, but also because of Brandes's outspoken public opposition to the war.

World War I seemed to confirm Brandes's bleakest fears, expressed in his response to Kaiser Wilhelm II's "Hun Speech" in 1900, that European culture would annihilate itself and regress to a state of barbaric militarism. Brandes had begun warning as early as 1881 that a world war was inevitable if Europe's nationalist fever did not abate, so he was not surprised by the outbreak of war, but he was deeply disappointed in the failure of European culture to restrain nationalism. Despite appeals from his friends to endorse the Triple Entente,

Brandes resolutely refused to legitimize the war by proclaiming either side to be in the right. He was not a pacifist in the traditional sense; he regarded most pacifist ideology as wishful thinking and scorned the Danish *Venstre* politicians who advocated complete disarmament for Denmark. In some cases, he felt that war was a justified and necessary evil, as he explains in his August 1914 article "The Fundamental Causes of the World War" (*Verdenskrigens Forudsætninger*).[71] However, he felt that World War I was being sold to the citizens of the belligerent nations on false premises, by means of governmental propaganda and biased media coverage, as a holy war intended to bring about the end of all warfare by achieving total victory over the other side. Brandes viewed the war as a competition between European imperialist powers over market share rather than the heroic struggle against evil it was presented as in the media. Both sides professed reluctance to fight and claimed the moral high ground, but neither was willing to moderate its inflammatory nationalistic rhetoric or seek a compromise to bring an end to the fighting. In a 1916 article titled "An Appeal" (*En Appel*), Brandes exclaims, "Since none of the powers wanted the war, let them make peace!"[72]

Brandes found it particularly galling that the early days of the war sparked a nationalistic euphoria among intellectuals in the belligerent countries. The ostensible torchbearers of modern, rational European culture seemed intoxicated by their sudden importance to the national cause and flocked to the banner of their respective fatherlands with enthusiastic declarations of patriotic ardor. Brandes regarded such glorifications of the war as the triumph of nationalist propaganda over reason, which he countered with an outpouring of carefully neutral articles analyzing the connection between domestic politics and global oppression, between the cultural and violent oppression by western European nationalism, imperialism, and capitalism. Since wartime conditions confined him to Copenhagen and drastically reduced his European correspondence, Brandes relied on newspapers to transmit his arguments, although many foreign newspapers were closed to him and he was limited to writing almost exclusively for a Danish audience.

Yet even as he relied on the media to convey his own opinions, Brandes was merciless in his denouncement of the complicity of the media, as lackeys of corporations and countries, in promoting and prolonging the war, either out of blind nationalism or calculated pragmatism. In the essay "Europe Now" (*Europa nu*), published in *Tilskueren* in February 1925, he charges, "Without the press of all countries the World War would have been impossible. Peoples, in general, love peace; the press awakens their warlike impulses. It does not need to be bribed by the great industrialists; it needs only to be patriotic, and that it was in almost all countries. Patriotism and world peace do not get on together."[73] As a writer, "truth's consecrated priest,"[74] Brandes felt an ethical responsibility to counteract this tendency toward nationalistic hysteria by providing rational, balanced consideration of the issues of the day.

The war years were a remarkably prolific period in Brandes's authorship, as a result of his geographically restricted lifestyle and his distress over world events. In addition to four massive biographies of Goethe, Voltaire, Napoleon, and Julius Caesar, he wrote extensively for *Politiken* and *Tilskueren,* including a monthly survey of foreign policy. He published his wartime articles in two volumes: *The World at War (Verdenskrigen)* in 1916 and *The Second Part of the Tragedy: The Peace Process (Tragediens anden Del. Fredsslutningen)* in 1919. Recurring themes include the role of nationalism in fanning the flames of war, the detrimental effect of the war on European culture, and apprehension about the postwar future.

The tone of his articles is urgent and often despairing, but he continually urges his (primarily Danish) readers to rise above partisanship and consider the war from a global perspective in order to understand the true magnitude of the disaster being enacted on the battlefields of France and Belgium. In February 1915 he lamented, "By stoking the hatred of the nations toward each other, Europe has been transformed into a lunatic asylum, a house of mourning, a field hospital, a cemetery, and a bankruptcy court."[75] In March 1915 he decried "the snorting national hatred that now divides Europe as an incalculable misfortune and the symptom of a terrible regression."[76] He noted soberly that "the belligerents are all optimists.... Every one hopes to win and is certain of success,"[77] and posed the prophetic question, "What if none of the belligerents should come out supreme? What if all the horrors now endured should leave the grave question unsettled which inspired the strife?"[78] As the war drew to a close, Brandes cautioned Britain and France against using victory as proof of the legitimacy of their cause and placing all of the blame for the war on Germany. He rightly foresaw that a punitive peace treaty, such as the Treaty of Versailles proved to be, would merely sow the seeds of the next global conflict.

Not everyone agreed with or appreciated Brandes's measured rationality. His categorical opposition to the war did not win him many admirers in the belligerent countries, aside from a few fellow antiwar activists, such as Romain Rolland in Switzerland and Edmund Morel in England. Nearly all of the prominent intellectuals across Europe, including Anatole France, Thomas Mann, Arthur Conan Doyle, Sigmund Freud, and Gerhart Hauptmann, had succumbed to nationalist propaganda and ardently defended their respective countries' causes. In 1917 the Scottish critic William Archer, who had introduced Ibsen to the British reading public, published an open letter to Brandes titled "Shirking the Issue," in which he accuses Brandes of "taking refuge behind a poor platitude in order to evade your intellectual and moral duty as one of the leaders of European thought."[79] His admiration for Brandes is as evident as his distress at what he interprets as Brandes's apologetics for Germany's crimes: "Who could have foreseen that in this great crisis of history George Brandes, the high-souled humanist, the daring outpost-fighter for political and social freedom, would be found snarling at the heels of the champions of his own ideals, and would have no word of outspoken condemnation for one of the most monstrous of recorded crimes against humanity?"[80] Even in Denmark, where the king and the government had expressly requested that citizens refrain from endangering Danish neutrality by taking sides, there were ardent supporters of both sides who felt that Brandes was being cowardly by refusing to endorse one side over the other.

Brandes's strict neutrality was motivated in part by allegiance to king and country, but even more so by his conviction that the war would "set humanity back more than a century,"[81] thereby negating the cause of cultural and social progress he advocated. According to Knudsen, Brandes "did not doubt for a moment that this war was a crime, for which all of the belligerents were responsible, and he maintained that position, in part out of loyalty toward the Danish government, which had declared the country neutral, but first and foremost because he *meant* it."[82] Despite the sincerity of his convictions, for which some of his friends privately commended him and a few Danish journalists publicly praised him, Brandes found himself ostracized by many of his former admirers and correspondents abroad. In an article in the left-leaning newspaper *Die Weltbühne* in 1925, Friedrich Sieburg reflected, "His compulsion to speak the truth is rather gruesome. This desperate faith that naked arguments must, in the end, be persuasive, places him outside his time, which does not want men of this type, because they disrupt business. As a result, Brandes has lost all of his friends—in

Germany, in France—and in his homeland."[83] In the past, his international status had compensated for the criticism he faced in Denmark, but now he stood alone on both the domestic and the international stage.

The most poignant and most publicized example of Brandes's precarious position was his estrangement from his longtime friend, French prime minister Georges Clemenceau, who broke with Brandes in a series of open letters published in his newspaper *L'Homme Libre* and reprinted in several major European and American newspapers. Knowing of Brandes's deep love for France and indebtedness to French culture, as well as his frequent warnings against German militarism, Clemenceau had expected Brandes to champion the Entente and was angered by Brandes's refusal to do so, interpreting his silence as tacit support for Germany. In his response to Clemenceau's charges, Brandes tried to explain that it was not love of Germany that kept him quiet about, for example, the brutal German invasion of Belgium, but rather his respect for Denmark's declared neutrality in conjunction with a fundamental unwillingness to choose sides in a conflict where all parties are in the wrong. He acknowledges Clemenceau's perspective— "For you the whole affair is simple and clear. Truth and freedom on the one side, injustice, force, barbarism on the other"[84]—but explains that all he can see is how the war is destroying the love of truth, requiring countries to lie to their populations in order to ensure their support.

In his well-publicized denouncement of Brandes's position, Clemenceau treated Brandes as representative of Denmark and accused the Danes of being "a nation without pride"[85] for refusing to declare war on Germany. Jørgen Stender Clausen explains that Clemenceau knew very well that Brandes could not dictate Danish foreign policy, but he hoped to provoke Brandes to a declaration of solidarity with the Entente that would suggest implicit Danish support.[86] Barring that, Clemenceau intended to undermine Brandes's influence and reputation throughout Europe, but especially in France.

Responding to Clemenceau, Brandes accepted the metacultural responsibility of representing Denmark, citing the Danish government's request to its citizens to avoid creating difficulties for the government by protesting its policy of neutrality and explaining that if such a request applied to the man on the street, how much more it applied to someone like himself, "whose name is widely known and who stands as a representative of the country in the eyes of the rest of the world."[87] He did not give in to Clemenceau's persuasion, but vigorously defended

Denmark's neutral position, outlining a very clear-sighted assessment, devoid of nationalist rhetoric, of the complex situation underlying the war. Clemenceau had held out the possibility of reclaiming Schleswig and Holstein as the incentive for Denmark to enter the war on the side of Britain and France, but Brandes countered with the assertion that the Danes not only didn't want the headache of dealing with a German minority in the duchies, especially not if they had been taken forcibly from Germany and were thus likely to be forcibly retaken, but that it was not even in the Entente's power to offer the duchies, which they did not control. Clemenceau's response was simply, and dismissively, "Adieu, Brandes."

Nevertheless, to a certain extent, Brandes's standing in Denmark improved, if only temporarily, as a result of his stubbornly neutral stance. As both Brandes and his Danish readers were aware, his international standing meant that his opinions would be interpreted abroad as expressions of Denmark's views. The Danish government, which closely monitored his correspondence and publications, approved of his careful avoidance of partisanship, while newspaper articles in Copenhagen praised him for being one of the few citizens of the ostensibly neutral Scandinavian states who took seriously the responsibility of building bridges between the belligerents by pointing out the warring countries' shared responsibility for the war. Brandes's frequent articles about and against the war resonated with his Danish readership more than anything else he had written; his article compilation *The World at War* sold out immediately, a rare experience for Brandes in Denmark.[88] When the Spanish journalist Pablo Diaz, who would later write one of the earliest biographies of Asta Nielsen, interviewed Brandes in Copenhagen in 1917, he described him as "one of the greatest representatives of world democracy, an important author, and a pioneer of the European spirit. The Copenhageners know this and remove their hats when they see him."[89] In this instance, most Danes could not fail to recognize the patriotic motivation and effect of Brandes's antiwar journalism.

Yet although many aspects of Danish society changed radically after the war, generally in the direction of the social liberalization that Brandes had long espoused, his standing in Danish society remained disputed. The old pro- and contra-Brandes camps had been quiescent during the war but soon reemerged, although in somewhat subdued fashion. Many of his fiercest opponents had died and younger Danes increasingly regarded him as an anachronism. Writing in 1925, Sieburg marvels that Brandes, despite having "spiritually represented this country for multiple generations . . . is laughed at or—even worse—overlooked."⁹⁰ Brandes's old student fan club, the *Studentersamfund*, had disbanded during the war but reformed in 1921, only to spawn a more radical daughter organization, *Det Ny Studenter Samfund*, when several members objected to the "old radicalism" of the original society.⁹¹ The fiftieth anniversary of *Main Currents* in 1921 was commemorated with parades, banquets, speeches, and seventy congratulatory telegrams from around Europe. However, the account of the festivities in the *Frederiksborg Amtstidende* concludes with the judgment, "His [Brandes's] students are dead and his power is broken. . . . Therefore, when the students light their torches, it is for a historical figure, a man whom time has passed by."⁹² For both his opponents and his supporters, Brandes was an influential but unwelcome figure, more important as a symbol than as an active participant in cultural debates.

The events surrounding the 1920 plebiscite in Schleswig-Holstein, which was mandated by the 1919 Treaty of Versailles, illustrates the ambiguity of Brandes's position. Although Brandes had espoused the cause of the Danes in Schleswig at a time when German oppression was most intense, the Schleswig Danes had always been suspicious of his efforts on their behalf. Brandes reissued his collected articles on the subject in 1919 in a collection titled *Southern Jutland under Prussian Pressure (Sønderjylland under prøjsisk Tryk)*, but when the reunification festivities were held in Sønderborg in 1920, Brandes was effectively excluded. He did receive an invitation to attend, but without a place on the dignitaries' ship or sleeping accommodations other than a train car, which was impractical for a man of seventy-eight years and disrespectful to a man of Brandes's stature.⁹³ The humiliating situation was reminiscent of 1909, when Brandes was made a knight of the Order of the Dannebrog and presented with the Commander's Cross by King Frederik IX at Fredensborg Palace. This distinction was intended to honor Brandes for what he had done for Denmark, but he was made only a commander second class, which offended Brandes so much that he rarely wore the medal.⁹⁴ Despite Brandes's valiant efforts to strengthen and improve Denmark's situation abroad, he continued to perceive himself as a second-class citizen in his homeland.

Much of Brandes's postwar journalism was aimed at an international audience, for his reputation in many places outside of Denmark recovered rapidly, particularly as the war-weary belligerent countries began to recover from their nationalistic intoxication and recognize the validity of Brandes's arguments against the war. His articulate articles about the war, available in a successful English translation published in 1917,[95] had raised his profile in the English-speaking press to the point that many of his Danish and German articles appeared in translation in American newspapers, while he was also frequently commissioned to write for others, including the *New Student,* the *Living Age,* the *New Republic,* and the *New York World.* His condemnation of the harsh conditions imposed by the Treaty of Versailles, of which his former friend Clemenceau had been a central architect, led to a renewal of his popularity in Germany, although not in France, where Clemenceau remained implacably hostile. As before, Brandes was bombarded with requests for support, for German prisoners of war, blockaded Hungarians, African Americans in the southern states, Zionists, and starving Ukrainians, among others.[96] Even when health problems confined him to his bed for days at a time, Brandes dictated hundreds of letters to his secretary, Gertrud Rung, in an attempt to satisfy the many demands on him.

In the final years of his life, Brandes contributed frequent articles to Danish, German, American, and British newspapers, primarily on the topic of global politics, continually striving to motivate his readers to take a more active role in shaping their national identities to reflect their own values, rather than their governments' interests. In 1922 a German journalist memorably dubbed Brandes "humanity's conscience."[97] In particular, Brandes advocated the strengthening of international ties as a means of combating the national self-deification that had survived the war and threatened to both dominate postwar European politics and cripple European intellectual culture. In the *Prager Tageblatt* in June 1925, he warned, "I am by no means certain that we can reconcile our present political condition with the existence of anything called culture. Estrangement and discord among nations and within nations are growing. Parties, classes, and religious factions hate and despise each other more bitterly than ever before."[98]

In his articles from this period, Brandes chastises the victors of the war for their harsh treatment of Germany, in particular their insistence that Germany alone was responsible for the war, and cautions that a vindictive peace must inevitably lead to another war.[99] Although he favored the concept of the League of Nations, he makes no secret of his conviction that it would fail without the participation of the world's most powerful countries, especially the United States. Finally, he condemns the hypocritical colonialism of Britain, France, and the United States, who claim to value democracy but in reality practice brutal oppression. He had little sympathy for the Bolsheviks in Russia, but he denounces the Western nations' armed intervention in the Russian Revolution, arguing that both sides would have been better served if they had sent bread instead of soldiers.[100] Ever the idealist, Brandes found himself disappointed by the self-interested direction taken by postwar European politics and culture.

At the same time, Brandes found himself also increasingly out of step with postwar Danish culture and politics. On the one hand, his interpretation of modern literature was outdated, while on the other, the social liberalization he advocated was still far from reality. The waves of cutting-edge artistic and literary movements, from dadaism to cubism, did not appeal to him, while the increasingly reactionary, inward-looking political climate in Copenhagen offered little hope of social progress or international activism. With his two last monographs, *The Legend of Jesus* (*Sagnet om Jesus*) and *Peter* (*Petrus*), published in 1925 and 1926, respectively, Brandes became involved in an ongoing debate among Danish intellectuals about the relative merits of a metaphysical versus a biological worldview.

To a certain extent, these final texts merely reprise Brandes's familiar critique of organized religion in general and Christianity in particular, but on another level, they are concerned with defending the importance of independent thought, which, Brandes felt, was not valued by the national-religious conservatives.[101] Although Brandes no longer had the energy to conduct a media blitz in support of his views, a new incarnation of Danish cultural radicalism, led by the architect-critic Poul Henningsen, among others, emerged in the mid-1920s and championed Brandes's twin causes of free-thinking and unconventional morals.

Brandes's death in February 1927 was commemorated with celebratory articles in newspapers across the globe, even one by Clemenceau in France, making it clear how far his reputation had spread. However, determining the depth of his effect on European society required many more decades, and was complicated by global war and the effectual erasure of his contributions to German literature by the anti-Semitism of the Nazis and the chaos of the postwar period. The social liberalization Brandes had advocated in Denmark was underway by the time he died, but the process was slow and halting and did not become mainstream until after World War II. Many of the negative mutations of nationalism Brandes had warned against were present in the late 1920s, especially in France, Germany, and Britain, and soon bore virulent fruit. His decades of advocacy work did not result in the end of oppression or persecution of minority ethnic and religious groups; on the contrary, the decades following Brandes's death witnessed the most efficient, highly organized genocides the world had ever seen. The trauma of World War II effectively eradicated the memory of Brandes from continental Europe, particularly Germany, even as his prophetic warnings were fulfilled, although he did serve as a symbol of freedom for some radical groups in Denmark during the German occupation. Despite opposition from the ostensibly independent Danish government, Brandes's hundredth birthday was celebrated in 1942 by such leftist organizations as *Clarté, Studentersamfundet,* and the student newspaper *Den jydske Akademiker.* Even the Nazi occupiers inadvertently commemorated Brandes's birthday and confirmed the continued potency of his ideas by issuing a warning, published in the newspaper *Fædrelandet* on February 2, 1942, against "the Jew Georg Brandes, ... one of the greatest deceivers of the people and destructors of society around the turn of the century."[102]

As the hundredth anniversary of Brandes's death approaches, the struggle to determine his legacy goes on. Danish conservatives still periodically demonize him as antinational, foreign, and un-Danish, as Hans Hertel has documented,[103] but his contributions to the establishment of Danish cultural modernity have become generally accepted. Since the mid-1960s, scholars in Denmark, as well as France and Germany to a lesser extent, have demonstrated both the revolutionary nature of Brandes's work and his importance to modern European literary and political culture. The gradual publication of Brandes's vast correspondence confirmed the extent of his close interaction with and influence on several generations of European writers. The secularization, sexual freedom, and pacifist-humanitarian orientation of Scandinavian society and politics in the 1960s found an echo in Brandes's critical and journalistic texts, thereby justifying both the rehabilitation of Brandes's reputation and the prominent positioning of his views in the construction of a Danish liberal tradition. What more than a century of debate makes clear, however, is that Brandes is still a celebrity whose expansively inclusive view of Danish national and cultural identity remains influential, relevant, and provocative today.

PART TWO
Asta Nielsen

CHAPTER FOUR

The Danish Diva

Identity Games in Prewar Silent Cinema

Much of the controversy surrounding Georg Brandes centered on his international orientation and liberal views of sexuality, religion, and aesthetics. His high-profile representation of Denmark abroad served to disseminate an image of Denmark as socially and culturally progressive, while his conflicted standing among Danes reflected the deep divisions this self-image sparked among his countrymen. Although Brandes was nearly forty years old by the time Asta Nielsen was born in 1881, these same issues continued to play a central, contentious role in Danish cultural politics almost three decades later, when Nielsen blazed her path to the heights of global silent cinema stardom with her uncommonly expressive acting and shockingly sensual dance performance in her debut film, *The Abyss / Afgrunden* (Urban Gad, 1910). Although Nielsen's on-screen eroticism, unconventional personal life, and naturalistic acting style were all factors that made her a controversial figure in Denmark, it was her decision to pursue a career in the burgeoning German film industry that played the most important role in determining her reception in her homeland. As one of the earliest objects of the movie-star craze launched by the film industry in the early twentieth century, Nielsen's celebrity was more frenzied and ephemeral than Brandes's, but no less influential abroad or contested at home, particularly in terms of her representation of Denmark.

Both in the early twentieth century and today, silent film is often described as inherently international or anational, due to the apparent absence of language (except for in the form of interchangeable intertitles) and the perceived universality of the visual language of gestures and facial expressions.¹ This lack of linguistic barriers had the economic benefit of facilitating the international circulation of silent films. Danish studios in particular eagerly exploited this global market, designing their products for international consumption by setting films in nonspecific locations and giving their protagonists generic names. Many early film critics also articulated the hope that silent film could serve to unite different nationalities. For example, Emma Gad, Nielsen's mother-in-law, wrote in a column for the Copenhagen newspaper *Politiken* in 1913 that film "brings people together, different races whose mutual comprehension has been hampered for millennia by heterogenous languages."² Writing immediately after World War I, her son, director Urban Gad, expressed a similar conviction that silent film had the power to "spread knowledge of a nation's everyday life from one people to another, and will do much to cause hate to vanish like the legacy of idiocy from the past that it is."³ Other Danes were less sanguine about the possible effects of the "cosmopolitan" character of silent film, however, a charge that echoes the criticism aimed at Brandes decades earlier; the conservative Student Union (*Studenterforening*) at the University of Copenhagen, which had been outspoken in its opposition to Brandes's radical views, was equally wary of the cinema, which "has a destructive effect on poetry, especially national poetry, because of its cosmopolitan orientation, which is not rooted in tradition and patriotic memories."⁴

Yet, from the earliest beginnings of cinema, national film industries have taken country- and culture-specificity into account. Films and film stars crossed borders with relative ease in this period, but they carried with them national attributes that informed discussions about cinema aesthetics, economics, and public morality. Certain acting styles and film genres came to be associated with particular countries, for example the feature-length erotic melodrama that originated in Denmark with Fotorama's thirty-five-minute sensation *The White Slave Trade / Den hvide Slavehandel* (Alfred Cohn, 1910). Producers often created different endings to a film for specific national markets or remade popular films; *The White Slave Trade* caused a commotion in the United States in its remade version, *Traffic in Souls* (George Tucker, 1913). Competition between national film industries for market share was fierce, with the French company Pathé and the Danish company Nordisk vying for dominance in the European market in the years prior to World War I, and played a significant role in determining the conditions for the importation of, for example, German films into Great Britain and the United States, in particular through the targeted use of censorship to restrict the circulation of certain types of films. Governmental support for and regulation of the film industry varied by country, leading to widely divergent censorship standards and different versions of films being produced for particular countries.

Although "national cinema" is a contested category that can encompass a range of definitions, it is often used somewhat simplistically, interchangeably with "domestic film industry," to denote the films produced by companies located within a particular country. However, such usage neglects the subtler connections between cinema and national identity and fails to account for several factors: the existence of stylistic or thematic commonalities between individual films and national traditions, the role of social and political ideologies, the effect of imported foreign films, and the classification of expatriate actors and directors who made films in countries other than their own homelands, as Nielsen did. Andrew Higson criticizes the concept of national cinema as an inadequate theoretical construction and suggests that it would be more effective to consider "to what extent [certain films] are engaged in 'exploring, questioning, and constructing a notion of nationhood' . . . in the films themselves and in the consciousness of the viewer."[5] If a national cinema were determined solely by place of production, Nielsen's films would be assigned almost exclusively to German national cinema, whereas a different standard that uses the nationality of either director or star as its guide would result in a much more varied but equally random pattern of classification. By contrast, employing Higson's more nuanced approach allows us to ask to what extent Nielsen's films can be understood as belonging to both the national culture of the country in which they were produced *and* the national culture of her own heritage and self-identification, due to their involvement in exploring, questioning, and constructing notions of both Danish and German national identity.

Nielsen's relationship to both the Danish and German film industries and markets is crucial to understanding her contributions to contemporary constructions of German and Danish national identity. She was an international star, but the differences in her reception in the land of her birth and the land where she worked are central to understanding her legacy for both cinema and society. It was on the strength of her first Danish film, with its use of Danish cinematic innovations, that Nielsen got her start in the German film industry in 1911, where she went on to play a decisive role in the development of silent film. Although she made only four films in Denmark before 1920, most of her German-made films from the pre–World War I period were widely screened in Denmark, with the result that Danish audiences were familiar with her name and face, while Danish newspapers frequently wrote about and interviewed her. For Danes, the fact that Nielsen was Danish initially trumped the fact that she worked in Germany, but this situation reversed itself after World War I due to a combination of economic, social, and cultural-political factors that will be discussed in chapter 5. Even while living in Germany for two and a half decades, Nielsen remained a Danish citizen; after fleeing Nazi Germany in 1937, she spent the final three and a half decades of her life in Denmark. She was recognized around the world as the most famous Danish actress, and her expressive acting style had a far more profound and lasting effect on continental European cinema than the erotic melodrama for which early Danish silent film was famous. Film historian Marguerite Engberg asserts that, thanks to Nielsen, the "Danish influence [on European cinema] became more of an influence of a great screen personality than a genre influence."[6] Yet despite her contributions to silent cinema and Denmark's international reputation, Nielsen received little official recognition in Denmark for her work and occupied a marginal position in Danish film scholarship until the 1970s.

One possible answer to the conundrum of Nielsen's conflicted reception lies in the way her career exploited the power of film to popularize particular values and identity constructions. By 1910 the cinema was becoming an increasingly lucrative industry and popular entertainment venue throughout Europe. From its humble beginnings as a carnival sideshow, film rapidly transformed itself into a sophisticated art form in its own right, as well as an influential medium for shaping public opinion, particularly with regard to notions of gender and national identity, in a time of social, economic, and political upheaval in Europe. As discussed in the introduction, the rise of the cinema is closely linked to the construction of social and cultural modernity. In 1944 German philosophers Theodor Adorno and Max Horkheimer identified the cinema as an integral part of modern society's "culture industry," by means of which certain values and ideals are commodified and marketed to audiences. Adorno's colleague Walter Benjamin, in his essay from 1936, "The Work of Art in the

Age of Its Technical Reproducibility" (*Das Kunstwerk im Zeitalter seiner technischen Reproduzierbarkeit*) posits an integral connection between the social changes associated with modernity and the mass media of photography and film, arguing that film is not just part of a culture industry designed to promote consumption by the masses but also a means of understanding and shaping the self-consciousness of the masses themselves.[7] Writing more than a decade before Benjamin, Siegfried Kracauer warned that visual media such as photography and film do not neutrally replicate the world but represent it in such a way as to "bring the world into conformity with its mediated image rather than the other way around."[8] As a powerful tool for shaping public perceptions of reality, the cinema can be manipulated by different groups to serve potentially contradictory aims.

While Adorno, Benjamin, and Kracauer explore this phenomenon primarily in connection with the dissemination of capitalist ideology, Heide Schlüpmann applies it to gender politics, arguing that "the disruption of the traditional order of gender and of traditional female role models brought about by industrialization and urbanization belatedly generated a social demand, especially among the female population, aimed at gaining a new self-confidence in gender relations."[9] This groundswell of interest in redefining the parameters of socially constructed female identity found an outlet in the cinema, which, due in part to Nielsen, became "a place of female self-determination, where gender relations might be redefined."[10] On screen, Nielsen generally chose to play independent, norm-transgressing women, thereby enacting both emancipated female identity and Danish cultural modernity. Her performance of womanhood is intextricable from the medium in which she worked; early silent cinema, once it had progressed past the nickelodeon stage, allowed for a combination of spectacle and storytelling that Nielsen exploited to its fullest extent. Nielsen was an influential participant in these discourses about identity not just by embodying strong women characters, but also by empowering her female viewers, thereby transforming the "public sphere of the cinema ... from a space of exhibition to a space of the reality of dreams."[11] Nielsen's initial success in film was linked to her ability to enact these emancipatory dreams on behalf of her female viewers.

Another important area in which early cinema served to challenge and redefine preexisting norms is national identity. Given the symbiotic relationship between modernity, nationalism, and mass media, it is not surprising that cinema would become a vehicle for promoting constructions of national identity, both as propaganda for governments, as was the case throughout Europe and America during both world wars, and in response to social movements. Indeed, cinematic depictions of revolutionary identity constructions are often so closely linked to the actualization of such models in particular societies, for example in the close chronological correspondence between women's emancipation movements and the provocative redefinition of gender roles on-screen discussed above, that it is nearly impossible to determine which came first, the social change itself or the cinematic popularization of it. Although Nielsen's films, like the majority of early silent films made in Germany in this period, are generally perceived as being apolitical, they nonetheless frequently and openly thematize national identity, particularly through the exploration of various national stereotypes. Viewed through the lens of Judith Butler's theorization of the social construction and performance of gender,[12] Nielsen's public and private enactment of both femininity and Danishness can be described as fundamentally performative, contributing to the creation of the very social reality that they describe. By playing identity games in her films, slipping between nationalities, ethnicities, ages, and genders, Nielsen demonstrated the artificiality and fluidity of identity constructions, entertaining and empowering her viewers at the same time.

At the same time as it facilitated the proliferation of individual identity constructions, however, the film industry itself became increasingly homogeneous during the first few decades of the twentieth century. The evolution of cinema into an independent artistic and economic force required both its institutionalization as a social practice and the standardization of filmic means. Thomas Elsaesser identifies several factors that contributed to the former development in Germany, in particular "the demand for longer films, the emergence of the star system, the drive for cultural status, the conflict with staged theater, and the need to attract loan capital to finance film production."[13] Sabine Hake, addressing the latter issue, singles out the importance of the shift from short films to multiple-reel narrative films that took place within a distinct space-time continuum and involved complex character development.[14]

These long, linear narratives relied heavily on individual actors and actresses, whose pantomimic performances in silent film conveyed a "strong sense of physical presence and, hence, of closeness and intimacy."[15] As a result, audiences felt an emotional connection to both the characters on screen and the actors who portrayed them. Hake explains the process underlying this phenomenon:

> Through their body types and facial expressions, [silent] film actors conveyed a unity of body and character not attainable on the stage. They gave new credence to older assumptions (for instance, taken from physiognomy) about outward appearance and inner self, while at the same time promoting more fluid definitions of identity based on the modern notion of self-transformation. In problematizing the body, actors played a key role in the construction of national identity, evoking the other as a temptation as well as a threat and defining Germanness in visual, narrative, and performative terms.[16]

By enacting particular "types" of identity on screen, many silent film actors and actresses attained not only tremendous fame and wealth but also representative status as the embodiment of particular identity constructions of gender, ethnicity, and national culture as well as examples of the infinite malleability of identity in the modern world.

These stylistic changes were made possible by the introduction of feature-length films starting in 1910, but they were also crucial to facilitating the "star culture" that studios and production companies began promoting at the same time. While the popularity of movie stars was facilitated by audiences' identification with individual actors and actresses as described above, the driving force behind the star system was an economic imperative generated by the emergence of the monopoly film-distribution system at the end of the first decade of the twentieth century.[17] In his study of the phenomenon of celebrity, David Gritten compares the systematic manufacturing of early movie stars to the mass production of Model T Fords, and notes that "the entertainment business became the first industry to treat the creation of fame as if it were an industrial process."[18] Under their new business model, film studios had a vested financial interest in establishing the drawing power of recognizable, famous faces in order to guarantee the success of entire series of films linked solely by the name of the leading actor or actress and presold to distributors and theaters. Prior to 1910, studios did not generally even release the names of the actors and actresses in their films, let alone disclose personal information about them, but the deliberate promotion of individual movie stars after 1910 by the studios generated a barrage of celebrity journalism and commercial tie-ins.

Movie stars rapidly became the focal point of the cinematic culture industry, forever unattainable on screen but indirectly accessible through a range of products bearing their names. Samantha Barbas explains that the film industry, together with publishers and advertisers, "urged fans to see consumption as a form of participation: rather than become personally involved in the movies, fans might vicariously participate by purchasing the cosmetics and clothing endorsed by the stars."[19] The frenzy of consumerism this inspired had farther-reaching consequences than just the proliferation of star-themed trinkets and the impoverishment of fans in pursuit of their idols, however. It also contributed to metacultural judgments by fans about the cultures depicted on screen, inspiring them to model their mannerisms, behaviors, and aspirations on movie stars, in order to feel a sense of belonging to imagined national, social, and gender communities.

Asta Nielsen was one of the first and most dynamic European female movie stars to occupy such a prominent place in the public eye and imagination. In this capacity, she was highly influential in terms of both the development of European cinema and European perceptions of Denmark in the early twentieth century. Although natural acting ability and hard work were integral to her success, Nielsen's meteoric rise to fame was also made possible by the serendipitous timing of her film debut in September 1910. The film industry in Europe was in a state of socioeconomic transition in 1910–11. The establishment of permanent, often luxurious "cinema palaces" in place of the earlier traveling and store-front cinemas made movie-going more attractive to middle-class audiences and expanded the size of the potential movie-going public, while the spread of the monopoly film distribution system enabled studios to realize much greater profits on the films they produced. Rather than making cheap films and selling as many prints as possible, producers now began to sell the distribution rights for a particular film or film series to a single national distributor, who, in turn, sold exclusive exhibition rights to local cinema managers. The exclusivity of the monopoly system allowed both producers and cinema managers to raise their prices, confident of making a predictable profit, and emboldened studios to bear the higher production costs of feature-length films.[20] However, ensuring the financial viability of the monopoly film distribution system necessitated creating a consistent supply of a product that would be sure to sell, which, in turn, required that audiences be able to choose films based on the actors in them, giving rise to the cultural and economic phenomenon of the movie star.[21]

Nielsen's debut film, *The Abyss,* was the first film to be distributed in Germany on the monopoly-distribution basis, and its tremendous success instantly made Nielsen a valuable commodity. As soon as she signed a contract with the German film company Deutsche Bioscop, they began building up her reputation as a star in order to ensure the success of the eight-film Nielsen series they would launch in 1911–12. The monopoly film system ensured that her films would be shown only in specific movie houses at strictly controlled times, so that cinema managers were willing to commit to purchasing the entire series of films sight unseen. Corinna Müller explains, "As long as films could be bought or sold, appearing here and there, in many cinemas all at once, or in none at all, the film star phenomenon was fundamentally impossible; it was not possible to create the necessary aura of uniqueness and exclusivity."[22] By magnifying Nielsen's celebrity status however possible and increasing demand for her films, producers could be sure of selling them for a large profit, while cinema owners could be sure of filling every seat in their theaters. The economic boost this gave the German film industry was immediate and unmistakable; according to Peter Jelavich, "In 1910 there were 456 cinemas in twenty-nine German cities; three years later, the number had swelled to 2,371."[23] Even more important, the production of films in Germany, for both domestic consumption and for export, increased exponentially from the 15 percent market share it commanded in 1910[24] to 67.6 percent by 1925.[25]

The process of creating a silent movie star was not predetermined, but it was subject to certain conditions, comparable to those demonstrated by the eighteenth- and nineteenth-century popularization of stage actresses such as Eleonora Duse and Sarah Bernhardt. Media historian Knut Hickethier defines a "star" as a person "who is not only able, through her physical presence, her demeanor, her gestures and mimicry to embody a role in a believable manner, but who can also fascinate an audience and cause it to fixate upon her person."[26] Talent and charisma are not, however, sufficient on their own. Stardom depends on the combination of several other factors as well: "audience expectations and taste for a particular type of woman; the perceived 'ideal' embodiment of these traits in a particular actress; her ability to present herself effectively in the medium [of film]; and finally the producers' interest in maintaining and exploiting this popularity by means of the continual production of films."[27] Yet stardom is not an absolute or immutable condition; theater and movie stars are bound to their particular historical eras and social contexts. Hickethier reminds us that "stars lose their attraction with the changing of social conditions and audience demands, and they are replaced by others unless they can successfully transform themselves into the embodiment of a new era."[28] When German newspapers heralded Nielsen as "the Duse of the North" and "the Scandinavian Sarah Bernhardt,"[29] both of the stage actresses to whom she was compared were still alive and professionally active, but their fame was being eclipsed by Nielsen's, just as the theater's popularity was losing ground to the cinema.

The stunning success of *The Abyss* confirmed Nielsen's mastery of the filmic medium and prompted distributors to invest in her success in order to ensure their own profits. Print media such as newspapers and, somewhat later, popular film journals played an instrumental role in aggressively marketing both her name and her films to cinema owners, while enticing readers to become audience members and devoted fans. Full-page ads for her films appeared frequently, laden with superlatives about both the star and her work; her name is often printed in larger type than the name of the particular film. Nielsen's on-screen enactment of strong, unconventional women resonated with contemporary women's emancipation movements throughout Europe and appealed to cinema audiences, particularly in Wilhelmine Germany, which included a high percentage of female viewers.[30] Hickethier explains, "Her cosmopolitanism, her simultaneously passionate and concise acting style made her a modern film star, who appealed to the new, urban, and above all intellectual audience."[31]

In some of the earliest advertisements for her German films, Nielsen was introduced to cinema owners and fans as "the Duse of the cinema." Although this moniker was initially employed as a marketing strategy, it also confirms the artistry of Nielsen's acting and her role in elevating the status of film to compete with the theater. In Poul Elsner's 1911 article "The Duse of Film," he exclaimed,

> From the silent theater in Denmark, a Duse has emerged, which this new art form has so long been lacking, a Duse who has made it her mission in life to elevate the art of film, which resides between photography, painting, and poetry, to a true, noble, and ennobling art, to a momentous moment in the spiritual development of the nations. This [Duse] is Asta Nielsen.[32]

Leopold Jessner, who directed Nielsen in two films in the 1920s, shared Elsner's admiration. He exclaimed that "a single tear from

Nielsen's eyes, a single sigh from her mouth says more than the most agitated expression of pain. She is and will remain the greatest actress to have appeared on the silver screen."[33] Although audiences and critics today might not be aware of Nielsen's erstwhile preeminence, her contemporaries clearly felt that the filmic medium owed her a great debt.

Unlike most Hollywood stars whose image was dictated by the studios, Nielsen was intimately involved in the creation of both her films and her public persona. Nielsen exercised a degree of control over her work on not just an artistic but also a technical and an economic level that was extraordinary for a woman in the 1910s. She had a hand in the pre- and postproduction phases of all of the films she made, from choosing the screenplays and designing her own costumes to splicing the negatives and helping to market the final product. During World War I, she formed her own production company, Neutral Film, entering into direct competition with the heavily male-dominated German film production industry, represented by men such as Paul Davidson of Projektions-AG "Union" (PAGU) and Carl Schleussner of Deutsche Bioscop, both of whom had helped her get her start in German film. Off-screen, she contributed to shaping her own mythology by means of publishing newspaper articles, letters to the editor, and autobiographical sketches. Her memoirs, published just after World War II, are a valuable source of information about her career but are also a tightly focused exercise in controlling information, telling only Nielsen's own side of the story and making no reference to any of the people who were important to her in her private life.

Throughout her film career, Nielsen's primary concern was maintaining a high level of artistry, an accomplishment that helped transform film into an art form that could compete with the theater. She pioneered a new style of cinematic acting, involving more realistic gestures, body language, and facial expressions than the histrionic pantomiming of very early film, that demonstrated the artistic possibilities inherent in silent cinema at a time when film was regarded as a vulgar imitation of the stage. The pioneering Danish film director Benjamin Christensen attributed his initial realization that "film, in the right hands, could be art,"[34] to watching Nielsen filming the final scene of her first movie. The innovations Nielsen pioneered were complemented by other interrelated developments in film style during this period, in particular the abandonment of the primarily spectacular and atemporal logic of early cinema in favor of linear narratives. Without the possibility of narrative development in cinema, early silent film could not have supported the characterization or national narrative elements that make Nielsen's films so artistically and thematically compelling. The increasing sophistication of editing techniques also served to crystallize storytelling norms and make possible the inclusion of more of the close-up head shots that showcased Nielsen's expressive face so effectively.

Nielsen's minimalist, naturalistic acting style contrasted sharply with the melodramatic posturing employed by her predecessors and influenced both an entire generation of silent film actresses and the evolution of a peculiarly European directorial and editing style. In *Theatre to Cinema,* Ben Brewster and Lea Jacobs explain how the slower cutting of early European films, in comparison to American films of the same period, "necessarily relied more upon the actor and the acting ensemble to provide dramatic emphasis. This mode of filmmaking also gave the actor the time to develop elaborate sequences of gestures and poses."[35] Such slow-cut early European silent films proved to be ideal vehicles for showcasing actresses and came to be known as "diva films," with a glamorous woman at the center of the film and its company, usually playing a sensuous, highly dramatic character. Asta Nielsen was one of the pioneers in this field, in the illustrious company of such other European silent film divas as Italian actresses Lyda Borelli and Francesca Bertini, as well as French actress Cécile Sorel, each of whom defined the genre in her own way.

The predominant shared attribute of "diva films" lay in the primary focus on the actress and her facial and body language, rather than fast-paced action or a complicated narrative. Nielsen's highly expressive eyes allowed her to convey a maximum of information in a single drawn-out shot and to dominate the screen in a way that would have been impossible in American films of the same period. The French poet Guillaume Apollinaire praised her expressivity, declaring, "She is everything! She is the drinker's vision and the lonely man's dream. She laughs like a happy young girl, and her eyes speak of things so tender and chaste that lips will never utter them. . . . When hate smolders in Asta Nielsen's eyes, we ball our fists, and when she opens her eyes, stars ignite."[36] Yet the emotional power of Nielsen's performances is only one aspect of her story, one that cannot be separated from the social and economic factors that shaped the reception of her films in various countries.

Part of the reason for Nielsen's problematic position in Danish film history today derives from her outsider status relative to the early

Danish film industry, which was dominated by Nordisk Films Kompagni throughout the 1910s. Nordisk was the first film company in Denmark, founded by a visionary entrepreneur named Ole Olsen in 1906. Relying on his business acumen and instinct for popular taste, Olsen launched the company with the controversial short film *Lion Hunt / Løvejagten* (Viggo Larsen, 1907), shot on location in the Copenhagen Zoo and Jægersborg Dyrhave, in which a lion savagely dismembers a goat and is shot, gutted, and skinned by hunters. The film caused a scandal, which brought it to the attention of European audiences, and sold an unprecedented 259 prints, making an enormous profit for Nordisk. Over the next few years, Olsen concentrated on building up a dynamic studio with talented actors and directors, including August Blom, Robert Dinesen, Forest Holger-Madsen, and Hjalmar Davidson.

By 1910, Nordisk was the largest film studio in Denmark and it controlled a disproportionate share of the European cinema market, due in part to its innovative approach to filmmaking and Olsen's well-developed distribution network in Germany and France. The company's logo, which depicts a polar bear perched on top of a globe, became an instantly recognizable brand. In the summer of 1910, Nordisk made a fortune with its unauthorized remake of Fotorama's erotic melodrama *The White Slave Trade / Den hvide Slavehandel* (August Blom, 1910), the sensationalistic story of a well-bred young girl who is lured to England to be sold into prostitution. Its financial position was so strong in 1912 that stockholders received a 60 percent dividend.[37]

Despite Nordisk's financial successes, film was still regarded by the Danish bourgeoisie as inferior to live theater, a situation that underpins the significance of Nielsen's spectacular film debut. Having trained to be a stage actress, Nielsen turned to film only after failing to find a niche in Copenhagen's competitive theater world. Initially, she hoped that a cinematic success would pay dividends in future theatrical roles in Copenhagen theaters, despite cinema's low status in Danish society. Poul Reumert, an actor at the Royal Theater and Nielsen's costar in her debut film, described the contemporary Danish opinion of film as "that miserable bastard, that despicable mix of photographic technique and penny-ante entertainment, the most outrageous antithesis to all spirit and art."[38] Twenty-nine years old and stuck in the wings, however, Nielsen had little to lose and everything to gain. In her own account of her fateful meeting with Urban Gad in the Town Hall Square in Copenhagen in 1910, she reputedly sighed, "I'll have to try film to prove that I'm not completely incompetent after all. I think I'll find some writer and ask him to write a film for me."[39] Urban Gad was the son of Emma Gad, one of Copenhagen's leading playwrights and society hostesses, and he rose to the challenge, writing the script for Nielsen's first film, *The Abyss*, that same night, or so the story goes, thus setting her destiny in motion.

The success of *The Abyss* defied all expectations and established Nielsen as a valuable commodity for the European film industry. Nielsen and Gad made the film on a shoestring budget without the support of any of Denmark's nine film companies, just an 8,000-kroner investment from the young Copenhagen cinema owner Hjalmar Davidson, who wanted a different actress to play the leading role but deferred to Gad's insistence on Nielsen. It was filmed outdoors over the course of a week with an inexperienced crew; only the cameraman, Alfred Lind, had ever even worked in film before. When *The Abyss* premiered in Copenhagen on September 12, 1910, it became an overnight sensation. It is one of the earliest and most successful Danish erotic melodramas, which became an extremely profitable genre not only for the Danish film industry but throughout Europe, particularly between 1910 and 1915. The film's plot line is melodramatic to a fault: Nielsen's character, the respectable bourgeois music teacher Magda Vang, becomes engaged to a pastor's son but runs away instead with a circus cowboy named Rudolph, who cheats on her with other women, forces her to play piano in cafés to support his drinking habit, and ultimately tries to extort money from her abandoned fiancé. When she protests, Rudolph tries to strangle her, forcing Magda to stab him to death with a table knife. The final scene of the film shows a dazed, dry-eyed Magda being led away by the police.

Although Nielsen's innovative, realistic acting, which is particularly evident in the memorable final scene, is responsible for making the film a classic, her highly provocatively sensual dance sequence, known as the "gaucho dance," is undeniably one of the main reasons the film remains somewhat scandalous. The gaucho dance was choreographed by a protégé of Royal Danish Ballet master August Bournonville, Anna Tardini, but it was Nielsen who transformed the scene into a self-consciously performative exploration of gender, sexuality, and cinema itself. Down on their luck, Magda and Rudolph have found work in a theater, performing a pantomime of a lover's quarrel in which Rudolph, playing a cowboy, spurns Magda and she retaliates by tying him up with his own lasso while writhing sensuously up

Figure 4.1. The "gaucho dance" sequence in *The Abyss*, featuring Asta Nielsen and Poul Reumert, shocked contemporary viewers but also ensured the film's notoriety and box-office success throughout the world, even when national censors had the scene removed. Credit: The Danish Film Institute, Stills Archive

against his body. Intent on creating a believable impression for viewers, Nielsen refused to wear stockings under her satin dress during the dance sequence in order to avoid garter lines that might mar the sleekness of her appearance, painting her legs black instead.[40] Yet the very mise-en-scène of the dance disrupts the illusion of reality, for the scene is filmed at a ninety-degree angle to the stage, so that the film audience enjoys privileged access to the events and extraneous people on stage, in contrast to the implied theater audience off to one side, and Nielsen performs her dance with her body oriented toward the camera, rather than the theater audience.

The scene is self-referential on multiple levels: the film audience watches the other characters in the scene watching Rudolph and Magda perform, while Nielsen plays Magda playing the gaucho girl under the gaze of fellow actors and the doubled audience of the theater and of the cinema. Relative to the film as a whole, the dance scene is so long that it is almost a film in itself, a vestige of the old cinema of attractions, "a little bit of vaudeville in a modern film."[41] At the same time, however, the gaucho dance sequence renegotiates the relationship between spectacle and storytelling in film. The strategies of controlling and multiplying the viewer's gaze call attention to film as spectacle and film viewing as spectatorship, while the dance itself, with its overt eroticism, highlights the ways in which gender and sexuality are constructed by the observed, embodied being. The entire sequence, however, is embedded within a narrative framework that lends emotional depth and complexity to the scene's obvious eroticism.

The blatant sensuality of Nielsen's performance in the gaucho dance still surprises modern audiences and embarrasses undergraduate film students, but it is worth noting that Nielsen's enactment of erotic desire is far more suggestive than explicit, leaving much to the imagination. In 1924 the influential Hungarian-born film commentator and theorist Béla Balázs described the subtlety of Nielsen's sexual appeal as "spiritualized eroticism":

> She is never undressed, she does not show her thighs like Anita Berber . . . , and yet this dancing harlot could take lessons from Asta Nielsen. Her belly dancing is tame compared to Asta Nielsen fully dressed. . . . [Asta Nielsen's] spiritualized eroticism is demonically dangerous, since it works at a distance through all of her clothes.[42]

Rather than attempting to shock audiences by baring her skin or depicting lewd behavior, Nielsen revealed her character's sensuality through her body language and smoldering gazes, as she later explained, "Unfamiliar as I was with the restraint required by film in erotic matters, I invested my rhythmic undertaking with all the longing, disappointed love, and burning passion that I could."[43] When she first saw the footage, Nielsen was taken aback by its "explosiveness" and was sure the dance would be censored, but the "pain and suffering" evident in her face throughout the dance provided "the fig leaf behind which the dance slipped past the censors."[44] Although censors in Norway, Sweden, and the United States continued to see Nielsen's eroticism, spiritualized or not, as a social danger, and cut the dance scene from the film entirely,[45] in Denmark and Germany the film was merely designated as forbidden for children.

Yet although *The Abyss* invested Nielsen with an instant reputation for eroticism, contemporary reviews of the film suggest that her popularity did not depend, either primarily or exclusively, on her sex appeal. In a characteristic review in the Danish journal *Masken* in November 1910, the author praises Nielsen's acting abilities and laments that the prevailing taste for Viennese operettas in Copenhagen could not effectively utilize her "Baroque" style. He rejoices, however, that the medium of film is able to maximize both the effect and extent of Nielsen's talents. Describing her performance in *The Abyss,* he exclaims,

> She tore out a piece of quivering human flesh and held it up to the light, so that everyone could see it. . . . Malicious people claimed that the film's popularity was primarily due to the dance, but no, that wasn't the case. It could easily have been omitted without minimizing her accomplishments. In Norway, where it was cut out, scores of people streamed to two theaters, which both stayed open with *The Abyss* on the program, and they never grew tired of watching the remarkable person in whose face they read so much about hope and despair.[46]

Nielsen's work was compelling not only for its sensuality or aesthetic innovations but also, even primarily, for her realistic portrayal of human emotions that viewers could identify with.

After a profitable debut in Denmark, with showings every three-quarters of an hour at the Kosmorama Theater in Copenhagen as well as at cinema houses around the country, *The Abyss* went on to take Europe by storm, playing for weeks on end as many as thirteen times a day, with crowds still waiting outside. As the test case for the monopoly distribution system, it was successful beyond even the wildest expectations. Ludwig Gottschalk, who bought the German monopoly distribution rights, earned 800,000 German marks on it, enough to "pave Düsseldorf with them," as contemporary newspapers trumpeted.[47] Nielsen's remuneration for the film had been only 200 Danish crowns, but it opened the door to much greater rewards. Her success generated its own momentum and directed her career into more ambitious paths than winning leading roles at the Danish Royal Theater. Job offers poured in, from the Danish production company Fotorama, the German studio Deutsche Bioscop, and, somewhat indirectly, Nordisk. In 1911 Nielsen, under the direction of Urban Gad, made two films in Germany for Deutsche Bioscop, *Burning Blood / Heisses Blut* (Gad, 1911) and *Retribution / Nachtfalter* (Gad, 1911), as well as two more films in Denmark, one for Fotorama, *The Black Dream / Den sorte Drøm* (Gad, 1911), and one for Nordisk, *The Ballet Dancer / Balletdanserinden* (Blom, 1911). Eager to secure a female star on a par with Valdemar Psilander, Ole Olsen finally gave in and hired Nielsen to star in a single film, at a salary of 5,000 Danish crowns, while her costars earned just 350 Danish crowns each.[48] It is, however, unclear whether Nielsen was ever under contract with Nordisk directly; her contract for *The Ballet Dancer* was signed by Frede Skaarup, who occupied a managerial position at both Fotorama and Nordisk in this period.[49]

Despite the ambiguity surrounding Nielsen's contractual status, however, the fact that she was finally hired to make a film for Nordisk reflects a significant shift in her status within the Danish film industry and in Ole Olsen's eyes. Under Olsen's leadership, Nordisk had turned down both the chance to produce *The Abyss* and international distribution rights to the finished film. In a letter to his London distribution office dated September 1911, Olsen noted that he did not find Nielsen particularly talented.[50] Even after *The Abyss* had been released, Olsen maintained his objections to the film. In a business letter to Nordische Films, the German subsidiary of Nordisk, on November 19, 1910, he explains, "We will not be sending out *The Abyss*. We are completely convinced that this film will be banned, at least the dance scene. The dance is such that no lady can watch it together with a gentleman. If the dance scene is removed, the film is unremarkable."[51] However, in a personal letter to Carl Süring two days earlier, he complains that Süring had told him that the German censor would not allow "scenes of murder, prostitution, theft, etc.,"[52] yet the censor's approval and the commercial success of *The Abyss* proved otherwise. Olsen explains, somewhat petulantly, that Nordisk could easily have made a film like *The Abyss* much earlier, if he had thought that a German audience would want "a picture of murder and perverse passions, such as *The Abyss* depicts."[53] Olsen's outrage seems to rest not on moral grounds but rather on frustration over his miscalculation about the censors and the market. The decision to hire Nielsen for *The Ballet Dancer* can be regarded as an attempt to rectify this error.

However, Nielsen's relationship with Nordisk in particular and Danish film in general came to an abrupt end in the summer of 1911, when Austrian film distributor Christoph Mülleneisen orchestrated an agreement among several film production companies, including PAGU, to establish a new monopoly distribution company, Internationale Film-Vertriebs-GmbH, based in Vienna and headed by Davidson of PAGU, which would distribute thirty-two Asta Nielsen films over the next four years. Although still under contract to Nordisk, Nielsen agreed, in exchange for an annual salary of 80,000 marks, 33.3 percent of film revenues, Urban Gad as her director, and full artistic freedom in choosing her screenplays, costumes, and supporting actors. While some Danish critics complained that Nielsen had abandoned Danish film out of greed, German film historian Andreas Hansert counters that the move was a professionally and artistically strategic one, as "the Danish film industry was clearly not in a position to realize the artistic ideas and concepts of Asta Nielsen and Urban Gad."[54]

Since Internationale Film was initially strictly a distribution company, the first dozen Asta Nielsen–series films were produced by Deutsche Bioscop, which gave Nielsen the chance to work closely with the talented cameraman Guido Seeber. Deutsche Bioscop built the first studios at Babelsberg specifically for the making of Nielsen's films. Internationale Film had to pay a penalty of 10,000 crowns for causing Nielsen to breach her contract, but it seemed a worthwhile investment. As Nielsen explained to an interviewer shortly thereafter, "The films we are going to make in 1912 have already been sold to the whole world, although the buyers have no idea what they will be about. All they know is that *I* am in them. . . . You can see that a 'World-Monopoly-Patent' has been taken out on me!"[55] Nielsen herself was commodified in order to become the first commercially constructed cinema celebrity, demonstrating the close connection between modern notions of celebrity and the power structure of capitalism.

The gamble paid off for both Nielsen and her investors; virtually overnight she emerged as the first world-renowned megastar of silent film, a household name recognized and capitalized on across the globe. In 1914 Davidson boasted to Spanish journalist Pablo Diaz,

> I immediately recognized Asta Nielsen's potential to be a global business. . . . In my office, we have calculated that Asta Nielsen is shown daily to around one-and-a-half-million people in ca. 600 theaters distributed around the world. We work like a precision machine: today, Asta Nielsen is the most famous woman in the world.[56]

Thanks to mass-media technology, Nielsen became iconic on a previously unprecedented global scale. Newspaper articles routinely referred to her as "the Queen of the Cinema,"[57] but Nielsen was not just a film star; she was a brand. Her name was attached to perfumes, cigarettes, champagne, harmonicas, corsets, and feather boas. Fans could buy Asta Nielsen pastries in Berlin, cutlets in Budapest, and hats in Melbourne, get an Asta Nielsen hairstyle in San Francisco, and visit Asta Nielsen movie theaters in Nagasaki and Saigon.[58]

This branding of Nielsen's name was the result of a deliberate and pioneering effort on the part of her film distribution company to create a star persona for her. Market saturation with a steady supply of Nielsen films was an integral part of the creation of Nielsen's stardom, with new films appearing every four to six weeks during the peak season,[59] so that she would never be out of the public eye for long. During the 1911/12 season, eight films appeared in the first Asta Nielsen/Urban Gad series, followed by eight more in 1912/13 and seven in 1913/14. Her film premieres were carefully staged, with an entire "Asta Nielsen" newspaper printed and mailed out to likely moviegoers on the day her film *A Strange Bird / Der fremde Vogel* (Gad, 1911) premiered in Germany. An "Asta Nielsen-Waltz" was commissioned from the Düsseldorf-based composer Mathieu Hofnagel for the opening of the Asta Nielsen Cinemas in Düsseldorf and Hannover. Not only were cinema palaces named after her, but so too was a popular restaurant dish: the "Asta Nielsen-Schnittchen," consisting of a slice of bread topped with salmon, caviar, and oysters for 1 mark 75.[60] During World War I, her picture consoled troops in the trenches on both sides, especially Danish speakers from Schleswig-Holstein who had been drafted into the German army.[61] In 1918 a contest in a German newspaper to determine the country's favorite film actress produced the result, submitted by Frau E. von Scheinpflug near Dresden, "Nur meine Asta! Und damit: basta!" (Only my Asta! And that's enough!).[62]

Nielsen's fame came at the cost of her privacy, however, and her personal experiences of international celebrity were unprecedented and often traumatic, although they have become commonplace for modern movie stars. On a visit to Budapest in 1914, adoring fans nearly tore her clothes to shreds and smashed the windows of her car, so that she rode away amid rose petals and glass shards.[63] As mentioned in chapter 1, a man in Spain felt so attached to Nielsen after watching one of her movies several nights in succession that he fired a pistol into her face on screen the last night to protest the end of the film's run.[64] When Nielsen sued an illustrated newspaper for publishing unauthorized pictures of her in her apartment, the court ruled that the pictures were legal if she appeared in them, as her fame made her image public property.[65] Aside from private gatherings with intimate friends, which included regular visits from Brandes on his frequent visits to Berlin, Nielsen lived an increasingly reclusive life in Berlin, a "prisoner of popularity."[66] Many years later, she described her popularity as "hell on earth," explaining, "I experienced my popularity as an invasion of my private life and complete isolation became necessary to preserve that. My life outside the studio was spent in the car or within four walls."[67]

The staggering dimensions of Nielsen's international fame magnified the significance of her Danish citizenship. Thanks largely to Nordisk, the Danish film industry was already a leader in European cinema, but Nielsen put a face to it, clinching the association between Denmark and the exciting new mass medium of public entertainment and edification. Even before her name was known to fans, she was "marketed as a Nordic foreign beauty,"[68] despite the fact that her dark hair and dark eyes did not conform to stereotypical images of blond Scandinavians. Looking back at the German release of *The Abyss*, Egon Jacobsohn noted that although no one had heard of Nielsen, the word on the street was to "go to the movies. A dark-haired Nordic woman is performing and she is absolutely wonderful."[69] Asta Nielsen stands out as the only Danish actress to achieve notable success in the German film industry. Although she was by no means the only Danish cinema star with a following in Germany, all the rest of the border-crossing Danes who made films in Germany were men. Nielsen's costar in the Fotorama film *The Black Dream*, Valdemar Psilander, was both the highest-paid Danish cinema star and the most popular cinema actor in Germany, according to a 1914 survey of German filmgoers by the magazine *Kino-Woche*.[70] Although Psilander's fame in Germany derived from his exclusively Danish-produced films, Nielsen's longtime friend Olaf Fønss made a very popular series of six *Homunculus* films for Deutsche Bioscop in 1916, although he, unlike Nielsen, made the majority of his films in Denmark. In addition to Urban Gad, whom Nielsen married in 1912, several Danish directors also worked in Wilhelmine Berlin, including Benjamin Christensen and Stellan Rye.

As the only Danish actress to achieve international silent cinema stardom, Nielsen was not simply a diva or a star but the most visible representative of Danish culture in Europe. Danish author Adolf Langsted, who wrote the first biography of Nielsen in 1916, marveled, "I sat in Paris and saw film's star rise: with wonder I discovered that it was—*Danish*. The first film actress to attain world renown was Asta Nielsen."[71] Similarly, in 1913, a German reviewer exclaimed, "The light came to us from the North. . . . The great Asta is simply a genius."[72] German film critic Lotte Eisner described Nielsen as "typically Nordic, as legendarily Nordic as Edda, and although she has filmed very little in her own country, Denmark, in German film she has remained representative of Scandinavia."[73] The matter of her Danish nationality is frequently mentioned in German newspaper reviews of her films, although most often as simply a descriptive attribute or in connection with her efforts to master German. It was her professional success and media prominence that made her Danish identity notable, particularly for other Danes, and allowed her to function as an influential icon of a modern, liberal Danish national identity throughout the world, at a time when Danish society was still struggling to realize the social and political reforms that would bring the country into the modern era.

The stunning success of *The Abyss* and Nielsen's subsequent meteoric rise to global stardom came as a tremendous surprise to her Danish contemporaries, most of whom knew her only from the minor roles she had played in Copenhagen theaters during the preceding decade. The Danish reception of Nielsen's German-made films between 1911 and 1914 reflected both Nielsen's countrymen's delighted amazement that a Danish actress had attained such global renown and their defensive refusal to accord her the same level of celebrity in Denmark. While most Danish critics appreciated the prestige that Nielsen's fame brought to her homeland, other Danes disparaged their countrywoman's international success and her cinematic work, for reasons ranging from aesthetic distaste to moral outrage. Close examination of the Danish print media's reception of Nielsen's films from this prewar period reveals a curious blend of approbation and disdain for Denmark's most famous export.

During this first phase of Nielsen's career, the Danish media basked in the glow of her success, celebrating their countrywoman's triumphs. In the immediate prewar years, Nielsen's German-made films received top billing in Danish newspapers and Copenhagen movie palaces. Danish newspapers in the early 1910s carried glowing reviews and sprawling advertisements for each new Asta Nielsen film, alongside detailed accounts of every visit that "our famous countrywoman,"[74] "the most world-famous of all Danish actresses," paid to Denmark.[75] The tone of these reviews could be rather spiteful on occasion, for example in an article heralding the Danish premiere of *A Romany Spy / Das Mädchen ohne Vaterland* (Gad, 1912) in *Politiken* on December 21, 1912, which begins with the statement, "The diva of film glides once more over the screen in the city of her birth, which now seems distant and small to her. Mrs. Asta Nielsen-Gad has conquered the world, her name is uttered with reverence in European metropolises and African villages, and on Monday evening Copenhagen must kneel before her art."[76]

The release of each of Nielsen's films in pre–World War I Denmark was an event, in which the screening of the feature film was preceded by orchestral music and various short films, which served as a type of psychological and emotional *amuse bouche*. A review of *Vengeance Is Mine / Das Feuer* (Gad, 1914) in *Berlingske Tidende* on May 10, 1914, reports that Mrs. Asta Nielsen-Gad's performance was the high point of the evening, crowning "an excellent, varied program, consisting of an exciting action movie with a car chase, a series of lovely nature images from the coast of Bretagne, a current events survey from Canada's snowy plains to the race in Auteuil and a wonderful children's film: a baby playing with its beloved household pets."[77] The mélange of genres and styles on what the reviewer in *Folkets Avis* on May 12 dubs "the Palace Theater's menu," which offers "something for every taste,"[78] recalls the variety-show style of the cinema before the advent of the feature-length film, but the tone of the cinema experience was elevated in the new movie palace. Embossed programs printed on thick paper provided a summary of the film, in the style of program notes for an opera or theater performance.

The Palace Theater in Copenhagen had the honor of hosting the Danish premiere of several of Nielsen's prewar films, which it did in grand style. The premiere of *A Romany Spy* in late December 1912 was a particularly high-profile affair, organized as a Christmas charity benefit. An energetic publicity campaign included a series of articles published in *Politiken* in the days leading up to the premiere and immediately afterward. On December 21, the announcement of the premiere advised that "several well-known authors, actors, and actresses have been invited. It is much like when old Ibsen had a premiere."[79] The article published on December 23, the day of the premiere, reads as if the author is reporting live from the red carpet (or white carpet, as they say in Danish) and explicitly foregrounds both the luxurious surroundings of the Palace Theater and the high artistic *niveau* of the evening: "At 8:15 this evening, as the new Asta Nielsen film 'The Girl Without a Fatherland' rolls across the screen in the Palace Theater, a very fine audience is present in both the box seats and the orchestra. The comfortable blue velvet chairs are filled with literature and art, which is naturally, in keeping with tradition, offered at a film premiere."⁸⁰ The cinema's position relative to the preeminence of the stage is also defended with the assertion that "in modern cinemas one now receives just as much art in two-three hours as in half a year's diligent attendance at the talking theaters."⁸¹

It was an era when Denmark viewed film as a means of extending Denmark's influence and enhancing its reputation abroad, a task to which Nielsen seemed peculiarly well suited. The announcement in the Danish newspaper *Politiken,* on April 16, 1911, of the Danish premiere of Nielsen's first German film, *Burning Blood,* notes that the film should be of particular interest to Danes because "the film industry in Berlin has selected a Danish actress, Miss Asta Nielsen, to perform the female lead. This is the first time such a thing has happened."⁸² Picking up the same theme, in the column "With the Film-Diva" in the same edition of *Politiken,* the columnist notes the significance of the fact that "Deutsche Bioscop, which is one of the world's largest film production companies, has become interested in Asta Nielsen, whose success in *The Abyss,* which has conquered the world from New Zealand to Hammerfest, has made her Denmark's first world-famous actress."⁸³ Describing the opening of the new Palace Theater (Palads-Teatret) in 1912, which Nielsen attended for the Danish premiere of her film *The General's Children / Kinder des Generals* (Gad, 1912), Niels Thomsen admitted, "There is something nationally pleasing in the fact that we here at home have not just been able to create one of Europe's largest theaters for moving pictures, but have also produced a true prima donna to adorn its inauguration."⁸⁴

The scale of Nielsen's global fame and its relevance to international perceptions of Denmark in this period is vividly illustrated in an article written by Danish journalist Jens Locher in 1916, giving an account of an encounter he had in a Paris café with a crowd of strangers from across Europe. The conversation turned to each person's respective homeland, but while everyone present knew something about Russia, Spain, the Balkans, and Germany, each of Locher's attempts to spark an association with Denmark failed; he mentioned Tivoli, Georg Brandes, Hans Christian Andersen, and King Christian IV, but with no success. Prepared to give up and allow his companions to continue doubting Denmark's existence, he tried Nielsen's name:

> And there I finally found the help I needed—why hadn't I thought of her immediately?—of course, Asta Nielsen, the Duse of the cinema, she is Danish, after all, and they'd have to know who she was. Then

there was great rejoicing. Asta Nielsen, of course, they knew her, she was a great artist, and they knew that she was from somewhere in Scandinavia, which I now explained was called Denmark. This sounded eminently plausible to them, but it must be a cultivated, if somewhat cold, place, to have fostered Asta Nielsen.[85]

Locher recounts his relief finally at being able to prove the existence of his homeland to the citizens of so many great powers, then chides his readers, "We here at home ought to appreciate to a higher degree than we have been accustomed our few world-famous countrymen; they make our country larger, and once in a while, you might find yourself in a situation where you feel that it needs it."[86] Locher's anecdote reveals that while Nielsen's significance for domestic consumption in Danish culture was not on par with Hans Christian Andersen or King Christian IV's, her prominence in European popular culture made her uniquely valuable to her countrymen.

Yet although Danes flocked to theaters to see the latest Asta Nielsen film, they remained somewhat perplexed by her popularity. An article in the *Maanedsmagasin* in late 1912 noted, "It came as somewhat of a surprise for Danish audiences a few years ago to suddenly learn that Miss Asta Nielsen was an actress who mattered because she enjoyed worldwide fame."[87] Nielsen's celebrity in Denmark in this period never equaled her fame in Germany, either in terms of brand marketing or as the object of a cult of adoration. In contrast to the situation in Germany and elsewhere in the world, no elaborate marketing apparatus in Denmark plastered her name on a cornucopia of wares to keep her in the public eye and demonstrate her exceptionality.

Such an undertaking as that would have been counterproductive in Denmark in any case, in light of the widespread resolutely egalitarian, sometimes rigidly narrow trait of not taking oneself or anyone else too seriously that Dano-Norwegian author Aksel Sandemose would dub the "Jante Law" (*janteloven*) in his 1933 novel *A Refugee Crosses His Tracks* (*En flygtning krysser sitt spor*).[88] In keeping with this attitude, Danes tried very hard not to make a fuss over Nielsen, particularly once she had become world-famous. Instead of encouraging adulation, the media made a point of reminding readers that Nielsen was no one special, "the same as when she lived on Bagerstræde in a rear building and had to fetch the cream and liqueur for her coffee herself."[89] In a profile of Nielsen in the Danish illustrated magazine *Verden og Vi* in 1915, the author reveals the deliberateness of the indifference with which Danes reacted to Nielsen's celebrity status:

> We Copenhageners, who are known for our tact and discretion, have perhaps glanced fleetingly over at the world famous star who glided past us like a dark, foreign mystery, but we did not allow ourselves to be more affected by the celebrated lady's presence. In Germany, people are very differently affected by being able to rub up against the Queen of Film. Ladies run after her on the street, touch her clothing, and people name cookies and sandwiches after her.[90]

This determination not to treat Nielsen any differently because of her fame can be read both as a manifestation of Danish "tact and discretion," as the author suggests, and as evidence of Danish society's unwillingness to acknowledge Nielsen's newly elevated social status. The contrast to Nielsen's imagined German audiences is clear—Danes are too level-headed to indulge in fan hysteria, even, or rather, especially toward a fellow Dane.

Many Danish critics took issue with the fact that German and other international ads for Nielsen's films frequently attributed to her a distinguished theatrical career at the Royal Theater in Copenhagen. Sometimes maliciously, other times regretfully, Danish critics were quick to correct any misapprehension that Nielsen had been an integral part of the Danish theater community. In *Politiken*'s review of *Retribution*, Nielsen's second German film, the reviewer comments disparagingly of Nielsen's dancing that her "abilities as such are only just adequate for the cinema; a real music hall would hardly hire her in that capacity."[91] *Politiken*'s review of her previous film, *Burning Blood*, six weeks earlier, had included a similar observation about Nielsen's unsuitability for Copenhagen theater, although with a more positive spin, noting that the film allowed Nielsen to demonstrate her talent, "which she has now dedicated to the service of international cinema, since the Copenhagen stages, with which she was affiliated, had no occasion to make use of it."[92] The implicit question that many of Nielsen's Danish critics seem to struggle with is how she could have become so famous around the world without being famous in Denmark first.

If anything about Nielsen seemed particularly noteworthy and admirable to the Danish press at the time, it was her connection, by marriage, to the highly respected Gad family, particularly her mother-in-law, Emma Gad, who had earned a reputation for herself not only as a successful playwright and hostess but also as an expert on polite society. Nielsen's marriage to Urban Gad, undertaken after their move to Germany, not only satisfied bourgeois morality by regularizing their highly productive collaborative working relationship and cohabitation, but it also enabled Nielsen to transcend her working-class origins in the eyes of class-conscious early twentieth-century Danish society. After her 1912 wedding to Gad, the Danish press generally referred to Nielsen as Mrs. Asta Nielsen-Gad, reminding readers of her membership in this rarefied social sphere.

The announcement of the Danish release of Nielsen's film *Death in Seville / Tod in Sevilla* (Gad, 1913), which appeared in *Politiken* on June 9, 1913, begins with mention of the fact that Mrs. Asta Nielsen-Gad was currently visiting her in-laws, Rear Admiral Urban and Mrs. Emma Gad, in Humlebæk,[93] while the review of the premiere a few days later devotes several lines to the fact that Nielsen delegated responsibility for receiving her admirers to her mother-in-law. It also points out Urban Gad's considerable contributions to making the film a success, in particular his ability to capture the essence of the Spanish landscape on film. Corinna Müller explains that German film distributors had been initially uncertain whether to market Nielsen or Gad in developing the star system, but quickly opted to foreground the actress instead of the director and stopped including Gad's name in ads for Nielsen's films after the first two.[94] In Denmark, however, the reviews of Nielsen's early films nearly always include Gad's name.

Though she made no secret of her Danish origins, Nielsen rarely appeared on screen in the role of a Dane in her prewar films. Instead, she insisted on playing a wide range of nationalities and character types, which allowed her to showcase the changeability of her identity constructions. In the nearly forty films she made in Germany between 1911 and 1917, she played an English suffragette, a French noblewoman, an American debutante, a Balkan rebel, an Italian bandit, a German film prima donna, a Spanish dancer, an impoverished Gypsy, the daughter of a German general, a seventeen-year-old girl pretending to be thirteen, a blind artist, and a Greenlander. It was not just national identity that Nielsen explored in her films but also psychological, social, and gender identity. Nielsen played young girls, middle-aged matrons, and old women, as well as several androgynous or masculine roles. In the highly self-referential film *The Wrong Asta Nielsen / Die falsche Asta Nielsen* (Gad, 1914), she plays the dual role of herself as a famous actress and a young girl who attempts to impersonate her. She was also fond of so-called "breeches parts" (*Hosenrollen*), in which a woman plays the part of a man, or at least dresses like one, which occurs in the films *Lady Madcap's Way / Jugend und Tollheit*

(Gad, 1912); *Zapata's Robber Band / Zapatas Bande* (Gad, 1913); and *The Alphabet of Love / Das Liebes-ABC* (Magnus Stifter, 1916).

The extreme diversity of the roles Nielsen played was feasible because early film allowed for a degree of improvisation and experimentation, in terms of both aesthetic and social norms, that was lost as the industry became increasingly institutionalized. Nielsen once explained, "This art form was so new back then that we had to explore new, unknown territory from film to film, literally from meter to meter."[95] The lack of established conventions, particularly with regard to feature-length narrative films, gave Nielsen latitude to shape her own characters and the revolutionary values they represented. This freedom encompassed both aesthetic and cultural elements of the films; according to Jelavich, "Early cinema conformed neither to bourgeois cultural ideals nor to the ideology of Social Democracy; rather, it offered a free and uncontrolled space for expressing nonbourgeois values—adventure, frivolity, sensuality, letting-go—a space that occasionally questioned the justice of every social order."[96]

Over the course of the 1910s, as the film industry developed into a powerful national economic force, this freedom to be spontaneous and provocative was replaced by centralized control. As the cost of filmmaking rose, producers began insisting, as Müller explains, on

> highly planned productions with detailed budgets. The earlier laissez-faire attitude to film-making where a director might sometimes sketch out a "screenplay" on his cuff, was no longer practical. Organisation had to be tight and painstaking, work had to be divided up amongst specialists who would realise a well-constructed, thoroughly filmic product. The long, monopoly feature film could no longer contend [sic] itself with filling up space . . . with a series of gags. It was much more a question of constructing the story as a carefully thought out, unified whole.[97]

This trend toward greater studio control and technical specialization, as well as the steadily increasing clout of predominantly male directors, had become the norm by the 1920s, and had the effect of "containing the potential anarchy of the film medium."[98] This development also made it much more difficult for an actress like Nielsen to determine the shape and message of her films, as the discussion of her later work in the next chapter illustrates.

While many American studios in this period deliberately tried to suppress depictions of ethnic difference in their films to attract a broader audience and preserve the perceived universality of silent film,[99] Nielsen's films often explicitly thematize both national identity and nationalism. Between 1910 and 1916, she made the most of the opportunities she had to depict a wide range of characters of different ethnic backgrounds and national origins. In *A Strange Bird,* she plays a cosmopolitan British girl, Miss May Wolton,[100] who falls in love with a rustic German peasant named Poul while vacationing in the Spreewald. May's tailored clothes and fashionable hats contrast sharply with the traditional folk costumes and kerchiefs of the German peasants, while her ignorance of the local language complicates communication and brands her an outsider. Love transcends linguistic boundaries, however, and May's infatuation prompts her, as the intertitle informs the audience, to take "German lessons" from Poul. When May's father and fiancé discover the budding cross-cultural romance, they intervene and threaten to send her home. In desperation, May and Poul attempt to run away together, but Poul's jilted fiancée persuades his mother to refuse to help them. Betrayed by a maid at the hotel, they are pursued by the British men in a frantic boat chase through the Spreewald, at the climax of which May falls into the river and drowns, the victim of star-crossed romance, class differences, and cultural incompatibility.

Several of Nielsen's other films from the years immediately preceding World War I are preoccupied with envisioning more ominous potential outcomes of transnational relationships. In *The Traitress / Die Verräterin* (Gad, 1912), long-standing national prejudices initially heighten the romantic tension between Nielsen's French character Yvonne and the German lieutenant who falls in love with her, but ultimately lead to tragedy when Yvonne betrays her lover's camp to the enemy, then regrets her betrayal and is killed saving his life. Nationalism and national security concerns also feature prominently in *Das Mädchen ohne Vaterland*. The English title, *A Romany Spy,* obscures the centrality of the issue of national identity that the original title, in literal translation "The Girl Without a Fatherland," makes explicit. Nielsen's character, a Gypsy girl named Zidra, accepts a bribe from enemy soldiers to steal a map from an army encampment. Using her feminine wiles, including a sultry dance reminiscent of the gaucho dance in *The Abyss,* Zidra ingratiates herself with a lieutenant and succeeds in stealing the map from him. When he discovers her betrayal, which promises to have disastrous consequences for him personally, he falls to his knees at her feet and appeals to her sense of patriotism. It is at this moment that the centrality of nationalism to the narrative emerges, for Zidra, a stateless Gypsy, proves to be immune to the call of duty to the state; her motives are purely self-interested. In response to the lieutenant's anguished pleas, she replies simply, "Fatherland? What is a fatherland?" The lieutenant is executed for his lapse in judgment, Zidra keeps her reward and her head, and the film ends with the Gypsy clan moving on to greener pastures. Patriotism is presented here as an admirable sentiment, but also a potential source of weakness.

In tandem with their exploration of national identities, Nielsen's early films also exploit the cinema's power to blur the boundaries between social classes and genders. Regardless of nationality or economic standing, her characters tend to be assertive, self-confident, and decisive, although often socially marginalized women, ranging from Magda in *The Abyss*, who stabs her abusive lover with a table knife, to the tailor's daughter Sabine in *Front Stairs, Back Stairs / Vordertreppe-Hintertreppe* (Gad, 1914), who wins the lottery but refuses to marry the financially strapped lieutenant who offers her social advancement in exchange for her money. The women she plays are individuals with "tumultuous, powerful feelings and passions, full of emotional and sexual power."[101] Hake argues that her "greatest successes were social dramas that placed her on the side of the underprivileged and the oppressed in powerful demonstrations of female strength and self-determination."[102]

In this period, Nielsen frequently plays women who, even in desperate straits, know their own minds and act decisively to defend their own interests, using whatever tools they have at their disposal, including their sexuality. Janet Bergstrom asserts that, in Nielsen's early films,

> Her sensuality is matched by the powerful impression of intelligence she conveys, and by her resourcefulness and physical agility. She excelled at embodying individualized, unconventional women who are convincingly "natural," whose stories convey their entanglement within—and their resistance to—an invisible web of confining class and sex roles.[103]

In many of her roles, Nielsen challenges these class and gender restrictions, both playfully, as in *Little Angel / Engelein* (Gad, 1913), and overtly, as in *The Militant Suffragette / Die Suffragette* (Gad, 1913). For example, in several of her films, including "The Film Prima Donna" / *Die Filmprimadonna* (Gad, 1913), *Engelein*, and *S1* (Gad, 1913), her character smokes in public. In *A Romany Spy*, Nielsen's character even turns down an offer of a cigarette in favor of a cigar. According to Hake, a woman smoking on-screen was a provocative gesture of liberation that "is a measure of her appropriation of male privilege."[104] Nielsen's performance of male identity in her various *Hosenrollen* takes this challenge to male authority even further, thematizing both sexual difference and women's liberation. Although comedic *Hosenrollen* demonstrate a playful attitude toward gender, they also allow women the freedom to invent for themselves emancipated sexual identities by putting on men's clothes.

Nielsen's boldness resonated with cinema audiences, particularly female viewers. In her doctoral dissertation "On the Sociology of the Cinema" (*Zur Soziologie des Kino*), the pioneering German sociologist Emilie Altenloh surveyed more than 2,400 moviegoers in Mannheim in 1913 to determine not only the statistical breakdown of cinema audiences in terms of occupation, social class, and gender, but also their motivations for attending the cinema and their film preferences. Altenloh reports that Nielsen's films were particularly popular among upper-class women regardless of age, laborer's wives (*Arbeiterfrauen*), and young women, who preferred romances, social dramas, and historical dramas.[105] Many of these women, particularly those who did not work outside the home, initially attended the cinema out of boredom, but quickly became addicted to the pleasure of "living for a time in another world, a world of luxury and extravagance, that allows them to forget the monotony of daily life."[106] In addition to the pure pleasure of escapism, however, Hake notes that these genres were particularly well suited to facilitating viewers' identification with characters depicted in the film:

> The early melodramas, and the social dramas even more critically, addressed the problems of female self-determination within a discernible social setting and with close attention to the performative aspects of femininity. Films . . . offered sustained reflections on modern marriage and motherhood and addressed social problems without the usual moralizing tone.[107]

Elsaesser agrees that early German cinema allowed its socially heterogeneous female audiences to "gain visual and vicarious access to social spaces and thus to experiences normally out of bounds for women, whether married or unmarried."[108] As Nielsen's female fans identified with the wide range of modern female characters that Nielsen depicted on screen, with all of the challenges they faced but also with the novel freedoms they enjoyed, they not only developed empathy with women of other social classes but were also empowered to imagine their own liberation from restrictive social and gender norms. Both as a strong female character on-screen and as a powerful, prominent woman in her own right, Nielsen challenged gendered relations of power, and her stardom was "shaped by its early articulation and questioning of the paradigmatic opposition between public and private power at a time when many women in her audiences sought to redraw those very boundaries."[109]

Yet Nielsen's performative construction of emancipated female identity was not universally admired, nor uncontested. On the level of marketing and audience identification, this was due in part to the difficulty of associating her with a single, formulaic identity construction, such as the Vamp, the Virgin, or the City Girl. The adoption of such personas proved to be central to the success of many early American cinema stars, such as Theda Bara (the Vamp) and Clara Bow ("The It Girl"). On screen, Nielsen shifted constantly from one identity to another, as Jörg Becker notes, "from good girl to vamp and femme fatale, from corrupter to the pitiably seduced. Sorrow alternated with sensuality, sensuality with rebellion. She is described as having challenged all traditional ideas of natural femininity, disclosing them in role plays and identity games."[110] Nielsen's screen personas were frequently sensual, but rarely vampish and often comic, leaving the image of the threatening femme fatale to be appropriated in the years after World War I by more overtly erotic stars such as the smoldering Polish actress Pola Negri, who had been "discovered" by Ernst Lubitsch. At the other extreme, another Lubitsch protégé, Ossi Oswalda, combined an emancipated, cheeky, girl-next-door image with slapstick comedy and childlike innocence that rendered her sexuality somewhat harmless, although her *Hosenrolle* in the homoerotically charged, cross-dressing comedy *I Don't Want to Be a Man / Ich möchte kein Mann sein* (Lubitsch, 1918) certainly pushes the limit. Hake suggests further that Oswalda's romantic comedies, such as *The Oyster Princess / Die Austernprinzesse* (Lubitsch, 1919), "presented the pitfalls of female desire through a highly filmic mixture of fairytale elements, slapstick humor, and narrative irony,"[111] thereby allowing viewers to discount the seriousness of Oswalda's claims to female emancipation.

Like Oswalda, Nielsen had a gift for comedic acting and delivered some of her most impressive performances in humorous roles, but without compromising her own emancipated image. The best example

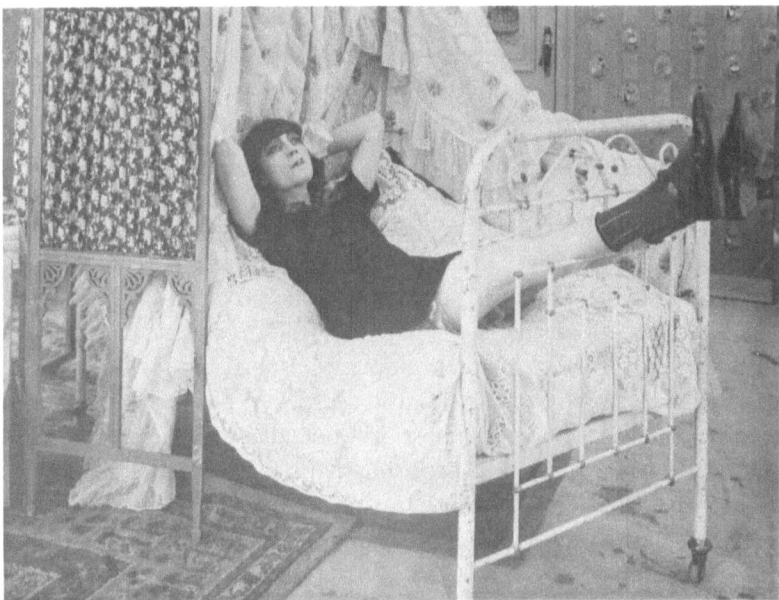

Figure 4.2. The film *Engelein* (1913) showcased Nielsen's considerable comic talents, with a thirty-two-year-old Nielsen playing the part of a seventeen-year-old girl pretending to be twelve years old in order to curry favor with a rich uncle. Credit: The Danish Film Institute, Stills Archive

of this is perhaps her 1913 film *Engelein,* in which the thirty-two-year-old Nielsen plays the part of a seventeen-year-old girl named Jesta, who is forced to pretend to be twelve in order to conceal from a rich uncle the fact that she had been born several years before her parents' wedding. Jesta first appears as a rebellious teenager at an all-girl boarding school who scandalizes the headmistress by smoking, playing cards, and sneaking out at night to meet her boyfriend. When she assumes the persona of a preadolescent, Jesta gets into a variety of comic predicaments. Her bedroom at her uncle's house is filled with children's furniture and Jesta gets stuck in one of the chairs, causing her to leap about the room with a chair affixed to her hips. In another scene, she lies on her bed, smoking, wearing a sailor dress, knee-high stockings, and ringlets in her hair.

Charged by her parents with ingratiating herself with her uncle in order to secure an inheritance from him, Jesta instead falls in love with him, but is unable to reveal her feelings because of her supposed youth. In despair, she decides to drown herself in the lake and leaves a suicide note for her uncle, but, after hitching up her skirts and taking a few steps into the cold water, grimacing all the while, she changes her mind and heads back to the house, where her secret is revealed, she is joyfully reunited with her uncle, and, over cognac and cigarettes, she decides, as the intertitle informs the audience, that "if he doesn't propose, I'll have to do it." Although tame by modern standards, the film teases the viewer with the obvious discrepancy between the rebellious maturity of the supposedly seventeen-year-old Jesta and the coquettish immaturity she pretends for her uncle. The film also titillates with the possibility of a romantic relationship between Jesta and Uncle Peter, despite the social taboos that would prohibit such a liaison were Jesta in fact the preadolescent she pretends to be. Given that the film skirts the edge of bourgeois acceptability so narrowly, it is not surprising that it faced careful scrutiny by film censors throughout Europe.

Official film censorship as a means of "taming cinema"[112] was instituted around 1906, and Nielsen's films, being as popular and provocative as they were, frequently attracted the negative attention of national film censors. The venerable German playwright Gerhart Hauptmann commented wryly, "The censor should intervene as soon as Asta lifts up her eyes."[113] At the time, censorship was carried out locally, often by the chief of police, so there was no consistent standard and decisions to allow or deny particular films varied from town to town within the same country, although national censorship boards were established in several countries in the early 1910s, partly in reaction to the influx of erotic melodramas such as *The Abyss*. This connection is evident in the fact that although *The Abyss* had already been screened in Sweden without any cuts in 1910 and 1911, one of the first actions of the Swedish National Censorship Board, established on June 22, 1911, was to cut out the gaucho dance scene.

Grounds for censorship of a film included the depiction of illegal actions, even something as innocent as picking flowers in a garden without permission or a young man's temptation to steal from his parents; real tears, "which could have too powerful an impact on nervous individuals";[114] a cross; or any suggestion of immodesty or sensuality. Nielsen's films often violated more than one of these guidelines, but the reaction of censorship boards still varied considerably by country. Danish film historian Marguerite Engberg explains, "In Norway the dance scene of *The Abyss* was deleted as being immoral. In Sweden many of the films with Nielsen were either cut or banned completely.

In France the Danish films were considered lascivious but their bad reputation often promoted the sale of a film."[115] In 1913 the German censors narrowly decided that Nielsen's character Jesta in *Engelein* had not violated the rules by revealing a very brief glimpse of a garter while climbing over a wall, then resolved to ban the film in any case, because of the implicit immorality of Jesta's illegitimate birth five years before her parents' wedding. Only after Paul Davidson at PAGU filed a storm of protests and dared to show the film at his theaters anyway was the ruling amended to simply "forbidden for children."[116]

Yet although many of the storylines of Nielsen's early films do incorporate sexuality to an extent, their most important common trait is her depiction of strong women who make difficult choices and stand by them, regardless of the consequences. Traditional gender roles in Nielsen's erotic melodramas are frequently reversed, setting a precedent for other films of the genre. Engberg explains,

> The woman in the Danish film melodrama is as a rule a cocksure, independent person, whereas the man is weak, without much willpower. He is often scared by the independent women of his own class, and therefore falls in love with a girl from the lower classes, to whom he feels superior. In this attitude to the woman of his own class he demonstrates modern man's fear of the modern woman. Moreover, the woman of the erotic melodrama is as a rule an active partner in the love story. It is often she who makes the decision, she who is the sexually active one.[117]

While romantic relationships do occupy a central position in Nielsen's films, it is not the romantic or erotic attraction between the characters that draws the viewer's attention, but rather the professional and sexual confidence that both her characters and she herself radiated.

Similarly, Bergstrom explains that even when Nielsen's sexually transgressive characters are punished and end as victims, they are not weak or pathetic:

> [Asta Nielsen] is never a conventional victim. The very naturalness with which she endows so many actions deemed unusual for women, her integrity, her depth of feeling, her active sense of intelligence, her particular kind of sensuality, mark her female roles with an individuality that resists the reduction to types that will become common during the 1920s in Germany.... The representation of Nielsen's characters as women who must think quickly and constantly in order to make sense of things, or to get what they want, serves to detract the censorious eye from the extremely sexual nature of many of these characters.[118]

In her films, as in her personal life, Nielsen set herself apart from the norm by daring to challenge conventions and take risks, but these choices came with professional and personal consequences that strained Nielsen's relationship to her homeland.

Many of Nielsen's films were censored in Denmark and other parts of Scandinavia, which reflects the latent tension between Nielsen's provocatively modern screen persona and the conservative morals of mainstream Scandinavian society. Although the situation would become acute in the 1920, Danish censors were already strict about approving her films in the 1910s, while audiences were on guard against transgressive behavior either depicted in the films or inspired by them. In an editorial in the *Aarhus Stiftstidende* on October 23, 1912, Nielsen is condemned as "the priestess of sensuality" and blamed for "awakening disturbing sensual joys in the viewer and making reprehensibility fashionable across Europe through her performance."[119] This puritanical view of Nielsen's films as a threat to bourgeois morality was not limited to Denmark but also influenced censors in the rest of Scandinavia, particularly Norway and Sweden.[120] Nielsen's association with cultural modernity, which made her so attractive to German audiences, had the opposite effect on Scandinavian audiences, who vividly recalled the cultural wars of the late nineteenth and early twentieth centuries over Brandes, Ibsen, Strindberg, and the Modern Breakthough.[121]

Even in the face of such disapproval, however, Nielsen proactively defended the merits of her work, protested censorship, and used the press to present her arguments to the broadest possible public. In 1911 her film *The Great Moment / In dem großen Augenblick* (Gad, 1911), which had been shown in German churches as an example of selfless maternal love, was banned by the Swedish censors. In response, Nielsen published an open letter to Marie Louise Gagner, the only female member of the Swedish censorship board. In the letter, she appeals to Ms. Gagner on the basis of their shared gender to reconsider the censorship board's decision, which she attributes to the fact that the child in the film is illegitimate, as well as to an attempted attack by one character on another with a pocket knife. In defense of both the film and her own performance in it, Nielsen explain that such details are irrelevant to the "great moment" to which the film's title refers, which is

> the greatest moment, that can occur in a woman's life,—the moment in which she must choose between her own existence and that of her child. I have done my best to portray the life of a young mother, her

despair when need forces her to entrust her child to strangers, and the great ecstasy that forces her, at the last moment, to give her life for her child's. You, as a woman, ought surely to be the first to recognize that a central action such as this most certainly always has human emotion and moral value enough to justify showing it to everyone—even the Swedish people.[122]

Nielsen argues that the film's focus on human emotions and choices elevates it above mere sensationalism. She dismisses the idea that "the world was pure and innocent, until Edison brought sin into the world with the invention of cinematography," and urges the censor to acknowledge, "as a woman," that her film is "exclusively a tribute to female heroism."[123]

Singled out to defend one decision among thousands that the three-person Swedish censorship board had made in the fall of 1911, Gagner offered the explanation that the ban was due to the shocking and brutalizing effect of the climactic scene in the film when the house burns down, with Nielsen's character trapped inside after having saved her child, which conformed to Swedish guidelines against "horror" films.[124] Yet despite this ostensibly justified objection, it is noteworthy that Gagner devoted the bulk of her response not to a discussion of this particular scene or even this film, but rather to a more general discussion of the cinema's influence in Sweden, especially among teenagers. In particular, she warns against the detrimental impact that scenes of sexuality can have on "vulnerable youths,"[125] implicitly acknowledging that the ban on Nielsen's film was due in part to the centrality of an illegitimate child in the story. Gagner's response triggered a wider debate in the Swedish press about the degree to which cinema could be considered art, the extent to which art should be subject to censorship, and how to safeguard Swedish society against the coarsening effect of erotic spectacles depicted on screen.

This emphasis on protecting Swedish youth from the dangerous immorality of Nielsen's films in particular and the genre of the erotic melodrama in general reinforces the gap between the prevailing endo- and exo-stereotypes about Scandinavian cinema and Scandinavian national identity at the time. Rather than being sexually permissive, as one might infer from certain literary works of the Modern Breakthrough or from erotic melodramas made in Denmark or by Nielsen in Germany, mainstream Danish and Swedish society was still very conservative, particularly with regard to sexuality, and was concerned that films would encourage immoral behavior among Scandinavian young people. As a result of this preoccupation, Scandinavian censors were often particularly strict in assessing the possible effect of Nielsen's films, although in the case of *The Great Moment,* this decision seems to have been unjustified.

Censorship also played a role in limiting the success Nielsen's films enjoyed in the English-speaking countries, particularly the United States, before the war. The importation of Nielsen's films to the United States was actively hampered by the American censors, who seemed motivated as much by the desire to protect their respective domestic film industries as their country's youth. Richard Abel documents the increasingly xenophobic attitude of the American film industry, reflected in the claim that American audiences would not tolerate foreign subjects on screen, in the years immediately preceding Nielsen's film debut.[126] Accordingly, American censors were quick to suppress foreign films that might offend American sensibilities, such as the erotic melodramas that had made Nielsen a star in Europe. Despite its success in Europe, *The Abyss* was not released in the United States until April 1912, distributed by Carl Laemmle's Imp Films Company, and the United Kingdom in June 1912, with a small, second-rate distributor. The film ran under the title *Woman Always Pays* and had been mutilated into incomprehensibility, at least in the United States, as indicated by a review in the *New York Dramatic Mirror,* which complained that "essential points ... have evidently been cut out by some overscrupulous authority."[127] Unsurprisingly, *The Abyss* was not at all successful in the United States and did little to boost Nielsen's American reputation. Other obstacles to the success of Nielsen's films in the United States were the states-rights system of distribution that was new in the United States at the time, in which a firm or person purchased the right to license a film's exhibition in a particular territory, and the widespread popularity of short-film variety programs and serials, such as *The Perils of Pauline* (Louis Gasnier, 1914), rather than multiple-reel feature films.

What little attention Nielsen did attract in the United States preceded the release of *The Woman Always Pays,* resulting from an "exclusive" Asta Nielsen series launched by the relatively small Tournament Film Company of Toledo, Ohio, beginning in March 1912. In keeping with its midwestern clientele, many of whom were of German origin, Tournament Films promoted Nielsen as "the foremost German actress," "the German Bernhardt."[128] Her films *Gipsy Blood / Zigeunerblut* (Gad, 1911) and *The Traitress* had their US premieres in the spring of 1912 as part of this series, which generated what Jennifer Bean has described as the first "wave" of Nielsen reception in the United States.[129] These two films circulated for more than a year in the United States,[130] but four additional Nielsen films for which Tournament Films had acquired the American distribution rights, including *The Great Moment* and *Retribution,* were never released. Scattered newspaper ads for *The Might of Gold / Die Macht des Goldes* (Gad, 1912) and *A Strange Bird* indicate that these films were also shown in various US locations during this period, through unidentified distributors. After the dissolution of Tournament Films in 1913, American distribution rights for Nielsen's films were acquired by Pathé-Frères, which chose to relaunch the series with the American premiere of *Lady Madcap's Way,* followed by five more films, including *The Devil's Assistant / Sünden der Väter* (Gad, 1912) and *A Romany Spy.*

Even when screened in the United States, however, Nielsen's films were subject to very specific interpretations by American critics and audiences. Whereas Nielsen's films could be marketed in Europe on the strength of her name, American critics paid much closer attention to the acceptability of the individual film narratives than to aesthetics or artistry. The cultural gap between Europe and America aggravated the already strained distribution conditions for European films in the United States, making it impossible for Nielsen to achieve the same level of fame or influence as she had in Germany. *Behind Comedy's Mask / Wenn die Maske fällt* (Gad, 1912) and *The Devil's Assistant* were regarded as "intemperance tales" that showcased the dangers of strong drink and the desire for vengeance, while *The Militant Suffragette* was interpreted as an antisuffrage tale rather than a defense of the extreme tactics of such British suffragists as Emmeline Pankhurst.

Some distributors tried to capitalize on the perception of Nielsen's exotic difference in order to tap into a niche market for European films in the United States, but this strategy ran afoul of the puritanical strains within American culture. Audience tastes and values differed from Europe to America, and the film engendered disapproval for the perceived moral depravity of Nielsen's character in *Lady Madcap's Way,* who smokes a cigar, dresses like a man, and flirts with other men. The ambiguity of Nielsen's film persona made it difficult for American critics and promoters to pigeonhole her as a particular "type," with the result that she was simply labeled "foreign." Bean notes that many of the American reviews of Nielsen's early films disseminated a view of her as "a flamboyant figure of European 'difference' inassimilable to the norms then constructing and constraining a particular version of mass-mediated America."[131] In short, Nielsen was perceived as being too foreign to be an American movie star.

Despite Nielsen's tremendous popularity in Germany, the tension between competing national identity constructions was also involved in shaping Nielsen's German reception. Although many other gifted actresses carved out a niche for themselves in the silent German film market, Nielsen's primary rival for the title of Germany's favorite cinema star throughout the 1910s was the buxom, blond-haired, blue-eyed actress Henny Porten, who was frequently described as "the blonde antithesis of Asta Nielsen"[132] and whom Hickethier identifies as the "symbol of the German woman in her most concentrated form."[133] The contrast between these two stars, particularly the heavily nationalistic symbolism associated with Porten, serves to illuminate some of the central issues related to Nielsen's differing reception in Denmark and Germany and justifies taking a few moments to compare both her work and her discursive positioning to Nielsen's.

Nielsen and Porten's rivalry contained a significant economic component, related primarily to competition over market share. Porten had been a child star in director Oskar Messter's early cinematic *Tonbilder,* which consisted of either reenactments of well-known scenes from operas and operettas or adaptations of musical numbers from Berlin's variety and cabaret theaters, which were screened accompanied by a prerecorded soundtrack. *Tonbilder* made up 90 percent of Messter's sales in 1908, before plummeting to 8 percent by 1911.[134] Anxious not to lose out to the new monopoly-distribution system, Messter "discovered" Porten and launched her career the same year as Nielsen's debut, putting them into direct competition. Porten's first feature film, *The Blind Girl's Romance / Das Liebesglück der Blinden* (Curt Stark, 1910),[135] appeared just a few weeks after Nielsen's debut film had premiered in the Palast Theater in Düsseldorf and caused a sensation due to its erotic content and unprecedented length of forty-five minutes. Messter's plan to promote Porten as the rising star of German cinema in early 1911 was further disrupted by the establishment of PAGU, which embarked on an aggressive marketing campaign to popularize Nielsen as "the Eleonora Duse of the Cinema" and to generate interest in the first Asta Nielsen Film series. Building on the resistance of the small film companies to the new monopoly distribution companies, Messter countered by positioning Porten as an "anti-star" to a distributor-backed star such as Nielsen.[136] This approach was not as profitable, however, and within a few years, Porten began receiving the same star treatment as Nielsen.

Although Porten's star career got off to a somewhat slower start than Nielsen's, she quickly gained a devoted following in Germany, though it was not until 1912 that Porten began to appear in longer films and to receive star treatment from Messter's company. This campaign included widespread marketing of her name, public appearances, higher-than-average wages, and the launching of a Henny Porten Film series in 1913–14. Porten soon eclipsed many other rising stars and secured her position in the top rank of film stars in Germany. In a magazine survey from early 1914, Porten ranked as the third most popular cinema personality in Germany, after Valdemar Psilander and Asta Nielsen.[137] However, although Porten was extremely popular in Germany and Austria throughout the early 1910s, her films gained far less traction overseas than Nielsen's, with the result that her international fame was largely limited to the Netherlands, Scandinavia, and Russia, aside from the isolated US success of *Anna Boleyn* (Lubitsch, 1920).

The competition between Nielsen and Porten did not stem exclusively from economic considerations, however, but to a large extent was due to the two stars' highly public embodiment of divergent ideals of gender roles as well. Porten and Nielsen appeared in some fairly similar types of roles, often as women caught between jealous lovers or feuding armies, but Porten's characters tended to be much more self-sacrificing and dutiful than Nielsen's. Hake explains,

> Whereas Nielsen was perceived as an almost disruptive presence in silent cinema, Henny Porten became identified with the normative force of traditional gender roles. With her long blonde hair, plain features, and buxom figure, Porten personified traditional Germanic womanhood even when she appeared in rustic comedies that showed off her considerable comic talents. . . . Her association with the maternal principle helped to placate widespread anxieties about women's emancipation and made her ideally suited for old-fashioned stories about female honour, duty, and sacrifice.[138]

Becker agrees that Porten was "typecast to roles that alternated between passion and heroism," proving most "successful as the wife and mother who was morally and ethically beyond reproach. . . . She was a model for those German women who tended toward a sense of duty and the suppression of instincts. Unbridled temperament and erotic advances, hedonism and sensuality, these were reserved for the other early stars."[139] In terms of both her acting style and the roles she played, Porten embodied a premodern, traditional image of womanhood, "a cinematic spectacle which signified at once a properly restrained female sexuality and German national identity: 'the *mother land*'"[140] that contrasted sharply with Nielsen's private and public enactment of modern feminism. By contrast, as Becker notes, Nielsen's roles "were characterized by violations of or digressions from the rules."[141] An early Porten film *In the Shadow of the Sea / Im Schatten des Meeres* (Stark, 1912) is based on a similar narrative premise as Nielsen's film *A Strange Bird*, the story of a city girl who steals the heart of a country boy from his devoted fiancé and thereby causes a tragedy, but the opening frames of the film reassure viewers that "if she [Porten's character Evelyne] causes unhappiness for others in this film, it is only because of external tragic circumstances," in contrast to the willful behavior of Nielsen's character in *A Strange Bird*.

Not only was Porten portrayed and perceived as more maternal, less emancipated, and therefore less socially disruptive than Nielsen, her ethnic identity was also much more reassuringly Germanic, "a prototype of Germanic femininity," as Karl Bleibtreu described her in his review of her 1913 film *The Enemy at Home / Der Feind im Land* (Stark, 1913).[142] Although Bleibtreu felt that Porten's Teutonic image distracted from her portrayal of a French revolutionary, other viewers were less concerned with verisimilitude in cinema than with the political potential of Porten's incarnation of nationalistic ideals. In an article in the journal *Das Tagebuch* in 1921, the prominent journalist, film critic, and director of the Reinhardt Theater in Berlin, Kurt Pinthus, satirically proposed Porten as a potential candidate for president of the new German republic:

> Henny Porten for President of the Republic! Here is a figure whom Germans feel is closer to the people than old Fritz [Frederick the Great] or Goethe the Olympian ever were or could be. . . . Here is a beautiful woman, who is admired by hundreds of thousands of her countrymen as the realization of their dreams and longings, who has long been silently acknowledged by the women of Germany as their queen. Here is a beautiful woman who appears to a devastated nation of seventy million people hungry for a future as a symbol of virtue, of the emotionally strong and yet cheerful woman. Here is a beautiful woman, Gretchen and Germania rolled into one, elevated to an ideal of the German people by the Germans themselves.[143]

Even tongue-in-cheek, Pinthus's praise for Porten's embodiment of nationalistic virtues supports Ramona Curry's argument that "early German film stars represent a visible site of the closely articulated foundations of national cinema and nationalistic politics and demonstrate the historical use of female images to sell both."[144] Porten's patriotic credentials included not only her personal virtue and beauty but also her contributions to the national film industry's support of the German war effort, both as a modest pinup girl, a war widow, and as the star of a short film in support of war bond sales, *Hann, Hein, und Henny* (Rudolf Biebrach, 1917). When antiwar and antigovernment riots broke out in Berlin in November 1918, Porten appeared in another short film, in which she rises out of flames in a cloud of billowing white robes "like the peace angel personally," urging viewers to "stay calm, be reasonable, spare your women and children."[145] The characterization of Porten as an angel striving to save the German nation underscores both the purity of Porten's image and the almost messianic qualities attributed to her in Pinthus's proposal.

Whatever her other strengths, Nielsen's foreign citizenship and dark coloring made it highly unlikely that she would ever be perceived as a benevolent goddess of Germanness. Her coloring was no more typical for Germany than it was for Denmark, and many German reviews of her films point out her foreignness. Instead of shaping German national identity by modeling its ideal incarnation, as Porten did, Nielsen influenced it by depicting otherness and offering an alternative to the nationalist ideal incarnated by Porten. Her star persona was identified with Scandinavia, in particular the image of a progressive, often transgressive, modern Scandinavian culture that had been established by the literature of the Modern Breakthrough around the turn of the century. In a collection of biographical sketches of Germany's greatest film stars of the 1910s and 1920s, Alex Binder remarks, "Asta Nielsen was always a stranger to us. One spoke unfailingly of the 'great Danish actress.'"[146]

In Denmark, however, critics found Nielsen to be anything but typically Nordic. Writing about a screening of *The Abyss* in Paris in an article in *Politiken* in 1911, Sophus Claussen objected to Nielsen's "southern complexion," which, he felt, threatened to convey an inaccurate impression of Denmark to the world, and argued that Danish film ought to show "a certain degree of blondness, [which] suits us and awakens affection. . . . Keep your films pure!"[147] Claussen's article reveals that Danes perceived Nielsen as looking exotic and foreign, although this did not always evoke negative connotations. After interviewing Nielsen in Berlin in 1912, Viggo Schiörring commented admiringly on her "magnificent, red silk kimono with gold embroidery, which looks so exotic that it could easily have come from The Mikado! But this Yum-Yum costume suits her dark, bizarre physiognomy perfectly and reminds me of Polaire one moment, Mistinguett the next."[148] By comparing Nielsen to these two sultry French singers, Schiörring's goal seems to be to convey a sense of her aura of sensuality and exoticism, yet in so doing he too reaffirms her failure to embody the Danish norm. Nielsen was aware of this perception of her foreignness by her own countrymen, as she notes in a letter to Claussen in 1917, "I remember well that you were once incensed that I, the opposite of the Danish type, represented *Danish* cinema in France."[149]

It was not just her dark coloring that did not conform to Danish ideals of beauty but also her body type. In a 1913 article in *Ekstrabladet* titled "Heroes of Our Time: Asta Nielsen-Gad," the future director Carl Theodor Dreyer, writing under the pseudonym Tommen, bluntly disparages Nielsen's physical appearance. He criticizes her for appearing in *Hosenrollen* that reveal "how terribly she is built" and explains,

> Asta Nielsen-Gad truly has some terribly unfortunate features. She is lanky and overgrown, flat like an ironing board in back, flat-chested and with no calves to speak of. . . . But what does Asta Nielsen-Gad do? In half of her films, she wears a tight jersey, and when she is no longer interested in the jersey, she dons men's clothing. She is determined . . . to reveal her scrawniness.[150]

At a time when the aesthetic ideal for a Danish woman was blond and buxom, Nielsen's slender figure was perceived as unattractive, although it corresponded very closely to the athletic, boyish body type that was already becoming fashionable in France, through the work of Paul Poiret and Coco Chanel,[151] and would take the world by storm in the 1920s.

The outbreak of World War I interrupted Nielsen's career trajectory, both as a result of the logistical difficulties of wartime conditions for the production and international distribution of German films, as well as the increasing alignment of the German film industry with German nationalist and propaganda aims. In her memoirs, Nielsen recounts that she was making a film near the Polish border when the war broke out. She immediately decided to return to Denmark, but a single day's journey turned into a two-week ordeal due to military checkpoints and train requisitions for troop transports. Thanks to her well-known face, she made it across the border, but the war continued to disrupt her work in a variety of ways: after her contract with Internationale Film expired, she had planned to start her own film company, but capital was unavailable; film studios throughout Germany and Denmark instituted production freezes; travel restrictions made the on-location filming she preferred impossible; and her marriage to Urban Gad disintegrated, with Nielsen filing for separation on October 19, 1914.[152]

Nielsen's and Gad's close collaboration on her prewar films had been instrumental in establishing both Nielsen's stardom and her film expertise, and ensuring a high quality product and artistic freedom for Nielsen, as well as enhancing the status of Danish film abroad. In 1927 Christian Engelstoft noted in the Danish newspaper *Aftenbladet* that it was their collaboration that deserves credit for the fact that "Danish film was respected on the world market for a short while."[153] Although Gad did not receive the same level of adoration as Nielsen, his role in her success was pivotal, as he noted himself, in his influential book on cinematic techniques from 1919. Explaining the distinction between the role of the director and that of the actor, Gad argues, "Unnoticed by the audience, the director holds the actor's embroidered puppet strings, carrying out the bulk of the work—he is the backbone of the film."[154] Their separation was amicable, on the whole, and Nielsen soon found both a new love interest, as well as the capital she needed to start her own film company, in the person of Freddy Wingårdh, a Swedish naval captain and son of a wealthy shipping magnate.

Restless at being unable to work, Nielsen seized every opportunity to flee war-torn Europe and its "daily, wearing news about horrors that one cannot change by a hair's breadth,"[155] but she could not escape her own fame. As Wingårdh's guest, she accompanied the freighter *Nautilus* on a dangerous voyage through mined Atlantic waters to deliver a load of cement to South America in 1915. When the ship encountered a German submarine off the English coast, the German sailors recognized Nielsen and sent them on their way with shouts of "Long live Asta!" Nielsen doesn't mention the encounter in her memoirs, published in Denmark just after World War II, and other scholars have doubted its veracity, but a letter written by Wingårdh from Las Palmas mentioning the incident was published in a

Danish newspaper in 1915.[156] It can also be confirmed by photographs of the sub taken by Wingårdh.[157] Two years later, Nielsen and Wingårdh visited New York, on the first leg of a planned around-the-world voyage that ended abruptly with America's entry into the war. Relatively unknown to American audiences, Nielsen's fame was not helpful in pacifying American authorities who suspected her of being a German spy and put her under surveillance.[158] Forced to stay in New York for six months, she made tentative plans to film a Strindberg play with Fox Films to support herself. She began going to the cinema frequently to improve her English, but ultimately dropped the project after a disheartening visit to a small, crowded, loud American film studio.

Nielsen's film career did not, however, come to a complete standstill because of the war. Between her sea voyages and with financial support from Wingårdh's family, Nielsen returned to Berlin in 1916 to make eight films under the auspices of her own independent film company, judiciously named Neutral Film. Based on scripts written primarily by Louis Levy and Martin Jørgensen, the series catered to audience demand for comedies with *The Alphabet of Love*, *The Eskimo Baby / Das Eskimobaby* (Walter Schmidthässler, 1916), *Queen of the Stock Market / Die Börsenkönigin* (Edmund Edel, 1916), and *The Guinea Pig / Das Versuchskaninchen* (Edel, 1916).[159] Some of the films premiered in Berlin in 1916, but others were not released until 1918. Despite the makeshift working conditions in wartime Berlin and the lack of involvement on the part of Urban Gad, who had been instrumental in almost all of Nielsen's previous films, these films were quite successful and represent some of Nielsen's best work from this early period. Any plans for additional films had to be dropped, however, when Nielsen's stay in Berlin ended abruptly after she came under suspicion of espionage because of her foreign citizenship and was advised by the police to leave Germany for the duration of the war.[160]

Of the films Nielsen made with Neutral Film, one of the most noteworthy, in terms of both its comic appeal and its playfully confrontational approach to questions of cultural identity, is *The Eskimo Baby*, which features a Greenlandic protagonist and overtly thematizes cultural otherness. Nielsen delivers a dynamic performance as Ivigtut, a young Inuit woman brought back to Berlin from Danish-controlled Greenland by a German ethnographer, Knud, whose name evokes the Danish Arctic explorer Knud Rasmussen. Throughout the film, she is dressed in a traditional Greenlandic costume of sealskin pants

Figure 4.3. *The Eskimo Baby* is one of Nielsen's most remarkable films from the period following her long collaboration with Urban Gad and is notable for both its slapstick humor and its bold treatment of postcolonial issues. Credit: The Danish Film Institute, Stills Archive

and beaded sweater, with her hair in a fabric-wrapped ponytail on the top of her head. Upon arriving in Berlin, Ivigtut refuses to shake Knud's father's hand, to his disapproving consternation, but the intertitle warns, "Do not doubt Ivigtut's manners [*Bildung*]! In Greenland we greet each other with smiles." Although the film is not politically correct by modern standards, it does not mock or denigrate Greenlandic culture, but rather shows how Ivigtut comes to terms with the new world she encounters in Berlin, winning the audience fully to her side. She explores the "civilized world," gets into trouble, and exposes the fundamental choices at the core of national and cultural identity. Many aspects of the film's depictions of Greenlandic culture are inaccurate—beginning with the name Ivigtut, which is not a female personal name at all but the name of a Danish cryolite mine in Greenland—or deliberately simplistic in order to maximize the comic potential in each new situation in which Ivigtut finds herself.[161]

Despite the film's use of stereotypical images of culture shock, Ivigtut's reactions demonstrate not only her unfamiliarity with Western culture but also her inherent intelligence, assertiveness, curiosity, and humor. Fascinated by technology, she pulls the emergency brake on the train, tries to climb under an automobile, clicks the electric lights in her room on and off incessantly, and drives the housemaid to distraction by continually ringing her service bell. However, when she is treated like an object, put on display alongside a polar bear head and three stuffed birds, she retaliates by playing the savage to the hilt. At a luncheon with Knud's parents and intended bride, she scandalizes her hosts by eating with her hands, grimacing at food she dislikes, and spitting it out onto her plate. The intended bride loathes her, telling Ivigtut, "In our society, one does not fall in love with a woman in fur pants," and warning Knud, "For God's sake, stay away from this wild woman!"

Yet Ivigtut, another of Nielsen's strong female characters, fights for her man and wins. After being chastised for wearing pants to a reception being held for Knud, she borrows a rowboat and makes her way down the river to the heart of Berlin to acquire proper European clothes. Unfamiliar with Western retail practices, she tries to walk out of a department store without paying for her goods and causes a commotion that ends with her crawling across the manager's desk while he telephones Knud. Despite her wildness, Knud prefers his Eskimo girl to the quintessentially German girl his parents had chosen. When the spurned bride tries to ship Ivigtut back to Greenland, the secret comes out that she is expecting Knud's child, making it clear that she and Knud have done more than just rub noses. At the end of the film, Knud returns to the Arctic with his wife and son, leaving Germany behind for good.

When Nielsen left Germany once more in 1916, she settled into an apartment in Copenhagen, where she found herself at the center of a vibrant social life, not only because of the prosperity enjoyed by Denmark's "goulash barons" that contributed to a lively atmosphere, but also because of her connections to Danish society through the Gad family. Prior to 1910, her working-class background had restricted her access to elite society in Copenhagen, but her marriage to Urban Gad had brought her into contact with the intellectual and cultural elite of Copenhagen. At the home of her in-laws, Nielsen encountered many of the prominent figures of the Danish literary world, including Georg and Edvard Brandes, Henri Nathansen, Henrik Cavling, Sophus Claussen, and Johannes V. Jensen, as well as Karin and Sophus Michaëlis.

Emma Gad was famous for her hospitality and receptivity to modern social and aesthetic ideas, particularly those associated with the Modern Breakthrough, and her salon was an oasis of liberal ideals in the midst of the generally conservative Danish bourgeoisie.[162] In a posthumously published memoir, Urban Gad recalled frequent discussions during his childhood of the most provocative new books about marriage, free love, and women's emancipation by Tolstoy, Ibsen, Bjørnson, and Strindberg.[163] This intellectual environment was instrumental in shaping both Urban Gad's positive view of modernity and the characters he helped Nielsen create on screen. After her separation and divorce from Urban Gad, Nielsen remained close friends with many of Emma Gad's guests, particularly Georg Brandes, his secretary Gertrud Rung, and Rung's husband Otto, as well as a few colleagues from the Danish acting community, notably Olaf Fønss and Clara Pontoppidan Wieth.

What wartime Copenhagen could not provide Nielsen with, however, was work. Her legendary energy had no outlet and her fortune was inaccessible in a Tokyo bank account.[164] She could not get a visa to return to Germany, but the only Danish film company actively producing films was Nordisk. Nielsen swallowed her pride and made one film for Nordisk, the drama *Toward the Light / Mod Lyset* (Holger-Madsen, 1918). Based on a belief that Danish audiences would welcome moralistic tales, Ole Olsen cast Nielsen as the callously flirtatious Countess Isabella, who is converted to evangelical Christianity by a humble priest. Although Nielsen's performance was adept, the film was not a success, largely, according to Engberg, because of the competence gap between Nielsen and her fellow cast members: "Asta makes the impression of being a peacock among sparrows."[165] When Nielsen was finally granted a visa to return to Germany in 1919, she seized the opportunity, but this time, the consequences of her decision would prove to be much greater than before, particularly with regard to her relationship to both her homeland and her adopted country, due to the profound changes in sociopolitical conditions in postwar Europe, as well as aesthetic and technical shifts within the film industry.

By the end of World War I, the golden era of Danish film was over. Of six Danish film companies operating in 1913, only three remained: Nordisk, Danmark, and Astra, and none of them was in a solid financial situation. Confident that business as usual would resume after the war, Olsen at Nordisk had increased the company's share capital from two to four million kroner in order to build a new studio, finance the production of over 150 films, and acquire a string of first-run cinemas in Germany via its German subsidiary, Nordische Films Company.[166] This endeavor was initially successful, allowing Nordisk to become Germany's largest distributor, but could not compensate for the losses occasioned by the closure of the export market to Great Britain, the United States, and Russia. Most of the backlogged Nordisk films were outdated after the war and had to be written off as a loss, causing significant financial damage to Nordisk.

The creation of Universum Film AG (UFA) in Germany in 1917, which served to unify the German film industry and cinema market, had an even more dramatic negative effect on the Danish film industry. Governmental support for UFA gave it a significant advantage over foreign companies such as Nordisk, most strikingly when, in 1917, the German government forced foreign film companies working in Germany, including Nordisk, to sell all of their assets, including first-run cinemas and shares in German film companies, to the state for extremely devalued German marks. Nordische Films merged with UFA in 1918, while Nordisk never recovered its former status. When these assets were turned over to UFA, the German film industry came out of the war in a much stronger position than it had enjoyed in 1914, while the Danish film industry was reduced to competing for only the regional Scandinavian market.

The end of the golden age of Danish film coincided with the end of the first phase of Nielsen's career and a transformation of both the types of film she made and the way she and her films were regarded in Denmark. The informal, exploratory atmosphere of early film studios was replaced by regimentation, transferring creative control of films and their social agendas from actors to directors. Nielsen could no longer exercise the same degree of influence on the tone of her films and the identity of her characters, let alone improvise entire scenes with a free hand. In an attempt to elevate the respectability of film, social dramas with minimal plots gave way to film adaptations of complex literary texts. The flourishing state of the Danish film industry during most of the 1910s had proved mutually beneficial to Nielsen and Denmark, each of whom gained by the other's success. This congenial situation, aside from some social discontent about Nielsen's sensual screen persona, allowed for a generally favorable reception of her films in Denmark. As Danish film went into decline, however, at the same time as Nielsen returned to Germany to restart her career there, she gradually came to be perceived by her countrymen as more of threat than an asset to Danish film, culture, and national identity. The nature of this paradigm shift in Nielsen's Danish reception is articulated very poignantly in a Danish review of Nielsen's film, *Crown of Thorns / I.N.R.I.* (Robert Wiene, 1923) in December 1923. The review confirms Nielsen's new status as an outsider, in contrast to the emphasis that had been placed on her Danish origins before the war, with the announcement that one of the film's main attractions is that it stars "our own, or rather the Germans' own Asta Nielsen."[167]

CHAPTER FIVE

The New Woman

Enacting Scandinavian Modernity on Screen

When Asta Nielsen moved back to Berlin in 1919 to rebuild her film career after World War I, she was greeted with enthusiasm by critics and audiences alike. In the first issue of the magazine *Bühne und Film,* published in early 1919, film critic Egon Jacobsohn reported a sighting of Nielsen in the streets of post–World War I Berlin and articulated the possessive sentiment felt by German audiences toward her upon her return:

> You're walking through the streets of Friedrichstadt [a Berlin neighborhood]. Suddenly you look up: who is the woman driving by? *Die Nielsen?* Impossible! She left Germany long ago, retreated into private life.... But it is *die Asta*! You can see it in her greeting: the small nod, the ephemeral smile that shows her dimples and teeth, and then—the large, the enormous, expressive eyes. There is no doubt: it is *die Nielsen*. So she has come home after all.[1]

The tone of affectionate intimacy that suffuses Jacobsohn's description of Nielsen's features and mannerisms suggests that his readers were already familiar with her dimples, smiles, and expressive eyes, as indeed they were. Despite her Danish origins, Nielsen was the first superstar of German silent cinema, and Jacobsohn claims her, on emotional, artistic, and economic grounds, for Germany. He continues,

> Yes, "come home" again. It is true that she is a Dane, from Copenhagen, but her artistic home, as far as the public is concerned, is here in our lovely Berlin, the Athens of film-making. She has admitted it a dozen times herself—here is where the young unknown actress found her first substantial support—here is where most of her films were

made—here—here in Berlin; countless memories tie her to the German Empire, make it her home, and pull her back again and again into the realm of the black and white posts. Now she is ours once again.[2]

Jacobsohn's insistence on Germany's claim to Nielsen is indicative of the nationalistic issues that would become acute during her second period of residence in Berlin, from 1919 until 1937, when Nielsen's personal and professional ties to Germany became a liability for her acceptance in Denmark, reminiscent of Brandes's situation while in Berlin in the late 1870s.

In contrast to Denmark's acceptance of silent film's cosmopolitan nature in the 1910s, Danish attitudes toward silent cinema became increasingly nationalized during the 1920s and 1930s, a development that led to both a closer identification between Nielsen and German culture than had been the case before the war and her resulting professional alienation from Danish society. Reacting to Nielsen's success in Germany in this period, at a time when Danish film had been displaced from its earlier prominence, Danish critics frequently raised the question, even decades after Nielsen had returned to Denmark, of where Nielsen's loyalties lay—to the land of her birth or the land of her professional success. This issue, including its implications for Nielsen's aesthetic, cultural, and political views, played a major role in shaping both her films from the 1920s and her relationship to her homeland from the 1920s until her death in 1972. Nielsen continued to embody modernity and feminism on screen, setting the trend for the flapper fashions of flat chests, sheath dresses, and bobbed hair, but her construction of modern female identity was both more mainstream in Germany and more contested in Denmark than her prewar experiments with identity manipulation had been. Danish resistance to Nielsen's postwar films is particularly ironic in light of the fact that her films from the 1920s are, to a large extent, exemplary of the kind of thematic engagement with social issues that Brandes had advocated for modern Danish literature.

The second phase of Nielsen's film career, which lasted from 1919 to 1932, followed a much more turbulent course than the first phase. Socioeconomic and political difficulties in Europe were exacerbated by the long war and the subsequent global financial crises, particularly the potent combination of inflation and recession. Intensified nationalist sentiment in both Germany and Denmark, along with

Nielsen's well-established reputation as a global movie star, invested her renewed decision to work in Germany with a much more significant political dimension than in 1911. At the same time, however, the concomitant shift in the German film industry from an actor-centric to a director- and distributor-centric system made it more difficult for her to exercise the same degree of artistic autonomy that she had enjoyed in her prewar career. Determined to have a say in her work, and with the financial backing of her second husband's wealthy family, Nielsen formed her own production company, Art Film, in 1920,[3] which she ran until it was dissolved in 1925. This venture gave her control over some of her film roles and finished films, but otherwise she felt that she was generally at the mercy of mediocre directors and that the originality and quality of the screenplays she was offered declined markedly during the 1920s.[4] As she told a reporter many years later,

> I wanted to play women who really lived, I wanted to capture on film everyday people, I wanted so much to embody problematic figures from world literature. . . . I fought a constant battle against incompetent directors, against banal manuscripts. The tasks offered me were worth less and less, the figures I was to depict more and more hypocritical and mechanical.[5]

Several factors contributed to the deterioration in the quality of scripts and roles at Nielsen's disposal. To a certain extent, she was a victim of her own popularity, as her characteristic short hair and slender build had become so fashionable that they had been adopted by many other actresses, so that her look was no longer distinctive. The constant influx of attractive, younger actresses into the industry made it difficult for an aging star such as Nielsen to land interesting roles and maintain her popularity, which, in turn, made her less of a sure thing at the box office. Furthermore, her importance as an inspirational feminist figure had waned with the success of women's emancipation movements during the war, which culminated in the legal establishment of women's suffrage in Denmark in 1915 and Germany in 1919, but stagnated somewhat during the 1920s.

The German film industry was far stronger and more institutionalized during the Weimar era than it had been before the war. Cinema was the most popular pastime in Berlin in the 1920s, with more than twice as many cinemas as stage theaters. The number of cinema houses increased from 3,500 in 1920 to over 5,000 by the end of the decade, serving approximately six million patrons per week.[6]

Domestic German film production vastly exceeded prewar levels and outpaced other European countries, whose combined market share of German box-office receipts shrank to a mere 13.1 percent of box-office returns between 1925 and 1930.[7]

However, although a handful of distributors still controlled the German market, production was distributed among dozens of small production companies that jockeyed for market share. According to the official *Guide to the Film Industry (Handbuch der Filmwirtschaft)*, in 1926, "Eighty-one German companies produced 185 feature-length films, and forty-two of these companies produced only a single film. Even the two largest German film companies of the 1920s, UFA and Emelka, produced only a relatively small number of films; in 1926, UFA made twelve and Emelka nine films."[8] Aside from the handful of films she made with her own Art Film company, Nielsen worked primarily on a freelance basis in the 1920s, making films for Cserépy-Film, Richard-Oswald-Film, Messter-Film, Bioscop, PAGU, Leopold-Jessner-Film, Sofar-Film, Internationale Film, Pantomim-Film, Illés-Film, and Märkische Film, among others.

The increase in domestic German film production and production companies caused a corresponding surge in the number of film stars in Germany. Whereas Nielsen's fame in the early 1910s had been unprecedented in its scope, the sheer numbers of stars vying for the spotlight in the 1920s made it difficult for any of them to attain such renown. Writing in the journal *Theater und Kunst* in 1925, Leopold Jacobson notes, "Instead of a single favorite, one now has ten, and uniqueness has become commonplace."[9] The competition had become brutal, and, as Jacobson explains, "one or two failures mean that [a film star] is thrust into the background of the production line sooner than expected."[10] Established stars such as Nielsen not only found themselves competing with famous directors such as Fritz Lang for top billing, but also with dozens of emerging starlets, many of whom enjoyed only brief moments of fame before sinking into obscurity. Looking back at his career as a young film reporter in the 1920s and 1930s, Wolfgang Fischer recalls the popularity of the American star Priscilla Dean, the Norwegian heartthrob Gunnar Tolnæs, and Germany's sweetheart Lilian Harvey, but he also mentions dozens of others who had already been largely forgotten, among them Rita Clermont, Stella Harf, Leontine Kühnberg, and Lya Mara.[11] Achieving star status required extensive marketing, which studios were not always willing or able to provide, leaving it up to the individual actors to accomplish. Fischer tells of one relatively unknown actor who plastered his own picture on every advertising column and subway station wall in Berlin for weeks, and of actress Lee Parry throwing hundreds of photographs of herself into the audience at the premiere of one of her films at the Schauburg cinema palace.[12]

The parameters of stardom had also altered in postwar Germany. Media exploitation of a star's private life gradually became much more common than had previously been the case in Germany. Joseph Garncarz explains that, in contrast to Hollywood's eagerness to disseminate movie star gossip, German publicists had traditionally been very parsimonious with the private information they dispensed, refusing, for example, to disclose a star's eye color or the name of her spouse.[13] He explains that German stars "wanted to be respected as artists and not simply be adored for their charming personalities."[14] Although German fans generally respected this position and tended not to pose questions about taboo subjects such as a star's love life, the outward appearance of stars often served to reinforce certain ideas about their personalities. For example, Henny Porten's conservative bun and sensible clothes in the rational dress style confirmed her positioning as a "German mother" figure, while Nielsen's fashionable shingled hair and flapper-style dresses reaffirmed her liberated, cosmopolitan modernity.[15]

Toward the end of the 1920s, however, as UFA's ties to Hollywood tightened in the wake of the Parufamet agreement of 1925, magazines with ties to UFA began to adopt a more American fanzine style of revealing more personal information about stars, following the position expressed by Dr. R. Roth in *Filmwoche* that "film stars do not have any 'private affairs.' They must not be allowed to have any. To whom they are engaged, to whom they are married, whom they divorce and why, and why there are no children—all this must be openly discussed in public."[16] For Nielsen, this meant that while her marriages to and divorces from both Urban Gad and Freddy Wingårdh had passed largely without commentary in the press, her long-term common-law relationship with Grigori Chmara, from the mid-1920s until the late 1930s, was a matter of public interest.

Yet Nielsen had long been the darling of the German press, a tendency that intensified during the Weimar era and prompted most reporters to maintain a respectful distance. The tone of most German media accounts of Nielsen in the 1910s had been enthusiastic, but in the 1920s they begin to demonstrate distinct hagiographic tendencies, praising Nielsen not only for her acting ability but also for her general brilliance and legendary status. The final sentence of Béla Balázs's profile of Nielsen in 1924 is characteristic of this effusiveness: "Lower the flags before her, for she is incomparable and unequaled."[17] Taking stock of the state of German art after World War I, the authors of *Our Time* (*Unsere Zeit*) express gratitude to "our Danish neighbors" for Nielsen, whom they describe as "an emissary who combines all feminine attractions and in addition—how extravagant Mother Nature often can be to chosen individuals!—must also be called a divinely favored actress, an artist equally distinguished by her delightful personal charm and her rare, perfect gift for pantomime."[18] Looking back in 1971, the Weimar-era film critic Willy Haas enthused that Nielsen was "the great genius of the silent film era. But she was more than that. She was a magician, a beautiful witch. She could transform her face whenever and however she desired."[19] Even as many new competitors challenged Nielsen's preeminence among film stars, the adulation of journalists and film critics ensured that her legend would endure.

Film critics occupied an increasingly important position in public discourses about not just film but also artistic, social, and political issues in general. Rather than the anonymous reviews of films or the use of only an author's initials that were common before the war, individual film critics, such as Haas and Fischer, became recognizable names, acquiring a degree of celebrity akin to that of the stars they wrote about. On one occasion, Haas had to resort to publishing an inquiry in *Film-Kurier* in January 1921 in an attempt to discover the identity of the admirer who had sent him a magnificent New Year's basket full of delicacies.[20] By virtue of their position as interpreters of the country's most popular objects of entertainment, film critics established themselves as authorities on questions of aesthetic and moral significance. Sabine Hake explains,

> Writing about film meant writing about mass culture and class society, questions of national and sexual identity, and the experience of modernity. Early German film criticism fulfilled a double function. It promoted and evaluated films, and it used their narratives to discuss problems relevant to culture and society at large.[21]

Nielsen's films tended to be popular with critics not only because of their high degree of artistry but also because of their social content, both factors that lent themselves to productive analysis by film critics. Her realistic filmic explorations of national and sexual identity constructions illustrated the challenges particular to modern, urban society and resonated with the critics' own interrogation of the experience of modernity.

Early German film criticism was deeply concerned with the question of the effects of this new mass media phenomenon on German culture. The cinema was frequently blamed for negative health effects, ranging from blindness to venereal disease,[22] as well as for posing a "threat to the emotional and intellectual well-being of the nation's youth."[23] While some critics feared the power of film to convey propagandistic ideological messages, others felt that it was a mindless pursuit that commercialized art and thereby cheapened it. The question of whether the cinema should strive to belong to high (generally defined as educated) culture or whether it was irrevocably bound up with low (generally defined as popular) culture recurs frequently in early film criticism. Competing developments within German cinema during the 1920s illustrated the tension between these two cultural spheres, with the most popular genres, such as war movies, mountain movies, and military comedies, competing with more aesthetically sophisticated and experimental projects, for example Robert Wiene's now legendary proto-Expressionist film *The Cabinet of Dr. Caligari / Das Cabinet des Dr. Caligari* (1920), sweeping historical dramas, including Ernst Lubitsch's *Anna Boleyn* (1920), and ambitious literary adaptations, such as F. W. Murnau's *Nosferatu* (1922), which was based on Bram Stoker's *Dracula*.

The majority of Nielsen's films from the 1920s belong to the category of German art film for which the Weimar era has since become famous, though it was not the most popular or profitable genre at the time. Capitalizing on the continued popularity of Scandinavian modern literature, Nielsen was involved in making film adaptations of several of the most iconic texts of the Scandinavian Modern Breakthrough and other modernist authors, drawing attention to her connections to Scandinavia and modernity far more explicitly than she had done in her prewar films. Her many film adaptations from this period include Strindberg's *Intoxication / Rausch* (Lubitsch, 1919), Fyodor Dostoevsky's *The Idiot / Irrende Seelen* (Carl Froelich, 1921), Strindberg's *Miss Julie / Fräulein Julie* (Felix Basch, 1922), Stendhal's *Vanina* (Arthur von Gerlach, 1922), Frank Wedekind's *Earth-Spirit / Erdgeist* (Leopold Jessner, 1922), Zweig's *The House by the Sea / Das Haus am Meer* (Fritz Kaufmann, 1924), Ibsen's *Hedda Gabler*

Figure 5.1. Nielsen capitalized on both the popularity of modern Scandinavian literature and the high-culture aspirations of the German film industry in the 1920s with several film adaptations of iconic texts of the Scandinavian Modern Breakthrough, including Ibsen's *Hedda Gabler,* pictured here. Credit: The Danish Film Institute, Stills Archive

(Franz Eckstein, 1925), and Karin Michaëlis's *The Dangerous Age / Das gefährliche Alter* (Eugen Illés, 1927). Such film adaptations were considered by many critics to be an effective means of elevating the status of film and gaining the approval of German intellectuals, who gradually overcame their disdain for the cinema in the 1920s in order to maintain their hold on the educated middle class "as a customer in the cultural marketplace."[24] In the later years of the decade, Nielsen starred in some of the most powerful and unforgettable examples of the Weimar street film, notably *The Joyless Street / Die freudlose Gasse* (G. W. Pabst, 1925), *Lusts of Mankind / Laster der Menschheit* (Rudolf Meinert, 1927), and *A Tragedy of the Streets / Dirnentragödie* (Bruno Rahn, 1927).

Nielsen's first postwar film, *Intoxication*, which she made with director Ernst Lubitsch in 1919, was also her first attempt at a film version of a modernist text, Strindberg's play *Crimes and Crimes (Brott och brott)*. The film was only moderately successful, but even its modest success was due largely to Nielsen's involvement. In his review of the film in *Film-Kurier* on July 11, 1919, B. E. Lüthge explains that just as Strindberg's talents elevated a banal story into a brilliant play, the film's cheap sensationalism is redeemed only by Nielsen's artistry: "Film is a curious thing. A young art form can only be improved by a great artist. But we now possess the artist who is capable of resolving this problem. That artist is *die Nielsen*."[25] In this reviewer's opinion, Nielsen's many years of screen-acting experience more than compensated for her relatively advanced age (for a film actress) of thirty-eight.

The new director-centric orientation of the German film industry meant that the experience of filming *Intoxication* was a fairly negative one for Nielsen, because of the lack of input she was allowed in the making of the film. Although she had approved an early version of the screenplay adapted by Svend Gade, the final screenplay, adapted by Hanns Kräly, had little to do with Strindberg's play. She complained to a journalist, "I protested, commented explicitly that I thought we had gathered to film Strindberg, and emphasized that it was not an unknown name to be exploited, but in vain. They didn't care at all about the author . . . and just wanted a series of impressive pictures like the Americans."[26] Lubitsch publicly disagreed, and the conflict between them became a matter of public interest. A column in *Film-Kurier* in October 1920 summarizes the dispute, quoting both Nielsen's complaints about the decline in the artistry of German filmmaking and Lubitsch's response that Nielsen's discontentment was due to a misconception about the nature of film. Lubitsch is quoted as exclaiming, "The real Strindberg cannot be filmed! Strindberg's art lies in the psychological, while the art of film is the optical. Psychological problems cannot be filmed!"[27] Ultimately, the author of the article sided with Lubitsch, arguing that German film demonstrated great improvement in both technique and artistry, but professing tremendous admiration for Nielsen nonetheless. Although a fairly trivial matter, the debate highlights both the reduced influence of actors on the filmmaking process, which Nielsen resented, and her unshakeable focus on the aesthetic quality of her films.[28]

In addition to artistry, Nielsen was also concerned with the social messages her films conveyed, particularly the representation of how female identity is affected by modern urban life. The epoch of the "New Woman" in Germany coincides almost exactly with the chronology of Nielsen's career, and Nielsen's screen persona was often associated with this image in the media.[29] Throughout the 1920s she continued to develop her screen persona of the emancipated modern woman, but from a more sobering perspective than before the war. However, Rainer Rother notes that Nielsen herself defied stereotyping as the "New Woman"; instead of conforming to an existing trend, she both anticipated and shaped it,[30] in particular through her cinematic explorations of sexual and gender identity.

In place of her earlier persona of the willful girl who playfully swapped ages, national identities, and genders, Nielsen now opted for more serious and nuanced portrayals of female identity, pitting various incarnations of independent, norm-transgressing modern women against traditional notions of docile femininity, yet also showing how modern women's options are still limited by their age and beauty. Although most German women had not yet embraced such radical views of women's sexual emancipation as they witnessed on-screen, Nielsen provided her viewers with glimpses of the social and emotional costs of such choices, ranging from Miss Julie's desperate suicide to Hedda Gabler's defiant one.

Nielsen's later films reprise the discomfiting Scandinavian naturalism that aroused debate among German theater audiences in the 1880s and 1890s, depicting the darker, rougher side of the modern life she had celebrated in her earlier films. Her characters in the 1920s tend to be fallen women, no longer confident and strong, but broken and defeated by society, time, and financial desperation. In her Weimar films, Nielsen frequently depicted prostitutes who, despite

Figure 5.2. Nielsen's interest in the socially realistic agenda of the modernist literature promoted by Brandes enlivens her stark performance as a down-on-her-luck aging prostitute in the Weimar street film *A Tragedy of the Streets*. Credit: The Danish Film Institute, Stills Archive

the degradation of their situation, are determined to fight for their happiness and ultimately end up murdering their rivals for a man's love. The noted film critic Siegfried Kracauer commented that Nielsen "portrayed the prostitute incomparably: not a realistic one, but that imaginary figure of an outcast who has discarded social conventions because of her abundance of love, and now, through her mere existence, defies the questionable laws of a hypocritical society."[31] Perhaps not coincidentally, film critics in the 1910s and early 1920s often made mention of the presence of prostitutes among cinema audiences. Miriam Hansen explains, "The image of the prostitute was actually used for the cinema as a whole—typical of the opportunistic double standard that characterized the attitude of the cultural bourgeoisie towards an openly commercial (venal) art."[32] Although such preconceptions of the lower-class origins of cinema-goers and the attendant disdain for film as a profitable art form had become passé by the mid-1920s, Nielsen's female characters enact the dichotomy of attraction and contempt that once characterized both the bourgeoisie's opinion of the cinema and the abstract projection of female identity it enshrined.

The first film Nielsen made with her new production company, Art Film, is also one of the most striking examples of her ability to combine virtuoso acting with the exploration of existential questions, while still managing to make a statement about both national identity and women's emancipation. Filmed in 1920, it is a groundbreaking adaptation of the story of Hamlet, Prince of Denmark, perhaps the most famous Dane of all time, with Nielsen playing the title role. Although *Hamlet* was hardly a modern subject even when first dealt with by Shakespeare, in Nielsen's hands it becomes an uncompromising exploration of contemporary issues of sexuality, gender, politics, and nationalism. Despite the dire predictions of some critics, Nielsen's *Hamlet: A Drama of Vengeance / Hamlet: Ein Rachedrama* (Svend Gade, 1920), which was directed by fellow Danish expatriate Svend Gade and premiered in Berlin's Mozart Hall on February 4, 1921, was both an artistic and commercial success in Germany and abroad. Guido Haller, writing for the trade journal *Der Kinematograph,* hailed it as Nielsen's best film;[33] *Film-Kurier* quoted the Italian publisher Eugenio Bogiano-Pico as exclaiming, "I have never seen a better film! Asta Nielsen as Hamlet is a phenomenon. I regard this woman as one of the most important personalities of our time!"[34]

Almost uniquely among Nielsen's post-WWI films, *Hamlet* was released in the United States to general critical acclaim.[35]

Several film versions of Hamlet had already been produced even at this early stage of film history, including a short film shot at Elsinore Castle by August Blom for Nordisk in 1910, but Nielsen's was groundbreaking for the simple fact that she was not just a woman playing the part of a man, as Sarah Bernhardt had done on film in 1900, but a woman playing the part of a woman pretending to be a man. Critics protested that Nielsen's female Hamlet would desecrate Shakespeare, but Nielsen insisted that her Hamlet adaptation was not based on Shakespeare. Instead, she claimed to be returning to the original Hamlet legend as recounted by the medieval Danish historian Saxo Grammaticus and supported by the arguments of an obscure American Shakespeare scholar, Edward P. Vining. Although the film's narrative is a pastiche of Saxo, Vining, Shakespeare, and Nielsen's own notions, her insistence on an original Danish source for her retelling of Hamlet is significant. *Hamlet* is an iconic text for the perception of Danish identity in the Western world, and in choosing to play Hamlet, Nielsen positioned herself as representative of Denmark. However, her depiction of Denmark is as disturbingly modern as her interpretation of Vining's theory is liberal—in his *Mystery of Hamlet,* he states that "some men (like our prince) are perfectly female in temperament and therefore irresolute, impulsive, sharp-tongued, and as averse to women as they are attracted to men,"[36] but stops short of actually declaring Hamlet a woman. Although Nielsen cites Vining in several interviews and newspaper articles as her source for depicting Hamlet as a woman, her reading both goes beyond Vining's hypothesis and disregards his implicit allegation of Hamlet's homosexuality.

In Nielsen's filmic version of the famous story, Hamlet's female gender is a biological fact, one that must be obscured for reasons of state but which endows the film with layers of tension and innuendo. At the beginning of the film, Hamlet's father, the king of Denmark, is engaged in battle against the king of Norway while Hamlet is being born. Soon after the birth of her baby girl, news reaches Gertrude that her husband has been killed; in order to ensure the succession to the throne, she announces that the newborn baby is male. By the time the king returns home, wounded but still alive, it is too late to retract the announcement, so the young princess is raised as a boy. She attends school at Wittenberg, where she masters swordplay and scholarship, while carousing with fellow students Fortinbras, Laertes,

Figure 5.3. In her performance as Hamlet, Prince of Denmark, Nielsen both underscored her representative Danishness and delivered a masterful, gender-þending performance as a woman required for dynastic reasons to live as a man, including courting Ophelia even though her heart belonged to Horatio. Credit: The Danish Film Institute, Stills Archive

and Horatio. Her disguise allows her access to both an education and a privileged male fellowship that would be denied her in feminine clothes.

The fact that Hamlet's freedom comes at the price of her own femininity transforms the story into a parable about modernity and female identity. Nielsen's treatment of gender issues is unrepentantly modern and provocative. Tony Howard notes that the other female characters, Gertrude and Ophelia, are turned into "grotesques": "Ophelia becomes a caricature of naivety and Gertrude a darkening image of voracious desire,"[37] while Hamlet herself appears as "a polymorphic woman in a stereotyped world."[38] Although a historical anachronism, Nielsen's Hamlet is the embodiment of the "New Woman," who was often depicted, both seriously and in caricatures, as androgynous or masculinized in appearance, while retaining the feelings of a woman. Anne Jerslev points out that Nielsen's Hamlet wears a tight bodysuit throughout the film, which both emphasizes the boyishness of her figure and the fact that she is a woman, thereby situating the duality of Hamlet's gender at the visual center of the film.[39] Hamlet's unacknowledged attraction to Horatio endows several scenes with sexual tension, and when he later confesses his attraction to Ophelia, Hamlet decides to pretend to court Ophelia herself in order to prevent Horatio from doing so. Confronted by her mother, Hamlet bemoans her impossible situation, crying out, "I am not a man! And must not be a woman!" The relevance of this dilemma to the feminist movement during the 1920s and today is unmistakable, as it poignantly poses the question of what sacrifices a woman must make in order to succeed in a male-dominated world and demonstrates that gender is both socially and performatively constructed.

The political side of the story demonstrates Hamlet's keen intelligence and command of statecraft, despite the traditional handicap of her gender. Returning home upon her father's death, Hamlet discovers her mother's remarriage and her uncle's treachery. No ghost warns her, but a gardener tips her off that snake venom killed her father, and later she finds Claudius's dagger beside the snake pit below the castle. The film's most powerful scenes take place in its latter half, when Hamlet wrestles with the question of how to avenge her father's murder. She grasps at "the subversive freedom of madness"[40] and plays the fool while laying her plans. After a diplomatic voyage to Norway that costs Rosenkrantz and Guildenstern their heads, Hamlet confronts her uncle and avenges her father, by trapping Claudius in the cellar room where he has been carousing, then setting it on fire. According to Howard,

> Asta Nielsen's Hamlet was more remorseless than any man's. She easily repels Claudius when he staggers awake and seizes her throat; she seals the door, leaving him to choke in the smoke of a personal hell with Expressionist zig-zag lightning on the walls. Thus Nielsen dismantles Shakespeare's ending: Hamlet has revenged her father's death on Claudius easily; now she must face her mother and take revenge for her own life.[41]

Through her mother's treachery, she is poisoned during her duel with Laertes, just as Gertrude dies of her own poison. Horatio, groping to stanch the wound in Hamlet's chest, discovers the secret of her physiology and suddenly understands the true nature of her love for him, crying out, "Hamlet, my beloved Hamlet. Death reveals thy tragic secret. Now I understand what bound me to that matchless form and feature—your true heart was a woman's," but it is too late; she is dead.

Nielsen's *Hamlet* continues a distinguished international tradition of female Hamlets, both on stage and on screen, from Sarah Siddons in eighteenth-century London to Sarah Bernhardt in a short film of the duel scene shown at the World's Fair in Paris in 1900, but it goes far beyond her predecessors in its contributions to contemporary discourses of women's emancipation, particularly the question of sexual identity. Judith Buchanan suggests that this long history of women playing Hamlet is due to the fact that, because of Hamlet's "thoughtfulness, sensitivity, capriciousness, vulnerability, and indecision," the "role lent itself to female actorly appropriation."[42]

The added dimension of Nielsen's insistence on Hamlet's actual female gender transforms Hamlet's predicament from that of an effeminate man struggling to retain his throne to that of a woman struggling to come to terms with her own gender identity. The film's challenges to gender stereotypes, in both comic and tragic ways, render it unmistakably modern, despite the antiquity of the tale. Howard explains that while all other cross-dressing Shakespearean heroines voluntarily adopt their disguises, Nielsen's Hamlet has no choice: "Nielsen shows first the arbitrary construction of gender—Hamlet is 'male' because she is trained to be—and then its instability.... Yet if Hamlet's masquerade both liberates and destroys her, the film is framed by our knowledge that what we are watching is Nielsen rewriting the canon to break 'the iron laws of gender.'"[43] Even as Nielsen's Hamlet breaks medieval gender rules in fraternizing with male students at Wittenberg and dueling, Nielsen herself challenged the patriarchal hegemony of the contemporary film industry by daring to craft her own roles and produce her own films, rather than deferring to directors and studios.

Unlike her prewar "breeches parts" (*Hosenrollen*), where crossdressing usually functioned as a comic device, Nielsen's Hamlet is a serious figure whose gender ambiguity is both painful and provocative. With her sensitive, expressive face and assertive, violent behavior, she supports constructs of both male and female identity. Rüdiger Schaper explains, "Asta Nielsen, as a man, demonstrated a modern female identity type. [She is] a knight with a slender, seductive figure, sharp nose, shaded eyes, and narrow, sensual mouth. [She is] a vision of the metropolitan night, before a medieval backdrop. Asta Nielsen could have been the inspiration for Virginia Woolf's *Orlando* novel of 1928."[44] Patrice Petro agrees with this estimation of the inspirational effect of Nielsen's androgyny, noting that her "appropriation of masculine styles and gestures and, in the case of *Hamlet* (1921), male identity, . . . [made her] a figure of sexual mobility—a figure who destabilizes the polarized opposition between masculine and feminine identities."[45] The film raises the stakes even higher by placing Nielsen's Hamlet in a series of sexually fraught situations—"at once heterosexual (the heroine loves Horatio), homosexual (Hamlet loves Horatio), heterosexual again (Hamlet woos Ophelia), and lesbian (Asta Nielsen woos Ophelia)"[46]—that explore the complex nature and infinite variations of desire.

In addition to positioning Nielsen as a pioneering figure for queer studies, *Hamlet* proved to be a media coup for Nielsen that once again brought both her acting and her Danish identity to the public's attention. The film's controversial premise ensured that it received extensive press coverage, even well before it premiered. Both Nielsen and screenwriter Erwin Gepard defended the film in frequent newspaper articles, with Gepard arguing in one column, "Who today is more suited to giving new life to Hamlet than Asta Nielsen, whose deepest longings are for the favorite hero of her homeland?"[47] The daily industry newspaper *Film-Kurier* emphasized this connection in the headline of the lead article on July 16, 1920, which read "From Denmark to the Moon,"[48] and July 30, 1920, which proclaimed, "Asta Nielsen—Prince of Denmark."[49] Nielsen's Danish citizenship was also prominent in the way the film was presented to American audiences, although *Hamlet* was only released in New York City. In contrast to the 1910s, when she was often described in American reviews as "the most prominent German actress" or "the German Bernhardt,"[50] reviews of *Hamlet* in the *Morning Telegraph*, the *Evening Telegram*, and the *New York Tribune* of November 8–9, 1921, repeatedly refer to Nielsen as the "Danish tragedienne."[51]

Although the film's artistic merits and the brilliance of Nielsen's performance were praised by critics across Europe and the United States, nationalistic tensions complicated its reception in both the United States and Denmark. In *Der Film*, Nielsen's *Hamlet* is proudly hailed as "a sign of the success of the German film industry in foreign countries,"[52] but none of the American reviews mention the film's German connections. *Film-Kurier* reported that *Hamlet* was being marketed in the United States as a Danish film,[53] most likely to avoid running afoul of residual anti-German sentiment. A similar anti-German attitude, although more economically motivated, pervades the film's Danish reception, even though a large part of the cast had Scandinavian connections: Asta Nielsen, director Svend Gade, and cameraman Axel Graatkjær were all Danes, while Nielsen's costars Lilly Jacobsson (Ophelia) and Anton de Verdier (Laertes) were Swedes who lived in Denmark and worked for Nordisk.

Yet although Danish audiences, including Georg Brandes, attended the film in droves, Danish critics, while acknowledging Nielsen's virtuosity, were generally dismissive of the film. They judged it, aside from Nielsen's performance, to be either ridiculous or poorly acted, and denounced it as a "tasteless German film"[54] and a plagiarism of Shakespeare.[55] One reviewer explained that Danish audiences, "in typical contrast to German ones," could not enjoy a film that relied so heavily on the main character's performance.[56] A German review in *B. Z. am Mittag* took note of the negative Danish press coverage, which it called "idiocy" and attributed to a competitive attitude toward the flourishing German film industry, as well as the "jealousy, gossip, and envy" that flourishes in every small community and from which Germany needed to protect Nielsen.[57]

Although the Danish critiques were not personal attacks on Nielsen, a letter to Henning Brøchner dated February 3, 1921, reveals that she shared the German journalist's opinion that Danish opposition to her films was rooted, at least in part, in petty nationalism:

> If anyone finds *this* film tasteless simply because it was filmed in Germany, then they are in a mess that can only have politics behind it, in which case all protests are useless. . . . If I take the Danish press

seriously in this case, then it has paid me a great compliment, for I am proud to have my film bear the label "Made in Germany": it has always been my goal to rise, through tireless work, to a level commensurate with the larger circumstances here. This is the reason I have chosen to work here rather than in Denmark, where it is common knowledge that all trees in the forest are required to be the same height.[58]

Behind the cloak of national self-interest, the widely admired Danish national character traits of equality and self-sufficiency show themselves here from a less positive angle, as socially mandated mediocrity and politically motivated resentment of Nielsen's success in Germany. As she explained to a group of Danish women journalists in a 1946 speech, Nielsen saw her international career as a patriotic act that "gave me the chance to carry Denmark's name beyond its borders,"[59] but over the course of the 1920s, Danish criticism (or outright rejection, in some cases) of Nielsen's work gradually became more targeted at Nielsen herself, as well as at the often distressingly modern image of Danish identity that she presented to the world.

Building on the success of *Hamlet*, Nielsen devoted her energy to starring in and producing a series of film versions of modernist texts, many of which thematize the harsh social consequences for women who assert their sexuality. In each of these films, Nielsen enacts the pleasures and penalties of sexual emancipation on screen, establishing a close association between the modernity of her roles and her own professional persona, although she continued to play young women well into her forties. Her compelling performances as iconic modern women in such films as *Miss Julie*, *Erdgeist*, and *Hedda Gabler* illustrate her statement that "I am what I play, completely."[60] Howard suggests that "*Hamlet* had freed her to explore gender and entrapment from unprecedented angles.... She made Hedda a repressed Dresden figurine; her Lulu, in geometrical jazz-age costumes, was Expressionist and angular, snapping between arch seduction and *ennui*."[61] In a similar vein, Balázs commented about *Erdgeist* that "the content of the film is the erotic charisma of this woman, who demonstrates the vast, complete lexicon of the actions of sensual love."[62]

In the decades after Nielsen retired from the silver screen, the press took Nielsen's words about being what she played at face value. Many retrospective newspaper accounts tend to conflate Nielsen as an individual with the unconventional but unhappy modern women she chose to depict in this period, rather than considering the ways in which Nielsen used film to contribute to contemporary discourses of women's liberation. By way of example, an article in the *Süddeutsche Zeitung* in 1961 explains, "In principle, she [Nielsen] was always only a Hedda Gabler, a woman who wanted to live her own life outside the rules of society. Asta was simultaneously the nightmare and fantasy of the bourgeoisie."[63] Unfortunately for scholars and film aficionados, the prints of many of her most iconically "modern" films have been lost, including her *Miss Julie* and *Hedda Gabler*, but still photographs and contemporary reviews provide insight into how Nielsen claimed these texts as her own. For example, her version of *Miss Julie* incorporated an additional three acts detailing Julie's unhappy childhood and disastrously unconventional upbringing by her mother, played by Lina Lossen.[64] As Birgitte Søland points out in *Becoming Modern*, the optimistic narrative identifying the 1920s as the era when women achieved political, economic, and sexual liberation falters in the face of feminist scholarship that has revealed how superficial, limited, and even illusory many of these gains for women actually were.[65] While the 1920s was a pivotal period in the struggle for women's rights, Nielsen's later films remind us that it was very much a struggle, not a triumphal processional, and that many women were casualties in the fight.

Some of Nielsen's most memorable films from the 1920s belong to the genre of Weimar street film, which, in keeping with the realistic aesthetic of postwar German New Objectivity, "concentrate[d] more directly on the conflict between the upper and lower classes and addresse[d] typical urban problems such as bad housing, poverty, unemployment, violence, and discrimination."[66] Weimar street films presented a particularly bleak view of women's options in a time of economic hardship. In general, ideals of emancipation give way to depictions of the harsh realities of survival and a reaffirmation of the importance of female sexual morality. One of Nielsen's best-remembered films, *The Joyless Street*, which was, coincidentally, the only film she made with Greta Garbo and Garbo's only German film, belongs to this genre.

Although the film was instrumental in launching Garbo's American career, critics and film scholars have long debated whether the film was primarily a star vehicle for Garbo or whether Nielsen's role is the more significant one. Looking back on his own changing perceptions of the film, Willy Haas, who wrote the screenplay for the film, confessed:

Figure 5.4. Thanks to its high-profile director and the involvement of rising Swedish star Greta Garbo, *The Joyless Street* is often regarded as one of Nielsen's most important later films. Even though her role is comparatively minor, it does afford her the opportunity to demonstrate her remarkable ability to convey powerful emotions with minimal facial movement. Credit: The Danish Film Institute, Stills Archive

> [I] recognized more clearly each time, that it was not Greta Garbo, but rather the much older Asta Nielsen who had achieved the great dramatic triumph, that she played the actual leading role, without particular effort aside from her power, while the "divine Garbo" collected the applause of the evening with a few enchanting glances from beneath her lashes. It was a duel between ravishing beauty and simple, overwhelming genius that played out on the screen on this evening.[67]

The contrast between Nielsen and Garbo's roles in the film reflects the diametrically opposed screen personas the actresses cultivated: Nielsen consistently opted for artistically challenging roles that would allow her to articulate social messages, while Garbo tended to concentrate on showcasing her physical attractiveness.

The screenplay of *The Joyless Street*, adapted by Haas from Hugo Bettauer's novel about the miserable living conditions in postwar Vienna, tells the story of two young women who are drawn into the Viennese underworld by financial desperation. In essence, the film tells two contrasting stories about the fate of women in an urban environment. While Nielsen's character, the working-class girl Maria Lechner, sinks into prostitution to raise money for Egon, the man she loves, Garbo's Grete Rumfort, the refined daughter of an unemployed bureaucrat, is saved from the street in the nick of time by a dashing American Red Cross officer. Petro interprets these two separate but interrelated dramas as reflecting the differences between German and American expressionism.[68] The virtuous Grete is selflessly prepared to sacrifice herself to save her father from financial ruin and is rewarded for her courage, while Maria flees into Egon's arms in order to escape her abusive father and is punished by Egon's faithlessness for giving into desire. Yet Maria does not surrender to her fate; determined to defend her interests, she murders her rival and blames Egon for the crime. Although Maria ultimately confesses to the crime to allow Egon to go free, she still represents, according to Petro, "the repressed anger that seeks expression in the text," which is evident in the final scenes of the film, when crowds of angry women seek revenge on the madame of the brothel and on a butcher who has exploited their poverty for sexual favors.[69] Garbo's character remains chaste but dependent on men, while Nielsen's character sacrifices her virtue and ultimately her freedom, but acts decisively and takes responsibility for her actions and their tragic consequences.

The German reception of *The Joyless Street* was positive, particularly among film critics, but the Danish reception was markedly unenthusiastic, with several references to the negative, peculiarly German, aspects of the film. A review in *Nationaltidende* in March 1926 reported that the audience hissed loudly at the film;[70] *Politiken* described it as "German fasting food";[71] and another review in *Berlingske Tidende* predicted that the film would not enjoy a long run, since the film demonstrates "a German realism that Danish audiences will find both ugly and tasteless."[72] It is of course ironic that Danish critics should take exception to the very same type of gritty realism on film that had been introduced into German literature by Brandes and the Scandinavian writers of the Modern Breakthrough in the late nineteenth century, but contemporary notions of modernist aesthetics had shifted enough to make those of Brandes's heyday seem outdated.

Just as German critics in 1879 had objected to the shocking outcome of Ibsen's play *A Doll's House* (*Et Dukkehjem*), forcing the writer to craft a new ending in which Nora repents her decision to leave her husband and children, Danish critics in 1926 objected to Nielsen's uncompromising, thoroughly unromantic depiction of the bleak fate of a girl forced into prostitution by socioeconomic circumstances. The increasingly conservative and culturally pessimistic orientation of the Danish bourgeoisie in the 1920s, which represented one of the poles in the "life view debate" (*livsanskuelsesdebat*) that pervaded Danish intellectual circles in this period,[73] had the effect of rendering the birthplace of the Modern Breakthrough hostile or, at the very least, indifferent to the very cultural modernity it had once fostered.

Although it is not as well-crafted a film as *The Joyless Street*, Nielsen's film version of Danish author Karin Michaëlis's controversial novel *The Dangerous Age* (*Den farlige Alder*, 1910) confirms the boldness of Nielsen's social agenda as well as her deliberate self-identification with Scandinavian cultural modernity. Radical for its time, the novel focuses on the emotional and sexual needs of a middle-aged woman, Elsie Lindtner, who divorces her husband and takes up with a younger man, only to send him away when she realizes that she will soon be old and his affection for her will fade. Although not as well known today as the works of Ibsen and Strindberg, the grand old men of Scandinavian modern literature, Michaëlis's work was immensely provocative and successful both in Denmark and Germany in the early twentieth century. Michaëlis was in the vanguard of a new generation of modern Danish writers, many of whom Nielsen had encountered in Emma Gad's home, making this a particularly appropriate text for Nielsen to film. August Blom made the first cinema adaptation of Michaëlis's novel for Nordisk already in 1911, but it diverges considerably from the novel, transforming the story into a programmatic erotic melodrama in which Elsie seduces and marries her daughter's fiancé, only to abandon him for an Italian singer. Just before Elsie dies, she is reconciled to her daughter, but her jilted husband tries to defend his own honor and is killed in a duel with the Italian singer.

Nielsen, who was both a friend of the author and in the same stage of life as the female protagonist, made her film version of *The Dangerous Age* in 1927, with director Eugen Illés. The film's visual look is an iconic depiction of 1920s fashion, with all of the women sporting bobbed hair and flapper dresses with long strings of pearls, but the thematic exploration of the emotional plight of women as they age and lose their beauty is timeless.[74] Nielsen's film adaptation downplays the dissolute sexuality foregrounded in Blom's version in favor of a more nuanced exploration of the psychological journey Elsie undergoes, articulated by intertitles drawn directly from the novel. Elsie is unhappy in her marriage to an absent-minded professor and falls in love with her husband's favorite student, Jörgen Malte. Afraid of a scandal, she asks her husband for a divorce and he agrees graciously, telling Jörgen that he hopes he can make Elsie happier than he himself had been able to do. Elsie consummates her relationship with Jörgen, but finds herself jealous of his friendship with Magda, a fellow student.

Despite Jörgen's protestations that he will love her forever, Elsie comes to the realization that her age will always be a factor in their relationship and preemptively ends it. She writes in her journal, "I don't fear age, but rather the transition, when the call of the heart only arouses laughter. Youth only lasts as long as the skin is smooth and the body attractive. A woman who dares to demand the right to love at an advanced age is despised." Jörgen follows her out to a remote summer house to plead his case, but Elsie sends him away. By the time she repents her decision, Jörgen has begun a relationship with Magda. At the end, the film diverges from Michaëlis's novel by allowing Elsie a tender reunification with her husband, who confesses, "I was blind to my wife's inner life." This unexpectedly harmonious resolution lacks the tragic drama of the many other films in which Nielsen's characters' lives end in suicide, murder, or prison, but it articulates the belief that the reality of women's emancipation can

Figure 5.5. Given that August Strindberg's play *Miss Julie* premiered in Copenhagen because of strict Swedish theater censorship in the late nineteenth century, it is ironic that Nielsen's film adaptation of the play was banned by the Danish censorship board. Credit: The Danish Film Institute, Stills Archive

only come about in cooperation, rather than competition, with men, a view that had been the basic premise of the quintessentially modern Scandinavian efforts to achieve gender equality since Brandes's day.[75]

Yet, ironically, the more Nielsen identified herself on screen with Scandinavian cultural modernity, the more Danish society tried to disassociate itself from her. Having been stripped of its European network by the new German film distribution system, the Danish film industry was smarting from the loss of its prewar European prominence and, as a result of the war and the reinvigoration of nationalistic sentiment in connection with the 1920 referendum on Schleswig, becoming increasingly nationally oriented, while Danish society and politics took a sharply conservative turn in the early 1920s. Nielsen's choice to pursue a career in Germany, once unquestioningly accepted as the logical route to international success, was now widely viewed by Danes as repudiation of the Danish film industry and of Danish culture in general, while her films were regarded as promoting an unsettling immorality antithetical to Danish social mores. The parallels to Brandes's conflict with the Danish bourgeoisie over similar issues of morality and national identity in the 1880s (discussed in chapter 2) are striking, although in this case the international crisis that prompted Danish society's renewed inward turn was an economic as well as a political one.

More than half of the thirty-one films Nielsen made in Berlin between 1919 and 1926 were never screened in Denmark, although only three were officially banned by the Danish censors. In 1922, Nielsen's film version of *Miss Julie* was banned in Denmark, although Strindberg's play itself had initially premiered in Copenhagen in 1889 after being banned by Swedish censors. The Danish film censor's assessment of Nielsen's *Miss Julie*, that "the film is just as repulsive as the Strindbergian play . . . , a Swedish writer's filthy product,"[76] suggests that Danish society and aesthetics had become more rather than less conservative in the intervening three decades. The censor's disdain for Strindberg's work may also reflect the fact that the rivalry between the Danish and Swedish film industries had intensified during the 1920s, when both national cinemas faced stiff competition from Germany and the United States for a dwindling market share. Two years later, Nielsen's *Hedda Gabler* met a similar fate, despite the long-established respectability of Ibsen's work in Denmark.

Although Nielsen was considered a role model for Danes in her early films, her later films gave rise to concerns about their possible negative influence on a society already destabilized by the effects of World War I and the economic downturn Denmark experienced in the 1920s. When Nielsen's critically acclaimed film *Lusts of Mankind*, which tells the story of a drug-addicted singer who sacrifices herself to protect her daughter from her dealer, was banned in Denmark, Norway, and Sweden in 1927, the Danish censor explained to a film critic from the Copenhagen newspaper *B. T.* that the film's depiction of the miserable fate of a cocaine addict "can easily come to have the opposite effect of the one it aims for," and that the film was altogether "too instructive with regard to cocaine abuse."[77] The censor's comments about this specific film reveal a fundamental fear about cinema's capacity to blur the distinction between lived and observed reality, as well as concerned awareness of film's metacultural potential.

This disapproval was based not only on moral but also on political, economic, and aesthetic grounds. Although it had been commonplace for Danes to work in Germany since the Middle Ages, the heightened nationalistic climate of the 1920s and the reduced state of the Danish film industry meant that Danish critics and audiences were particularly critical of Nielsen's perceived disloyalty to Denmark by working in Germany. Ib Monty argues, "It was in Germany that she became world famous, and we in Denmark have never forgiven her for it."[78] As had been the case with Brandes, it was not even necessarily anti-German sentiment that poisoned the well of Danish public opinion, but a more fundamental anti-internationalism and patriotic provincialism. In a 1922 article, Danish journalist Andreas Winding explains, with reference to Nielsen's costar in *The Abyss*, "Poul Reumert remained loyal to the Danish theater, Asta Nielsen chose the world."[79] Similarly, an article by Christian Engelstoft in *Aftenbladet* on November 27, 1927, bears the title "Asta Nielsen, the Actress who Abandoned her Fatherland" and the subtitle "Born in [the working-class Copenhagen district] Nørrebro—as the daughter of a washerwoman—Asta Nielsen became the first great artist of the cinema. Her fame has spread around the entire world, but she never quite managed to conquer her fatherland."[80] Although the title seems to suggest that Engelstoft approves of Denmark's unenthusiastic attitude toward Nielsen, the article itself expresses the author's perplexity over the lukewarm reception given to the most illustrious movie star Denmark had produced.

Another factor in the disinterest of Danish audiences in Nielsen's later films is the question of genre. Danish audiences were simply less interested in the serious, literary films Nielsen made after the war than they had been in her earlier romantic dramas and comedies. American films constituted between 64 and 70 percent of Danish cinema programming in the 1920s,[81] while the few successful Danish films produced during this period were slapstick comedies, often starring the duo Fyrtårnet (lighthouse) and Bivognen (sidecar), played by Carl Schenstrøm and Harald Madsen and known in Germany and elsewhere as Pat and Patachon. Dressed in torn, vagabond clothes with rope belts, Fy and Bi made more than fifty films together, including thirteen produced outside of Denmark, and became nearly as popular as Charlie Chaplin, in Denmark at least. Even Urban Gad, Nielsen's ex-husband and former director, jumped on the bandwagon; his final film was the Fy and Bi vehicle *The Wheel of Fortune / Lykkehjulet* (Gad, 1926). The enduring popularity of comedic cinema in Denmark beyond the 1920s is evidenced by the fact that one of the brightest stars of Danish cinema in the 1930s was the fresh-faced comedienne Marguerite Viby, who got her start with roles in four Fy and Bi films. Nielsen's weighty social and literary dramas held little attraction for audiences accustomed to such frothy fare.

In contrast to the many positive articles about Nielsen and her early films in the prewar Danish press, the media coverage of her work in Denmark in the 1920s and 1930s dwindled to a trickle and took on a somewhat supercilious tone, illustrating the increasing alienation between the star and her homeland. Although Danes were still aware of Nielsen's status as "the only world-renowned Danish name in cinema,"[82] they were increasingly resentful of her success in Germany and began to identify her as more German than Danish. Although the reviews of those of her films that were shown in Denmark tended to speak highly of her performance, a fundamental although subtle shift in Danish perceptions of Nielsen took place, as Stephan Michael Schröder argues, when the Danish press began to discursively "Germanize" her.[83] In the German press, as illustrated in the quote by Egon Jacobsohn in 1919 at the beginning of this chapter, Nielsen was commonly referred to, if not by her full name, as either "die Nielsen," in keeping with the German custom of referring to great actresses by their last names preceded by a definite pronoun, or, more rarely, "die Asta."

The Danish press in the 1910s generally spoke of Miss (*Frøken*) Asta Nielsen, Mrs. (*Fru*) Asta Nielsen (-Gad), or simply *Fru* Asta. Beginning in the early 1920s, however, it became increasingly common for Danish newspapers to refer to their famous countrywoman as "die

Asta."[84] Schröder points out that, although most Danes believed the term was simply adopted from German newspapers, it was used with much greater frequency by Danish writers from the 1920s on than it ever was in Germany, with the deliberate aim of expressing cultural distance from their most famous actress.[85] That the term was often used pejoratively by Danish critics, and understood as such by Danish audiences, is clear from the 1927 article in *B.T.* about the banning of Nielsen's latest film, where the author clarifies that he is speaking of the actress Asta Nielsen, "or, as she is known in her second fatherland, 'die Asta.'"[86] Danes reacted with irritation to Nielsen's oft-repeated acknowledgment that Germany had become "her second fatherland," which they increasingly took to mean that Germany was in fact the nation with which she identified herself.[87] Schröder suggests that Nielsen's use of the term "fatherland" rather than "nation" indicates an attempt to reject the prevailing nationalized discourse of identity in favor of an older model of patriotism, but to no avail.[88] The notion that Nielsen had chosen Germany over Denmark is implicit in the consistent Danish use of the moniker "die Asta," expressing Danish society's quid pro quo rejection of her.

This charge was not without a basis in reality, for Nielsen had developed a strong sense of loyalty to Germany over the years. During the 1910s, Nielsen had frequently traveled back to Denmark, both to visit family and scout out film locations, but in the 1920s she remained in Berlin the majority of the time. As she told an interviewer from *Politiken* while visiting Denmark in January 1930, "It is cozy and festive here [in Copenhagen], but there is nothing going on. Berlin is a whirlwind of art, work, and life."[89] The enthusiastic welcome she received from German fans upon her return in 1919 had also moved her, particularly in contrast to the restrained manner in which she was customarily treated in Denmark, while the repeated failure of the Danish industry to accommodate her abilities and ambition had reinforced how much she owed to the German film industry for the professional opportunities it had afforded her. In an interview with her old friend and colleague Olaf Fønss that appeared in *Politiken* on March 16, 1930, Nielsen explained why she regarded Germany as her home: "The country in which an artist has found work and activity—where she is understood and appreciated and where she thereby receives the spiritual nourishment and artistic stimulation that she *must* have in order to develop her art—*this* country must become her homeland."[90] In giving Germany its due for having provided her with professional opportunities and acceptance, Nielsen did not reject Denmark, but refused to limit herself to a single, rigid national identity.[91]

But although Nielsen's explanation of her attachment to Germany is logical, the negative Danish response to her was more emotionally laden than rational. In his article about Nielsen, Fønss is generous in his recognition of her accomplishments and fame, but chastises his readers for Denmark's small-minded unwillingness to give her the same credit:

> Asta Nielsen conquered the whole world—but not quite completely— for there was a small country that would not succumb—a country, most of whose inhabitants believe that one raises one's own status by not admiring others, and who greet those of their countrymen who have managed to create a name for themselves abroad with self-congratulatory skepticism and petty criticism—this little land, by whose walls censorship with scissors and pencil and the idiocy of the licensing system still grow like weeds, has never wanted to treat Asta Nielsen as she deserves.[92]

Ten years after Nielsen's letter to Henning Brøchner about her *Hamlet* film, in which she expressed her disgust for Danish insistence on "all trees in the forest [being] the same height," Fønss repeats the same criticism of the unwritten Danish social code, dubbed the "Jante Law" by Aksel Sandemose in 1933, that implicitly punishes those individuals who stood out from the masses.

By way of illustration, Fønss recounted an anecdote about the German actor Poul Wegener, who had attended a party in Copenhagen in the 1920s after the Danish premiere of one of his films. A close friend of Nielsen's, Wegener mentioned to some of the Danish actresses present that he had a picture in his pocket of their most famous actress. When they became curious and asked whom he meant, he said Asta Nielsen, and one of the actresses immediately replied, "God, do you really think she's something special? She's never been anything here in Denmark," while another commented, "Honestly, I think she's terrible—she has cow's eyes!"[93] After telling Fønss about the encounter, Wegener noted that he had heard more malicious gossip about Nielsen in the few hours he was at the party in Copenhagen than in the previous ten years in Berlin.

Although the much larger scale of German society meant that Nielsen did not have to endure the jealousy of her fellow Danes, her relationship with the German film industry was not without its challenges. The growing dominance of American film imports in Germany during the 1920s rendered it virtually impossible for an individual actress to exercise any significant degree of control over the production of her films. Although a 1925 law restricted imports to 50 percent of films shown, the financially unstable Universum Film AG (UFA) made a deal with Paramount and Metro-Goldwyn the same year, arranging to borrow four million dollars and, in return, dedicate 50 percent of the screen time in its German cinemas to American films.[94] In the meantime, Nielsen was losing interest in churning out films without aesthetic or sociopolitical value, as well as wearying of the burdens of film stardom. Confident in her own aesthetic judgment, Nielsen was known for being extremely selective about screenplays and outspoken in her criticism of the Americanization of German film, both of which made her unpopular with producers and film distributors.

In her autobiography, Nielsen offers her version of the events that precipitated her most serious breach with the German film industry. It came about in 1924, when Nielsen attended the premiere of her latest film, *The Butterfly Battle / Der Schmetterlingsschlacht* (Eckstein, 1924), in Leipzig, at the explicit request of the producer, National Films. Due to a poorly planned program, the film didn't finish until 1:30 A.M., after which Nielsen made her appearance, exhausted from a day of rehearsing for a live pantomime engagement, so that she "walked around almost like a sleepwalker." As she was sitting in her dressing room removing her makeup at 2 A.M., the theater director knocked on her door and told her that he and the film distributors were waiting for her in a nearby pub. She tendered a polite refusal on grounds of fatigue and went to bed. The next day, she was informed that the distributors, annoyed at her refusal to come, had decided to boycott her films. Although Nielsen was flabbergasted that they could be so juvenile, they followed through on their threat, she claimed, with the result that "no company dared to hire me, since the distributors refused either to finance the film, if that was required, or to accept it for distribution."[95] While the release dates of several of Nielsen's films fall in the period that she claimed to have been blacklisted, suggesting that the boycott was not absolute, this anecdote at least confirms that Nielsen resented being perceived as a servant who should be waiting at their beck and call, a situation that was closely connected to the centralization of the film industry in the hands of directors and producers.

This state of affairs lasted approximately two years, during which time both Nielsen and the representatives of the German film industry pretended indifference to each other, but their estrangement revealed fundamental differences of opinion over the kind of films produced and the way in which films should be made. Mariann Lewinsky explains that Nielsen and Weimar cinema "were incompatible and boycotted each other reciprocally." She continues,

> [Asta Nielsen] knew precisely what she no longer approved of in the film industry; for the first, she disliked the "vainglorious intellectual pomposity that was gaining ground," and second, that she was continually offered the same role, "in which I am to personify and defend sinfulness for the God-knows-how-many-th time." Thirdly, the "psyche of European films has been completely altered by the onslaught of the avalanche of American films. The excessive cutting has ruined every artistic accomplishment of the actor, leading to the golden age of dilettantism . . . two meters atmosphere, two meters gaze, one meter neck sprain."[96]

For Nielsen, film acting was not simply a job but a calling, yet the tendency in German film in the 1920s was toward greater compartmentalization of responsibility behind the scenes, which disempowered actors from shaping their own films.

Nielsen was not alone in her disapproval of the state of German film, and her long absences from the screen encouraged others to speak out as well. In 1926 film critic Herbert Jhering complained,

> Nothing makes the capitulation of European film to America more apparent than the fact that Asta Nielsen cannot find work these days. The female "type" preferred in American films, the smooth, round, smiling doll-face, has made such inroads into Europe that talented actresses like *die Nielsen* are no longer employed. . . . And that is a scandal.[97]

Although Nielsen was by no means the only actress affected by the shifting aesthetic paradigms of German cinema toward an American model, she was such a high-profile figure with such a loyal fan base that she became closely associated in the public mind with the artistic integrity of European cinema, in contrast to the perceived superficiality and homogeneity of American cinema.

Always pragmatic, Nielsen used her enforced hiatus from filmmaking to her own advantage and returned to her first love, stage acting, where she was finally able to command leading roles. She toured Germany and Austria in critically acclaimed productions of *Rita Cavallini*, written by Edward Sheldon (originally published as *Romance* in 1913), and Alexandre Dumas's *Lady of the Camellias*. Although her

German was, as most press coverage of her stage acting mentions, marred by her Danish accent and grammatical errors, it was irrelevant to her success, as both of the characters she played were foreigners as well. Critic Walter Kordt points out that neither piece is particularly well written, but he describes "die Nielsen's" performance as masterful, transforming mediocre, sentimental schmaltz into high art on stage as she had always done on screen. He gushes, "This talent was the most amazing thing about her films from the beginning. It elevated the most impossible screenplays into the realm of art, an art that contributed to determining the standard of European film."[98]

Nielsen had performed in stage pantomimes before the war, such as her production of *The Death of Prince Harlequin / Prinz Harlekins Tod* in Vienna in 1913, but her return to the stage in the mid-1920s was viewed as a momentous decision, affirming the value of the theater in an age when cinema had become predominant. The 1925/26 program of the Leipziger Schauspielhaus notes,

> Many important actors have moved from theater to film, without finding their way back to the stage. Now, after a brilliant and successful career, Asta Nielsen, the "Mother of Film," as she has been called, is appearing on the stage. Some will describe this as a victory of the stage over film, while others will claim that theater has finally become ready for film.[99]

Just as Nielsen's initial move from stage to screen had been seen as risky, her return to the stage a decade and a half later was an unusual choice for a film actress, particularly one who had not spoken a single word in any of her roles over the past fifteen years. Fortunately for her career, Nielsen managed the transition very well, despite the language obstacles. Anton Sahm, writing for the *Münchener Illustrierte Presse,* explained, "We were surprised to suddenly hear this woman, whose silent articulation of harrowing emotions made speech superfluous, speaking on stage; but the words, that sound charmingly foreign, are incidental."[100] Her much-vaunted expressiveness on screen proved equally captivating on the stage, regardless of her pronunciation of the text.

Despite the success of her theatrical endeavors, Nielsen returned to film in 1927, making five more films, including the above-mentioned *Lusts of Mankind, A Tragedy of the Streets,* and *The Dangerous Age.* However, her enthusiasm for the cinema continued to wane, accelerated by the advent of sound films, which, in Nielsen's opinion, deprived film acting of its uniqueness. Sound film was too close an imitation of theater, she felt, and artistically inferior to silent film: "Instead of exploiting the optical accomplishments that silent film had achieved and combining these with sounds and words, it threw everything overboard and photographed endless theater dialogues."[101] Nevertheless, she was willing to give it a chance and, in 1932, made her first and only sound film, titled *Impossible Love / Unmögliche Liebe* (Erich Waschneck, 1932), in which she plays a middle-aged sculptor who falls in love but, out of deference to her grown daughters' wishes, gives up the relationship and resigns herself to lonely old age.

Counter to speculation by later biographers that the film was a failure due to Nielsen's husky voice or Danish accent, the film was very successful in Germany, despite its fairly weak plot, thanks primarily to Nielsen's consummate skill. In his review in the *Frankfurter Zeitung,* Kracauer chastises the German producers for their unfounded opposition to Nielsen, which had deprived German audiences of her talents for so long, and praises both Nielsen's artistry, "which has not diminished in the intervening years," and her voice, "the supple austerity of which lends itself to all kinds of situations and melds imperceptibly with the rest of the piece. Frau Nielsen is particularly wonderful in her mastery of the interplay between language and gesture."[102] Kracauer's praise makes it clear that Nielsen's foray into the new world of sound film was a critical success and suggests that Nielsen could very well have made several more sound films, if she had so chosen, despite the residual traces of her Danish mother tongue in her speech.

While it did not detract from her performance, Nielsen's accent did underscore her Nordic identity; however, as several critics noted, it did so in a positive way. Lene Voigt, writing for the *Frankfurter Allgemeine Zeitung,* rejoiced over the chance to see and hear her "beautiful, serious sister from the North" once more,[103] while another reviewer compared Nielsen's voice to that of Garbo, "her almost-countrywoman," and pronounced it "the completely personal expression of a great artist with a very faint echo of the Nordic."[104] Ironically, however, the film had a very limited distribution in Denmark because of low expectations for its commercial success. This was Denmark's loss, not Nielsen's; one Danish review lamented, "Unfortunately it appears that we cannot expect to get to see this film in any Danish cinema, although one would think it would be a film that would interest the Danish public."[105] Disregarding Nielsen's films had become habitual for Danish cinema houses, and even the novelty of Nielsen in a "talking picture" failed to arouse enough interest to justify a wider release in Denmark.

Despite the critical success of *Impossible Love*, however, it was to be Nielsen's last feature film; although she continued to explore possible ideas for films during the following years, none of them came to fruition. One factor that contributed to her retirement was her conviction that sound film could not equal the artistry of silent film; another was the fact that she was fifty-one years old by the time *Impossible Love* premiered in December 1932 and few leading roles were available to women of that age. She continued to appear in live theater guest performances throughout the 1930s, earning very positive reviews in both Germany and Denmark, but her private letters reveal her frustration over her reduced professional activity.

The rise of the National Socialist party in Germany also affected Nielsen's career, as the government's role in the German film industry soon became much more intrusive. Film production during the Third Reich was essentially nationalized, and, as Ramona Curry notes, "the audience loyalty the stars evoked could be, and was, readily deployed in support of nationalist aims."[106] This state of affairs drove many of the actors and directors she had worked with into exile, generally in Hollywood, and made the prospect of working in German cinema unpalatable to Nielsen. Other Scandinavian actresses, notably the Swedes Zarah Leander and Kristina Söderbaum, did not share Nielsen's antipathy to working for the Nazis, however, and rose to prominence in the cinema of the Third Reich.

The final years that Nielsen lived in Berlin were marred by the deterioration in the political and cultural climate in Berlin after 1933. The number of film studios actively producing films fell from twenty-nine in 1932 to eleven in 1933. Nielsen's decision to remain in Berlin after the seizure of power by the Nazi Party in 1933, in contrast to the many artists, actors, and directors who fled into exile, made her a target for the attention of the Nazi propaganda minister Joseph Goebbels. In the postwar years, Nielsen's oft-repeated account of her consistent rejection of Goebbels' offers served to confirm her contempt for the Nazi agenda. Keenly aware of the power of film to shape public opinion and Nielsen's global celebrity status, Goebbels actively solicited Nielsen's cooperation, along with that of other leading cinema personalities, on several occasions. Her most memorable encounter with the Nazi leadership took place in early 1933, when Goebbels invited Nielsen, along with many other prominent members of the film industry, to a reception at the Ministry of Propaganda.

In a full-page article in *Berlingske Tidende* on October 10, 1945, Nielsen sketched the dramatic scene that she would later flesh out in extensive detail in her autobiography, but not until the second edition was issued in 1966.[107] Having been given a slip of paper printed with the number one, Nielsen found herself seated to the right of the *Führer* himself, who urged her to resume her film career in the service of the Reich. "The time has now come once more," he allegedly said, "that we need our greatest artists on screen." Nielsen protested that she did not play political roles, but Hitler countered that she would not need to. He explained, "People are so stupid. I can speak unin-terruptedly for two hours without anyone understanding a word of it. But you make a single gesture—and hundreds of thousands see it and understand it." Nielsen allegedly replied, "Oh, do you mean this one?" and lifted her arm in a mock Nazi salute, though she assured the reporter that was "the only time I raised my hand in that gesture." According to Nielsen, Hitler's face went stiff, like "someone from the Salvation Army." She then claims to have underscored her close association with several Jewish artists and defended the accomplishments of Jewish actors and journalists. In her memoirs, Nielsen recalls that she had "openly expressed support for my Jewish friends to the highest levels."[108] Later in the evening, Goebbels reportedly offered Nielsen a film company of her own, financed by the state, if she would turn her talents to building Germany's renown, but she declined, as she explained to her interviewer, "for I knew the price."[109] Nielsen never explained why she chose to attend the party at all, but her statement to the reporter suggests that she took a pragmatic view of the situation and resisted committing herself either way.

Aside from their ninety-minute conversation at Goebbels' tea party, Nielsen never met Hitler again, but Goebbels continued to solicit her cooperation, both before and after her return to Denmark. In April 1935, he sent her a fairly generic but strongly-worded invitation to attend the International Film Ball. The letter conveys Goebbels' insistence "that members of the film industry must absolutely attend, in order to give this event the appropriately representative character" and informs Nielsen that Goebbels "regards it as your professional duty to attend and requests that you sign the attached contract and return it immediately."[110] Malmkjær affirms that Nielsen did not sign, yet in November 1938, Nielsen received another more personalized, engraved invitation from Goebbels and Berlin mayor Julius Lippert to attend a performance of Schiller's *Kabale und Liebe* to commemorate the re-opening of the Schiller Theatre in Berlin. In the *Berlingske Tidende* interview, Nielsen revealed that Goebbels also contacted her in Copenhagen in 1943 by proxy, having commissioned a Director Horn from UFA to bestow a sum of money on Nielsen and obtain her permission for a retrospective montage of her old films as part of UFA's twenty-fifth anniversary celebrations. Nielsen rejected the money and refused the request for the retrospective film, with the explanation that "you must understand that I am a Dane."[111] Nielsen's foregrounding of her Danish identity and equation of Danishness with non-cooperation with Nazi Germany implicitly refutes the charge that she self-identified as German. Nielsen's refusal to accommodate Goebbels' and Hitler's requests eventually crippled her career, resulting in repeated rejections of her proposed theatre performances. Unable to work and unwilling to collaborate, Nielsen had little choice but to move back to Denmark, which she did in 1937, at the cost of two-thirds of her personal fortune, which she was not allowed to take with her out of the country.

Despite her insistence that she had left Germany because of the Nazis, however, suspicions about Nielsen's possible sympathies for Germany plagued her in Denmark until long after the war. For the most part, this sentiment seems to have been conveyed in meaningful winks and gossipy whispers, but in October 1933, the Danish anti-Nazi journal *Aandehullet* accused her publicly of being a Nazi sympathizer. The first issue of the journal, which was edited by the satirical artist Hans Bendix, was a special issue entitled "The Collapse of German Culture," with contributions from prominent Danish cultural radicals, including Poul Henningsen and Andreas Vinding. Between articles about Nazi censorship of jazz music and a warning about the growing popularity of Nazi ideology in Denmark, a page of illustrations titled "Heil Hitler!" features a photograph of Asta Nielsen, under the subheading 'Church! Kitchen! Children!-Women,' alongside a photograph of a plump, blond Saxon housewife and accompanied by the caption: "Asta Nielsen, who is an enthusiastic Nazi supporter in interviews. –That's also typical!"[112] It is unclear to which interviews Bendix was referring, but Nielsen was unsuccessful in her attempts to persuade Bendix to retract his accusation and had to find other ways to defend her reputation.[113] Publishing her autobiography immediately after the war was a major part of this effort, as evidenced by high-profile articles about her anti-Nazi stance such as the abovementioned account of her abortive tea party with Hitler.

While no evidence indicates that Nielsen ever seriously affiliated herself with the Nazi party, Nielsen did admit to complying with Nazi demands to affirm her support for them in exchange for the right to work. In 1947 she wrote a statement on behalf of her longtime friend, the dime novelist, screenwriter, and playwright Heinrich Rumpff, attesting that he had never truly been a Nazi, even though he had become a member of the NSDAP during the Third Reich. She alleged that he had only done so in order to be able to continue earning a living, not because he endorsed Nazi policies or ideology, and assigns herself to the same group of pragmatists:

> All of us who worked in Germany as artists and authors were forced to complete a questionnaire, in which we were required to declare our support for the Nazi government, if we wanted permission to continue working. Naturally, we ALL declared our support! EVEN I did, when I was preparing for a guest performance at the Comedy Theater in Berlin, together with Paul Wegener. We gladly gave the Nazis what they forced us to give; we artists did not take it seriously; we laughed over every question, and those of us whose names were already on the black list were, in light of current conditions, especially enthusiastic about emphasizing our inside jokes. We could not, in our wildest fantasies, imagine that it would become deadly serious within a few years.[114]

Such protestations of innocence and internal resistance meant for public consumption were very common among actors and writers in postwar Germany and it is nearly impossible to determine their accuracy without consulting the individual in question's private documents.

Nielsen's extensive correspondence with Rumpff and his wife Tilla, which begins in 1926 and ends in 1965, reveals that her own feelings toward Nazi Germany were not as uncompromisingly disdainful as she claims in her published accounts. From the late 1920s onward, Nielsen spent the summers in her beloved house *Karusel* (Carousel) on the island of Hiddensee, in the company of such eminent friends as Paul Wegener and Joachim Ringelnatz. In her memoirs, she describes the militarization of the island in 1933 and notes derisively that once the "brown shirts" appeared on the island and "the dark-haired, intellectual artist types were replaced by robust blond men and wide-hipped women with Gretchen-hairstyles, ... I had nothing more to do with it [the island]."[115] Yet Nielsen continued spending her summers on Hiddensee until as late as 1943, explaining in a letter to Heinrich Rumpff on June 24, 1943, that she had applied for permission to spend at least part of the summer there and noting that she "longs for all of you and for Germany. It is so odd."[116] The persistence of Nielsen's strong emotional ties to Hiddensee are further demonstrated by a letter to Heinrich Rumpff dated August 22, 1946, in which she reports that a bombed-out family is occupying Karusel and that she plans to appeal to the Russian embassy for the return of the property: "As a Dane, it *must* be possible to obtain my rights."[117]

Even more problematic than Nielsen's half-truths about Hiddensee, however, is a private letter she wrote on September 12, 1936 from Hiddensee, which suggests that she did, at one point at least, feel a certain degree of admiration for Hitler and his vision for a new Germany. Writing to the Rumpffs, she reports,

> We derived much pleasure from the newspapers about the Party rally. The Führer's brilliant speech *must* surely make it clear to everyone how great his idea is. He is truly correct, when he calls himself a prophet and says the people are fortunate to have him. I often think about what a pity it is that I did not have myself naturalized as a German earlier. If I did it now, it would appear to be sycophancy. I would very much have liked to be a part of the nation that was able to place such a man at its head.[118]

Nielsen's comments can be interpreted in a variety of ways: taken at face value as a positive personal opinion of Hitler, read between the lines as an ironic caricature of nationalistic fervour, or presumed to be a calculated effort to appear positively disposed toward the Nazi regime for personal or professional reasons. In light of the fact that Heinrich Rumpff had become a member of the NSDAP, it is possible that Nielsen's sentiments were sincere, echoing the widespread approval that Hitler enjoyed among the German people at this relatively early stage in his tenure, well before the atrocities committed by the Nazi regime reached their full, horrific proportions.

Even if Nielsen did admire Hitler in 1936, she did not act on that sentiment, either in terms of lending the weight of her celebrity to the Nazi cause or throwing in her lot with the Third Reich, nor did it motivate her to remain in Germany. Nielsen had already determined that her future did not lie with either the German film industry or Germany's leader, however charismatic or prophetic he might have been. On December 9, 1936, she wrote to Tilla Rumpff, expressing her longing for Denmark and her eagerness to return. "In my thoughts, I already no longer live here, but in Denmark," she writes,[119] suggesting that she was beginning to sever her emotional ties to the country she had called home for so many years and to look ahead to re-establishing herself in the land of her birth, which she did in the spring of 1937.

Whether Nielsen's return to Denmark was indeed the heroic defiance she later claimed or merely a pragmatic choice, it may have saved her life. In contrast to Nielsen's defiance of Goebbels, her friend and fellow actor Heinrich George, who had been a prominent communist in Weimar Germany and a frequent guest in Nielsen's home on Hiddensee, chose to cooperate with the Nazi regime. Despite having been labelled "undesirable" in the early 1930s, George was designated a "national actor" (*Staatsschauspieler*) in 1937 and given central roles in some of the most notorious Nazi propaganda films, including *Jud Süß* (Veit Harlan, 1940). Malmkjær claims that Nielsen refused to see George when he came to Denmark to perform for Nazi troops,[120] but her correspondence reveals that their friendship survived George's change of allegiance. A letter from George dated December 31, 1940, thanks Nielsen for her letter of November 25 and mentions an unsuccessful attempt to see Nielsen on a recent trip and his relief to learn that she had been traveling at the time: "I have of late been saddened by the thought that our beautiful and longstanding friendship had come to an end."[121] His fears seem to have been unfounded; in a letter dated June 24, 1943, Nielsen mentions a recent visit by George.[122]

As the war ended, however, George's decision to collaborate earned him harsh treatment at the hands of the Soviets, and Nielsen no longer acknowledged him as a friend. George was incarcerated at Sachsenhausen in 1945, where he died of starvation on September 25, 1946. In her October 1945 interview in *Berlingske Tidende,* Nielsen takes pains to distance herself from George, naming him offhandedly as the only one of her acquaintances who became a Nazi party member and noting dispassionately, "I read yesterday that he has been shot."[123] A private letter to Tilla and Heinz Rumpff from June 6, 1946, confirms that Nielsen was concerned about her own reputation; she makes a point of reassuring her friends that "I for one know who fought with me against the Nazi scoundrels and you both were in the front line," unlike "Heinrich George, [who] is sitting in a Russian jail, you know;

he was lucky that he wasn't immediately put up against the wall."[124] Two months later, on August 22, Nielsen confesses her continuing compassion for George: "Despite all his mistakes, Heinrich was very loyal. I'm sure he'll come out all right, he always knew how to use circumstances to his advantage, but perhaps he was too visible under the Nazi regime. It would be difficult for him to suddenly assert himself as a Communist."[125] Yet in a letter dated January 21, 1947, Nielsen seems ambivalent about George's death. She describes him as "a true friend," with whom she associates many memories, but concludes, "as a person, he had been dead for me a long time. And yet a tear followed him."[126]

However fortunate Nielsen was to be safe at home, the Denmark to which she returned in the spring of 1937 was very different from the country she had left a quarter-century earlier. Denmark had been in the throes of a cultural crisis for most of the preceding two decades, a process in which Nielsen had not participated but by which her reception in Denmark was still affected. One of the likely reasons that Nielsen's films had received such limited attention in Denmark during the 1920s was Danish society's preoccupation with its own cultural politics rather than broader European trends. In the wake of World War I, Danish culture went through a period of upheaval that manifested itself in a variety of forms, ranging from an inward turn reflected in the concern of Danish filmmakers with depicting Danish landscapes and domestic narratives[127] to the popularization of Marxist ideals of proletarian political equality by, among others, Hans Kirk, Rudolf Broby-Johansen, and Otto Gelsted in the journals *Clarté* and *Monde*.[128] The election of Denmark's first Social Democratic government in 1924, led by Thorvald Stauning, also contributed to a climate of political receptivity to social change.

Beginning around 1926, a movement that eventually came to be known as cultural radicalism revived the individualistic, socially revolutionary ideals of the Modern Breakthrough that Brandes and his cohort had promoted, particularly the quest for women's rights and sexual freedom, but with more success. Although the Brandesians had not been able to alter the conservative foundations of Danish society, the cultural radicals' efforts were assisted by both the destabilization of the Danish conservative bourgeoisie after the war and the endorsement of the movement's agenda by not just artists and writers but also doctors, educators, and psychologists, which lent it an air of scientific authority.[129]

Cultural radicalism emphasized both individual freedom and social solidarity, striving for the improvement of all people by means of the expansion of individual rights. Unlike the Brandesians in the previous century, the cultural radicals had a defined program with which to replace the fossilized Victorianism of the previous century, which resulted in gradual but far-reaching shifts in the ideological foundations of Danish society. This program was primarily disseminated through print media but also through art (particularly political cartoons), music (especially jazz), and theater, with film playing a fairly marginal role. One of the leading cultural radicals was the architect, designer, and cultural critic Poul Henningsen, whose mother, the writer Agnes Henningsen, had been a friend of Georg Brandes.

In addition to writing for the mainstream newspaper *Politiken*, Henningsen was one of the founders of the architectural journal *Kritisk Revy*, which became the mouthpiece of Danish cultural radicals in their campaign against both traditionalism, in particular the perpetuation of Victorian pseudoclassicism, and architectural modernism, which tended toward a highly technical, artificial style.[130] Henningsen regarded functional but stylish applied architecture as a tool of social reform for achieving "a happier humanity despite increasingly difficult living conditions."[131] The extent to which cultural radicalism had succeeded in permeating Danish political and social discourse is evident in the manifesto issued in 1935 by the antifascist organization National Association for Liberal Cultural Politics (Frisindet Kulturkamp), which calls for a "rational attitude toward the world and all people" as well as "equal rights for all people regardless of gender, race, or age."[132] Although the NALCP manifesto does not, of course, stand for the cultural attitudes of the whole of Denmark, it is a fairly high-profile, mainstream endorsement of the kind of liberal humanitarian attitudes that Brandes had advocated in the early twentieth century.[133]

By the mid-1930s, however, the cultural climate in Denmark was becoming less accommodating to social and artistic innovations, largely in reaction to the unsettling political developments across Europe that had become impossible to ignore, including the Italian invasion of Abyssinia, the Spanish Civil War, and Germany's aggressively nationalistic expansionism. A conservative reaction against cultural radicalism manifested itself in the formation of fascist political parties and the spread of a cautious attitude among Danish newspapers, for example *Politiken*, which ceased to employ Henningsen in

1938.[134] The tensions at work in Danish society became visible during a scandal that erupted over a propaganda film commissioned from Henningsen in 1935 by the Danish foreign ministry. Intended as an introduction of Denmark to possible investors, trading partners, and tourists in a tradition of national propaganda films inaugurated ten years earlier by Richard Lund, Henningsen's film *Denmark / Danmark* (Henningsen, 1935) focuses on working-class Danes, depicting the production of milk, cheese, herring, bacon, beer, and other Danish exports, as well as capturing both vast swaths of the Danish land- and seascape and hectic scenes of urban life in Copenhagen, accompanied by an original jazz score written by Danish composer Bernhard Christensen. The finished film received governmental approval,[135] but when it was screened for representatives of the Danish tourism industry, it was condemned by several newspapers as an unacceptable distortion of Danish national identity.

The controversy over Henningsen's film, which is generally referred to as *The Denmark Film / Danmarksfilmen*, exhibits the effect of the historical context and its attendant political ideologies on viewers' reactions to Henningsen's film and its depiction of Danish culture. The film had been commissioned in 1932, before Hitler came to power in Germany, but was released after Nazism had become firmly entrenched along Denmark's southern border. Pro-German sympathies were fairly common among Danes at this early period, many of whom found Henningsen's left-leaning radicalism highly suspect and threatening to traditional Danish values. Newspaper critiques of the film reflect this mistrust. For example, a typical review in *Politiken* complained, "All beauty was lacking. The Danish people were chiefly depicted as stout men and broad-bottomed matrons. The shadow sides of existence were too prominently displayed through back alleys and triviality."[136] Some reviewers complained about the lack of Danish tourist attractions, such as Tivoli and Hamlet's castle in Elsinore, and others about the scarcity of blond, smiling Danish girls.[137] Many critics were particularly disapproving of the musical score's jazz elements, which the Danish American editor of the journal *Redsted* described as "a mockery of every patriotic Danish man or woman who had looked forward to hearing good Danish music."[138] One notable exception was the socialist newspaper *Arbejderbladet*, which chastised Henningsen for acting as a marketing agent for the "royal capitalist Denmark," but also praised the film's optimistic and poetic depiction of both Danish weather and Danish workers.[139]

The blame for the fiasco was laid on Henningsen, who was described as "a man without a fatherland" because of his socialist views and was therefore deemed incapable of understanding or depicting Danish culture or national identity.[140] As a result of the uproar, Henningsen was asked to remove eighteen scenes, revise several others to remove all explicit and implicit social criticism, and incorporate traditional Danish folk songs into the score. The revised film received highly positive reviews abroad, particularly in Poland, France, Belgium, Germany, and Canada, and even elicited standing ovations from some Danish audiences,[141] but it still displeased many Danes, as well as many Danish Americans, who pleaded with the Danish government to retract the film because of its failure to depict traditional Danish culture.[142] Accordingly, the film was pulled out of circulation and was not rehabilitated and rereleased in Denmark until the 1960s, still in the revised format, although the idea of the *Danmarksfilm* as a periodic filmic diagnosis of Danish culture and identity has persisted until the present day.[143] Like Nielsen's films from the 1920s, with their bold representations of both emancipated femininity and urban misery, Henningsen's particular *Danmarksfilm* was unacceptable to the conservative elite in Denmark because of the unsettling nature of its depiction of Danish national identity as working-class, industrialized, and rapidly modernizing.

Unlike Henningsen's film Nielsen's return home elicited no public uproar, positive or negative, other than a few matter-of-fact newspaper articles, but the very anonymity of her life in Copenhagen after 1937 testifies to the Danish public's persistent indifference toward her. In a certain sense, the three and a half decades Nielsen lived in Copenhagen were a kind of exile, "in a provincial Denmark that did not recognize her as a world star and offered her no opportunities for work, because she was too 'great' for this small country."[144] Living in Denmark, she lived like any other ordinary Dane. The nameplate on her door stated simply "A. Nielsen," but the apartment inside was filled with valuable antiques, tapestries, and works of art she had collected during her years in Berlin. Initially, she frequently expressed a desire to work in Danish theater and film, but little came of it, due to the difficulty of finding roles that appealed to her, combined with her low opinion of the technical and artistic quality of Danish film, which she described as being twenty-five years behind German film.[145] She did appear in a supporting role in a light comedy in 1938, *Tony Draws a Horse* (*Tony tegner en hest*) at the Folketeater in Copenhagen, but remained otherwise uninvolved in Danish theater and film. The greatest actress Denmark had given to European audiences was completely excluded from Danish cultural production.

The most explicit evidence that Danes were not prepared to forgive or forget Nielsen's affiliation with Germany emerged in the press debates surrounding her repeated applications for a cinema license in Copenhagen. It had long been mandatory in Copenhagen to acquire a license to run a particular cinema, a system that was centralized by a 1922 law. The intention of the law was to ensure "that only such films are shown as will have an ennobling and instructive effect on the audience," but its secondary effect was to severely limit the number of cinema houses in Denmark.[146] Initially, however, the law did not specify any particular qualifications, and it became customary to grant cinema licenses to retired actors and film technicians as a de facto pension in recognition of their contributions to Danish film culture. The fact that Nielsen, despite her undeniable cinematic accomplishments, was denied a cinema license on thirteen separate occasions says volumes about the attitude of the Danish cultural elite toward her, particularly their resentment of her work in Germany. For her first application, she had enlisted Brandes to write a letter of recommendation, which he agreed to do, but with the caveat that his influence in Copenhagen was limited, as he had never even been invited to meet the Danish king.[147]

After her return to Denmark, when her financial situation was so precarious that she had to take in lodgers, Nielsen routinely applied for the cinema licenses that came available in Copenhagen, but without success. No official reason was ever given, but the implicit justification seemed to be that Nielsen did not deserve a Danish cinema license, since her professional work had primarily benefited German cinema. By contrast, licenses were granted to such locally prominent Danes as actor Hilmar Clausen in 1936, cameraman Leo Hansen in 1937, director Emanuel Gregers in 1943, cameraman Johan Ankerstjerne in 1945, actress Johanne Fritz-Petersen in 1947, and actress Agnes Nørlund in 1948.[148] Nielsen's ex-husband Urban Gad had received one of the earliest cinema licenses, for Copenhagen's Grand Theater, in 1923, which he ran until his death in 1947, after which the license was granted to his German-born widow, Ester. Licenses could also be withheld as punishment. It is possible that Nielsen's close friend Olaf Fønss did not get his license until 1946, twenty-nine years after he first applied, because of his unwavering support for her.[149]

The denial of Nielsen's twelfth application, for the Triangel Theater in Copenhagen in 1948, sparked a highly publicized controversy, with partisans on both sides making impassioned arguments in Danish newspapers about her respective merits and demerits as an actress and as a Dane. As reported in *Berlingske Tidende,* after Nielsen was "not found worthy to be granted a cinema license,"[150] Fønss asked minister of justice Niels Busch-Jensen, who was responsible for the decision, for an explanation. On public radio, Busch-Jensen replied, "It could just be for the same reason she didn't get a license the other eleven times."[151] Nielsen responded with an open letter to Busch-Jensen requesting further clarification, but Busch-Jensen demurred. In *Berlingske Aftenblad* on November 11, Fønss declared, "It is my firm conviction that the country has a duty of special proportions toward Asta Nielsen. It was she, who, in her day, lifted Danish silent film up to an artistically respectable niveau; it was she who carried Denmark's name out into the whole film world and created us a position."[152]

His defense of Nielsen angered her critics, however; on November 14, Ole Dalsgaard-Olsen, the director of Nordisk Film, responded in *Politiken* and *Social Demokraten:*

> Denmark does not owe Asta Nielsen a cinema license. Mrs. Asta Nielsen was employed by the Danish film industry in 1910, but left Denmark already in 1913 [sic], when she received an offer to perform in Germany for a very large salary. . . . It is doubtlessly correct that the lady was a good advertisement for Denmark when she appeared in Danish films, but it is also a fact that the lady has been known over the whole world for the past thirty-five years as "die Asta," the great star of the German cinema, and not as a Dane.[153]

Furthermore, Olsen argued, not only did Nielsen's lack of business experience render her legally unqualified for a license, but if one intended to follow the precedent of awarding licenses based on the applicant's cultural merit, he did not believe she had done enough for Danish film to deserve consideration. Unsurprisingly, this Ole Olsen was the son of the same Ole Olsen who missed out on the chance to earn a fortune on *The Abyss,* and whose grudging offer of employment Nielsen had accepted in 1911, only to break her contract when offered a better situation by Paul Davidson, so his opposition to honoring Nielsen is understandable, evoking the French proverb that "revenge is a dish best served cold."[154]

Olsen's derogatory use of the moniker "die Asta" and his insistence that Nielsen was known worldwide as a German film star reveal the crux of the issue, namely the extent to which Nielsen qualified as a true Dane. The commotion surrounding Nielsen's cinema license denial rekindled old antagonisms over her description of Germany as her "second fatherland" many years earlier, intensified by residual anti-German sentiment from the World War II years. In the wake of Olsen's remarks, several journalists asked Nielsen about her attitude toward her fatherland, and she replied, "*I* have always known and still know, what *I, as a Dane,* owe Denmark."[155] In an interview with Knud Poulsen in *Politiken* on November 29, 1948, she downplayed her association with Germany in explaining her view of her own nationality, "I was a Danish artist who worked in Germany for a number of years."[156]

Neither Nielsen nor the international press made any secret of her Danish origins, but rather, when advisable, as in the case of marketing her *Hamlet* film in the United States, made a point of foregrounding her Danishness. As Danish director Ella Laugesen points out, Nielsen had always managed out in the world with "her good, simple Danish name—*Nielsen*—and her *Danish* citizenship."[157] In an editorial in *Politiken* on November 18, 1948, Danish author Josef Petersen defends Nielsen's qualifications, comparing her to other famous Danes who worked abroad, such as the sculptor Bertel Thorvaldsen, whose atelier was located in Rome, or explorer Vitus Bering, who was employed by the Russian tsar, both of whom received great honor from their countrymen. Petersen takes a dig at Nielsen's critics in the Danish film industry, asserting that, "among artists, it is often the mediocrities that remain at home and are respected."[158] He urged that Nielsen be granted a cinema license as a "modest expression of affection and gratitude" for the "luster she has cast over the land of her birth, which she loves with all of her warm heart."[159]

Nielsen recognized the absurdity of the situation, but could do little about it, telling a friend in a letter dated December 1, 1948, "I have been attacked in the newspapers here for the past two months, because I acted in German movies. They are trying to persuade the public that I have been fundamentally AGAINST Denmark, just because I dared to apply for a cinema license."[160] Given the strong anti-German sentiment in Denmark at the time, however, she had little choice but to finally give up her quest for a cinema license.

The decades following the license debacle were lonely ones for Nielsen, who lived in humble obscurity in her modest apartment in Copenhagen. She had few friends, especially after the death of Olaf Fønss in 1949, followed by that of both her son-in-law, Poul Vermehren, and her daughter Jesta in 1963. Her financial situation was dire, so she tried to find creative ways to supplement her income. Following the advice of Danish writer Johannes V. Jensen, who had encouraged her to write her memoirs, Nielsen wrote several short stories and novellas for publication in Danish magazines.[161] She also began painting again, a hobby she had first taken up at her summer house on Hiddensee in the 1930s, using material from her old costumes to make collages.

She had not been forgotten by the world, however, even if her countrymen seemed generally uninterested in her accomplishments. On her eightieth birthday, in 1961, Nielsen received more than 1,000 telegrams and 300 letters from fans across the world, primarily Germany, but the only official acknowledgment of the occasion in Denmark came from the Danish Film Museum,[162] which had made several efforts to rehabilitate her legacy in Denmark. Two years later, after West Germany presented her with a medal of honor, the Danish Parliament voted to grant her an annual pension of 5,817 Danish crowns, in recognition of "her outstanding artistic qualities and highly significant involvement in the refinement of the art of film," despite the fact that she was a practicing (*udøvende*) and not a creating (*skaffende*) artist.[163] Her memoirs were republished in a single-volume edition in 1968 and sold very well, earning her a distinction from the Danish Writers' Guild. Her paintings were also much in demand, which brought her into contact with art dealer Christian Theede, eleven years her junior, whom she married in January 1970. Her advanced age and obvious happiness captured the imagination of the global media, bringing her back into the spotlight for a few years before her death on May 25, 1972, at the age of ninety-one.

Aside from occasional newspaper articles about her during the 1950s, it was not until the final decade of Nielsen's life that the Danish cultural establishment began to recognize the value of her contributions to Denmark's international reputation in the field of film. Her eighty-fifth and ninetieth birthdays, in 1966 and 1971, respectively, received extensive coverage in various Danish newspapers, both stimulating and satisfying the growing public interest in her legacy. Author Henrik Stangerup attempted to make a biographical film about Nielsen in 1968, building on the popularity of her memoirs, but irreconcilable differences of perspective led to an abrupt end of the project. After firing Stangerup and pursuing legal action to be sure that his footage would never be made public, Nielsen made the film herself, in time to be screened at the Berlin Film Festival in 1968.

Since her death, she has been the subject of several theater and film productions in Denmark, including a one-woman stage play by Vivian Nielsen titled *Asta—Die Asta* (1999), and two films by Torben Skjødt-Jensen, a documentary titled *The Talking Muse / Den talende Muse* and a television drama titled *Afgrunden / The Tenth Muse*, both of which premiered in 2003.[164] Memorial plaques have been installed outside of both the apartment she was born in and the apartment she lived in until her death, while a street was named after her in 1994 in the Copenhagen suburb of Valby, where the Danish film industry has long been headquartered. She has even been depicted on two series of stamps in Denmark: a portrait in 1996, and a still photograph of the gaucho dance from *The Abyss* in 2000.[165] However, although the name Asta has become increasingly common for babies born in Denmark since 1991, many Danes are not familiar with Asta Nielsen's name or works, nor were her films deemed worthy of inclusion in the Danish Ministry of Culture's "Cultural Canon" project in 2005.

This renaissance of interest in Asta Nielsen, however belated or inadequate, testifies to her unique status as Denmark's only film actress of international stature as well as the concurrence of contemporary Danish cultural identity with Nielsen's groundbreaking enactment of on- and off-screen modernity. In today's Denmark, where border-crossing female filmmakers such as Susanne Bier are lauded for their international success, Nielsen's ambition and initiative in making a name for herself in German cinema are no longer automatically interpreted as a self-interested rejection of Danish film and culture. Instead, modern Danish newspaper articles and film scholarship have begun to depict her as a strong woman who achieved artistic independence and commercial success on her own terms, outside the sheltering but also limiting confines of Denmark. Anecdotal evidence for Nielsen's rehabilitated standing in Denmark's cultural memory comes from a marketing campaign conducted in 1998 by Denmark's oldest newspaper, *Berlingske Tidende,* which had been outspoken in its contempt for Nielsen in the immediate postwar years. The full-page ad featured Nielsen's image beneath the slogan "We played a role for *Die Asta*," completing a series that showcased the newspaper's role in advancing the careers of such other iconic Danes as sculptor Bertel Thorvaldsen and theologian N. F. S. Grundtvig.[166] As its use in this instance demonstrates, the moniker "die Asta" is no longer understood in a derogatory way but rather as an expression of pride in Nielsen's steadfast representation of her homeland abroad.

Conclusion

Over the course of their long and highly productive lives, both Georg Brandes and Asta Nielsen played many different professional roles. Brandes began his career as an academic; earned notoriety as a literary and social revolutionary; tried his luck at journalism in Denmark, Germany, England, Austria, and France; marketed Scandinavian literature throughout Europe; mentored dozens of aspiring writers and bitterly disappointed others; scolded most of Europe for human-rights abuses and warmongering; and finished off his lengthy list of publications with biographies of Julius Caesar, the apostle Peter, and Jesus Christ himself. Nielsen started out on the Danish stage; made the leap to the silent screen and conquered it; tried her hand at costume design, editing, and film production; returned to the stage in Germany; contributed to a variety of German newspapers; debuted as a memoirist; wrote a series of novellas; and found true love as an octogenarian through her fabric collage artworks. Yet, as this catalogue of their diverse interests makes plain, there is little overlap between their accomplishments beyond a general interest in the arts. They admired each other's work and shared a bond of personal affection, but had little professional interaction with each other. The unifying factor that justifies their joint treatment in this book is their shared experience of celebrity and the connotative cultural meanings with which their celebrity personas and performances were invested, particularly with regard to representation of Danish identity. Both Brandes and Nielsen made important professional contributions to their respective fields, but they also shaped world history and global culture in their roles as icons of Danish modernity.

As popular but controversial media personalities in the decades before and after the turn of the twentieth century, Brandes and Nielsen functioned as signifiers of Danish modernity to the world at a time when Western society as a whole was undergoing massive paradigm shifts in connection with such hallmarks of modernity as industrialization, urbanization, secularization, and democratization. They exemplified the progressive, innovative artistry of Danish culture, even when social, economic, and political conditions in Denmark constrained such innovation. The ambiguity that characterizes their reception in their homeland reflects a perceived "tension between authentic and false cultural value"[1] in their very public, symbolically charged enactments of modern Danish cultural and national identity. As celebrities, Brandes and Nielsen ceased to be regarded primarily as private individuals and became instead cultural signs or icons representing particular ideologically determined constructions of reality. However, P. David Marshall warns that "the celebrity sign . . . is never fully determined or 'naturalized.' It is subject to a process of negotiation of signification. . . . The stability of a celebrity representation signifies the degree of conventionalization of the sign and the establishment of a stable consensus of its signification."[2] As celebrity signs, Brandes and Nielsen are subject to ongoing negotiations about what they represent, in terms of Danish cultural identity and Denmark's place within the larger discourse of European and global cultural politics. This process is reflected not just in the plurality of the roles played by Brandes and Nielsen themselves, but also, even more importantly, in the shifting attitudes toward Brandes and Nielsen in Denmark and Germany, as well as within the fields of literary history and film studies, over the course of their lives and in the decades since their deaths.

The emotional intensity with which this process of reception and interpretation has been conducted in Denmark varies noticeably with regard to Brandes and Nielsen, reflecting the different stakes involved in the cultural connotations of their respective legacies. Brandes continues to arouse controversy in Denmark today because he was a homegrown provocateur with ardent opponents and supporters who continue to carry his flag. His "cosmopolitan" views represented (and still represent) a distinct countercultural challenge to a nationalistic narrative of ethnically and religiously homogenous Danish identity. Much of Brandes's notoriety at home stemmed from his outspoken interference in his homeland's social and cultural affairs, while his European renown derived from his defense of more universal, and therefore more palatable (to Danes, at least) causes such as human rights, antiimperialism, and pacifism. By contrast, Danes most commonly view Nielsen with indifference rather than hostility. Since she had not made a name for herself in Copenhagen before moving to Germany, Nielsen's fame was never deeply rooted in Danish culture but came primarily from external sources, including the targeted advertising done by her German film distributors and the media reports of the irrational adoration of faceless masses in far-flung lands who thronged to her films. Even at the height of her global fame, Nielsen's Danish contemporaries distanced themselves from both her cult of fandom and the modernity of her personal and professional enactment of female identity, allowing that aloofness to harden into contempt in the context of the geopolitical stratification connected with World War II and to soften again as the passage of time eased those national traumas. At the same time, however, the magnitude of her international reputation, as an actress who happened to be Danish, was too great and potentially beneficial for Denmark's own standing in the world to be completely ignored by Danes, who then had to justify their previous unwillingness to acknowledge the most famous cinema actress the country had ever produced.

Yet despite the attention they have received in Denmark and Germany in recent years, it cannot be asserted that Brandes's or Nielsen's global fame has endured, particularly in the English-speaking world, despite the international acclaim they both enjoyed during their lifetimes. By nature, celebrity is fleeting, linked etymologically to the word "celerity," which means "swift."[3] By writing about contemporary literature and current events of his day, Brandes bound his work to the specific historical context in which he lived and worked. While the texts of many of the authors he promoted and analyzed, from Søren Kierkegaard to J. P. Jacobsen, continue to be read in countries across the globe, few people read Brandes anymore. Views that were revolutionary for the time have become antiquated and no longer resonate with readers. Aside from his one brief visit to the United States and his scattered publications in English-language newspapers and journals, Brandes made relatively little effort to establish a reputation outside of continental Europe, but the divisive political climate of Europe in the decades following his death quickly drowned out the echo of his words and obliterated public memories of his works.

Similarly, Nielsen's fame was closely tied to the fate of European silent cinema, which she was instrumental in elevating to an art form, despite the fact that many of the films in which she starred fell far short of her own and her critics' artistic standards. Unlike Brandes's texts, which continued to be reprinted for decades after his death, silent films were rarely recirculated more than a few years after their initial release, with the result that the immediacy of the visual experience of cinema could not be replicated for later generations. The industry's shift to sound film, in conjunction with Nielsen's own advancing age by the late 1920s and early 1930s, further constrained the perpetuation of Nielsen's reputation. Her brief foray into talking pictures confirmed her disdain for a genre that replaced gestures with speech, but audiences didn't share her opinion. Sound films rapidly eclipsed their quieter predecessors, and Nielsen retired from the screen. The destruction of many of her film negatives during the world wars made it even more difficult for audiences to become familiar with her work, with the result that her legacy to cinema was relegated to the relative obscurity of academic textbooks, particularly in the United States, where her films had never received wide distribution.

So why bother bringing Brandes and Nielsen to the attention of English-speaking readers now? Why not simply allow them to remain the private preoccupation of Danish academics and silent film aficionados? One could argue that the world today has celebrities enough to deal with without reviving the memory of celebrities of ages past, from obscure European countries no less. The purpose of this book has been to demonstrate that it is the very connectedness of particular celebrities to their historical and cultural contexts that lends them significance for the present day. The complicated, contradictory lives and careers of Brandes and Nielsen and their status as cultural icons, however contested, have a great deal to contribute not just to our understanding of how Danish national identity was constructed and construed in the early twentieth century, but also to our own efforts to define our collective national and cultural identities by means of the celebrities that crowd our public sphere. Given that many of Brandes's books are riddled with contradictions and errors and many of Nielsen's films are melodramatic and predictable, it is important to remember that it is not solely the intellectual or artistic merit of their works that justifies the rehabilitation of Brandes's and Nielsen's reputations now, a century after the peak of their renown, but also their energetic and effective participation in the ongoing process of national identity construction via the mass media, both directly, in Brandes's case, and indirectly, in Nielsen's.

Although their fame was partly the result of being in the right place at the right time—Brandes in Berlin in the 1870s and 1880s, Nielsen in Berlin in the 1910s and 1920s—Brandes and Nielsen also owed their success to the fact that they possessed the skills and ambition to take full advantage of the favorable circumstances in which they found themselves. Brandes's keen literary acumen, his immense productivity, and his fierce determination to defend the causes he believed in, especially in the face of virulent opposition, enabled him to climb to the top of the European literary heap, but it helped that he peddled his ideas to the upwardly mobile, culture-hungry German middle class via the newspaper at a time when German literature was rather stagnant and Scandinavian texts were inexpensive to publish. Similarly, Nielsen's radically expressive acting, sensuality, and assertive involvement in all aspects of her film career facilitated her conquest of the German film industry in the prewar years, but her natural talents were greatly enhanced by both the relevance of her portrayals of strong women to an increasingly self-aware audience of female moviegoers, and her suitability to the monopoly film distribution system's urgent need for marketable stars.

As a result of their respective combinations of ability and opportunity, Brandes and Nielsen came to play a central role in informing public discourse with regard to a new conception of Danish culture that reflected the emerging, though disputed, reality of Denmark as a democratic, liberal, egalitarian society. Although neither was a political figure per se nor particularly nationalistic in ideological orientation, they each had a profound effect, as celebrity representatives of their homeland, on both Denmark's self-perception and outsiders' assessments of the modernity of Danish culture. By challenging the status quo and typifying new national cultural norms, Brandes and Nielsen were instrumental in shaping the character of modern Danish society, if only by demonstrating the receptivity of the larger world to such ideas. The social, political, and economic turbulence associated with the advent of modernity in Denmark in the late nineteenth and early twentieth centuries invested the task of national identity construction with particular consequence, especially in light of Denmark's diminished size and precarious geopolitical position. The unequal political relationship between Denmark and the ascendant German Empire added an additional symbolic dimension to all cultural exchanges between the two countries, at least from the Danish perspective. In this context, it is unsurprising that Brandes's and

Nielsen's perceived influence on international perceptions of Danish cultural identity remains contested, particularly when the image they projected did not harmonize with mainstream Danish society's view of itself. Collective, especially national, identities are inherently resistant to fixed determinacy, making them subject to constant processes of (re-)negotiation of meaning and signification, such that any large-scale paradigm shift takes so much time that is difficult to recognize except in hindsight. In the case of Brandes and Nielsen, therefore, it is precisely their controversiality that confirms their continuing relevance, not only to Danish culture and society but also to the ongoing, universal struggle we all face to define our identities in a world of constantly shifting value parameters.

NOTES

INTRODUCTION

1. Mary Hilson, *The Nordic Model: Scandinavia since 1945* (London: Reaktion Books, 2008), 19.
2. Søren Mørch, *Den sidste Danmarkshistorie* (Copenhagen: Gyldendal, 1996), 62–63. Unless otherwise noted, all translations from German and Danish are my own.
3. Anthony D. Smith, *National Identity* (Reno: University of Nevada Press, 1991), 99.
4. Jürgen Habermas, *The Structural Transformation of the Public Sphere: An Inquiry into a Category of Bourgeois Society*, trans. Thomas Burger and Frederick Lawrence (Cambridge, MA: MIT Press, 1989).
5. Benedict Anderson, *Imagined Communities*, 2nd ed. (London: Verso, 1991), 25.
6. Benjamin Lee, foreword to *Metaculture: How Culture Moves through the World*, by Greg Urban (Minneapolis: University of Minnesota Press, 2001), xv.
7. Ole Feldbæk, "Dansk Identitet, 1740–1992," in *Dansk Identitet?* ed. Uffe Østergård (Aarhus: Aarhus Universitetsforlag, 1992), 60.
8. Mørch, *Danmarkshistorie*, 50.
9. Steven Sampson, "Please: No More Danskhed," in *Dansk Identitet?* ed. Uffe Østergård (Aarhus: Aarhus Universitetsforlag, 1992), 228.
10. Ibid., 226.
11. Ibid., 228.
12. In their anthology of interpretations of Benedict Anderson's theory of the imagined community, *Grounds of Comparison: Around the Work of Benedict Anderson* (New York: Routledge, 2003), editors Jonathan Culler and Pheng Cheah argue that Anderson implicitly acknowledges the inherence of comparability in his subsequent book *The Spectre of Comparisons: Nationalism, Southeast Asia, and the World* (London: Verso, 1998).
13. Ernest Gellner, *Nations and Nationalism* (Oxford: Blackwell, 1983).
14. John Hutchinson, *Modern Nationalism* (London: Fontana Press, 1994), 7.
15. Anderson, *Imagined Communities*, 22.

16. Bernd Henningsen, "'O Danmarck!' Det danske ved den danske politiske tradition," in *Dansk Identitet?* ed. Uffe Østergård (Aarhus: Aarhus Universitetsforlag, 1992), 85. See also Claus Bjørn, "Modern Denmark: A Synthesis of Converging Developments," *Scandinavian Journal of History* 25, nos. 1–2 (June 2000): 123.

17. One of the representative organs of the antifascist wing of the cultural radicalist movement was the National Association for Liberal Cultural Politics (*Frisindet Kulturkamp*), which existed from 1935 to 1940 and published the journal *Kulturkamp*. Much of the Danish scholarship about cultural radicalism tends to draw, as Elias Bredsdorff puts it, "an unbroken line in Danish intellectual life from the cultural radicalism of Brandes's day to the journal *Kulturkamp* in the 1930s," but Olav Harsløf's treatment of the Monde Group documents the political and ideological differences between the various left-oriented cultural groups of 1930s Denmark. Olav Harsløf, *Mondegruppen: Kampen om Kunsten og Socialismen i Danmark, 1928–1932* (Copenhagen: Museum Tusculanum Press, 1997), 14.

18. P. David Marshall, *Celebrity and Power: Fame in Contemporary Culture* (Minneapolis: University of Minnesota Press, 1997), 6.

19. Ibid., 7.

20. Ibid., x.

21. Hans Hertel, "Georg Brandes' Dobbeltblik: Nationalisme, antisemitisme, internationalisme—og litteraturhistorien som kulturkamp, 1871–2003," in *Kampen om Litteraturhistorien: Festskrift til Pil Dahlerup,* ed. Marianne Alenius et al. (Copenhagen: Dansklærerforeningen, 2004), 307.

22. Malcolm Bradbury and James McFarlane, "The Name and Nature of Modernism," in *Modernism: A Guide to European Literature, 1890–1930,* ed. Malcolm Bradbury and James McFarlane (London: Penguin, 1976), 39–41.

CHAPTER 1. THE CRITIC AND THE ACTRESS

1. The *Vaterland* was impounded by the US Navy in 1914, stored in a New Jersey shipyard until being commandeered by the US government in 1917, rechristened *Leviathan*, and put into service in the US Navy for the duration of the war and on into the 1920s.

2. Friedrich Sieburg, "Brandes und Dänemark," *Die Weltbühne* 21, no. 13 (31 March 1925): 468.

3. Greg Urban, *Metaculture: How Culture Moves through the World* (Minneapolis: University of Minnesota Press, 2001), 255.

4. Benjamin Lee, foreword to *Metaculture: How Culture Moves through the World,* by Greg Urban (Minneapolis: University of Minnesota Press, 2001), xi.

5. Despite the establishment of Greenlandic self-rule in June 2009, Denmark retains control of Greenlandic defense, foreign policy, and monetary policy, and provides significant financial subsidies.

6. The iconic phrase appeared on a decorative coin issued in conjuction with an art exhibition in Copenhagen in 1872. Although it is commonly

attributed to Enrico Mylius Dalgas, it was actually written by the poet Hans Peter (H. P.) Holst. Kjeld Hansen, *Det tabte land: Den store fortælling om magten over det danske landskab* (Copenhagen: Gads Forlag, 2008), 82.

7. Quoted in Michael Meyer, introduction to *Ghosts and Three Other Plays* (New York: Anchor Books, 1966), 108.

8. Ibid., 115.

9. Ibid., 116.

10. Urban, *Metaculture*, 1.

11. As Russian American sociologist Pitrim Sorokin (1889–1968) noted in 1927, "While in the past there was necessary a period of several hundreds or thousands of years for the diffusion of a definite value (custom, belief, ideology, religion) within a rather limited area or for its penetration from one group to another one, now this diffusion is achieved within a few months, or for the whole world within a few years." Pitrim Sorokin, *Social Mobility* (New York: Harper, 1927), 392.

12. Theodor Adorno and Max Horkheimer, *Dialectic of Enlightenment: Philosophical Fragments*, ed. Gunzelin Schmid Noerr, trans. Edmund Jephcott (Stanford, CA: Stanford University Press, 2002).

13. Mette Hjort, *Small Nation, Global Cinema: The New Danish Cinema* (Minneapolis: University of Minnesota Press, 2005), 113.

14. Paul A. Taylor and Jan Ll. Harris, *Critical Theories of Mass Media Then and Now* (Maidenhead, England: Open University Press, 2008), 93.

15. Walter Benjamin, *Das Kunstwerk im Zeitalter seiner technischen Reproduzierbarkei: Drei Studien zur Kunstsoziologie* (Frankfurt am Main: Suhrkamp, 1977).

16. Benedict Anderson, *Imagined Communities*, 2nd ed. (London: Verso, 1991), 24–25.

17. Mary Ann Doane, *The Emergence of Cinematic Time: Modernity, Contingency, the Archive* (Cambridge, MA: Harvard University Press, 2002). See also Philip Rosen, *Change Mummified: Cinema, Historicity, Theory* (Minneapolis: University of Minnesota Press, 2001).

18. Urban, *Metaculture*, 272.

19. Ibid., 255.

20. Anderson, *Imagined Communities*, 35.

21. Jonathan Auerbach, *Body Shots: Early Cinema's Incarnations* (Berkeley: University of California Press, 2007), 17.

22. Robert C. Allen, "Contra the Chaser Theory," *Wide Angle* 3, no. 1 (1979): 4–11.

23. Quoted in Charles Musser, *Before the Nickelodeon: Edwin S. Porter and the Edison Manufacturing Company* (Berkeley: University of California Press, 1991), 163.

24. P. David Marshall, *Celebrity and Power: Fame in Contemporary Culture* (Minneapolis: University of Minnesota Press, 1997), 58.

25. Ibid., 245.

26. Taylor and Harris, *Media*, 136.

27. Asta Nielsen, "Der Schuss im Kino," in *Film Photos wie noch nie*, ed. Edmund Bucher (Giessen: Kindt & Bucher, 1929), 21.

28. Ibid.

29. Marshall, *Celebrity*, xi.

30. The Modern Breakthrough in Scandinavia and Brandes's promotion of modern Scandinavian literature in Germany is covered in greater detail in chapter 2.

31. Cie, "Marathondisputats på 375 minutter: Elias Bredsdorffs forsvar for sin doktorafhandling," *Politiken* (Copenhagen), 1 July 1964.

32. Poul Malmkjær, *Asta: Menneket, myten og filmstjernen* (Copenhagen: P. Haase & Søn, 2000), 46.

33. Olaf Fønss, *Danske Skuespillerinder: Erindringer og Interviews* (Copenhagen: Nutids Forlag, 1930), 113.

34. Fønss, *Skuespillerinder*, 117.

35. Quoted in Erik Ulrichsen, "Asta Nielsens fire danske film," *Kosmorama* 19 (1956): 7.

36. Hjort, *Cinema*, ix. Among the criteria for defining a small nation's film tradition as "minor cinema," Hjort identifies a small population, a less commonly spoken language, and significant competition from American films.

37. Mette Winge, *Alle tiders Emma Gad* (Copenhagen: Politikens Forlag, 2005), 59.

38. Asta Nielsen, *Den tiende Muse*, vol. 2 (Copenhagen: Gyldendal, 1946), 42. The Danish title of the book can be translated as either *The Silent Muse* or *The Tenth Muse*, but most translations use the former.

39. Nielsen, *Muse*, vol. 2, 43.

40. Ibid.

41. Unpublished letter from Bandes to Asta Nielsen, dated 23 Decemnber, 1916, Asta Nielsen Collection, Danish Film Institute, Copenhagen. A few of Brandes's letters to Nielsen are reprinted in Ib Monty, ed., *Asta Nielsen: Breve 1911–71* (Copenhagen: Gyldendal, 1998). Most of the unpublished letters are accessible in the Asta Nielsen Collection at the Danish Film Institute in Copenhagen.

42. Unpublished letter dated 24 December 1919, Asta Nielsen Collection, Danish Film Institute, Copenhagen.

43. Willy Haas, "Die schöne Hexe der Stummfilmzeit," *Die Welt* (Frankfurt), 11 September 1971.

44. Nielsen, *Muse*, vol. 2, 134.

45. Ibid.

46. Ibid.

47. Georg Brandes, "Tale til Asta Nielsen," 1918, unpublished manuscript, Brandes Collection, Danish Royal Library Manuscript Department, Copenhagen.

48. Georg Brandes, speech for Asta Nielsen, 1920, unpublished manuscript, Brandes Collection, Danish Royal Library Manuscript Department, Copenhagen.

49. Nielsen, *Muse*, vol. 2, 136.

50. Ibid.

51. Claus Bjørn, "Modern Denmark: A Synthesis of Converging Developments," *Scandinavian Journal of History* 25, nos. 1–2 (June 2000): 123.

52. Quoted in Allen Hagedorff and Renate Seydel, *Asta Nielsen: Ihr Leben in Fotodokumenten, Selbstzeugnissen, und zeitgenössischen Betrachtungen* (Berlin: Henschelverlag, 1981), 69.
53. Nielsen's biographer, Poul Malmkjær, contends that if she had any foreign blood, it was likely to have come from one of the Spanish soldiers who invaded Jutland under general Albrecht von Wallenstein during the Thirty Years' War, or perhaps from a shipwrecked Scottish sailor. Malmkjær, *Asta*, 24.
54. Bjørn, "Synthesis," 123–24.
55. Aksel Sandemose, *En flygtning krysser sitt spor* (Oslo: Tiden Norsk Forlag, 1933).
56. Malmkjær, *Asta*, 305.
57. Quoted in Ella Laugesen, "Asta Nielsen og Danmark," *Information* (Copenhagen), 20 November 1948.
58. Marguerite Engberg, *Asta Nielsen* (Copenhagen: Det danske filmmuseum, 1966).
59. Stephan Michael Schröder, "Die Duse des Kinos as 'Frau Nielsen': In Dänemark," in *Unmögliche Liebe: Asta Nielsen, ihr Kino*, ed. Heide Schlüpmann et al. (Vienna: Film Archiv Austria, 2009), 435.

CHAPTER 2. THE LITERARY REVOLUTIONARY

1. Quoted in Niels Neergaard, *Under Junigrundloven: En Fremstilling af det danske Folks politiske Historie fra 1848 til 1866*, vol. 2 (Copenhagen: Selskabet for Udgivelse af Kilder til Dansk Historie, 1973), 1532.
2. Uffe Østergård, *Europas ansigter: Nationale stater og politiske kulturer i en ny, gammel verden* (Copenhagen: Munksgaard-Rosinante, 1992), 42.
3. Vibeke Winge, "Dänemark—Ein fortgesetztes Teutschland? Sprachliche Grenzgänger in Kopenhagen," in *Grenzgänge: Skandinavisch-deutsche Nachbarschaften*, ed. Heinrich Detering, vol. 1., Grenzgänge: Studien zur skandinavisch-deutschen Literaturgeschichte (Göttingen: Wallstein Verlag, 1996), 53, 57.
4. Edward W. Said, *Culture and Imperialism* (New York: Vintage, 1994), xiii.
5. Østergård, *Europas ansigter*, 42.
6. Johann Gottfried Herder, *Journal meiner Reise im Jahr 1769* (Stuttgart: Philipp Reclam Jr., 1976), 119.
7. Johann Meerman, *Reise durch den Norden und Nordosten von Europa in den Jahren 1797 bis 1800*, Gravenhaage 1804–06, trans. Rühs, vol. 1 (Vienna: B. Ph. Bauer, 1811), 39.
8. See Anne Scott Sørensen, "Den nordiske kredsen dansk-tysk aristokratisk salonkultur," *Nordisk salonkultur*, ed. Anne Scott Sørensen (Odense: Odense Universitetsforlag, 1998), 147–70.
9. Said, *Culture*, 200.
10. Østergård, *Europas ansigter*, 44.
11. Said, *Culture*, 200.

12. Ibid., 209.

13. Johannes Ewald, *Harlequin Patriot eller den uægte Patriotismus* (Copenhagen, 1772), 80.

14. Quoted in Flemming Lundgreen-Nielsen, "Danskhed i krige og kriser, 1800–1864," in *På sporet af dansk identitet*, ed. Flemming Lundgreen-Nielsen (Copenhagen: Spectrum, 1992), 139.

15. Hans Hertel, "Georg Brandes' Dobbeltblik: Nationalisme, antisemitisme, internationalisme—og litteraturhistorien som kulturkamp, 1871–2003," in *Kampen om Litteraturhistorien: Festskrift til Pil Dahlerup*, ed. Marianne Alenius et al. (Copenhagen: Dansklærerforeningen, 2004), 308.

16. Said, *Culture*, 210.

17. Leopold Magon, "Nordische Literatur- und Geistesgeschichte: Dänemark," *Euphorion* (1926): 610.

18. The nature of Brandes's role in Ibsen's success in Germany, whether he attempted to promote or in fact hinder Ibsen's breakthrough, was the subject of a heated debate between Jørgen Knudsen and Erik M. Christensen in the late 1980s. See Erik M. Christensen, *Henrik Ibsens realisme: Illusion, katastrofe, anarki* (Copenhagen: Akademisk Forlag, 1985), and *Henrik Ibsens anarkisme: De samlede værker* (Copenhagen: Akademisk Forlag, 1989).

19. Stefan Zweig, *Europäisches Erbe* (Frankfurt am Main: S. Fischer, 1960), 138.

20. Georg Brandes, *Hovedstrømninger i det 19de Aarhundredes Litteratur*, 1st ed., vol. 1: *Emigrantlitteraturen* (Copenhagen: Gyldendal, 1872), 9.

21. Uwe Englert, "Der Moderne Durchbruch," in *Wahlverwandtschaft: Skandinavien und Deutschland 1800 bis 1914* (Berlin: Jovis, 1997), 209.

22. Jørgen Knudsen, *GB: En Brandes-biografi* (Copenhagen: Gyldendal, 2008), 78.

23. Brandes, *Emigrantlitteraturen*, 15.

24. Ibid.

25. Georg Brandes, *Hauptströmungen der Literatur des Neunzehnten Jahrhunderts*, trans. Adolf Strodtmann, 2nd ed., vol. 1 (Leipzig: H. Harsdorf, 1897), vii.

26. Brandes, *Emigrantlitteraturen*, 13.

27. Ibid., 14–15.

28. Knudsen, *GB*, 75.

29. Quoted in Poul Bagge, "Nationalisme, Antinationalisme og Natio-nalfølelse i Danmark omkring 1900," in *Festskrift til Astrid Friis*, ed. Svend Ellehøj, Svend Gissel, and Knud Vohn (Copenhagen: Rosenkilde og Bagger, 1963), 6.

30. Hans Hertel and Sven Møller Kristensen, eds., *The Activist Critic* (Copenhagen: Munksgaard, 1980), 5.

31. Henry J. Gibbons, "Georg Brandes: The Reluctant Jew," in Hertel and Kristensen, *The Activist Critic*, 64.

32. Said, *Culture*, 209.

33. Niels Finn Christiansen, "Folkets danskhed, 1864–1920," in *På sporet af dansk identitet*, ed. Flemming Lundgreen-Nielsen (Copenhagen: Spectrum, 1992), 171.

34. Georg Brandes, *Levned*, vol. 2: *Et Tiaar* (Copenhagen: Gyldendal, 1907), 116.
35. Georg Brandes, *Berlin som tysk Rigshovedstad* (Copenhagen: Philipsens Forlag, 1885), 1.
36. Ibid., 2.
37. Jørgen Knudsen, *Georg Brandes: I modsigelsernes tegn, 1877–83* (Copenhagen: Gyldendal, 1988), 11.
38. Sven Møller Kristensen, "Aktivisten Georg Brandes," in *Den politiske Georg Brandes*, ed. Hans Hertel and Sven Møller Kristensen (Copenhagen: Hans Reitzel, 1973), 11.
39. Quoted in Hans-Joachim Sandberg, "Tradition und/oder Fortschritt? Zum Problem der Wandlung Thomas Manns im Lichte der Brandes-Rezeption des Dichters," in *The Activist Critic*, ed. Hans Hertel and Sven Møller Kristensen (Copenhagen: Munksgaard, 1980), 186.
40. Klaus Bohnen, "Georg Brandes og de intellektuelle miljøer i Tyskland og Østrig," in *Georg Brandes og Europa* (Copenhagen: Museum Tusculanum Press, 2004), 159.
41. Bernhard Glienke, "Gründerjahre eines Großkritikers: Der Däne Georg Brandes in Berlin," in *Grenzgänge: Skandinavisch-deutsche Nachbarschaften*, ed. Heinrich Detering (Göttingen: Wallstein Verlag, 1996), 152.
42. Adolf Strodtmann, *Das geistige Leben in Dänemark: Streifzüge auf den Gebieten der Kunst, Literatur, Politik, und Journalistik des skandinavischen Nordens* (Berlin: Paetel, 1873), 259.
43. Ibid., xiii.
44. Ibid., 80.
45. Torben Nielsen, ed., *Georg Brandes: Breve til Forældrene, 1872–1904*, vol. 1: *1872–1879* (Copenhagen: C. A. Reitzel, 1994), 34.
46. Ibid., 40.
47. Ibid., 51.
48. Jørgen Knudsen, *Georg Brandes: Frigørelsens vej, 1842–77* (Copenhagen: Gyldendal, 1985), 313.
49. Strodtmann, *Leben*, xiii.
50. Otto Brahm, *Kritische Schriften: Über Drama und Theater* (Berlin: S. Fischer Verlag, 1915), 74.
51. Ibid.
52. Paul Krüger, ed., *Correspondance de Georg Brandes*, vol. 3: *L'Allemagne* (Copenhagen: Rosenkilde og Bagger, 1966), 279.
53. Friedrich Kreyssig, "Literarische Rundschau: Die Hauptströmungen der Literatur des neunzehnten Jahrhunderts," *Deutsche Rundschau* (October 1874): 139.
54. Ibid.
55. Wilmont Haacke, *Julius Rodenberg und die Deutsche Rundschau* (Heidelberg: Kurt Vowinckel, 1950), 196–97.
56. Ibid., 197.
57. Along with August Strindberg, Dagny Juel, Edvard Munch, and Knud Hamsun, Hansson and his wife, Laura Marholm, were part of the famous

Nordic émigré community in Berlin in the 1890s that gathered at the pub The Black Pig (Zum schwarzen Ferkel).

58. Georg Brandes, "Bjørnstjerne Bjørnson: *En Fallit og Redaktøren*," *Det nittende Aarhundrede* (2 June 1875): 241.

59. Brahm, *Schriften*, 74.

60. Georg Brandes, *Om Nationalfølelse* (Copenhagen: Gjellerup, 1894), 12.

61. Klaus Bohnen, "*Niels Lyhne* in Deutschland: Unveröffentlichter Briefwechsel zwischen Georg Brandes und Theodor Wolff," *Skandinavistik* 9, no. 1 (1979): 12.

62. Brandes's claim on Jacobsen did not go unchallenged. In 1903 Jacobsen's longtime translator Marie Herzfeld tried to disassociate Jacobsen from Brandes, arguing that Brandes "only claimed Jacobsen for his own movement when his fame appeared to Brandes to be advantageous" (quoted in Conny Bauer, "Die Rezeption Jens Peter Jacobsens in der deutschsprachigen Kritik, 1890–1910," in *Fin de siècle: Zu Naturwissenschaft und Literatur der Jahrhundertwende im deutsch-skandinavischen Kontext*, Text & Kontext, Sonderreihe Band 20 (Copenhagen: Fink, 1984), 145.

63. Recognizing Brandes's central focus on the sociopolitical function of literature, M. M. Meyer suggested that Brandes should in fact be considered a "literary politician" instead of a "literary historian"; see Magon, "Dänemark," 604.

64. Bengt Algot Sørensen, "Georg Brandes als 'deutscher' Schriftsteller," in *The Activist Critic*, ed. Hans Hertel and Sven Møller Kristensen (Copenhagen: Munksgaard, 1980), 135.

65. Morten Borup, ed., *Georg og Edv. Brandes: Brevveksling med nordiske Forfattere og Videnskabsmænd*, vol. 2 (Copenhagen: Gyldendal, 1940), 350.

66. Niels Barfoed, ed., *Omkring "Niels Lyhne"* (Copenhagen: Hans Reitzel, 1970), 104.

67. Ibid., 101.

68. Borup, *Brevveksling*, 374.

69. Krüger, *Correspondance*, 239.

70. Georg Brandes, "Nachwort," *Deutsche Rundschau* 35 (May 1883): 300.

71. Georg Brandes, *Det Moderne Gjennembruds Mænd* (Copenhagen: Gyldendal, 1883), 141.

72. Theodor Wolff, "Jens Peter Jacobsen," in *Niels Lyhne*, trans. Marie von Borch (Leipzig: Philipp Reclam, 1889), 3.

73. Ibid., 20.

74. Ibid., 27.

75. Krüger, *Correspondance*, 182.

76. Ibid., 195.

77. Ibid., 193.

78. The speech was published in German that same year in 10,000 copies as part of an attempt to stimulate the development of German literature by means of a literary prize named in Brandes's honor. In his foreword

to Brandes's speech, publisher Albert Langen confirms Brandes's legacy in Germany, explaining, "We believe that Georg Brandes, whom Scandinavia's greatest thinkers regard as their teacher, the man who discovered Ibsen and Nietzsche, is so well-known and respected in Germany to justify our intention of founding a Georg-Brandes-Prize," funded by the sale of copies of the speech. See Albert Langen, foreword to *Nationalgefühl: Vortrag gehalten bei der Einweihung der neuen Räume des Freisinnigen Studenten-Vereins in Kopenhagen am 1. Februar 1894* (Cologne: Albert Langen, 1894), 4.

79. Brandes, *Nationalfølelse*, 10.
80. Ibid., 12.
81. Ibid., 14.
82. Ibid., 16.
83. Ibid., 30. Although he was criticised in Denmark for attempting to denigrate Denmark in an unpatriotric manner, Brandes's speech appeared in various European newspapers within a few days and awakened precisely the response that Brandes had hoped for. On February 5, 1894, he received a letter from a Dutch woman named Margaretha Mayboom, who expressed frustration over the lack of awareness of Danish literature in the Netherlands and requested that Brandes write a few articles about leading Danish writers for Dutch newspapers and give her permission to translate their works. She had just read Brandes's speech and concluded, "You are well known here and I believe that your name will make your articles welcome in our best newspapers" (*Politiken*, 17 February 1894). Mayboom went on to become one of the primary mediators of Scandinavian literature in the Netherlands in the first decades of the twentieth century, as Petra Broomans documents in "Hur skapas en litteraturhistorisk bild? Den nordiska litteraturens 'fräschhet' i Nederländerna och Flandern," in *Videnskab og National Opdragelse: Studier i nordisk litteraturhistorieskrivning*, part 2 (Copenhagen: Nordisk Ministerråd, 2001), 487–542.

84. Brandes made his most significant contribution to Scandinavian perceptions of German national identity through more than eighty articles about the new German Empire and its capital that he wrote for Swedish and Norwegian newspapers while in Berlin. The articles were reprinted collectively in 1885 under the title *Berlin som tysk Rigshovedstad*, though they were not translated into German until 1989, when they appeared as *Berlin als deutsche Reichshauptstadt* (Berlin: Colloquium, 1989). Bohnen elaborates on Brandes's patriotic intentions of correcting Denmark's ignorance of Germany and motivating young Danes with a cultural-anthropological image of Germany by which they could orient themselves. See Klaus Bohnen, "Über das 'Seelenleben' einer Stadt," in *Ästhetik der skandinavischen Moderne*, ed. Klaus Bohnen et al. (Frankfurt am Main: Peter Lang, 1998), 203–13.

85. Georg Brandes, "Den danske Literatur efter 1870," *Samlede Skrifter*, vol. 15: *Tanker og Skikkelser, Første Bind* (Copenhagen: Gyldendal, 1905), 197.
86. Said, *Culture*, 210.
87. Ibid., 209.

CHAPTER 3. THE OUTSPOKEN RADICAL

1. Georg Brandes, "Hunnertalen," in *Samlede Skrifter*, vol. 17: *Tanker og Skikkelser, Tredie Bind* (Copenhagen: Gyldendal, 1906), 75.
2. Ibid., 77.
3. Ibid., 76.
4. Quoted in Hans Grössel, "Nachwort," in *Der Wahrheitshass*, ed. Hans Grössel (Berlin: Berenberg, 2007), 172.
5. Jørgen Knudsen, *GB: En Brandes-biografi* (Copenhagen: Gyldendal, 2008), 458.
6. Quoted in Jørgen Knudsen, "Georg Brandes og de intellektuelle i Norden og Europa," in *Georg Brandes og Europa* (Copenhagen: Museum Tusculanum, 2004), 22.
7. Uffe Østergård, "Georg Brandes og Europa i dag," in *Georg Brandes og Europa* (Copenhagen: Museum Tusculanum, 2004), 34.
8. Ibid., 34.
9. Ib Monty, ed., *Asta Nielsen: Breve 1911–71* (Copenhagen: Gyldendal, 1998), 36.
10. Olav Harsløf, "Fra kulturpolitik til politisk journalistik," in *Den politiske Georg Brandes*, ed. Hans Hertel and Sven Møller Kristensen (Copenhagen: Hans Reitzel, 1973), 136.
11. Henning Fenger, "Har Københavns kommune mon hørt om Brandes?" *København City*, no. 1 (February 1977): 12.
12. Knudsen, *GB*, 264.
13. Knudsen, "Intellektuelle," 19.
14. Knudsen, *GB*, 325.
15. Georg Brandes, "Tale i Sorø," in *Samlede Skrifter*, vol. 15: *Tanker og Skikkelser, Første Bind* (Copenhagen: Gyldendal, 1905), 436.
16. Harsløf, "Kulturpolitik," 136.
17. Jørgen Knudsen, *Georg Brandes: Magt og Afmagt, 1896–1914* (Copenhagen: Gyldendal, 1998), 34.
18. Ibid., 40.
19. Thomas Nordby, "Georg Brandes og imperialismen: Georg Brandes' politiske journalistik fra det 20. århundrede," in *Den politiske Georg Brandes*, ed. Hans Hertel and Sven Møller Kristensen (Copenhagen: Hans Reitzel, 1973), 142.
20. Ibid., 139.
21. Georg Brandes, "Tale paa Møen," *Samlede Skrifter*, Vol. 15: *Tanker og Skikkelser, Første Bind* (Copenhagen: Gyldendal, 1905), 443.
22. Knudsen, *GB*, 351.
23. Grössel, "Nachwort," 173.
24. Georg Brandes, "Tanker ved Aarhundredeskiftet," in *Samlede Skrifter*, vol. 12: *Politik og Nationalitet* (Copenhagen: Gyldendal, 1902), 144–45.
25. Knudsen, *GB*, 207.
26. Georg Brandes, "Das Dänentum in Südjütland," in *Der Zukunft*, ed. Maximilian Harden, 7, no. 27 (1 April 1899); reprinted in *Der Wahrheitshass*, ed. Hans Grössel (Berlin: Berenberg, 2007), 50–68.

27. Knudsen, *GB*, 548.
28. Augustus Oakes and R.B. Mowat, eds. *The Great European Treaties of the Nineteenth Century* (Oxford: Clarendon, 1918), 208.
29. Grössel, "Nachwort," 175.
30. Brandes, "Dänentum," 51.
31. Ibid., 53.
32. Ibid., 59.
33. Ibid., 63.
34. Ibid., 63.
35. Ibid., 66.
36. Ibid., 67.
37. Knudsen, *GB*, 448.
38. Østergård, "Brandes," 33.
39. Ernst Richard Eckert, "Georg Brandes," *Das Interview: Weltkritik* (Berlin), no. 15/16 (1922): 9.
40. Knudsen, *GB*, 292.
41. Ibid.
42. Ibid., 294.
43. Ibid., 296.
44. Ibid., 297.
45. Georg Brandes, "Pogromhetze," in *Der Wahrheitshass*, ed. Hans Grössel (Berlin: Berenberg, 2007), 119.
46. Knudsen, *GB*, 451.
47. Georg Brandes, "Armenien og Europa," in *Samlede Skrifter*, vol. 17: *Tanker og Skikkelser, Tredje Bind* (Copenhagen: Gyldendal, 1906), 13.
48. Ibid., 14.
49. Ibid., 20.
50. Ibid., 15.
51. "Brandes, Denmark's Foremost Personality," *American Review of Reviews* (New York) 43 (January 1911): 100.
52. Poul Houe, "Georg Brandes i Amerika," *Weekendavisen* (Copenhagen), 11 August 2000, 9.
53. Quoted in Einar Haugen, "Georg Brandes and his American Translators," *Journal of English and Germanic Philology* 37, no. 4 (October 1938): 468.
54. Quoted in C. H. W. Hasselriis, *Georg Brandes: Besøg i Amerika* (Chicago: The Danish-American Association, 1914), 6.
55. "Georg Brandes i Amerika: Danskerne træffer store Forberedelser," *Politiken* (Copenhagen), 8 May 1914.
56. Ibid.
57. "Georg Brandes i Chicago," *Berlingske Tidende* (Copenhagen), 27 May 1914.
58. H. Arnold Barton, *A Folk Divided: Homeland Swedes and Swedish-Americans, 1840–1940* (Carbondale: Southern Illinois University, 1994), 264.
59. Barton, *Folk*, 264.
60. Emil Opffer, "Georg Brandes i Amerika," *Politiken* (Copenhagen), 3 June 1914.

61. Emil Opffer, "Georg Brandes fortæller om sine Indtryk i Amerika," *Politiken* (Copenhagen), 6 June 1914.
62. Hasselriis, *Besøg*, 6.
63. "Georg Brandes hyldet i New York," *Nordlyset* (New York), 11 June 1914.
64. Quoted in Hasselriis, *Besøg*, 17.
65. Kate Parsons, "Georg Brandes: 'Big, Strong, Unamiable, Yet Lovable,'" *New York Times*, 31 May 1914, 3.
66. Quoted in Hasselriis, *Besøg*, 18.
67. Hasselriis, *Besøg*, 9.
68. C. H. W. Hasselriis, "Georg Brandes blandt sine Landsmænd i Amerika," *Politiken* (Copenhagen), 28 May 1914.
69. Hasselriis, *Besøg*, 14.
70. Houe, "Brandes," 9.
71. Georg Brandes, "The Fundamental Causes of the World War," in *The World at War*, trans. Catherine D. Groth (New York: Macmillan, 1917), 32–54.
72. Georg Brandes, "En Appel," in *Georg Brandes: Den mangfoldige*, ed. Jørgen Knudsen (Copenhagen: Gyldendal, 2005), 221.
73. Georg Brandes, "Europa nu," *Tilskueren* (February 1925): 90; partially reprinted in "Brandes Despairs," *The Nation* 120, no. 3122 (6 May 1925): 529–30.
74. Georg Brandes, "Svar til Georges Clemenceau," in *Politiske Taler* (Copenhagen: Tiderne Skifter, 1987), 77; Georg Brandes, "Georg Brandes on Denmark's Neutrality," trans. M. Wreschner, *Evening Post* (New York), 6 July 1915.
75. Brandes, "Pogromhetze,"117.
76. Brandes, "Svar," 74.
77. Ibid.
78. Ibid., 75.
79. William Archer, *Shirking the Issue: A Letter to Dr. George Brandes* (London: Hodden & Stoughton, 1917), 2.
80. Ibid., 4.
81. Georg Brandes, "Folgen des Weltkriegs," in *Der Wahrheitshass*, ed. Hans Grössel (Berlin: Berenberg, 2007), 135.
82. Knudsen, *GB*, 27.
83. Friedrich Sieburg, "Brandes und Dänemark," *Die Weltbühne* 21, no. 13 (31 March 1925): 469.
84. Brandes, "Svar," 74.
85. Ibid., 72.
86. Jørgen Stender Clausen, *Det nytter ikke at sende hære mod ideer* (Copenhagen: C. A. Reitzel, 1984), 61.
87. Brandes, "Svar," 70.
88. Knudsen, *GB*, 585.
89. Pablo Diaz, *Asta Nielsen: Eine Biographie unserer populären Künstlerin*, trans. from Spanish (Berlin: Verlag der Lichtbild-Bühne, [1927]), 16.
90. Sieburg, "Brandes," 468.
91. Olav Harsløf, *Lysår: Kunstens kulturhistorie i Danmark i det 20. Århundrede* (Copenhagen: Høst & Søn, 2000), 144.

92. Knudsen, *GB*, 624.
93. Ibid., 605.
94. Georg Brandes, "Lebenslauf," in *Der Wahrheitshass*, ed. Hans Grössel (Berlin: Berenberg, 2007), 166.
95. Georg Brandes, *The World at War*, trans. Catherine D. Groth (New York: Macmillan, 1917).
96. Knudsen, *GB*, 603.
97. Eckert, "Brandes," 10.
98. Georg Brandes, "A Great Danish Critic Finds a Deficit," *Living Age* (Boston) 326, no. 4232 (22 June 1925): 351.
99. Georg Brandes, "Germany Today," *New Republic* (New York) 32, no. 416 (22 November 1922): 327.
100. Knudsen, *GB*, 616.
101. Harsløf, *Lysår*, 155.
102. Hertel, "Dobbeltblik," 310.
103. Ibid., 311.

CHAPTER 4. THE DANISH DIVA

1. Stephan Michael Schröder connects the perceived linguistic universality of silent film and its emphasis on visual language to both the crisis of language that modernist German writers such as Hugo von Hoffmannsthal thematized and the burgeoning global interest in international languages, such as Esperanto and Volapyk. Stephan Michael Schröder, "Fra Babel til Nørrebro, fra Berlin til Frederiksberg: Filmens Internationalisering og Nationalisering," in *Kultur på kryds og tværs*, ed. Henning Bech and Anne Scott Sørensen (Aarhus, Denmark: Klim, 2005), 122–25.
2. Emma Gad, "Kronik: Film-Eventyret," *Politiken* (Copenhagen), 6 March 1913.
3. Peter Urban Gad, *Filmen, dens Midler og Maal* (Copenhagen: Gyldendal, 1919), 283.
4. Gad, "Kronik."
5. Andrew Higson, "The Concept of National Cinema," *Screen* (Autumn 1989): 36.
6. Marguerite Engberg, "The Erotic Melodrama in Danish Silent Films, 1910–1918," *Film History* 5 (1993): 67.
7. Walter Benjamin, *The Work of Art in the Age of Its Technical Reproducibility, and Other Writings on Media*, ed. Michael W. Jennings et al., trans. Edmund Jephcott et al. (Cambridge, MA: The Belknap Press of Harvard University Press, 2008), 26.
8. Paul A. Taylor and Jan Ll. Harris, *Critical Theories of Mass Media Then and Now* (Maidenhead, England: Open University Press, 2008), 46.
9. Heide Schlüpmann, "Asta Nielsen and Female Narration: The Early Films," in *A Second Life: German Cinema's First Decades*, ed. Thomas Elsaesser and Michael Wedel (Amsterdam: Amsterdam University Press, 1996), 118.
10. Ibid.

11. Ibid., 118–19.

12. Gill Jagger, *Judith Butler: Sexual Politics, Social Change, and the Power of the Performative* (London: Routledge, 2008).

13. Thomas Elsaesser, "National Subjects, International Style: Navigating Early German Cinema," *Before Caligari: German Cinema, 1895–1920*, ed. Paolo Cherchi Usai and Lorenzo Codelli (Madison: University of Wisconsin Press, 1990), 346.

14. Sabine Hake, *German National Cinema* (London: Routledge, 2002), 13.

15. Ibid., 16.

16. Ibid., 16.

17. Corinna Müller, *Frühe deutsche Kinematographie* (Stuttgart: Metzler, 1994), 148.

18. David Gritten, *Fame: Stripping Celebrity Bare* (London: Allen Lane, 2002), 19.

19. Samantha Barbas, *Movie Crazy: Fans, Stars, and the Cult of Celebrity* (New York: Palgrave, 2001), 5.

20. Corinna Müller, "Emergence of the Feature Film in Germany between 1910 and 1911," in *Before Caligari: German Cinema, 1895–1920*, ed. Paolo Cherchi Usai and Lorenzo Codelli (Madison: University of Wisconsin Press, 1990), 100.

21. Müller, *Kinematographie*, 143–55.

22. Müller, "Emergence," 102.

23. Peter Jelavich, "'Am I Allowed to Amuse Myself Here?': The German Bourgeoisie Confronts Early Film," in *Germany at the Fin de Siècle: Culture, Politics, and Ideas,* ed. Suzanne Marchand and David Lindenfeld (Baton Rouge: Louisiana State University Press, 2004), 231.

24. Ibid., 235.

25. Joseph Garncarz, "Art and Industry: German Cinema of the 1920s," in *The Silent Cinema Reader,* ed. Lee Grieveson and Peter Krämer (London: Routledge, 2004), 390.

26. Knut Hickethier, "Theatervirtuosinnen und Leinwandmimen: Zum Entstehen des Stars im deutschen Film," in *Die Modellierung des Kinofilms: Zur Geschichte des Kinoprogramms zwischen Kurzfilm und Langfilm, 1905/6–1918,* ed. Corinna Müller and Harro Segeberg (Munich: Vilhelm Fink Verlag, 1998), 335.

27. Knut Hickethier, "Schauspieler zwischen Theater und Kino in der Stummfilmzeit," in *Grenzgänger zwischen Theater und Kino: Schauspielerporträts aus dem Berlin der Zwanziger Jahre,* ed. Knut Hickethier (Berlin: Edition Mythos, Verlag Ästhetik und Kommunikation, 1986), 30.

28. Hickethier, "Theatervirtuosinnen," 336.

29. W. N., "'Schweigende Muse': Asta Nielsen erzählt ihr Leben," *Freie Presse* (Zwickau), 23 October 1961.

30. Miriam Hansen, "Early Silent Cinema: Whose Public Sphere?" *New German Critique*, no. 29 (Spring–Summer 1983), 175.

31. Hickethier, "Theatervirtuosinnen," 352.

32. Poul Elsner, "Die Duse des Films," *Reklams Universum Weltrundschau* (Leipzig) [1911]: 517.

33. Quoted in Ib Rehné, *Løvindens Pote: Et essay om myten og mennesket* (Frederiksberg, Denmark: Fiskers Forlag, 1993), 13.
34. Arnold Hending, *Lygterne tændes langs vejen: Om mange jeg mødte* (Copenhagen: Kandrup & Wunsch Forlag, 1961), 269.
35. Ben Brewster and Lea Jacobs, *Theatre to Cinema: Stage Pictorialism and the Early Feature Film* (New York: Oxford University Press, 1997), 111.
36. Poul Malmkjær, *Asta: Menneket, myten og filmstjernen* (Copenhagen: P. Haase & Søn, 2000), 168.
37. Lisbeth Richter Larsen, "Valdemar Psilander: Una star internazionale del cinema danese," trans. Cristiana Querze, *Cinegrafie* 17 (2004): 175.
38. Malmkjær, *Asta*, 63.
39. Ibid., 63.
40. Ibid., 76.
41. Maren M. Pust, "That's Why the Lady Is a Vamp: The Danish Origins of the Screen's First Dangerous Lady," in *Fleshpot: Cinema's Sexual Myth Makers and Taboo Breakers* (Manchester, England: Headpress, 2000), 85.
42. Béla Balázs, *Der Sichtbare Mensch oder die Kultur des Films* (Vienna: Deutsch-Österreichischer Verlag, 1924), 162.
43. Asta Nielsen, *Den tiende Muse*, vol. 1 (Copenhagen: Gyldendal, 1946), 131.
44. Nielsen, *Muse*, vol. 1, 132–33.
45. When the Danish Film Institute decided to restore the badly damaged negative of *The Abyss* in the early 2000s, they were able to use a pristine copy of the gaucho dance sequence that had been removed by the Swedish censors.
46. "Asta Nielsen," *Masken* 1, 8 (19 November 1910): 72.
47. Malmkjær, *Asta*, 78.
48. Ibid., 89.
49. Unpublished handwritten contract between Asta Nielsen and Frede Skaarup, signed in Aarhus, Denmark, dated 2 May 1911, courtesy of Isak Thorsen and Nordisk Film Archives.
50. Business letter no. 822 from Ole Olsen in September 1911, Danish Film Institute (DFI) Nordisk Films Kompagni Collection, Copenhagen. Partially reprinted in Marguerite Engberg, *Dansk Stumfilm*, vol. 1 (Copenhagen: Rhodos, 1977), 260.
51. Business letter no. 238 from Ole Olsen to "Nordische Films, Berlin," dated 19 November 1910, DFI Nordisk Films Kompagni Collection, Copenhagen.
52. Business letter no. 211 from Ole Olsen to "Herrn Carl Süring," dated 17 November 1910, DFI Nordisk Films Kompagni Collection, Copenhagen.
53. Ibid.
54. Andreas Hansert, *Asta Nielsen und die Filmstadt Babelsberg: Das Engagement Carl Schleussners in der Deutschen Filmindustrie* (Petersburg, Germany: Michael Imhof Verlag, 2007), 48.
55. Viggo Schiörring, "Kino-Kunstens Duse," unidentified Danish newspaper, 1912, DFI Asta Nielsen Collection, Copenhagen.

56. Pablo Diaz, *Asta Nielsen: Eine Biographie unserer populären Künstlerin*, trans. from Spanish (Berlin: Verlag der Lichtbild-Bühne, [1927]), 35.
57. "Urteile der Frankfurter Zeitungen über Asta Nielsen," *Colosseum-Theater Essen, Rheinpreußen*, (1913): 7.
58. Malmkjær, *Asta*, 118.
59. Müller, *Kinematographie*, 149.
60. Corinna Müller, "Der Weg zum Star: Versuch einer Rekonstruktion," in *Henny Porten: Der erste deutsche Filmstar, 1890–1960*, ed. Helga Belach (Berlin: Haude & Spener, 1986), 36.
61. Adolf Langsted, *Asta Nielsen* (Copenhagen: Nyt Nordisk Forlag, 1918), 47.
62. "Unsere Preisrundfrage: Wer ist die beliebteste Filmkünstlerin? V. Asta Nielsen," unidentified German newspaper, 4 May 1918, DFI Asta Nielsen Collection.
63. Nielsen, *Muse*, vol. 2, 66.
64. Malmkjær, *Asta*, 120.
65. Nielsen, *Muse*, vol. 2, 26.
66. Hending, *Lygterne*, 270.
67. Nielsen, *Muse*, vol. 2, 26.
68. Hickethier, "Theatervirtuosinnen," 352.
69. Egon Jacobsohn, "Asta Nielsen," *Bühne und Film*, no. 1 (1919): 6.
70. Müller, "Weg," 32.
71. Langsted, *Asta Nielsen*, 11.
72. Fritz Güttinger, *Kein Tag ohne Kino: Schriftsteller über den Stummfilm* (Frankfurt: Deutsches Filmmuseum, 1984), 255.
73. Lotte Eisner, "Zu Ehren von Asta Nielsen," *Kosmorama* 50, no. 7 (October 1960): 6.
74. "Teater og Tribune," *Politiken* (Copenhagen), 24 August 1912.
75. A characteristic example of such an article appeared in *Politiken* on 8 October 1912, under the byline Hektor and the title "The Visit of a Famous Artistic Couple: Asta Nielsen Gad and Peter Urban Gad: Brief Interview."
76. Helge, "En ny Asta Nielsen-Film: Paa Mandag Premiere i Paladsteatret: Hele Indtægter gaar til Juleindsamlingen," *Politiken* (Copenhagen), 21 December 1912.
77. "Paladsteatret: Asta Nielsen Premiere," *Berlingske Tidende* (Copenhagen), 10 May 1914.
78. "Paladsteatret: Ny Asta Nielsen Film i Paladsteatret," *Folkets Avis* (Copenhagen), 12 May 1914.
79. Helge, "En ny Asta Nielsen-Film: Paa Mandag Premiere i Paladsteatret: Hele Indtægter gaar til Juleindsamlingen," *Politiken* (Copenhagen), 21 December 1912.
80. Smut, "Filmen i Aften. Kl. 8¼ er der Premiere paa Paladsteatret," *Politiken* (Copenhagen), 23 December 1912.
81. Ibid.
82. "Teater og Tribune," *Politiken* (Copenhagen), 16 April 1911.
83. "Hos Film Divaen," *Politiken* (Copenhagen), 16 April 1911.

84. Niels Th. Thomsen, "Asta Nielsen-Gad," *Masken* 3, no. 27 (1912): 23.
85. Jens Locher, "Asta Nielsen," unidentified Danish magazine, 1916, 9, DFI Asta Nielsen Collection.
86. Locher, "Nielsen," 10.
87. "Asta Nielsen," *Maanedsmagasin*, 24 November 1912.
88. Aksel Sandemose, *En flygtning krysser sitt spor* (Oslo: Tiden Norsk Forlag, 1933).
89. Thomsen, "Asta Nielsen-Gad," 24.
90. V. S., "Mellem Film-Slagene: Et Besøg hos Asta Nielsen," *Verden og Vi* 1 (1915): 20.
91. "Levende Billeder," *Politiken* (Copenhagen), 30 May 1911.
92. "Panoptikon-Teatret," *Politiken* (Copenhagen), 18 April 1911.
93. "En Tyrefægtnings-Film med Asta Nielsen i Hovedrollen," *Politiken* (Copenhagen), 9 June 1913.
94. Müller, *Kinematographie*, 150.
95. Mariann Lewinsky, "Stummfilmdiva Asta Nielsen: Frauenbilder von nachhaltiger Modernität," *Filmpodium* (November/December 1994): 6.
96. Jelavich, "Amuse," 236–37.
97. Müller, "Emergence," 106.
98. Jelavich, "Amuse," 247.
99. Hansen, "Cinema," 151.
100. The names and national identities of the characters in this film varied according to the country in which the film was being screened, as was very often the practice during this period when marketing silent films to different national audiences. In some copies of *A Strange Bird*, for example, Nielsen's character is introduced as an American girl from New York.
101. Lewinsky, "Frauenbilder," 6.
102. Hake, *Cinema*, 16.
103. Janet Bergstrom, "Asta Nielsen's Early German Films," *Before Caligari: German Cinema, 1895–1920*, ed. Paolo Cherchi Usai and Lorenzo Codelli (Madison: University of Wisconsin Press, 1990), 162.
104. Sabine Hake, "Self-Referentiality in Early German Cinema," *A Second Life: German Cinema's First Decades*, ed. Thomas Elsaesser (Amsterdam: Amsterdam University Press, 1996), 139.
105. Emilie Altenloh, *Zur Soziologie des Kino: Die Kinounternehmung und die sozialen Schichten ihrer Besucher* (Leipzig: Spamerschen Buchdruckerei, [1913]), 94.
106. Ibid., 79.
107. Hake, *Cinema*, 19.
108. Thomas Elsaesser, "Early German Cinema: A Second Life?" in *A Second Life: German Cinema's First Decades,* ed. Thomas Elsaesser (Amsterdam: Amsterdam University Press, 1996), 22.
109. Kirsten Drotner, "Asta Nielsen: A Modern Woman Before Her Time?" in *Is There a Nordic Feminism? Nordic Feminist Thought on Culture and Society,* ed. Drude von der Fehr et al. (London: UCL Press, 1998), 306.

110. Jörg Becker, "Diven und Fans / Divas and Fans," in *Filmmuseum Berlin*, ed. Wolfgang Jacobsen et al. (Berlin: Nicolai, 2000), 33.

111. Hake, *Cinema*, 33.

112. Jelavich, "Amuse," 241.

113. Malmkjær, *Asta*, 130.

114. Nielsen, *Muse*, vol. 2, 23.

115. Engberg, "Melodrama," 67.

116. Nielsen, *Muse*, vol. 2, 24.

117. Engberg,"Melodrama," 66.

118. Janet Bergstrom, "Asta Nielsen's Early German Films," *Frauen und Film* 62 (2000): 43.

119. Malmkjær, *Asta*, 130.

120. In Sweden at this time, the perception of the Danish film industry as particularly decadent prompted the emergent Swedish cinema to consciously define itself in opposition to Danish film. For more on this topic, see Patrick Vonderau, *Bilder vom Norden* (Marburg, Germany: Schüren, 2007).

121. See chapter 2 for an in-depth discussion of Brandes and the Modern Breakthrough.

122. Ib Monty, ed., *Asta Nielsen: Breve, 1911–71* (Copenhagen: Gyldendal, 1998), 20.

123. Ibid., 22.

124. Dr. C. A., "Schwedische Kinozensur-Sensation: Asta Nielsen gegen die Zensur," *Lichtbild-Theater* 3, no. 46 (1911).

125. Ibid.

126. Richard Abel, *The Red Rooster Scare: Making Cinema American, 1900–1910* (Berkeley: University of California Press, 1999), 126.

127. "Woman Always Pays," *New York Dramatic Mirror*, 24 April 1912, 27.

128. Jennifer Bean, "'Übers Meer gebracht': In Amerika, 1912–1914," in *Unmögliche Liebe: Asta Nielsen, ihr Kino*, ed. Heide Schlüpmann et al. (Vienna: Film Archiv Austria, 2009), 338.

129. Ibid.

130. Ibid., 342.

131. Ibid., 338.

132. Becker, "Diven," 28. The enduring resonance of this comparison is evident in the fact that it is stated outright in some introductory footage appended by the East German National Film Archive to a copy of an early Henny Porten film, "In the Shadow of the Sea" / *Im Schatten des Meeres* (Curt Stark, 1912).

133. Hickethier, "Schauspieler," 33.

134. Michael Wedel, "Towards an Archaeology of the Early German Music Film," *Le son en perspective: Nouvelles recherches*, ed. Dominique Nasta and Didier Huvelle (Brussels: Peter Lang, 2004), 119.

135. Like Nielsen, Porten also married her director. Curt Stark directed nearly all of Porten's films until he was deployed to the Western Front during World War I, where he died in 1916.

136. Müller, "Weg," 36.

137. Müller, "Weg," 32.
138. Hake, *Cinema*, 16–17.
139. Becker, "Diven," 28.
140. Ramona Curry, "How Early German Film Stars Helped Sell the War(es)," *Film and the First World War*, ed. Karel Dibbets and Bert Hogenkamp (Amsterdam: Amsterdam University Press, 1995), 144.
141. Becker, "Diven," 30.
142. Karl Bleibtreu, "Der Feind im Land," *Die Ähre*, 21 September 1913; reprinted in *Henny Porten: Der erste deutsche Filmstar, 1890–1960*, ed. Helga Belach (Berlin: Haude & Spener, 1986), 41.
143. Kurt Pinthus, "Henny Porten als Reichspräsident," *Das Tagebuch*, no. 41 (1921); reprinted in *Henny Porten: Der erste deutsche Filmstar, 1890–1960*, ed. Helga Belach (Berlin: Haude & Spener, 1986), 83–84.
144. Curry, "Stars," 146.
145. Ibid., 145–46.
146. Alex Binder, ed., *Unsere Filmsterne* (Berlin: Buch-Film Verlag, 1922), 11.
147. Sophus Claussen, "Kronik: Films," *Politiken* (Copenhagen), 5 May 1911.
148. Schiörring, "Duse," 20.
149. Monty, *Breve*, 30.
150. Carl Theodor Dreyer, "Vor Tids Helte: Asta Nielsen-Gad," *Ekstrabladet* (Copenhagen), 2 October 1913; reprinted in Peter Schepelern, *Tommen: Carl Th. Dreyers filmjournalistiske virksomhed* (Copenhagen: C. A. Reitzel, 1982), 36.
151. José Teunissen, "Mode und Modernität," in *Unmögliche Liebe: Asta Nielsen, ihr Kino*, ed. Heide Schlüpmann et al. (Vienna: Film Archiv Austria, 2009), 245.
152. Malmkjær, *Asta*, 168.
153. Christian Engelstoft, "Asta Nielsen, Kunstnerinden der forlod sit fædreland," *Aftenbladet* (Copenhagen), 27 November 1927.
154. Gad, *Midler*, 239.
155. Nielsen, *Muse*, vol. 2, 104.
156. Freddy Wingårdh, "Med Asta Nielen over Atlanten," unidentified Danish newspaper, [1916], DFI Asta Nielsen Collection.
157. Malmkjær, *Asta*, 170.
158. Nielsen, *Muse*, vol. 2, 142.
159. One of the dramas in the series was *Dora Brandes* (Stifter, 1916), but despite the coincidence of the title character's surname being identical with Georg Brandes's, no connection has been established between Brandes and the film.
160. Nielsen, *Muse*, vol. 2, 132.
161. Inge Klevian, "Kultursammenstød som lystspil," *Kosmorama* 232 (2003): 107–9.
162. Otto Rung, "Københavnsk Selskabsliv ved Aarhundredeskiftet," in *Danmark i Fest og Glæde*, ed. Julius Clausen and Torben Krogh, vol. 5: *Tiden 1870–1914* (Copenhagen: Chr. Erichsens Forlag, 1935), 62.

163. Peter Urban Gad, *Klunketiden paa en anden Maade* (Copenhagen: Gyldendal, 1949), 38.

164. Malmkjær, *Asta*, 184.

165. Engberg, *Asta Nielsen*, [8].

166. Marguerite Engberg, "Nordisk in Denmark," in *Film and the First World War*, ed. Karel Dibbets and Bert Hogenkamp (Amsterdam: Amsterdam University Press, 1995), 44.

167. Felix, "Hvad Verden Taler Om: I Julen skal Kæmpefilmen INRI gaa over hele Jorden med Asta Nielsen som Magdalena," unidentified Danish newspaper, [1923], 10, DFI Asta Nielsen Collection.

CHAPTER 5. THE NEW WOMAN

1. Egon Jacobsohn, "Asta Nielsen," *Bühne und Film* 1 (1919): 3.
2. Ibid.
3. In the United States the company was known as Asta Film.
4. Stefan Lorant, *Wir vom Film: Das Leben, Lieben, Leiden der Filmstars* (Berlin: Böhm, 1928), 83.
5. Werner Fiedler, "Magie des stummen Spiels: Huldigung an die 80jährige Asta Nielsen," *Der Tag* (Berlin).
6. Joseph Garncarz, "Art and Industry: German Cinema of the 1920s," in *The Silent Cinema Reader*, ed. Lee Grieveson and Peter Krämer (London: Routledge, 2004), 389.
7. Ibid., 390.
8. Ibid.
9. Leopold Jacobson, "Asta Nielsen als Schauspielerin: Raimund-Theater," *Theater und Kunst*, [1925].
10. Ibid.
11. Wolfgang Fischer, *Von Asta Nielsen bis Sonja Ziemann* (Berlin: Wolfgang Fischer, 1958), 11.
12. Ibid, 8.
13. Garncarz, "Art," 392.
14. Ibid.
15. Knut Hickethier, "Theatervirtuosinnen und Leinwandmimen: Zum Entstehen des Stars im deutschen Film," in *Die Modellierung des Kinofilms: Zur Geschichte des Kinoprogramms zwischen Kurzfilm und Langfilm, 1905/6–1918*, ed. Corinna Müller and Harro Segeberg (Munich: Vilhelm Fink Verlag, 1998), 355.
16. Quoted in Garncarz, "Art," 397.
17. Béla Balázs, *Der Sichtbare Mensch oder die Kultur des Films* (Vienna: Deutsch-Österreichischer Verlag, 1924), 167.
18. Curt Michaelis et al., *Unsere Zeit* (Berlin: Mundus-Verlag, [1919]), [5].
19. Willy Haas, "Die schöne Hexe der Stummfilmzeit," *Die Welt* (Frankfurt), 11 September 1971.
20. Karl Prümm, "Mit den Sinnen denken: Der Filmkritiker Willy Haas," in *Willy Haas: Der Kritiker als Mitproduzent: Texte zum Film, 1920–1933,*

ed. Wolfgang Jacobsen, Karl Prümm, and Benno Wenz (Berlin: Edition Hentrich, 1991), 9.

21. Sabine Hake, *The Cinema's Third Machine* (Lincoln: University of Nebraska Press, 1993), x.

22. Ibid., 49.

23. Ibid., 50.

24. Miriam Hansen, "Early Silent Cinema: Whose Public Sphere?" *New German Critique*, no. 29 (Spring–Summer 1983), 165.

25. B. E. Lüthge, "Asta Nielsen in *Rausch*," *Film-Kurier* 31 (11 July 1919): 1

26. Niels Th. Thomsen, "Hos Asta Nielsen: Et Interview med den verdensberømte Filmdiva, inden hun rejste til Berlin," *Palads-Teatret Program*, [1919].

27. "Asta Nielsen und Ernst Lubitsch: Star, Strindberg, und Filmregie," *Film-Kurier* 2, no. 235 (19 October 1920): 1.

28. In *Filmgeschichte als Krisengeschichte*, Michael Wedel offers both an in-depth account of the dispute between Lubitsch and Nielsen and an analysis of Nielsen's aesthetic views and filmic practices, in particular her insistence on the difference between real and forced tears. Michael Wedel, *Filmgeschichte als Krisengeschichte: Schnitte und Spuren durch den deutschen Film* (Bielefeld: transcript Verlag, 2011).

29. Patrice Petro, *Joyless Streets: Women and Melodramatic Representation in Weimar Germany* (Princeton, NJ: Princeton University Press, 1989), 153.

30. Rainer Rother, "Glücksversprechen," in *City Girls: Frauenbilder im Stummfilm*, ed. Gabriele Jatho and Rainer Rother (Berlin: Stiftung Deutscher Kinemathek, 2007), 9.

31. Siegfried Kracauer, *From Caligari to Hitler: A Psychological History of the German Film* (Princeton, NJ: Princeton University Press, 1947), 158.

32. Hansen, "Cinema," 174.

33. Guido Haller, "Aus der Praxis," *Der Kinematograph* (Düsseldorf), no. 733 (6 March 1921).

34. "Aus dem Glashaus," *Film-Kurier* (Berlin), 22 November 1920.

35. For several decades, the New York Museum of Modern Art owned one of the only extant prints of the film, until the German Film Museum acquired and restored another, slightly different print in 2007.

36. Anthony R. Guneratne, *Shakespeare, Film Studies, and the Visual Cultures of Modernity* (New York: Palgrave Macmillan, 2008), 155.

37. Tony Howard, *Women as Hamlet: Performance and Interpretation in Theatre, Film, and Fiction* (Cambridge, MA: Cambridge University Press, 2007), 151.

38. Ibid., 152.

39. Anne Jerslev, "Asta Nielsen, kvindeligheden og de store følelser," *Kosmorama* 41, no. 213 (1995): 32.

40. Howard, *Hamlet*, 151.

41. Ibid., 153.

42. Judith Buchanan, *Shakespeare on Film* (Harlow, England: Pearson Longman, 2005), 60.

43. Howard, *Hamlet*, 156.

44. Rüdiger Schaper, "Die Helsingöre: Asta Nielsens 'Hamlet' in der Retrospektive," *Tagesspiegel* (12 February 2007): 25.
45. Petro, *Streets,* 153.
46. Howard, *Hamlet,* 152.
47. Erwin Gepard, "Hamlet von heute," *Neues vom Film,* [1920].
48. "Von Dänemark bis in den Mond," *Film-Kurier* (Berlin) 2, no. 155 (16 July 1920): 1.
49. "Asta Nielsen—Prinz von Dänemark," *Film- Kurier* (Berlin) 2, no. 166 (30 July 1920): 1.
50. Jennifer Bean, "'Übers Meer gebracht': In Amerika, 1912–1914," in *Unmögliche Liebe: Asta Nielsen, ihr Kino,* ed. Heide Schlüpmann et al. (Vienna: Film Archiv Austria, 2009), 339.
51. "Beilage," *Der Film* (Berlin), no. 51 (18 December 1921).
52. "Der Hamlet-Film in italienischen Königsschloss," *Der Film* (Berlin), no. 46 (13 November 1920).
53. "Filmspionage," *Film-Kurier* (Berlin), 16 September 1921.
54. "Einige Pressestimmen nach der Berliner Uraufführung im Mozartsaal am 4. Februar 1921 über das unbestrittenen größte Ereignis der Saison, der Welterfolg Hamlet mit Asta Nielsen," *Film-Kurier* (Berlin), 16 February 1921.
55. "Der angefeindete Hamletfilm," *Film-Kurier* (Berlin), 3 February 1921.
56. "Asta Nielsen-Filmen 'Hamlet,'" unidentified Danish newspaper, [1921], DFI Asta Nielsen Collection.
57. "Pressestimmen."
58. Ib Monty, ed., *Asta Nielsen: Breve 1911–71* (Copenhagen: Gyldendal, 1998), 40.
59. Ibid., 69.
60. Diaz, "Künstlerin," 62.
61. Howard, *Hamlet,* 156–57.
62. Béla Balázs, "Die Erotik der Asta Nielsen," *Der Tag* (Berlin), 6 April 1923.
63. "Die Stimme des stummen Films: Asta Nielsen zum 80. Geburtstag," *Süddeutsche Zeitung* (Munich), 11 September 1961.
64. Ej, "Fräulein Julie," unidentified German newspaper, [1922], DFI Asta Nielsen Collection.
65. Birgitte Sølund, *Becoming Modern: Young Women and the Reconstruction of Womanhood in the 1920s* (Princeton: Princeton University Press, 2000), 6.
66. Hake, *Cinema,* 41.
67. Caliban [Willy Haas], "Astas Tränen hörten nimmer auf...," *Die Welt* (Frankfurt), *Ausgabe B.*, 19 February 1973.
68. Petro, *Streets,* 201.
69. Ibid., 213.
70. "Bag Glædernes Maske," *Nationaltidende* (Copenhagen), 23 March 1926, 9.
71. Hj., "Bag Glædernes Maske," *Politiken* (Copenhagen), 23 March 1926.

72. Eric, "Syndens Gade," *Berlingske Tidende* (Copenhagen), March 1926.

73. Olav Harsløf, *Lysår: Kunstens kulturhistorie i Danmark i det 20: Århundrede* (Copenhagen: Høst & Søn, 2000), 147.

74. Nielsen had explored a similar theme several years earlier in *The Fall* (*Der Absturz*, 1922), which tells the story of an aging opera singer whose young lover goes to prison for a murder he committed for her, but who doesn't recognize the decrepit old woman she has become when he is released ten years later, as well as in *A Tragedy of the Streets* (1926), in which her character, the aging prostitute Auguste, falls in love with a young bourgeois man and dreams of settling down with him into comfortable respectability. When her pimp, afraid of losing business, introduces Auguste's lover to the younger, prettier prostitute Clarissa, Auguste is distraught, persuades her pimp to murder Clarissa, and poisons herself, freeing her young lover to return to his parental home.

75. This ideological position is supported by Brandes's own efforts to bring about political reforms to legalize civil marriage, as well as both Henrik Ibsen's and August Strindberg's divergent but equally provocative arguments for sensible gender relations in such texts as *A Doll's House* (*Et Dukkehjem*, 1879), *Getting Married* (*Giftas*, 1884), and *Miss Julie* (*Fröken Julie*, 1888).

76. Malmkjær, *Asta*, 206.

77. Mr. Screen, "Asta Nielsen forbudt," *B. T.* (Copenhagen), 17 May 1927.

78. Monty, *Breve*, 7.

79. Andreas Winding, "Hemmeligheden ved Asta Nielsen," unidentified Danish magazine, 1922, 6, DFI Asta Nielsen Collection.

80. Christian Engelstoft, "Asta Nielsen, Kunstnerinden der forlod sit fædreland," *Aftenbladet* (Copenhagen), 27 November 1927.

81. Kristin Thompson, *Exporting Entertainment: America in the World Film Market, 1907–1934* (London: British Film Institute, 1985), 129.

82. Eric, "Filmens eneste danske Verdensnavn: Asta Nielsen i den tyske Storfilm *Gadens Moral*," *Søndags B. T.* (Copenhagen), 27 September 1925, 18.

83. Stephan Michael Schröder, "Die Duse des Kinos as 'Frau Nielsen': In Dänemark," in *Unmögliche Liebe: Asta Nielsen, ihr Kino*, ed. Heide Schlüpmann et al. (Vienna: Film Archiv Austria, 2009), 430.

84. Schröder dates the first documented usage of "die Asta" to the 1922 article by Danish journalist Andreas Winding, "Hemmeligheden ved Asta Nielsen." This Danish example is, however, predated by both German journalist Egon Jacobsohn's 1919 article and the events from 1920 described in Svend Gade's 1941 autobiography, *The Screenplay of My Life*, where he writes about traveling around Germany with Nielsen while filming *Hamlet*: "'Die Asta! Die Asta!' they whispered wherever we walked, wherever we stood"; quoted in Allen Hagedorff and Renate Seydel, *Asta Nielsen: Ihr Leben in Fotodokumenten, Selbstzeugnissen, und zeitgenössischen Betrachtungen* (Berlin: Henschelverlag, 1981), 158.

85. Schröder, "Duse," 429.
86. Mr. Screen, "Asta Nielsen forbudt," *B. T.* (Copenhagen), 17 May 1927.
87. Eric, "Verdensnavn," 18.
88. Stephan Michael Schröder, "Fra Babel til Nørrebro, fra Berlin til Frederiksberg: Filmens Internationalisering og Nationalisering," in *Kultur på kryds og tværs,* ed. Henning Bech and Anne Scott Sørensen (Aarhus, Denmark: Klim, 2005), 127.
89. Merete, "Asta Nielsen taler ud," *Politiken* (Copenhagen), 6 January 1930.
90. Olaf Fønss, *Danske Skuespillerinder: Erindringer og Interviews* (Copenhagen: Nutids Forlag, 1930), 122.
91. Schröder, "Babel," 126.
92. Fønss, *Skuespillerinder,* 120.
93. Ibid., 120.
94. Garncarz, "Art," 397.
95. Asta Nielsen, *Den tiende Muse,* vol. 2 (Copenhagen: Gyldendal, 1946), 185–86.
96. Mariann Lewinsky, "Stummfilmdiva Asta Nielsen: Frauenbilder von nachhaltiger Modernität," *Film Podium* (November–December 1994): 6.
97. Quoted in Rolf Lehnhardt, "Sie ist schon Legende," *Welt der Arbeit* (Cologne), 9 September 1966.
98. Walter Kordt, "Asta Nielsen: Ein betrübliches Kapitel der deutschen Filmproduktion," unidentified German newspaper, [late 1920s], DFI Asta Nielsen Collection.
99. *Blätter des Leipziger Schauspielhauses* 3, 1925–26.
100. Anton Sahm, "Asta Nielsen," *Münchener Illustrierte Presse,* no. 1 (1926): 2.
101. Nielsen, *Muse,* vol. 2, 203.
102. Siegfried Kracauer, "Zwei große Filmpremieren: Asta Nielsen," *Frankfurter Zeitung,* 28 December 1932.
103. Lene Voigt, "Wiedersehen mit Asta Nielsen," *Frankfurter Allgemeine Zeitung,* 2 May 1933.
104. K. Gl. "Wieder Asta Nielsen: 'Unmögliche Liebe' im Mozartsaal," unidentified German newspaper, [1932], Bundesfilmarchiv Berlin.
105. "Asta Nielsens første Talefilm," unidentified Danish newspaper, [1932], DFI Asta Nielsen collection.
106. Ramona Curry, "How Early German Film Stars Helped Sell the War(es)," in *Film and the First World War,* ed. Karel Dibbets and Bert Hogenkamp (Amsterdam: Amsterdam University Press, 1995), 146.
107. Nls, "Da Asta Nielsen havde Hitler til Bords hos Göbbels," *Berlingske Tidende* (Copenhagen), 10 October 1945.
108. Nielsen, *Muse,* vol. 2, 207.
109. Nls, "Göbbels."
110. Malmkjær, *Asta,* 244.
111. Nls, "Göbbels."
112. Hans Bendix, ed., "Heil Hitler!" *Aandehullet,* 1 (October 1933), 39.
113. Malmkjær, *Asta,* 249.

114. Quoted in Malmkjær, *Asta*, 236.
115. Nielsen, *Muse*, 372.
116. Unpublished letter from Nielsen to Heinrich Rumpff, dated 24 June 1943. Deutsches Institut für Filmkunde, Frankfurt.
117. Unpublished handwritten letter from Nielsen to Heinrich Rumpff, dated 22 August 1946. Deutsches Institut für Filmkunde, Frankfurt.
118. Unpublished letter from Nielsen to Heinrich and Tilla Rumpff, dated 12 September 1936, Deutsches Institut für Filmkunde, Frankfurt; partially reprinted in Klaus Kirst, "Die schweigende Muse in Wort und Bild: Filmmuseum Potsdam mit Asta Nielsen," *Berliner Zeitung*, 3 September 1992.
119. Unpublished letter from Nielsen to Tilla Rumpff, dated 9 December 1936. Deutsches Institut für Filmkunde, Frankfurt.
120. Malmkjær, *Asta*, 254.
121. Monty, *Breve*, 61.
122. Unpublished letter from Nielsen to Heinrich Rumpff, dated 24 June 1943. Deutsches Institut für Filmkunde, Frankfurt.
123. Nls, "Göbbels."
124. Unpublished letter from Nielsen to Heinrich and Tilla Rumpff, dated 6 June 1946. Deutsches Institut für Filmkunde, Frankfurt.
125. Unpublished letter from Nielsen to Heinrich Rumpff, dated 22 August 1946. Deutsches Institut für Filmkunde, Frankfurt.
126. Unpublished letter from Nielsen to Heinrich Rumpff, dated 21 January 1947. Deutsches Institut für Filmkunde, Frankfurt.
127. Schröder, "Babel," 120.
128. Johan Fjord Jensen, *Homo Manipulatus* (Copenhagen: Gyldendal, 1966), 18.
129. Ibid., 22.
130. Ibid., 19.
131. Ibid., 20.
132. Ibid., 29.
133. See chapter 3 for an in-depth discussion of Brandes's humanitarian advocacy work.
134. Jensen, *Homo Manipulatus*, 28.
135. "Hvad de sagde om Danmarks-Filmen," unidentified Danish newspaper, Danish Film Institute Archives, 30 April 1935.
136. Jens Kistrup, "Ingen grund til forargelse," *Berlingske Tidende* (Copenhagen), 6 September 1994.
137. Paul Hammerich, *Lysmageren* (Copenhagen: Gyldendal, 1986), 273–74.
138. Trafic, "Danmarksfilmen er et uhørt Skandale," *Nationaltidende*, 2 November 1937.
139. E. H., "Danmarksfilmen," *Arbeiderbladet*, 30 April 1935.
140. Hammerich, *Lysmageren*, 273.
141. Ibid., 276.
142. Vidi, "Dansk-Amerikaners Dom over Danmarks-Filmen," *Politiken* (Copenhagen), 2 November 1937.

143. This tradition of both official and unofficial Danish national propaganda films includes many other provocative films, including Klaus Rifbjerg's *Danske billeder* (1970), Jørgen Leth's *Livet i Danmark* (1971), and Suzanne Brøgger's *Kort fra Danmark* (1973). For more on this topic, see Lars Henriksen, "Danmarks mange ansigter," *Kristeligt Dagblad*, 8 September 2006, 12.

144. Schröder, "Duse," 432.

145. "Pengene dræber Kunsten," *Uge Journalen*, 13 March 1938.

146. Niels Jørgen Dinnesen and Edvin Kau, *Filmen i Danmark* (Copenhagen: Akademisk Forlag, 1983), 33.

147. Monty, *Breve*, 35.

148. Malmkjær, *Asta*, 251.

149. Ibid., 249.

150. Liber, "Triangel-Bevillingen givet til Knud Jørgensen," *Berlingske Tidende* (Copenhagen), 14 October 1948.

151. "Åbent brev fra Asta Nielsen til justitsminister Busch-Jensen," *Social Demokraten* (Copenhagen), 10 November 1948.

152. Olaf Fønss, "Vi har en Forpligtelse over for Asta Nielsen," *Berlingske Aftenblad* (Copenhagen), 11 November 1948.

153. Ole Dalsgaard-Olsen, "Asta Nielsen og dansk film," *Politiken* (Copenhagen), 14 November 1948.

154. This proverb is first documented as "La vengeance est un plat qui se mange froid" in the novel *Les Liaisons Dangereuses* by Pierre Choderlos de Laclos (Dangerous Liaisons, 1782).

155. Ella Laugesen, "Asta Nielsen og Danmark," *Information* (Copenhagen), 20 November 1948.

156. Knud Poulsen, "Filmkameraet var som hele verdens øje," *Politiken* (Copenhagen), 29 November 1948.

157. Laugesen, "Danmark."

158. Josef Petersen, "Asta Nielsen," *Politiken* (Copenhagen), 18 November 1948.

159. Ibid.

160. Unpublished letter from Asta to Tilla [Rumpff], dated 1 December 1948, Deutsches Institut für Filmkunde, Frankfurt.

161. A collection of these stories, translated into German, was published as *One Day in Paradise* (*Ein Tag im Paradies*) (Munich: Ullstein Verlag, 1996).

162. Malmkjær, *Asta*, 292.

163. Inge Byrjalsen, *Asta Nielsen—Filmens dronning* (Copenhagen: Gyldendal, 1994), 60. "Asta Nielsen kommer på finansloven en principsag," *Berlingske Tidende* (Copenhagen), 5 September 1963.

164. Skjødt-Jensen capitalizes on the ambiguity of the title of Nielsen's memoirs, *The Silent/Tenth Muse*, in the English titles of his films. The documentary is based on taped telephone conversations between Nielsen and her confidante, Frede Schmidt, in which a far more personal portrait of Nielsen emerges than in her memoirs. Thus the title, *The Talking Muse*, refers to both the chance to hear Nielsen's voice on film, and the confessional tone of

the film. The television movie utilizes the alternate translation of the title of Nielsen's autobiography, *The Tenth Muse,* in order to underscore the legitimacy of film as the equal of the classical arts, thanks in part to Nielsen's work. The Danish title of the movie is identical to that of Nielsen's first Danish film.

 165. Schröder, "Duse," 434.
 166. Ibid., 435.

CONCLUSION

 1. P. David Marshall, *Celebrity and Power: Fame in Contemporary Culture* (Minneapolis: University of Minnesota Press, 1997), xi.
 2. Ibid., 57–58.
 3. Ibid., 6.

BIBLIOGRAPHY

A., Dr. C. "Schwedische Kinozensur-Sensation: Asta Nielsen gegen die Zen-sur," *Lichtbild-Theater* 3, no. 46 (1911).
Abel, Richard. *The Red Rooster Scare: Making Cinema American, 1900–1910*. Berkeley: University of California Press, 1999.
"Åbent brev fra Asta Nielsen til justitsminister Busch-Jensen." *Social-Demokraten* (Copenhagen), 10 November 1948.
Adorno, Theodor, and Max Horkheimer. *Dialectic of Enlightenment: Philosophical Fragments*. Edited by Gunzelin Schmid Noerr. Translated by Edmund Jephcott. Stanford, CA: Stanford University Press, 2002.
Allen, Robert C. "Contra the Chaser Theory." *Wide Angle* 3, no. 1 (1979): 4–11.
Altenloh, Emilie. *Zur Soziologie des Kino: Die Kinounternehmung und die sozialen Schichten ihrer Besucher*. Leipzig: Spamerschen Buchdruckerei, [1913].
Anderson, Benedict. *Imagined Communities*. 2nd ed. London: Verso, 1991.
"Der angefeindete Hamletfilm." *Film-Kurier* (Berlin), 3 February 1921.
Archer, William. "Shirking the Issue: A Letter to Dr. George Brandes." London: Hodden & Stoughton, 1917.
"Asta Nielsen." *Maanedsmagasin*, 24 November 1912.
"Asta Nielsen." *Masken*, no. 8 (19 November 1910): 71–73.
"Asta Nielsen—Filmen 'Hamlet.'" Unidentified Danish newspaper, [1921]. DFI Asta Nielsen Collection.
"Asta Nielsen kommer på finansloven en principsag." *Berlingske Tidende* (Copenhagen), 5 September 1963.
"Asta Nielsen—Prinz von Dänemark." *Film-Kurier* (Berlin) 2, no. 166 (30 July 1920): 1.
"Asta Nielsens første Talefilm." Unidentified Danish newspaper, [1932]. DFI Asta Nielsen collection.
Asta Nielsen und Ernst Lubitsch: Star, Strindberg, und Filmregie." *Film-Kurier* (Berlin) 2, no. 235 (19 October 1920): 1.
Auerbach, Jonathan. *Body Shots: Early Cinema's Incarnations*. Berkeley: University of California Press, 2007.

"Aus dem Glashaus." *Film-Kurier* (Berlin), 22 November 1920.

Bagge, Poul. "Nationalisme, Antinationalisme og Nationalfølelse i Danmark omkring 1900." In *Festskrift til Astrid Friis*, edited by Svend Ellehøj, Svend Gissel, and Knud Vohn, 1–28. Copenhagen: Rosenkilde og Bagger, 1963.

"Bag Glædernes Maske." *Nationaltidende* (Copenhagen), 23 March 1926, 9.

Balázs, Béla. "Die Erotik der Asta Nielsen." *Der Tag* (Berlin), 6 April 1923.

———. *Der Sichtbare Mensch oder die Kultur des Films*. Vienna: Deutsch-Österreichischer Verlag, 1924.

Barbas, Samantha. *Movie Crazy: Fans, Stars, and the Cult of Celebrity*. New York: Palgrave, 2001.

Barfoed, Niels, ed. *Omkring "Niels Lyhne."* Copenhagen: Hans Reitzel, 1970.

Barton, H. Arnold. *A Folk Divided: Homeland Swedes and Swedish-Americans, 1840–1940*. Carbondale: Southern Illinois University, 1994.

Bauer, Conny. "Die Rezeption Jens Peter Jacobsens in der deutschsprachigen Kritik, 1890–1910." In *Fin de siècle: Zu Naturwissenschaft und Literatur der Jahrhundertwende im deutsch-skandinavischen Kontext. Vorträge des Kolloquiums am 3. und 4. Mai 1984*, edited by Klaus Bohnen, Uffe Hansen, and Friedrich Schmöe, 128–46. Text & Kontext Sonderreihe. Vol. 20. Copenhagen: Fink, 1984.

Bean, Jennifer. "'Übers Meer gebracht': In Amerika, 1912–1914." In *Unmögliche Liebe: Asta Nielsen, ihr Kino*, edited by Heide Schlüpmann et al., 337–52. Vienna: Film Archiv Austria, 2009.

Becker, Jörg. "Diven und Fans/Divas and fans." In *Filmmuseum Berlin*, edited by Wolfgang Jacobsen, 21–34. Berlin: Nicolai, 2000.

"Beilage." *Der Film* (Berlin), no. 51 (18 December 1921).

Belach, Helga, ed. *Henny Porten: Der erste deutsche Filmstar, 1890–1960*. Berlin: Haude & Spener, 1986.

Bendix, Hans. "Heil Hitler!" *Aandehullet* 1 (October 1933): 39.

Benjamin, Walter. *Das Kunstwerk im Zeitalter seiner technischen Reproduzierbarkeit: Drei Studien zur Kunstsoziologie*. Frankfurt am Main: Suhrkamp, 1977.

———. *The Work of Art in the Age of Its Technological Reproducibility, and Other Writings on Media*. Edited by Michael W. Jennings, Brigid Doherty, and Thomas Y. Levin. Translated by Edmund Jephcott et al., 19–55. Cambridge, MA: The Belknap Press of Harvard University Press, 2008.

Bergstrom, Janet. "Asta Nielsen's Early German Films." *Before Caligari: German Cinema, 1895–1920*. Edited by Paolo Cherchi Usai and Lorenzo Codelli, 162–84. Madison: University of Wisconsin Press, 1990.

———. "Asta Nielsen's Early German Films." *Frauen und Film* 62 (2000): 42–44.

Binder, Alex. *Unsere Filmsterne*. Berlin: Buch-Film Verlag, 1922.

Bjørn, Claus. "Modern Denmark: A Synthesis of Converging Developments." *Scandinavian Journal of History* 25, nos. 1–2 (June 2000): 119–30.

Blätter des Leipziger Schauspielhauses 3, 1925–26.

Bleibtreu, Karl. "*Der Feind im Land.*" *Die Ähre.* 21 September 1913. Reprinted in *Henny Porten: Der erste deutsche Filmstar, 1890–1960.* Edited by Helga Belach, 41–42. Berlin: Haude & Spener, 1986. Citations refer to the 1986 edition.

Bohnen, Klaus. "Georg Brandes og de intellektuelle miljøer i Tyskland og Østrig." In *Georg Brandes og Europa*, edited by Olav Harsløf, 155–62. Copenhagen: Museum Tusculanum, 2004.

———. "*Niels Lyhne* in Deutschland: Unveröffentlichter Briefwechsel zwischen Georg Brandes und Theodor Wolff." *Skandinavistik* 9, no. 1 (1979): 1–20.

———. "Über das 'Seelenleben' einer Stadt." In *Ästhetik der skandinavischen Moderne: Bernhard Glienke zum Gedenken*, edited by Annegret Heitmann and Karin Hoff, 203–13. Frankfurt am Main: Peter Lang, 1998.

Borup, Morten, ed. *Georg og Edv. Brandes: Brevveksling med nordiske Forfattere og Videnskabsmænd.* 8 vols. Copenhagen: Gyldendal, 1940.

Bradbury, Malcolm, and James McFarlane. "The Name and Nature of Modernism." In *Modernism: A Guide to European Literature, 1890–1930*, edited by Malcolm Bradbury and James McFarlane, 19–55. London: Penguin, 1976.

Brahm, Otto. *Kritische Schriften: Über Drama und Theater.* Berlin: S. Fischer Verlag, 1915.

"Brandes, Denmark's Foremost Personality." *American Review of Reviews* (New York) 43 (January 1911): 100.

Brandes, Georg. "En Appel." *Georg Brandes: Den mangfoldige.* Edited by Jørgen Knudsen, 221–25. Copenhagen: Gyldendal, 2005.

———. "Armenien og Europa," In *Samlede Skrifter*, 11–20. Vol. 17. Skikkelser og Tanker, Tredie Bind. Copenhagen: Gyldendal, 1906.

———. *Berlin som tysk Rigshovedstad.* Copenhagen: Philipsens Forlag, 1885.

———. "Bjørnstjerne Bjørnson: *En Fallit* og *Redaktøren.*" *Det nittende Aarhundrede* (Copenhagen) 2 (June 1875): 241.

———. "Das Dänentum in Südjütland." In *Der Zukunft*, edited by Maximilian Harden, vol. 7, no. 27 (1 April 1899). Reprinted in *Der Wahrheitshass*, edited by Hans Grössel, 50–68. Berlin: Berenberg, 2007. Citations refer to the 2007 edition.

———. "Den danske Literatur efter 1870." 1901. In *Samlede Skrifter*, 191–200. Vol. 15. Skikkelser og Tanker, Første Bind. Copenhagen: Gyldendal, 1905.

———. *Det Moderne Gjennembruds Mænd.* Copenhagen: Gyldendal, 1883.

———. "Europa nu." *Tilskueren* (February 1925): 89–92. Partially reprinted in "Brandes Despairs," *The Nation* 120, no. 3122 (6 May 1925): 529–30. Citations refer to the *Nation* edition.

———. "Folgen des Weltkriegs." In *Der Wahrheitshass*, edited by Hans Grössel, 135. Berlin: Berenberg, 2007.

———. "The Fundamental Causes of the World War." In *The World at War*, translated by Catherine D. Groth, 32–54. New York: Macmillan, 1917.

———. "Georg Brandes on Denmark's Neutrality." Translated by M. Wreschner. *Evening Post* (New York), 6 July 1915.

———. "Germany Today." *New Republic* (New York) 32, no. 416 (22 November 1922): 327.

———. "A Great Danish Critic Finds a Deficit." *Living Age* (Boston) 326, no. 4232 (22 June 1925): 351.

———. *Hauptströmungen der Literatur des Neunzehnten Jahrhunderts*. Translated by Adolf Strodtmann. 2nd ed. Vol. 1. Die Emigrantenliteratur. Leipzig: H. Harsdorf, 1897.

———. *Hovedstrømninger i det 19de Aarhundredes Litteratur*. 1st ed. Vol. 1. *Emigrantlitteraturen*. Copenhagen: Gyldendal, 1872.

———. "Hunnertalen." In *Samlede Skrifter*, 74–77. Vol. 17. Skikkelser og Tanker, Tredie Bind. Copenhagen: Gyldendal, 1906.

———. "Lebenslauf." In *Der Wahrheitshass*, edited by Hans Grössel, 166–71. Berlin: Berenberg, 2007.

———. *Levned*. Copenhagen: Gyldendal, 1907.

———. "Nachwort." *Deutsche Rundschau* 35 (May 1883): 300.

———. *Om Nationalfølelse*. Copenhagen: Gjellerup, 1894.

———. "Pogromhetze." In *Der Wahrheitshass*, edited by Hans Grössel, 117–20. Berlin: Berenberg, 2007.

———. "Svar til Georges Clemenceau." In *Udvalgte Skrifter*. Vol. 9: *Politiske Artikler og Taler*, edited by Sven Møller Kristensen, 70–76. Copenhagen: Tiderne Skifter, 1987.

———. "Tale i Sorø." In *Samlede Skrifter*, 436–39. Vol. 15. Skikkelser og Tanker, Første Bind. Copenhagen: Gyldendal, 1905.

———. "Tale paa Møen." In *Samlede Skrifter*, 440–45. Vol. 15, Skikkelser og Tanker, Første Bind. Copenhagen: Gyldendal, 1905.

———. "Tanker ved Aarhundredeskiftet." In *Samlede Skrifter*, 142–62. Vol. 12: *Politik og Nationalitet*. Copenhagen: Gyldendal, 1902.

———. *The World at War*. Translated by Catherine D. Groth. New York: Macmillan, 1917.

Brewster, Ben, and Lea Jacobs. *Theatre to Cinema: Stage Pictorialism and the Early Feature Film*. New York: Oxford University Press, 1997.

Broomans, Petra. *Videnskab og National Opdragelse: Studier i nordisk litteraturhistorieskrivning*. Part 2, 487–542. Copenhagen: Nordisk Ministerråd, 2001.

Buchanan, Judith. *Shakespeare on Film*. Harlow, England: Pearson Longman, 2005.

Byrjalsen, Inge. *Asta Nielsen—filmens droning*. Copenhagen: Gyldendal, 1994.

Caliban, [Willy Haas]. "Astas Tränen hörten nimmer auf...." *Die Welt* (Frankfurt) / *Ausgabe B.*, 19 February 1973.

Christensen, Erik M. *Henrik Ibsens anarkisme: De samlede værker*. Copenhagen: Akademisk Forlag, 1989.

———. *Henrik Ibsens realisme: Illusion, katastrofe, anarki*. Copenhagen: Akademisk Forlag, 1985.

Christiansen, Niels Finn. "Folkets danskhed, 1864–1920." In *På sporet af dansk identitet*, edited by Flemming Lundgreen-Nielsen, 153–90. Copenhagen: Spectrum, 1992.

Cie. "Marathondisputats på 375 minutter: Elias Bredsdorffs forsvar for sin doktorafhandling." *Politiken* (Copenhagen), 1 July 1964.

Clausen, Jørgen Stender. *Det nytter ikke at sende hær mod ideer*. Copenhagen: C. A. Reitzel, 1984.

Clausson, Sophus. "Kronik. Films." *Politiken* (Copenhagen), 5 May 1911.

Culler, Jonathan, and Pheng Cheah, eds. *Grounds of Comparison: Around the Work of Benedict Anderson*. New York: Routledge, 2003.

Curry, Ramona. "How Early German Film Stars Helped Sell the War(es)." In *Film and the First World War*, edited by Karel Dibbets and Bert Hogenkamp, 139–48. Amsterdam: Amsterdam University Press, 1995.

Dalsgaard-Olsen, Ole. "Asta Nielsen og dansk film." *Politiken* (Copenhagen), 14 November 1948.

Diaz, Pablo. *Asta Nielsen: Eine Biographie unserer populären Künstlerin*. Translated from Spanish. Berlin: Verlag der Lichtbild-Bühne, [1927].

Dinnesen, Niels Jørgen, and Edvin Kau. *Filmen i Danmark*. Copenhagen: Akademisk Forlag, 1983.

Doane, Mary Ann. *The Emergence of Cinematic Time: Modernity, Contingency, the Archive*. Cambridge, MA: Harvard University Press, 2002.

Dreyer, Carl Theodor. "Vor Tids Helte: Asta Nielsen-Gad." *Ekstrabladet* (Copenhagen), 2 October 1913. Reprinted in Peter Schepelern, *Tommen: Carl Th. Dreyers filmjournalistiske virksomhed* (Copenhagen: C. A. Reitzel, 1982), 36. Citations refer to the 1913 edition.

Drotner, Kirsten. "Asta Nielsen: A Modern Woman Before Her Time?" In *Is there a Nordic Feminism? Nordic Feminist Thought on Culture and Society*, edited by Drude von der Fehr et al., 294–309. London: UCL Press, 1998.

Eckert, Ernst Richard. "Georg Brandes." *Das Interview: Weltkritik* (Berlin), no. 15/16 (1922): 9.

"Einige Pressestimmen nach der Berliner Uraufführung im Mozartsaal am 4. Februar 1921 über das unbestrittenen größte Ereignis der Saison, der Welterfolg Hamlet mit Asta Nielsen." *Film-Kurier* (Berlin), 16 February 1921.

Eisner, Lotte. "Zu Ehren von Asta Nielsen." *Kosmorama* 50, no. 7 (October 1960): 6–7.

Ej. "Fräulein Julie." Unidentified German newspaper, [1922]. DFI Asta Nielsen Collection.

Elsaesser, Thomas. "Early German Cinema: A Second Life?" In *A Second Life: German Cinema's First Decades*, edited by Thomas Elsaesser, 9–37. Amsterdam: Amsterdam University Press, 1996.

———. "National Subjects, International Style: Navigating Early German Cinema." In *Before Caligari: German Cinema, 1895–1920*, edited by Paolo Cherchi Usai and Lorenzo Codelli, 338–54. Madison: University of Wisconsin Press, 1990.

Elsner, Poul. "Die Duse des Films." *Reclams Universum Weltrundschau* (Leipzig), [1911]: 517.

Engberg, Marguerite. *Asta Nielsen.* Copenhagen: Det danske filmmuseum, 1966.

———. *Dansk Stumfilm.* 2 vols. Copenhagen: Rhodos, 1977.

———. "The Erotic Melodrama in Danish Silent Films, 1910–1918." *Film History* 5 (1993): 63–67.

———. "Nordisk in Denmark." In *Film and the First World War,* edited by Karel Dibbets and Bert Hogenkamp, 43–49. Amsterdam: Amsterdam University Press, 1995.

Engelstoft, Christian. "Asta Nielsen, Kunstnerinden der forlod sit fædreland." *Aftenbladet* (Copenhagen), 27 November 1927.

Englert, Uwe. "Der Moderne Durchbruch." In *Wahlverwandtschaft: Skandinavien und Deutschland 1800 bis 1914,* edited by Bernd Henningsen, et al., 209–13. Berlin: Jovis, 1997.

Eric. "Filmens eneste danske Verdensnavn: Asta Nielsen i den tyske Storfilm *Gadens Moral.*" *Søndags B. T.* (Copenhagen), 27 September 1925, 18.

———. "Syndens Gade." *Berlingske Tidende* (Copenhagen), March 1926.

Ewald, Johannes. *Harlequin Patriot eller den uægte Patriotismus.* Copenhagen, 1772.

Feldbæk, Ole. "Dansk Identitet, 1740–1992." In *Dansk Identitet?* edited by Uffe Østergård, 57–77. Aarhus: Aarhus Universitetsforlag, 1992.

Felix. "Hvad Verden Taler Om: I Julen skal Kæmpefilmen INRI gaa over hele Jorden med Asta Nielsen som Magdalena." Unidentified Danish newspaper, [1923], 10. DFI Asta Nielsen Collection.

Fenger, Henning. "Har Københavns kommune mon hørt om Brandes?" *København City,* no. 1 (February 1977): 12.

Fiedler, Werner. "Magie des stummen Spiels: Huldigung an die 80jährige Asta Nielsen. " *Der Tag (Berlin),* 10 September 1961.

"Filmspionage." *Film-Kurier* (Berlin), 16 September 1921.

Fischer, Wolfgang. *Von Asta Nielsen bis Sonja Ziemann.* Berlin: Wolfgang Fischer, 1958.

Fønss, Olaf. *Danske Skuespillerinder: Erindringer og Interviews.* Copenhagen: Nutids Forlag, 1930.

———. "Vi har en Forpligtelse over for Asta Nielsen." *Berlingske Aftenblad* (Copenhagen), 11 November 1948.

Gad, Emma. "Kronik: Film-Eventyret." *Politiken* (Copenhagen), 6 March 1913.

Gad, Peter Urban. *Filmen, dens Midler og Maal.* Copenhagen: Gyldendal, 1919.

———. *Klunketiden paa en anden Maade.* Copenhagen: Gyldendal, 1949.

Garncarz, Joseph. "Art and Industry: German Cinema of the 1920s." In *The Silent Cinema Reader,* edited by Lee Grieveson and Peter Krämer, 389–400. London: Routledge, 2004.

Gellner, Ernest. *Nations and Nationalism*. Oxford: Blackwell, 1983.
"Georg Brandes hyldet i New York." *Nordlyset* (New York), 11 June 1914.
"Georg Brandes i Amerika: Danskerne træffer store Forberedelser." *Politiken* (Copenhagen), 8 May 1914.
"Georg Brandes i Chicago." *Berlingske Tidende* (Copenhagen), 27 May 1914.
Gepard, Erwin. "Hamlet von heute." *Neues vom Film*, [1920].
Gibbons, Henry J. "Georg Brandes: The Reluctant Jew." In *The Activist Critic: A Symposium on the Political Ideas, Literary Methods, and International Reception of Georg Brandes*, edited by Hans Hertel and Sven Møller Kristensen, 55–89. Orbis Litterarum, supplement no. 5. Copenhagen: Munksgaard, 1980.
Gl., K. "Wieder Asta Nielsen: 'Unmögliche Liebe' im Mozartsaal." Uniden-tified German newspaper, [1932]. Bundesfilmarchiv Berlin.
Glienke, Bernhard. "Gründerjahre eines Großkritikers: Der Däne Georg Brandes in Berlin." In *Grenzgänge: Skandinavisch-deutsche Nachbarschaften*, edited by Heinrich Detering, 147–60. Grenzgänge: Studien zur skandinavisch-deutschen Literaturgeschichte. Göttingen: Wallstein Verlag, 1996.
Gritten, David. *Fame: Stripping Celebrity Bare*. London: Allen Lane, 2002.
Grössel, Hans. "Nachwort." In *Der Wahrheitshass*, ed. by Hans Grössel, 172–76. Berlin: Berenberg, 2007.
Guneratne, Anthony R. *Shakespeare, Film Studies, and the Visual Cultures of Modernity*. New York: Palgrave Macmillan, 2008.
Güttinger, Fritz. *Kein Tag ohne Kino: Schriftsteller über den Stummfilm*. Frankfurt: Deutsches Filmmuseum, 1984.
H., E. "Danmarksfilmen." *Arbeiderbladet* (Copenhagen), 30 April 1935.
Haacke, Wilmont. *Julius Rodenberg und die Deutsche Rundschau*. Heidelberg: Kurt Vowinckel, 1950.
Haas, Willy. "Die schöne Hexe der Stummfilmzeit." *Die Welt* (Frankfurt), 11 September 1971.
Habermas, Jürgen. *The Structural Transformation of the Public Sphere: An Inquiry into a Category of Bourgeois Society*. Translated by Thomas Burger and Frederick Lawrence. Cambridge, MA: MIT Press, 1989.
Hagedorff, Allen, and Renate Seydel. *Asta Nielsen: Ihr Leben in Fotodokumenten, Selbstzeugnissen, und zeitgenössischen Betrachtungen*. Berlin: Henschelverlag, 1981.
Hake, Sabine. *The Cinema's Third Machine*. Lincoln: University of Nebraska Press, 1993.
———. *German National Cinema*. London: Routledge, 2002.
———. "Self-Referentiality in Early German Cinema." In *A Second Life: German Cinema's First Decades*, edited by Thomas Elsaesser, 237–45. Amsterdam: Amsterdam University Press, 1996.
"Der Hamlet-Film in italienischen Königsschloss." *Der Film* (Berlin), no. 46 (13 November 1920).

Haller, Guido. "Aus der Praxis." *Der Kinematograph* (Düsseldorf), no. 733 (6 March 1921).

Hammerich, Paul. *Lysmageren*. Copenhagen: Gyldendal, 1986.

Hansen, Kjeld. *Det tabte land: Den store fortælling om magten over det danske landskab*. Copenhagen: Gads Forlag, 2008.

Hansen, Miriam. "Early Silent Cinema: Whose Public Sphere?" *New German Critique*, no. 29 (Spring–Summer 1983): 147–84.

Hansert, Andreas. *Asta Nielsen und die Filmstadt Babelsberg: Das Engagement Carl Schleussners in der Deutschen Filmindustrie*. Petersburg, Germany: Michael Imhof Verlag, 2007.

Harsløf, Olav. "Fra kulturpolitik til politisk journalistik." In *Den politiske Georg Brandes*, edited by Hans Hertel and Sven Møller Kristensen, 135–38. Copenhagen: Hans Reitzel, 1973.

———. *Lysår: Kunstens kulturhistorie I Danmark i det 20. århundrede*. Copenhagen: Høst & Søn, 2000.

———. *Mondegruppen: Kampen om Kunsten og Socialismen i Danmark, 1928–1932*. Copenhagen: Museum Tusculanum Press, 1997.

Hasselriis, C. H. W. *Georg Brandes: Besøg i Amerika*. Chicago: The Danish-American Association, 1914.

———. "Georg Brandes blandt sine Landsmænd i Amerika." *Politiken* (Copenhagen), 28 May 1914.

Haugen, Einar. "Georg Brandes and his American Translators." *Journal of English and Germanic Philology* 37, no. 4 (October 1938): 462–87.

Hektor. "The Visit of a Famous Artistic Couple: Asta Nielsen Gad and Peter Urban Gad: Brief Interview." *Politiken* (Copenhagen), 8 October 1912.

Helge. "En ny Asta Nielsen-Film: Paa Mandag Premiere i Paladsteatret: Hele Indtægter gaar til Juleindsamlingen." *Politiken* (Copenhagen), 21 December 1912.

Hending, Arnold. *Lygterne tændes langs vejen: Om mange jeg mødte* Copenhagen: Kandrup & Wunsch Forlag, 1961.

Henningsen, Bernd. "'O Danmarck!' Det danske ved den danske politiske tradition." In *Dansk Identitet?* edited by Uffe Østergård, 79–101. Aarhus: Aarhus Universitetsforlag, 1992.

Henriksen, Lars. "Danmarks mange ansigter." *Kristeligt Dagblad* (Copenhagen), 8 September 2006, 12.

Herder, Johann Gottfried. *Journal meiner Reise im Jahr 1769*. Stuttgart: Philipp Reclam Jr., 1976.

Hertel, Hans, and Sven Møller Kristensen, eds. *The Activist Critic: A Symposium on the Political Ideas, Literary Methods, and International Reception of Georg Brandes*, edited by Hans Hertel and Sven Møller Kristensen, 55–89. Orbis Litterarum, supplement no. 5. Copenhagen: Munksgaard, 1980.

Hertel, Hans. "Georg Brandes' Dobbeltblik: Nationalisme, antisemitisme, internationalisme—og litteraturhistorien som kulturkamp, 1871–2003." In *Kam-*

pen om Litteraturhistorien: Festskrift til Pil Dahlerup, edited by Marianne Alenius et al., 305–44. Copenhagen: Dansklærerforeningen, 2004.

Hickethier, Knut. "Schauspieler zwischen Theater und Kino in der Stummfilmzeit." In *Grenzgänger zwischen Theater und Kino: Schauspielerporträts aus dem Berlin der Zwanziger Jahre,* edited by Knut Hickethier, 11–42. Berlin: Edition Mythos, Verlag Ästhetik und Kommunikation, 1986.

———. "Theatervirtuosinnen und Leinwandmimen: Zum Entstehen des Stars im deutschen Film." In *Die Modellierung des Kinofilms: Zur Geschichte des Kinoprogramms zwischen Kurzfilm und Langfilm,*1905/6–1918, edited by Corinna Müller and Harro Segeberg, 333–57. Vol. 2 of *Mediengeschichte des Films.* Munich: Vilhelm Fink Verlag, 1998.

Higson, Andrew. "The Concept of National Cinema." *Screen* (Autumn 1989): 36–46.

Hilson, Mary. *The Nordic Model: Scandinavia since 1945.* London: Reaktion Books, 2008.

Hj. "Bag Glædernes Maske." *Politiken* (Copenhagen), 23 March 1926.

Hjort, Mette. *Small Nation, Global Cinema: The New Danish Cinema.* Minneapolis: University of Minnesota Press, 2005.

"Hos Film Divaen." *Politiken* (Copenhagen), 16 April 1911.

Houe, Poul. "Georg Brandes i Amerika." *Weekendavisen* (Copenhagen), 11 August 2000, 9.

Howard, Tony. *Women as Hamlet: Performance and Interpretation in Theatre, Film, and Fiction.* Cambridge, MA: Cambridge University Press, 2007.

Hutchinson, John. *Modern Nationalism.* London: Fontana Press, 1994.

"Hvad de sagde om Danmarks-Filmen." Unidentified Danish newspaper, 30 April 1935. Danish Film Institute Archives.

Jacobsohn, Egon. "Asta Nielsen." *Bühne und Film* 1 (1919): 3–6.

Jacobson, Leopold. "Asta Nielsen als Schauspielerin: Raimund-Theater." *Theater und Kunst,* [1925].

Jagger, Gill. *Judith Butler: Sexual Politics, Social Change, and the Power of the Performative.* London: Routledge, 2008.

Jelavich, Peter. "'Am I Allowed to Amuse Myself Here?': The German Bourgeoisie Confronts Early Film." In *Germany at the Fin de Siècle: Culture, Politics, and Ideas,* edited by Suzanne Marchand and David Lindenfeld, 227–49. Baton Rouge: Louisiana State University Press, 2004.

Jensen, Johan Fjord. *Homo Manipulatus.* Copenhagen: Gyldendal, 1966.

Jerslev, Anne. "Asta Nielsen, kvindeligheden og de store følelser." *Kosmorama* 41, no. 213 (1995): 26–35.

Kirst, Klaus. "Die schweigende Muse in Wort und Bild: Filmmuseum Potsdam mit Asta Nielsen." *Berliner Zeitung* (Berlin), 3 September 1992.

Kistrup, Jens. "Ingen grund til forargelse." *Berlingske Tidende* (Copenhagen), 6 September 1994.

Klevian, Inge. "Kultursammenstød som lystspil." *Kosmorama* 232 (2003): 99–112.

Knudsen, Jørgen. *GB: En Brandes-biografi*. Copenhagen: Gyldendal, 2008.

———. *Georg Brandes: Frigørelsens vej, 1842–77*. Copenhagen: Gyldendal, 1985.

———. *Georg Brandes: I modsigelsernes tegn, 1877–83*. Copenhagen: Gyldendal, 1988.

———. *Georg Brandes: Magt og Afmagt, 1896–1914*. Copenhagen: Gyldendal, 1998.

———. "Georg Brandes og de intellektuelle i Norden og Europa." In *Georg Brandes og Europa*, edited by Olav Harsløf, 17–30. Copenhagen: Museum Tusculanum, 2004.

Kordt, Walter. "Asta Nielsen: Ein betrübliches Kapitel der deutschen Filmproduktion." Unidentified German newspaper, [late 1920s]. DFI Asta Nielsen Collection.

Kracauer, Siegfried. *From Caligari to Hitler: A Psychological History of the German Film*. Princeton, NJ: Princeton University Press, 1947.

———. "Zwei große Filmpremieren: Asta Nielsen," *Frankfurter Zeitung*, 28 December 1932.

Kreyssig, Friedrich. "Literarische Rundschau: Die Hauptströmungen der Literatur des neunzehnten Jahrhunderts." *Deutsche Rundschau* (October 1874): 139.

Kristensen, Sven Møller. "Aktivisten Georg Brandes." In *Den politiske Georg Brandes*, edited by Hans Hertel and Sven Møller Kristensen, 9–26. Copenhagen: Hans Reitzel, 1973.

Krüger, Paul, ed. *Correspondance de Georg Brandes*. Vol. 3: *L'Allemagne*. Copenhagen: Rosenkilde og Bagger, 1966.

Langen, Albert. Foreword to *Nationalgefühl: Vortrag gehalten bei der Einweihung der neuen Räume des Freisinnigen Studenten-Vereins in Kopenhagen am 1. Februar 1894*, by Georg Brandes, 3–4. Köln: Albert Langen, 1894.

Langsted, Adolf. *Asta Nielsen*. Copenhagen: Nyt Nordisk Forlag, 1918.

Larsen, Lisbeth Richter. "Valdemar Psilander: Una star internazionale del cinema danese." Translated by Cristiana Querze. *Cinegrafie* 17 (2004): 168–91.

Laugesen, Ella. "Asta Nielsen og Danmark." *Information* (Copenhagen), 20 November 1948.

Lee, Benjamin. Foreword to *Metaculture: How Culture Moves through the World*, by Greg Urban, ix–xvi. Minneapolis: University of Minnesota Press, 2001.

Lehnhardt, Rolf. "Sie ist schon Legende." *Welt der Arbeit* (Cologne), 9 September 1966.

"Levende Billeder." *Politiken* (Copenhagen), 30 May 1911.

Lewinsky, Mariann. "Stummfilmdiva Asta Nielsen: Frauenbilder von nachhaltiger Modernität." *Filmpodium* (November–December 1994): 6–7.

Liber. "Triangel-Bevillingen givet til Knud Jørgensen." *Berlingske Tidende* (Copenhagen), 14 October 1948.

Locher, Jens. "Asta Nielsen." Unidentified Danish magazine, 1916, 9-12. DFI Asta Nielsen Collection.
Lorant, Stefan. *Wir vom Film: Das Leben, Lieben, Leiden der Filmstars*. Berlin: Böhm, 1928.
Lundgreen-Nielsen, Flemming. "Danskhed i krige og kriser, 1800–1864." In *På sporet af dansk identitet*, edited by Flemming Lundgreen-Nielsen, 109–52. Copenhagen: Spectrum, 1992.
Lüthge, B. E. "Asta Nielsen in *Rausch*." *Film-Kurier* (Berlin) 31 (11 July 1919): 1.
Magon, Leopold. "Nordische Literatur- und Geistesgeschichte: Dänemark." *Euphorion* (1926): 610.
Malmkjær, Poul. *Asta: Menneket, myten og filmstjernen*. Copenhagen: P. Haase & Søn, 2000.
Marshall, P. David. *Celebrity and Power: Fame in Contemporary Culture*. Minneapolis: University of Minnesota Press, 1997.
Meerman, Johann. *Reise durch den Norden und Nordosten von Europa in den Jahren 1797 bis 1800*. 6 vols. Gravenhaage: I. Van Cleef, 1804–1806. Translated by Rühs. Vienna: B. Ph. Bauer, 1811.
Merete. "Asta Nielsen taler ud." *Politiken* (Copenhagen), 6 January 1930.
Meyer, Michael. Introduction to *Ghosts and Three Other Plays*, 1–17. New York: Anchor Books, 1966.
Michaelis, Curt, et al. *Unsere Zeit*. Berlin: Mundus Verlag, [1919].
Monty, Ib, ed. *Asta Nielsen: Breve 1911–71*. Copenhagen: Gyldendal, 1998.
Mørch, Søren. *Den sidste Danmarkshistorie*. Copenhagen: Gyldendal, 1996.
Müller, Corinna. "Emergence of the Feature Film in Germany between 1910 and 1911." In *Before Caligari: German Cinema, 1895–1920*, edited by Paolo Cherchi Usai and Lorenzo Codelli, 94–112. Madison: University of Wisconsin Press, 1990.
———. *Frühe deutsche Kinematographie*. Stuttgart: Metzler, 1994.
———. "Der Weg zum Star: Versuch einer Rekonstruktion." In *Henny Porten: Der erste deutsche Filmstar, 1890–1960*, edited by Helga Belach, 32–39. Berlin: Haude & Spener, 1986.
Mungenast, E. M. (Ernst Moritz). *Asta Nielsen*. Stuttgart: Walter Hädecke Verlag, 1928.
Musser, Charles. *Before the Nickelodeon: Edwin S. Porter and the Edison Manufacturing Company*. Berkeley: University of California Press, 1991.
N., W. "'Schweigende Muse': Asta Nielsen erzählt ihr Leben." *Freie Presse* (Zwickau), 23 October 1961.
Neergaard, Niels. *Under Junigrundloven: En Fremstilling af det danske Folks politiske Historie fra 1848 til 1866*. 1916. Vol. 2. Copenhagen: Selskabet for Udgivelse af Kilder til Dansk Historie, 1973.
Nielsen, Asta. "Der Schuss im Kino." In *Film Photos wie noch nie*, edited by Edmund Bucher, 21. Giessen: Kindt & Bucher, 1929.
———. *Ein Tag im Paradies*. Munich: Ullstein Verlag, 1996.

———. *Den tiende Muse*. 2 vols. Copenhagen: Gyldendal, 1945–1946.
Nielsen, Torben, ed. *Georg Brandes: Breve til Forældrene, 1872–1904*. Copenhagen: C. A. Reitzel, 1994.
Nls. "Da Asta Nielsen havde Hitler til Bords hos Göbbels." *Berlingske Tidende* (Copenhagen), 10 October 1945.
Nordby, Thomas. "Georg Brandes og imperialismen: Georg Brandes' politiske journalistik fra det 20. århundrede." In *Den politiske Georg Brandes*, edited by Hans Hertel and Sven Møller Kristensen, 139–56. Copenhagen: Hans Reitzel, 1973.
Oakes, Augustus and R.B. Mowat, eds. *The Great European Treaties of the Nineteenth Century*. Oxford: Clarendon Press, 1918.
Opffer, Emil. "Georg Brandes fortæller om sine Indtryk i Amerika." *Politiken* (Copenhagen), 6 June 1914.
———. "Georg Brandes i Amerika." *Politiken* (Copenhagen), 3 June 1914.
Østergård, Uffe. *Europas ansigter: Nationale stater og politiske kulturer i en ny, gammel verden*. Copenhagen: Munksgaard-Rosinante, 1992.
———. "Georg Brandes og Europa i dag." In *Georg Brandes og Europa*, edited by Olav Harsløf, 31–46. Copenhagen: Museum Tusculanum, 2004.
"Paladsteatret: Asta Nielsen Premiere." *Berlingske Tidende* (Copenhagen), 10 May 1914.
"Paladsteatret: Ny Asta Nielsen Film i Paladsteatret." *Folkets Avis* (Copenhagen), 12 May 1914.
"Panoptikon-Teatret." *Politiken* (Copenhagen), 18 April 1911.
Parsons, Kate. "Georg Brandes: 'Big, Strong, Unamiable, Yet Lovable.'" *New York Times*, 31 May 1914, 3.
"Pengene dræber Kunsten." *Uge Journalen* (Copenhagen), 13 March 1938.
Petersen, Josef. "Asta Nielsen." *Politiken* (Copenhagen), 18 November 1948.
Petro, Patrice. *Joyless Streets: Women and Melodramatic Representation in Weimar Germany*. Princeton, NJ: Princeton University Press, 1989.
Pinthus, Kurt. "Henny Porten als Reichspräsident." *Das Tagebuch*, no. 41 (1921). Reprinted in *Henny Porten: Der erste deutsche Filmstar, 1890–1960*, edited by Helga Belach, 82–85. Berlin: Haude & Spener, 1986. Citations refer to the 1986 edition.
Poulsen, Knud. "Filmkameraet var som hele verdens øje." *Politiken* (Copenhagen), 29 November 1948.
Prümm, Karl. "Mit den Sinnen denken: Der Filmkritiker Willy Haas." In *Willy Haas: Der Kritiker als Mitproduzent: Texte zum Film, 1920–1933*, edited by Wolfgang Jacobsen, Karl Prümm, and Benno Wenz, 9–25. Berlin: Edition Hentrich, 1991.
Pust, Maren M. "That's Why the Lady Is a Vamp: The Danish Origins of the Screen's First Dangerous Lady." In *Fleshpot: Cinema's Sexual Myth Makers and Taboo Breakers*, edited by Jack Stevenson, 77–89. Manchester, England: Headpress, 2000.

Rehné, Ib. *Løvindens Pote: Et essay om myten og mennesket*. Frederiksberg, Denmark: Fiskers Forlag, 1993.

Rosen, Philip. *Change Mummified: Cinema, Historicity, Theory*. Minneapolis: University of Minnesota Press, 2001.

Rother, Rainer. "Glücksversprechen." In *City Girls: Frauenbilder im Stummfilm*, edited by Gabriele Jatho and Rainer Rother, 6–9. Berlin: Stiftung Deutscher Kinemathek, 2007.

Rung, Otto. "Københavnsk Selskabsliv ved Aarhundredeskiftet." In *Danmark i Fest og Glæde*, edited by Julius Clausen and Torben Krogh, 45–120. Vol. 5: *Tiden, 1870–1914*. Copenhagen: Chr. Erichsens Forlag, 1935.

S., V. "Mellem Film-Slagene: Et Besøg hos Asta Nielsen." *Verden og Vi* 1 (1915): 20.

Sahm, Anton. "Asta Nielsen." *Münchener Illustrierte Presse*, no. 1 (1926): 2.

Said, Edward W. *Culture and Imperialism*. New York: Vintage, 1994.

Sampson, Steven. "Please: No More Danskhed." In *Dansk Identitet?* edited by Uffe Østergård, 225–37. Aarhus: Aarhus Universitetsforlag, 1992.

Sandberg, Hans-Joachim. "Tradition und/oder Fortschritt? Zum Problem der Wandlung Thomas Manns im Lichte der Brandes-Rezeption des Dichters." In *The Activist Critic: A Symposium on the Political Ideas, Literary Methods, and International Reception of Georg Brandes*, edited by Hans Hertel and Sven Møller Kristensen, 169–90. Orbis Litterarum, supplement no. 5. Copenhagen: Munksgaard, 1980.

Sandemose, Aksel. *En flygtning krysser sitt spor*. Oslo: Tiden Norsk Forlag, 1933.

Schaper, Rüdiger. "Die Helsingöre: Asta Nielsens 'Hamlet' in der Retrospektive." *Tagesspiegel* (Berlin), (12 February 2007): 25.

Schiörring, Viggo. "Kino-Kunstens Duse." Unidentified Danish newspaper, 1912, 20. DFI Asta Nielsen Collection.

Schlüpmann, Heide. "Asta Nielsen and Female Narration: The Early Films." In *A Second Life: German Cinema's First Decades*, edited by Thomas Elsaesser and Michael Wedel, 118–22. Amsterdam: Amsterdam University Press, 1996.

———. "Cinema as Anti-theater: Actresses and Female Audiences in Wilhelminian Germany." In *Silent Film*, edited by Richard Abel, 125–41. New Brunswick, NJ: Rutgers University Press, 1996.

Schröder, Stephan Michael. "Die Duse des Kinos as 'Frau Nielsen': In Dänemark." In *Unmögliche Liebe: Asta Nielsen, ihr Kino*, edited by Heide Schlüpmann et al., 427–35. Vienna: Film Archiv Austria, 2009.

———. "Fra Babel til Nørrebro, fra Berlin til Frederiksberg: Filmens Inter-nationalisering og Nationalisering." In *Kultur på kryds og tværs*, edited by Henning Bech and Anne Scott Sørensen, 114–32. Aarhus, Denmark: Klim, 2005.

Screen, Mr. "Asta Nielsen forbudt." *B. T.* (Copenhagen), 17 May 1927.

Sieburg, Friedrich. "Brandes und Dänemark." *Die Weltbühne* (Berlin) 21, no. 13 (31 March 1925): 468–72.

Smith, Anthony D. *National Identity*. Reno: University of Nevada Press, 1991.

Smut. "Filmen i Aften. Kl. 8¼ er der Premiere paa Paladsteatret." *Politiken* (Copenhagen), 23 December 1912.

Sørensen, Anne Scott. "Den nordiske kreds: En dansk-tysk aristokratisk salonkultur." In *Nordisk salonkultur*, edited by Anne Scott Sørensen, 147–70. Odense: Odense Universitetsforlag, 1998.

Sørensen, Bengt Algot. "Georg Brandes als 'deutscher' Schriftsteller." In *The Activist Critic: A Symposium on the Political Ideas, Literary Methods and International Reception of Georg Brandes*, edited by Hans Hertel and Sven Møller Kristensen, 127–45. Orbis Litterarum, supplement no. 5. Copenhagen: Munksgaard, 1980.

Sorokin, Pitrim. *Social Mobility*. New York: Harper, 1927.

"Die Stimme des stummen Films: Asta Nielsen zum 80. Geburtstag." *Süddeutsche Zeitung* (Munich), 11 September 1961.

Strodtmann, Adolf. *Das geistige Leben in Dänemark: Streifzüge auf den Gebieten der Kunst, Literatur, Politik, und Journalistik des skandinavischen Nordens*. Berlin: Paetel, 1873.

Taylor, Paul A., and Jan Ll. Harris. *Critical Theories of Mass Media Then and Now*. Maidenhead, England: Open University Press, 2008.

"Teater og Tribune." *Politiken* (Copenhagen), 16 April 1911.

"Teater og Tribune." *Politiken* (Copenhagen), 24 August 1912.

Teunissen, José. "Mode und Modernität." In *Unmögliche Liebe: Asta Nielsen, ihr Kino*, edited by Heide Schlüpmann et al., 241–51. Vienna: Film Archiv Austria, 2009.

Thompson, Kristin. *Exporting Entertainment: America in the World Film Market, 1907–1934*. London: British Film Institute, 1985.

Thomsen, Niels Th. "Asta Nielsen-Gad." *Masken* 3, no. 27 (1912): 23–24.

———. "Hos Asta Nielsen: Et Interview med den verdensberømte Filmdiva, inden hun rejste til Berlin." *Palads-Teatret Program* (Copenhagen), [1919].

Trafic. "Danmarksfilmen er et uhørt Skandale." *Nationaltidende*, 2 November 1937.

"En Tyrefægtnings-Film med Asta Nielsen i Hovedrollen." *Politiken* (Copenhagen), 9 June 1913.

Ulrichsen, Erik. "Asta Nielsens fire danske film." *Kosmorama* 19 (1956): 7.

"Unsere Preisrundfrage: Wer ist die beliebteste Filmkünstlerin? V. Asta Nielsen." Unidentified German newspaper, 4 May 1918. DFI Asta Nielsen Collection.

Urban, Greg. *Metaculture: How Culture Moves through the World*. Minneapolis: University of Minnesota Press, 2001.

"Urteile der Frankfurter Zeitungen über Asta Nielsen." Bundesfilmarchiv Berlin. *Colosseum-Theater Essen, Rheinpreußen*, 1913, 7.

Vidi. "Dansk-Amerikaners Dom over Danmarks-Filmen." *Politiken* (Copenhagen), 2 November 1937.

Voigt, Lene. "Wiedersehen mit Asta Nielsen." *Frankfurter Allgemeine Zeitung*, 2 May 1933.
"Von Dänemark bis in den Mond." *Film-Kurier* 2, no. 155 (16 July 1920): 1.
Vonderau, Patrick. *Bilder vom Norden*. Marburg, Germany: Schüren, 2007.
Wedel, Michael. *Filmgeschichte als Krisengeschichte: Schnitte und Spuren durch den deutschen Film*. Bielefeld: transcript Verlag, 2011.
———. "Towards an Archaeology of the Early German Music Film." In *Le son en perspective: Nouvelles recherches*, edited by Dominique Nasta and Didier Huvelle, 115–34. Brussels: Peter Lang, 2004.
Wetzig-Zalkind, Birgit. *Das ist Berlin: Eine Stadt und ihre Stars*. Berlin: Westkreuz Verlag, 2005.
Winding, Andreas. "Hemmeligheden ved Asta Nielsen." Unidentified Danish magazine, 1922, 6. DFI Asta Nielsen Collection.
Wingårdh, Freddy. "Med Asta Nielen over Atlanten." Unidentified Danish newspaper, [1916]. DFI Asta Nielsen Collection.
Winge, Mette. *Alle tiders Emma Gad*. Copenhagen: Politikens Forlag, 2005.
Winge, Vibeke. "Dänemark—Ein fortgesetztes Teutschland? Sprachliche Grenzgänger in Kopenhagen." In *Grenzgänge: Skandinavisch-deutsche Nachbarschaften*, edited by Heinrich Detering, 46–59. Vol. 1. Grenzgänge: Studien zur skandinavisch-deutschen Literaturgeschichte. Göttingen: Wallstein Verlag, 1996.
Wolff, Theodor. "Jens Peter Jacobsen." Foreword to *Niels Lyhne*, translated by Marie von Borch, 1–27. Leipzig: Philipp Reclam, 1889.
"Woman Always Pays." *New York Dramatic Mirror*, 24 April 1912, 27.
Zweig, Stefan. *Europäisches Erbe*. Frankfurt am Main: S. Fischer, 1960.

UNPUBLISHED SOURCES

Brandes, Georg. Private letter to Asta Nielsen, dated 23 December 1916. Asta Nielsen Collection, Danish Film Institute, Copenhagen.
———. Private letter to Asta Nielsen, dated 24 December 1919. Asta Nielsen Collection, Danish Film Institute, Copenhagen.
———. Speech for Asta Nielsen, 1920. Unpublished manuscript, Brandes Collection, Danish Royal Library Manuscript Department, Copenhagen.
———. "Tale til Asta Nielsen," 1918. Unpublished manuscript. Brandes Collection, Danish Royal Library Manuscript Department, Copenhagen.
Nielsen, Asta. Handwritten contract between Asta Nielsen and Frede Skaarup, signed in Aarhus, Denmark, dated 2 May 1911. Courtesy of Isak Thorsen and Nordisk Film Archives.
———. Private letter to Heinrich and Tilla Rumpff, dated 12 September 1936. Deutsches Institut für Filmkunde, Frankfurt.
———. Private letter to Tilla Rumpff, dated 9 December 1936. Deutsches Institut für Filmkunde, Frankfurt.

———. Private letter to Tilla Rumpff, dated 24 June 1943. Deutsches Institut für Filmkunde, Frankfurt.

———. Private letter to Heinrich and Tilla Rumpff, dated 6 June 1946. Deutsches Institut für Filmkunde, Frankfurt.

———. Private letter to Heinrich Rumpff, dated 22 August 1946. Deutsches Institut für Filmkunde, Frankfurt.

———. Private letter to Heinrich Rumpff, dated 21 January 1947. Deutsches Institut für Filmkunde, Frankfurt.

———. Private letter to Tilla Rumpff, dated 1 December 1948. Deutsches Institut für Filmkunde, Frankfurt.

Olsen, Ole. Business letter no. 211 from Ole Olsen to "Herrn Carl Süring," dated 17 November 1910. Nordisk Film Collection, Danish Film Institute Archives, Copenhagen.

———. Business letter no. 238 from Ole Olsen to "Nordische Films, Berlin," dated 19 November 1910. Nordisk Film Collection, Danish Film Institute Archives, Copenhagen.

———. Business letter no. 822 from Ole Olsen, September 1911. Nordisk Film Collection, Danish Film Institute Archives, Copenhagen.

FILM REFERENCES

Basch, Felix. 1922. *Fräulein Julie*. Art-Film GmbH, Germany.

Biebrach, Rudolf. 1917. *Hann, Hein, und Henny*. Messter Film, Germany.

Blom, August. 1910. *Den hvide Slavehandel*. Nordisk Film, Denmark.

———. 1911. *Balletdanserinden*. Nordisk Film, Denmark.

Cohn, Alfred. 1910. *Den hvide Slavehandel*. Fotorama, Denmark.

Eckstein, Franz. 1924. *Der Schmetterlingsschlacht*. National-Film AG, Germany.

———. 1925. *Hedda Gabler*. National-Film AG, Germany.

Edel, Edmund. 1916. *Das Versuchskaninchen*. Neutral-Film GmbH, Germany.

———. 1916. *Die Börsenkönigin*. Neutral-Film GmbH, Germany.

Froelich, Carl. 1921. *Irrende Seelen*. Decla-Bioscop AG, Germany.

Gad, Urban. 1910. *Afgrunden*. Kosmorama, Denmark. DVD, Denmark: Det Danske Filminstitut, 2005.

———. 1914. *Das Feuer*. Projektions AG "Union," Germany.

———. 1912. *Das Mädchen ohne Vaterland*. Deutsche Bioscop, Germany.

———. 1911. *Den sorte Drøm*. Fotorama, Denmark.

———. 1911. *Der fremde Vogel*. Deutsche Bioscop, Germany.

———. 1914. *Die falsche Asta Nielsen*. Projektions AG "Union," Germany.

———. 1913. *Die Filmprimadonna*. Projektions AG "Union," Germany.

———. 1912. *Die Macht des Goldes*. Deutsche Bioscop, Germany.

———. 1913. *Die Suffragette*. Projektions AG "Union," Germany.

———. 1912. *Die Verräterin*. Deutsche Bioscop, Germany.

Bibliography

———. 1913. *Engelein*. Projektions AG "Union," Germany.
———. 1911. *Heisses Blut*. Deutsche Bioscop, Germany.
———. 1911. *In dem großen Augenblick*. Deutsche Bioscop, Germany.
———. 1912. *Jugend und Tollheit*. Deutsche Bioscop, Germany.
———. 1912. *Kinder des Generals*. Deutsche Bioscop, Germany.
———. 1926. *Lykkehjulet*. Palladium, Denmark.
———. 1911. *Nachtfalter*. Deutsche Bioscop, Germany.
———. 1913. *S1*. Projektions AG "Union," Germany.
———. 1912. *Sünden der Väter*. Deutsche Bioscop, Germany.
———. 1913. *Tod in Sevilla*. Projektions AG "Union," Germany.
———. 1914. *Vordertreppe-Hintertreppe*. Projektions AG "Union," Germany.
———. 1912. *Wenn die Maske fällt*. Deutsche Bioscop, Germany.
———. 1913. *Zapatas Bande*. Projektions AG "Union," Germany.
———. 1911. *Zigeunerblut*. Deutsche Bioscop, Germany.
Gade, Svend. 1920. *Hamlet: Ein Rachedrama*. Art-Film GmbH, Germany.
Gasnier, Louis. 1914. *The Perils of Pauline*. Pathé, USA.
Gerlach, Arthur von. 1922. *Vanina*. Projektions AG "Union," Germany.
Harlan, Veit. 1940. *Jud Süß*. UFA, Germany.
Henningsen, Paul. 1935. *Danmark*. Danish Foreign Ministry, Denmark.
Holger-Madsen, Forest. 1918. *Mod Lyset*. Nordisk Film, Denmark.
Illés, Eugen. 1927. *Das gefährliche Alter*. Illés-Film GmbH, Germany.
Jessner, Leopold. 1922. *Erdgeist*. Leopold Jessner-Film GmbH, Germany.
Kaufmann, Fritz. 1924. *Das Haus am Meer*. Metro Film AG, Germany.
Larsen, Viggo. 1907. *Løvejagten*. Nordisk Film, Denmark.
Lubitsch, Ernst. 1920. *Anna Boleyn*. Messter Film and Universum Film (UFA), Germany. DVD, Germany: Kino Video, 2006.
———. 1919. *Die Austernprinzessin*. UFA, Germany.
———. 1918. *Ich möchte kein Mann sein*. UFA, Germany.
———. 1919. *Rausch*. Argus-Film GmbH, Germany.
Meinert, Rudolf. 1925. *Laster der Menschheit*. Internationale Film-AG, Germany.
Murnau, F. W. 1922. *Nosferatu*. Prana Film, Germany.
Pabst, G. W. 1925. *Die freudlose Gasse*. Sofar-Film-Produktion GmbH, Germany. DVD, Germany: Deutsches Filmmuseum, 2009.
Rahn, Bruno. 1927. *Dirnentragödie*. Pantomim-Film AG, Germany.
Schmidthässler, Walter. 1916. *Das Eskimobaby*. Neutral-Film GmbH, Germany.
Stark, Curt. 1910. *Das Liebesglück der Blinden*. Messters Projektion GmbH, Germany.
———. 1913. *Der Feind im Land*. Messters Projektion GmbH, Germany.
———. 1912. *Im Schatten des Meeres*. Messters Projektion GmbH, Germany.
Stifter, Magnus. 1916. *Das Liebes-ABC*. Neutral-Film GmbH, Germany.

———. 1916. *Dora Brandes*. Neutral-Film GmbH, Germany.

Tucker, George. 1913. *Traffic in Souls*. Independent Moving Pictures Company, United States.

Waschneck, Erich. 1932. *Unmögliche Liebe*. Märkische Film GmbH, Germany.

Wiene, Robert. 1920. *Das Cabinet des Dr. Caligari*. Decla-Bioscop, Germany.

———. 1923. *I.N.R.I.* Neumann-Produktion GmbH, Germany.

INDEX

Adorno, Theodor, 24, 130–31
Afgrunden (*The Abyss*), 33, 127, 135–36, 140–44, 147–48, 150, 155–56, 160, 164, 169, 204, 223, 226, 247
Altenloh, Emilie, 157
Andersen, Hans Christian (H. C.), 4, 11–12, 22, 28, 41, 48, 54, 70–71, 105, 150–51
Andersen, Vilhelm, 96
Anderson, Rasmus B., 111
Antonsen, Carl, 114
Apollinaire, Guillaume, 138
Armenia, 32, 92, 99, 101, 103, 109–10
Art Film, 180–81
Die Austernprinzesse (*The Oyster Princess*), 158

Babelsberg film studios, 145
Baggesen, Jens, 53–55
Balázs, Béla, 142, 183, 196
Balletdanserinden (*The Ballet Dancer*), 143–44
Bang, Herman, 20, 33, 61
Bara, Theda, 158
Bendix, Hans, 214–15
Benjamin, Walter, 25, 130–31
Berlin som tysk Rigshovedstad (*Berlin as the German Capital*), 66, 241
Bern Convention, 72
Bernhardt, Sarah, 135–36, 164, 190, 193, 195
Bernstorff, A. P., 53, 55
Bertini, Francesca, 138
Bettauer, Hugo, 199
Bier, Susanne, 43, 226
Bismarck, Otto von, 10, 47, 66, 69
Bjørnson, Bjørnstjerne, 84, 87–88, 91, 94, 187
Blom, August, 139, 143, 190, 201
Borelli, Lyda, 138

Die Börsenkönigin (*Queen of the Stock Market*), 172
Bournonville, August, 140
Bow, Clara, 158
Brandes, Edvard, 70, 78, 97–98, 174
Brandesianism, 10, 50, 59, 61, 98, 100, 115, 218–19
Bredsdorff, Elias, 32, 234
Broby-Johansen, Rudolf, 218
Brøchner, Henning, 195, 207
Busch-Jensen, Niels, 223, 258
Butler, Judith, 132

Das Cabinet des Dr. Caligari (*The Cabinet of Dr. Caligari*), 184
Cavling, Henrik, 12, 98, 174
celebrity: Brandes's and Nielsen's international, x, 11, 16–17, 111, 127, 146, 151, 212; cult of, 11, 26–27, 133, 135, 146, 183, 227, 229; definition of, 11, 27, 145, 229; power, ix, 11–12, 15, 27–28; sign, ix, 6, 11, 13, 27, 145, 148, 151, 216, 228, 231
censorship, national, 24, 95, 129, 141–42, 144, 160–64, 202–4, 207, 214, 247
Chmara, Grigori, 39, 182
Christensen, Benjamin, 137, 147
Christensen, Bernhard, 220
Christensen, Theodor, 42
Claussen, Sophus, 169–70, 174, 251
Clemenceau, Georges, 32, 91, 119–20, 122–23, 244
culture industry, 24, 27, 130–31, 133

Dalgas, Enrico Mylius, 235
Das Dänentum in Südjütland (*Danishness in Southern Jutland*), 104–5
Danish-American Association of Chicago, 126, 255

Danmarksfilmen (*The Denmark Film*),
    220–21, 258
danskhed (Danishness), 5–7, 9, 11–13,
    22, 28, 31, 40–41, 44, 56, 79, 132,
    191, 214, 224
Davidson, Hjalmar, 139–40
Davidson, Paul, 137, 144–45, 161, 223
Deutsche Bioscop, 135, 137, 143, 145,
    147, 150, 181
Deutsche Rundschau, 68, 71, 73–75,
    78, 81
de Verdier, Anton, 195
Diaz, Pablo, 120, 145
Dinesen, Robert, 139
Dirnentragödie (*A Tragedy of the
    Streets*), 186, 210, 255
Disraeli, Benjamin, 71, 73
diva film, 138
Dora Brandes, 251
Dostoevsky, Fyodor, 184
Doyle, Arthur Conan, 118
Drachmann, Holger, 61, 70, 82
Dreyer, Carl Theodor, 4, 170, 251
Dumas, Alexandre, 209
Duse, Eleonora, 135–36, 166

Eisner, Lotte, 147–48
endo-stereotypes, 7–8, 11–22, 18–19,
    21–22, 28, 60, 163
Engberg, Marguerite, 43, 130, 160–61,
    175
Engelein (*Little Angel*), 156, 159, 161
Erdgeist (*Earth-Spirit*), 184, 196
erotic melodrama, 128, 130, 139–40,
    157, 160–61, 163–64, 201, 245,
    250, 253
Eskesen, Echard V., 113–14
Das Eskimo Baby (*The Eskimo Baby*),
    172–74
Estrup, J. B. S., 91, 96
Ewald, Johannes, 58
exo-stereotypes, 7–8, 11–12, 18–20, 22,
    28, 48, 163

Die falsche Asta Nielsen (*The Wrong
    Asta Nielsen*), 153
Der Feind im Land (*The Enemy at
    Home*), 168
Das Feuer (*Vengeance Is Mine*), 149
film industry: American, 27, 138, 154,
    158, 164–66, 172, 181–82, 186,
    194–95, 205, 207–9; Danish, 15,
    139–40, 144–45, 147, 176, 203–4,
    206, 223–24, 226, 250; in general,
    26–27, 129, 130, 132, 133–34, 138,
    140, 154, 175, 180, 194, 208–9,
    230; German, 15, 33–34, 127, 130,
    135, 137, 147, 150, 169–70, 176,
    180–81, 185–86, 194–95, 207–8,
    212–13, 217, 231
Die Filmprimadonna (*The Film Prima
    Donna*), 153, 156
Fischer, Wolfgang, 181–83,
Fønss, Olaf, 147, 175, 206–7, 222–24
Fotorama, 128, 139, 143–44, 147
France, Anatole, 89, 118
Fräulein Julie (*Miss Julie*), 184, 187,
    196, 197, 202–3
Der fremde Vogel (*A Strange Bird*), 146,
    155
Freud, Sigmund, 118
Die freudlose Gasse (*The Joyless Street*),
    186, 197–200
Frisindet Kulturkamp (National
    Association for Liberal Cultural
    Politics), 219, 234
Fyrtårnet og Bivognen (Pat and
    Patachon), 205

Gad, Emma, 128, 140, 152–53, 175, 200
Gad, Peter Urban, 128, 139–40, 143,
    145–47, 152–53, 171–75, 182, 205,
    222
Gade, Svend, 186, 189, 195
Gagner, Marie Louise, 162–63
Garbo, Greta, 35, 197–99, 211
Das gefährliche Alter (*The Dangerous
    Age*), 39, 186, 200–201
Gelsted, Otto, 218
George, Heinrich, 217–18
German Circle, 53
Gladstone, William, 109
Goebbels, Joseph, 212–14, 217
Gorki, Maxim, 109
Gottschalk, Ludwig, 143
Goulash Age, 38, 174
Graatkjær, Axel, 195
Grammaticus, Saxo, 190
Greenland, 19, 32, 52, 153, 172–74, 234
Grundtvig, N. F. S., 58–59, 105, 226
Guldalderen (Golden Age), 19, 48–49

Haas, Willy, x, 37, 183, 197–9
Hage, Alfred, 49, 58
Hamid, Abdul, 109
Hamlet: ein Rachedrama, 37, 189–96,
    207, 224, 255
Hamsun, Knud, 75, 239
Hann, Hein, und Henny, 169
Hansson, Ola, 75, 239
Harden, Maximilian, 104
Hasselriis, C. H. W., 111, 114
Hauch, Carsten, 64
Hauptmann, Gerhart, 68, 118, 160

Index

Das Haus am Meer (*The House by the Sea*), 184
Hedda Gabler, 184–85, 187, 196, 197, 203
Heiberg, Johan Ludvig, 48
Heiberg, P. A., 55
Heisses Blut (*Burning Blood*), 150
Henningsen, Agnes, 219
Henningsen, Poul, 219–21
Herder, Johann Gottfried, 52, 54, 58
Herzfeld, Marie, 240
Heyse, Paul, 73, 77–78, 80–81
Hickethier, Knut, 135–36, 166
Hiddensee, 215–17, 225
Hitler, Adolf, 213–16, 220
Hofmannsthal, Hugo von, 68
Hofnagel, Mathieu, 146
Holberg, Ludvig, 54, 58, 71, 73, 105
Holger Danske ("Holger the Dane"), 55
Holger-Madsen, Forest, 139
Holger Tydske ("Holger the German"), 55
Holmsen, Bjarne P., 72
Holst, H. P., 235
Holstein, 9–10, 19, 48–49, 52–53, 56–57, 65, 70, 81, 86, 90, 105, 120–21, 146
Holz, Arno, 72
Homunculus, 147
Horkheimer, Max, 24, 130
Hørup, Viggo, 64, 91, 97
Hosenrollen (breeches parts), 153, 157, 170, 194
Hovedstrømninger (*Main Currents*), 29, 50, 61, 63–64, 68–69, 71–74, 80, 83, 121
Den hvide Slavehandel (*The White Slave Trade*), 128, 139

Ibsen, Henrik, 31, 59–60, 69–72, 75–77, 79, 82, 118, 149, 162, 175, 184–85, 200, 203, 238, 241, 255
Ich möchte kein Mann sein (*I Don't Want to Be a Man*), 158
Illés, Eugen, 181, 186, 201
Im Schatten des Meeres (*In the Shadow of the Sea*), 168
In dem großen Augenblick (*The Great Moment*), 162
Indtryk fra Polen (*Impressions from Poland*), 108–9
Internationale Film, 144–45, 171, 181
Irrende Seelen (*The Idiot*), 184

Jacobsen, J. P., 20, 31, 61, 69, 72, 74–75, 77–80, 82–83, 106, 178–79, 229, 240
Jacobsohn, Egon, 147, 178, 205
Jacobson, Leopold, 181
Jacobsson, Lilly, 195

Janteloven (Jante Law), 41, 151, 207
Jensen, Johannes V., 225
Jernsdorff, Peter, 33
Jessner, Leopold, 136, 181, 184
Jørgensen, Johannes, 96
Jørgensen, Martin, 172
Jud Süß, 217
Jugend und Tollheit (*Lady Madcap's Way*), 153, 165

Kielland, Alexander, 77
Kierkegaard, Søren, 4, 41, 47–48, 67, 69, 71, 105, 229
Kinder des Generals (*The General's Children*), 150
Kirk, Hans, 12, 218
Klopstock, Friedrich, 53
Köller, E. M. von, 105
Kracauer, Siegfried, x, 131, 189, 211
Krag, Thomas, 33
Kräly, Hanns, 186
Kulturkampe (culture wars), 10
Kulturradikalismen (cultural radicalism), 10

Lady of the Camellias, 209
Laemmle, Carl, 164
Lang, Fritz, 181
Langen, Albert, 241
Langsted, Adolf, 147
Lassalle, Ferdinand, 73
Laster der Menschheit (*Lusts of Mankind*), 186
Leander, Zarah, 35, 212
Lee, Benjamin, 18, 233, 234
Levy, Louis, 172
Lie, Jonas, 82
Das Liebes-ABC (*The Alphabet of Love*), 154
Das Liebesglück der Blinden (*The Blind Girl's Romance*), 166
Lind, Alfred, 140
livsanskuelsesdebat (life view debate), 200
London Protocol of 1852, 48, 56–57
Lossen, Lina, 197
Løvejagten (*The Lion Hunt*), 139
Lubitsch, Ernst, 158, 167, 184, 186–87, 253
Lykkehjulet (*The Wheel of Fortune*), 205

Die Macht des Goldes (*The Might of Gold*), 165
Das Mädchen ohne Vaterland (*A Romany Spy*), 148–49, 155–57, 165
Madsen, Harald, 205
Malmkjær, Poul, 33, 41, 43, 214, 217, 237

Mann, Thomas, 68, 118
Marvin, Harry, 26
Mayboom, Margaretha, 241
McLuhan, Marshall, 24–25
Meerman, Johann, 52
Melnik, Joseph, 16–17
Messter, Oskar, 166–67, 181
metaculture, ix, 18–20, 22, 25, 27–28, 40–41, 95, 111, 119, 134, 204
meta-stereotypes, 7–8, 12
Michaëlis, Karin, 36, 39, 174, 186, 200–201
Michaëlis, Sophus, 36, 174
Mill, John Stuart, 50
Mod Lyset (*Toward the Light*), 175
Modern Breakthrough, 20, 30–31, 47, 50, 56, 61, 69, 75, 79, 82, 85, 115, 163, 169, 175, 184–85, 200, 218
Moderne Geister (*Creative Spirits of the Nineteenth Century*), 71
Det Moderne Gjennembruds Mænd (*Men of the Modern Breakthrough*), 79
modernity: agents of, 9–10, 24, 73, 131, 183, 228, 231; cultural, 12, 14–15, 18–20, 23, 29, 43, 56, 78, 124, 131, 162, 200, 203; definition of, 8–9, 14, 50, 61, 75, 80; discourses about, 7–8, 14, 24–25, 130–31, 184; performance of, 13–14, 22–23, 40, 175, 179, 182, 192, 196, 226–27; Scandinavian, 22, 35, 178, 184, 200, 203, 228, 231
monopoly film-distribution system, 33, 133–35, 143–45, 154, 166, 231
Morel, Edmund, 118
Mülleneisen, Christoph, 144
Murnau, F. W., 184

Nachtfalter (*Retribution*), 143, 152, 165
Nathansen, Henri, 36, 100, 174
national cinema, 35–36, 94, 128–30, 169, 179, 203, 220, 258
national identity: construction of, 4–7, 10, 15, 18, 21, 28, 35, 43, 48, 57–59, 61, 81, 83–84, 89, 122, 129–33, 155, 189, 230–32; Danish, ix, 4–10, 12, 18–19, 21–22, 35, 40–43, 48–49, 55–60, 63–64, 74, 78–79, 81–86, 89–92, 95, 97, 100, 124, 129, 148, 177, 220–21, 228, 230; German, 73–75, 129, 166, 168–9
nationalism, 4–5, 7–9, 15, 31–32, 40–41, 48–49, 51, 53–58, 63, 66, 73–74, 77, 81–84, 87–92, 95, 97, 99–105, 107, 115–18, 120–21, 123, 131, 155–56, 166, 168–70, 179, 189, 195–96, 203–4, 212, 216, 219, 228, 231
naturalism, 29, 50, 56, 68, 72, 75–76, 80, 187
Nazarbék, Avetis, 110
Neble, Sophus, 111
Negri, Pola, 158
Neutral Film, 137, 172
Nielsen, Harald, 96
Nielsen, Jesta, 33, 225
Niels Lyhne, 77–80, 83
Nietzsche, Friedrich, 31, 47, 60, 65, 68–69, 73, 75, 95, 241
Nordisk Film, 128, 139, 143–44, 147, 175–76, 190, 195, 201, 223
Det Ny Studenter Samfund (The New Student Society), 121

Oehlenschläger, Adam, 48, 54, 73
Olsen, Ole, 139, 143–44, 175, 223–24
Om Nationalfølelse ("Concerning National Sentiment"), 81, 100
Oswalda, Ossi, 158
Ottoman Empire, 87, 110

Paludan-Müller, Frederik, 70–71
Pankhurst, Emmeline, 165
Parry, Lee, 182
Pathé-Frères, 128, 165
The Perils of Pauline, 164
Politiken, 94, 97–98, 112, 117, 128, 148–50, 152–53, 169, 200, 206, 219–20, 223–24
Porten, Henny, 166–69, 182, 250
Projektions-AG Union (PAGU), 137, 144, 161, 166, 181
provisorietid (provisional period), 91
Psilander, Valdemar, 143, 147, 167

Radikale Venstre (Radical Left), 98
Rasmussen, Knud, 172
Rausch (*Intoxication*), 184
Reumert, Poul, 139, 141, 204
Reventlow, C. D. F., 53
Reventlow, J. L., 53
Reventlow, Sophie, 53
Rita Cavallini, 209
Rodenberg, Julius, 68, 73–75
Rolland, Romain, 118
Roth, Dr. R., 182
Rumpff, Heinrich and Tilla, 215–18
Rung, Gertrud and Otto, 39, 122, 175
Rye, Stellan, 147

S1, 156
sædelighedsfejden (morality feud), 96, 98

Sagnet om Jesus (The Legend of Jesus), 123
Said, Edward, 51, 54, 57–59, 63, 65, 85–86
Sainte-Beuve, Charles Augustin, 50
Sandemose, Aksel, 151, 207
Schandorph, Sophus, 78, 82
Schenstrøm, Carl, 205
Schimmelmann, Charlotte, 53
Schimmelmann, Ernst, 53
Schiörring, Viggo, 170
Schlaf, Johannes, 72
Schlegel, Johann Elias, 53
Schleswig, 9–10, 19, 32, 48–49, 52–53, 56–57, 65, 70, 81, 86, 90, 99, 103–9, 120–21, 146, 203
Schleussner, Carl, 137
Der Schmetterlingsschlacht (The Butterfly Battle), 208
Schmidt, Frede, 258
Der schwarze Traum (The Black Dream), 143, 147
Seeber, Guido, 145
Sheldon, Edward, 209
Siddons, Sarah, 193
Sieburg, Friedrich, 18, 118, 120–21
Skaarup, Frede, 144
Skjødt-Jensen, Torben, 226, 258
Söderbaum, Kristina, 35, 212
Sønderjylland under prøjsisk Tryk (Southern Jutland under Prussian Pressure), 121
Sorel, Cécile, 138
Sorokin, Pitrim, 235
Stangerup, Henrik, 42, 225
Stark, Curt, 166, 168, 250
Stauning, Thorvald, 218
Steffens, Henrik, 54
Stendhal, 184
Strindberg, August, 162, 172, 175, 184, 186–87, 200, 202–3, 239
Strodtmann, Adolf, 69–71, 74
Struensee, Johann Friedrich, 54–55
Studenterforening (Student Union), 99, 128
Studentersamfund (Student Society), 81, 99–100, 102, 106, 121, 124
Die Suffragette (The Militant Suffragette), 153, 156, 165
Sünden der Väter (The Devil's Assistant), 165
Süring, Carl, 144
systemskifte (system change), 91, 97–98, 100

Taine, Hippolyte, 50, 61, 69
Tardini, Anna, 140
Tegnér, Esias, 71, 73

Theede, Christian, 225
Thorvaldsen, Bertel, 105, 224, 226
Tod in Sevilla (Death in Seville), 153
Tolnæs, Gunnar, 181
Tonbilder, 166
Traffic in Souls, 128
Turgenev, Ivan, 61
Tyskerfejden (the German Feud), 55

Universum Film AG (UFA), 176, 181–82, 208, 214
Unmögliche Liebe (Impossible Love), 21
Urban, Greg, 5, 18, 23, 25, 27

Vanina, 184
Vaterland (Leviathan), 16–17, 24, 27, 36, 38, 42, 111, 234
Venstre (Left [Party]), 91, 96–100, 116
Vermehren, Poul, 224
Die Verräterin (The Traitress), 155, 164
Das Versuchskaninchen (The Guinea Pig), 172
Viby, Marguerite, 205
Vining, Edward P., 190
Vordertreppe-Hintertreppe (Front Stairs, Back Stairs), 156

Walkley, A. B., 21
Wedekind, Frank, 184
Wegener, Poul, 207, 215
Weimar street film, 186, 188, 197
Wenn die Maske fällt (Behind Comedy's Mask), 165
Wied, Gustav, 36
Wiene, Robert, 177, 184
Wieth, Clara Pontoppidan, 175
Wilhelm II, Kaiser, 28, 84, 88, 115
Wingårdh, Freddy, 37–38, 171–72, 182
Winther, Sophus Keith, 113
Wolff, Eugen, 75
Wolff, Theodor, 77, 79–80
The Woman Always Pays (see *Afgrunden*)
World War I, 10, 15–16, 29, 32–33, 35, 38, 41, 88, 94–95, 100, 111–12, 115–17, 128, 130, 132, 137, 146, 149, 155, 158, 170, 175, 178, 183, 204, 218, 251
World War II, 10, 123–24, 132, 137, 171, 224, 229

Zahle, Carl Theodor, 94
Zapatas Bande (Zapata's Robber Band), 154
Zigeunerblut (Gipsy Blood), 164
Zola, Émile, 63, 69, 71, 73
Zweig, Stefan, 60, 184

www.ingramcontent.com/pod-product-compliance
Lightning Source LLC
Chambersburg PA
CBHW031800220426
43662CB00007B/479